Living and Working
in
Switzerland

A Survival Handbook

By
David Hampshire

SURVIVAL BOOKS • LONDON • ENGLAND

First published 1988
Second Edition 1989
Third Edition 1991
Fourth Edition 1993
Fifth Edition 1995
Sixth Edition 1997
Seventh Edition 1999
Eighth Edition 2002
Ninth Edition 2004

Copyright © Survival Books 1988, 1989, 1991,
1993, 1995, 1997, 1999, 2002, 2004

Survival Books Limited, 1st Floor,
60 St James's Street, London SW1A 1ZN, United Kingdom
☎ +44 (0)20-7493 4244, 🖷 +44 (0)20-7491 0605
✉ info@survivalbooks.net
🖳 www.survivalbooks.net
To order books, please refer to page 444.

British Library Cataloguing in Publication Data.
A CIP record for this book is available
from the British Library.
ISBN 1 901130 13 4

Printed and bound in Finland by WS Bookwell Ltd

ACKNOWLEDGEMENTS

My sincere thanks to all those who contributed to the publication of this book and to the many people who took the trouble to read and comment on the draft versions. In particular I would like to thank Erik Gottschalk and Adèle Kelham, without whose unstinting assistance and advice this book may never have seen the light of day. Also special thanks to Gabrielle Grether (Grether Consulting) for updating this edition, Kerry and Joe Laredo (proof-reading and desktop publishing), Nigel MacGeorge, Nicolas Vivion and Patric Eisele (all Grether Consulting), Dianne Kiefer-Dicks (Bergli Books), Christian Tromp (*Die Schweizerische Post*), Philipp Dubach (Bundesamt für Statistik) and Rolf Beeler (Strassenverkehrsamt Zurich). Also a special thank you to Jim Watson for the superb illustrations, cartoons and cover design.

OTHER TITLES BY SURVIVAL BOOKS

Living and Working Series

Abroad; America; Australia;
Britain; Canada; France;
Germany; the Gulf States &
Saudi Arabia; Holland,
Belgium & Luxembourg;
Ireland; Italy; London; New
Zealand; Spain .

Buying a Home Series

Abroad; Britain; Florida;
France; Greece & Cyprus;
Ireland; Italy;
Portugal; Spain

Other Titles

The Alien's Guide to Britain;
The Alien's Guide to France;
The Best Places to Live
in France;
The Best Places to Live
in Spain;
How to Avoid Holiday &
Travel Disasters;
Retiring Abroad;
Rioja and its Wines;
The Wines of Spain

Order forms are on page 444.

WHAT READERS & REVIEWERS

When you buy a model plane for your child, a video recorder, or some new computer gizmo, you get with it a leaflet or booklet pleading 'Read Me First', or bearing large friendly letters or bold type saying 'IMPORTANT – follow the instructions carefully'. This book should be similarly supplied to all those entering France with anything more durable than a 5-day return ticket. It is worth reading even if you are just visiting briefly, or if you have lived here for years and feel totally knowledgeable and secure. But if you need to find out how France works then it is indispensable. Native French people probably have a less thorough understanding of how their country functions. – Where it is most essential, the book is most up to the minute.

LIVING FRANCE

Rarely has a 'survival guide' contained such useful advice. This book dispels doubts for first-time travellers, yet is also useful for seasoned globetrotters – In a word, if you're planning to move to the USA or go there for a long-term stay, then buy this book both for general reading and as a ready-reference.

AMERICAN CITIZENS ABROAD

It is everything you always wanted to ask but didn't for fear of the contemptuous put down – The best English-language guide – Its pages are stuffed with practical information on everyday subjects and are designed to complement the traditional guidebook.

SWISS NEWS

A complete revelation to me – I found it both enlightening and interesting, not to mention amusing.

CAROLE CLARK

Let's say it at once. David Hampshire's *Living and Working in France* is the best handbook ever produced for visitors and foreign residents in this country; indeed, my discussion with locals showed that it has much to teach even those born and bred in l'Hexagone. – It is Hampshire's meticulous detail which lifts his work way beyond the range of other books with similar titles. Often you think of a supplementary question and search for the answer in vain. With Hampshire this is rarely the case. – He writes with great clarity (and gives French equivalents of all key terms), a touch of humour and a ready eye for the odd (and often illuminating) fact. – This book is absolutely indispensable.

THE RIVIERA REPORTER

A mine of information – I may have avoided some embarrassments and frights if I had read it prior to my first Swiss encounters – Deserves an honoured place on any newcomer's bookshelf.

ENGLISH TEACHERS ASSOCIATION, SWITZERLAND

HAVE SAID ABOUT SURVIVAL BOOKS

What a great work, wealth of useful information, well-balanced wording and accuracy in details. My compliments!

THOMAS MÜLLER

This handbook has all the practical information one needs to set up home in the UK – The sheer volume of information is almost daunting – Highly recommended for anyone moving to the UK.

AMERICAN CITIZENS ABROAD

A very good book which has answered so many questions and even some I hadn't thought of – I would certainly recommend it.

BRIAN FAIRMAN

We would like to congratulate you on this work: it is really super! We hand it out to our expatriates and they read it with great interest and pleasure.

ICI (SWITZERLAND) AG

Covers just about all the things you want to know on the subject – In answer to the desert island question about the one how-to book on France, this book would be it – Almost 500 pages of solid accurate reading – This book is about enjoyment as much as survival.

THE RECORDER

It's so funny – I love it and definitely need a copy of my own – Thanks very much for having written such a humorous and helpful book.

HEIDI GUILIANI

A must for all foreigners coming to Switzerland.

ANTOINETTE O'DONOGHUE

A comprehensive guide to all things French, written in a highly readable and amusing style, for anyone planning to live, work or retire in France.

THE TIMES

A concise, thorough account of the DOs and DON'Ts for a foreigner in Switzerland – Crammed with useful information and lightened with humorous quips which make the facts more readable.

AMERICAN CITIZENS ABROAD

Covers every conceivable question that may be asked concerning everyday life – I know of no other book that could take the place of this one.

FRANCE IN PRINT

Hats off to *Living and Working in Switzerland*!

RONNIE ALMEIDA

THE AUTHOR

David Hampshire was born in the United Kingdom, where after serving in the Royal Air Force he was employed for many years in the computer industry. He has lived and worked in many countries, including Australia, France, Germany, Malaysia, the Netherlands, Singapore, Switzerland and Spain, where he now resides most of the year. It was while working in Switzerland that he wrote his first book, *Living and Working in Switzerland*, in 1987. To date, David is the author of 15 books, including *Buying a Home in France, Buying a Home in Italy, Buying a Home in Spain, Living and Working in France, Living and Working in Spain* and *Retiring Abroad*.

CONTENTS

8. TELEVISION & RADIO 137

9. EDUCATION 149

10. PUBLIC TRANSPORT 175

11. MOTORING 201

12. HEALTH   241

13. INSURANCE   255

14. FINANCE 277

15. LEISURE 303

IMPORTANT NOTE

Switzerland is a diverse country with many faces. It has four national languages, both federal and canton laws, a variety of religions and customs, and continuously changing rules and regulations, particularly with regard to foreigners.

Always check with an official and reliable source (not always the same) before making any major decisions or undertaking an irreversible course of action. However, don't believe everything you're told or read, even, dare it be said, herein. Comprehensive lists of useful addresses, publications and useful websites are included in Appendices A, B and C respectively, to help you obtain and verify information. Throughout this book certain points have been emphasised in bold print. Ignore them at your peril or cost.

Unless specifically stated, a reference to any company, organisation or product in this book doesn't constitute an endorsement or recommendation. Any resemblance to any place or person (living or dead) is purely coincidental. There's no Swiss town called Geneva.

AUTHOR'S NOTES

- Times are shown using am for before noon and pm for after noon (see also **Time Difference** on page 387).

- His/he/him/man/men (etc.) also mean her/she/her/woman/women (no offence ladies!). This is done simply to make life easier for both the reader and, in particular, the author, and isn't intended to be sexist.

- Spelling is (or should be) British English and not American English. Names of Swiss towns and foreign words are generally shown in their English spelling, e.g. Basle (Basel), Berne (Bern), Geneva (Genf, Genève), Lucerne (Luzern) and Zurich (Zürich).

- Prices quoted usually include value added tax (VAT) and should be taken only as estimates, although they were mostly correct when going to print and fortunately don't usually change overnight in Switzerland.

- Warnings and important points are shown in bold type.

- The following symbols are used in this book: ☎ (telephone), ▤ (fax), 🖳 (Internet) and ✉ (e-mail).

- Lists of Useful Addresses, Further Reading and Useful Websites are contained in **Appendices A, B** and **C** respectively.

- For those unfamiliar with the metric system of weights and measures, conversion tables are included in **Appendix D**.

- A map of Switzerland showing the 26 cantons is included in **Appendix E**.

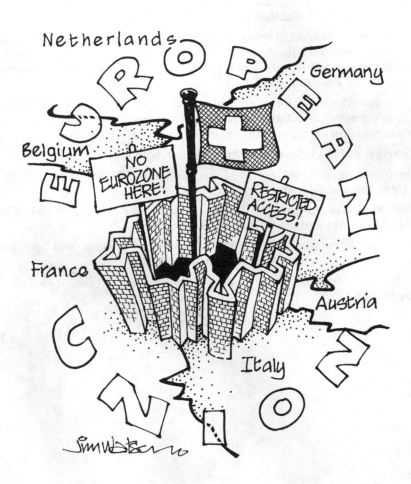

INTRODUCTION

Whether you're already living or working in Switzerland or just thinking about it – this is **THE BOOK** you've been looking for. Forget about those glossy guide books, excellent though they are for tourists. This amazing book was written especially with you in mind and is worth its weight in Swiss watches.

In sharp contrast to the abundant information provided by Switzerland Tourism (ST), information for foreigners living and working in Switzerland is often hard to come by – particularly in the English language. My aim in writing this book was to help redress the balance and try to fill the void (chasm?) that exists between the paucity of information available and the knowledge necessary for a relatively trouble-free life.

You may have visited Switzerland as a tourist, but living and working there's a different matter altogether. Moving to a new job and making a home in any foreign country can be a traumatic and stressful experience – and Switzerland is no exception. You need to discover the Swiss way of doing things – for example, finding an apartment, paying bills and obtaining insurance – and to adapt to your new surroundings.

For most foreigners in Switzerland, finding out how to overcome the everyday obstacles of Swiss life was previously a case of pot luck. However, with a copy of *Living and Working in Switzerland* to hand, you will have a wealth of information at your fingertips. Information derived from a variety of sources, both official and unofficial – not least the hard won personal experiences of the author, his friends, colleagues and acquaintances. This book isn't simply a monologue of dry facts and figures, but an entertaining, practical and occasionally humorous look at life in Switzerland. However, don't be mislead by the subtle and sophisticated witticisms – this is serious stuff!

Living and Working in Switzerland represents the most up-to-date source of information available to foreigners in Switzerland – in any language. It doesn't contain all the answers (most of us don't even know the questions), but it will help you to make informed decisions instead of costly mistakes, calculated judgements rather than uneducated guesses, and, most important, it will help you save time, trouble and money.

A period spent in Switzerland is a wonderful way to enrich your life, broaden your horizons and hopefully please your bank manager. I trust that this book will help to smooth your way to a happy and rewarding life in your new home in Switzerland.

Viel Glück/Bon courage!

David Hampshire
October 2003

1.

FINDING A JOB

Finding a job in Switzerland isn't as difficult as official Swiss policy may lead you to believe, although obtaining a permit can prove a problem. Switzerland is known for its restrictive immigration policy and permit quota system, although the rules regarding executives and certain 'specialists' have been eased in recent years. A bilateral agreement between the EU countries and Switzerland will eventually allow the free movement of people and remove the need for permits. Switzerland's economic success is largely dependent upon the influx of foreign labour and foreigners are found in almost every walk of life. Many companies have a sizeable foreign labour force and foreigners fill almost half the top positions at the largest 25 Swiss companies. Foreign employees in Switzerland number around 1,052,000 or some 25 per cent of the workforce.

The world-wide recession curbed immigration in the early 1990s, during which many Swiss companies slashed their workforces in an effort to become 'lean and mean' and compete more effectively (where previously redundancies were a sign of weak management, they became viewed as courageous decisiveness). Since 1992, over half of Swiss companies have reduced their workforces and many large employers have subcontracted services, often to former employees. At the same time, companies have been increasingly moving their production and research facilities abroad in order to reduce further costs. However, despite the upheavals in many companies, labour relations remain excellent and there are fewer strikes than in any other industrialised country.

For many years a 'jobless Swiss' was a contradiction in terms, although in the early 1990s unemployment reached around 6 per cent or some 200,000 people – a level not experienced in Switzerland since the 1930s. By 2002 the unemployment rate had gone down to around 2.9 per cent, although it was much higher in some cantons.

Despite the recession, the number of foreigners and has reached record levels and in 2002 there was a resident population of over 1.5 million foreigners or some 20 per cent of the population (Geneva has the highest percentage at around 43 per cent). This figure doesn't include employees of international organisations, foreign embassies and consulates (and their families), or seasonal workers and asylum seekers, who together total a further 100,000. An additional 175,000 foreigners cross the borders each day to work in Switzerland. Around 60 per cent of foreigners are from the EU and EEA countries, 24.1 per cent from the former Yugoslavia and some 5.5 per cent from Turkey. Switzerland also exports workers and some 550,000 Swiss live and work abroad.

The employment of foreigners, albeit an economic necessity, is something of a political hot potato. The Swiss generally live and work harmoniously with their foreign 'guests', although there's a vociferous minority who would like to see the number of foreign workers drastically reduced. During the last 30 years they've gained sufficient support to stage a number of national referendums in an attempt to reduce the resident foreign population. All have been defeated but they've served to strain relations between the Swiss and resident foreigners. An attempt to prohibit foreign workers in sectors with over 3 per cent unemployment was also rejected in the canton of Zurich in 1996.

Most positions held by foreigners fall into two main categories: seasonal jobs for a maximum of nine months a year and permanent staff positions. Seasonal jobs include hotel and catering staff, building and construction workers, factory hands, farm workers, and most jobs associated with the tourist industry. They're available throughout Switzerland and aren't usually difficult to find. Permanent jobs are generally reserved for senior managers, professionals and specialists (e.g. computer experts and engineers), and require annual residence permits. Residence permits are also required by au pairs, students and trainees, for whom there are no quota restrictions (although permits are generally valid only for one year).

Switzerland And The European Union

In a landmark referendum on 6th December 1992, the Swiss voted against joining the European Economic Area (EEA), created to allow free movement of goods, services, capital and people between member states. The EEA comprises the 15 European Union (EU) members (Austria, Belgium, Denmark, Finland, France, Germany, Greece, Ireland, Italy, Luxembourg, the Netherlands, Portugal, Spain, Sweden and the United Kingdom) plus Iceland, Liechtenstein and Norway. The EEA vote (seen as a precursor to full EU membership by the Swiss people) highlighted a serious split between the Swiss Germans and Swiss French over Switzerland's future, and created an acrimonious divide between them. While the French-speakers of western Switzerland voted overwhelmingly in favour of the EEA, the majority of Swiss Germans and Swiss Italians came out firmly in opposition. **However, a further referendum on starting negotiations to become a member of the European Union was heavily defeated by 77 to 23 per cent on 4th March 2001.**

If Switzerland joined the EU it would need to make a number of far-reaching changes to it laws and institutions, although membership would have helped liberate the economy and remove the 'traditional' cartels, monopolies, anti-competitive practices, price fixing and red tape – while adding lots more of its own! However, there remains a mood for change in the country and rejection of the EEA didn't alter the need for Switzerland to 'revitalise' its economy and business practices. In the wake of the EEA vote the Swiss government took steps to institute many of the conditions contained in the EEA package (although opponents have declared that they won't hesitate to force another referendum if deals are made of which they don't approve).

The 'no' vote prompted a period of agonising soul-searching in Switzerland, regarding its future role in Europe and the world. The EEA vote called into question Switzerland's seemingly permanent prosperity and stability, coming as it did during the recession that had already resulted in higher inflation, unemployment and negative growth. The government and most business leaders believe that membership of the EU is vital to Switzerland's long-term economic survival and that Swiss industry will suffer from the country's decision not to join (although there's little indication of this to date). The Swiss government hasn't withdrawn its application for membership of the EU and plans to hold another referendum when it feels it can gain public support.

In the meantime, Switzerland has negotiated a bilateral agreement with EU countries whereby the citizens of EU countries will eventually have full free movement within Switzerland (and Swiss citizens in EU countries). The agreement is to be phased in over a period of 12 years having started on 1st July 2002.

In the past, Switzerland has been successful in attracting foreign companies to invest or relocate to Switzerland (despite high labour costs and a lack of qualified personnel), although this is now more difficult. In addition, more Swiss companies have been expanding abroad, particularly within EU countries, and the anti-EEA vote accelerated this policy. The main losers (in addition to Swiss industry) are Switzerland's younger generation, who are disadvantaged by their inability to study and work in EEA countries. Nevertheless, Switzerland has risen to the challenges posed by life outside the EEA and the economy has made a strong recovery (led by record exports) following the recession in the early 1990s. GDP growth was a healthy 4.1 per cent in 2000, but is expected to fall to only 0.3 per cent by the end 2003.

With Austria joining the EU and Liechtenstein joining the EEA, Switzerland has never looked so politically and economically isolated, and it resembles a missing jigsaw piece in the middle of Europe. With the introduction of the common currency Switzerland has also become a 'currency island' completely surrounded by the euro – the nice side effect being that you now only need one extra currency for all these cross-border shopping trips to Germany, France, Austria and Italy. Since the rejection of the EEA, it has had an uneasy relationship with the EU, although most 'differences of opinion' have now been resolved. Following the EEA vote, the EU was in no hurry to treat Switzerland as a special case, although it's too valuable a trading partner to ignore. It's one of the EU's most important export markets (some 78 per cent of Swiss imports are from the EU) and its third-largest supplier after the US and Japan (the EU takes around 59 per cent of Swiss exports). Furthermore, around 50 per cent of Swiss investments are in EU countries and almost a million EU citizens work in Switzerland.

There will inevitably be another referendum on joining the EEA/EU, although it's likely to be some time before the government dares to risk another vote. However, there are already signs that a majority may eventually be willing to vote in favour of membership and many Swiss believe that Switzerland will become a member of the EU within the next decade. What is certain, is that the topic of European integration and EU membership is here to stay and it will dominate Swiss politicians' thinking for the foreseeable future.

SEASONAL JOBS

The majority of seasonal jobs in Switzerland are available in the tourist industry. Most seasonal jobs last for the duration of the summer or winter tourist seasons, i.e. April to October and December to April respectively.

Switzerland used to have a special 'seasonal work permit' for a maximum of nine months per year. With the change of the work permit system in 2002 these have been abolished and it therefore is necessary to either get a (non-renewable) L permit for a maximum of 12 months or a normal annual B permit. Special short-term permits (see page 64) that allow foreigners to work in Switzerland for a maximum of three or four months a year are also available.

Although salaries are higher in Switzerland than in most other countries, you're expected to work **hard and long hours**, particularly in hotels and restaurants in winter resorts (summer is generally more relaxed). Many businesses must survive for a whole year primarily on their winter earnings and employers expect everyone to earn their keep. Language fluency is required for all but the most menial and worst paid jobs, and is equally or more important than experience and qualifications (not that language proficiency alone will get you a well paid job). **The local language in Switzerland may be French, German or Italian, depending on the area** (see **Languages** on page 39).

If accommodation, if necessary with cooking facilities, isn't provided with a job, it can be expensive and difficult to find. Ensure that your salary is sufficient to pay for accommodation, food and other living expenses, and hopefully save some money (see **Cost of Living** on page 298). You may be able to find a job on the spot, although you should bear in mind that you need a residence permit to work in Switzerland. Seasonal Jobs include the following:

Year Round	**Winter Only**
Hotels & Restaurants	Chalet Girls
Bars & Clubs	Ski Technicians
Couriers or Resort Representatives	Ski Instructors or Guides
Sports Instructors	
Manual Workers	
Voluntary Workers	

Year Round Jobs

Hotels & Restaurants

Hotels and restaurants are the largest employers of seasonal workers and jobs are available at all levels, from managers to kitchen hands. Experience, qualifications and language fluency are required for all the best and highest paid positions, however, a variety of jobs are available for the untrained and inexperienced. These include chambermaids, waiters and waitresses, cleaners, dishwashers, handymen, porters, messengers, drivers, kitchen assistants and MBOs (muscle bound oafs).

The standards required by Swiss employers are high and hard work and long hours are demanded, although the pay is usually good. The minimum monthly wage for employees in the hotel/restaurant industry is around SFr. 2,500 and a 13th month's salary (see page 50) is paid to full-time employees (but isn't usually paid to seasonal workers). All employees in hotels are usually provided with full board and you should avoid any job that doesn't include it as the cost can be prohibitive. Reductions from gross salaries for board and lodging and compulsory insurance amount to some 50 per cent.

Official working hours vary from between 44 and 48 hours a week (or higher) depending on the particular job, or around nine to nine and a half hours a day. Your contract will contain a stated maximum number of working hours a week (normal working hours should be a maximum of 45 per week), although in reality this may be the minimum. You're entitled to two free days each week and four weeks' paid holiday a year (around one and a half days a month). Between Christmas and New Year you may be expected to work 12 hours a day, seven days a week, for which you will usually receive time off in January. Most jobs include a two-week trial period with a notice period of three days, after which the notice period is one month.

Waiters and waitresses are expected to supply their own 'uniform', special wallet and a cash float of around SFr. 200. The salary is often on a commission basis, where you're paid a percentage of your takings (plus tips – provided all your customers aren't Swiss). Aprons, hats and oven gloves are normally supplied for kitchen staff, and a free laundry service is usually provided for working clothes and uniforms. Other dress requirements vary depending on the particular job, for example waiters require black trousers and shoes, white shirts and often jackets. Waitresses require black skirts, shoes and stockings, white blouses and possibly small aprons. In addition to jobs in Swiss hotels and restaurants, jobs are available in hotels and chalets run by British and other foreign tour operators, where local language ability may be unnecessary. Work is generally easier and the atmosphere more relaxed, but salaries are usually lower than those paid by Swiss-run hotels and may even be half the minimum wage.

Many agencies and a number of trade newspapers are available in Switzerland to help you find a job in a hotel or restaurant. Union Helvetia is the official Swiss union for hotel and restaurant staff, and anyone who has training or qualifications in the hotel and catering trades may become a member. Union Helvetia publish an official rule book (*Obligationenrecht, droit des obligations*) for employers and employees and a list of official minimum salaries for all jobs. They also publish a weekly newspaper, *Hotel & Gastro Union*, containing job vacancies. It's available from news kiosks in Switzerland or on subscription from *Hotel & Gastro Union*, Zentralsekretariat, Adligenswilerstr. 22, Postfach 4870, CH-6002 Lucerne (☎ 041 418 22 22). *Hotel & Gastro Union* have their own employment agency at their head office in Lucerne and regional offices in Geneva, Lausanne, Sion and Zurich.

The Swiss Hotel Association (*Schweizer Hotelier-Verein, Société Suisse des Hôteliers*) publish their own newspaper, *Hotel + Touristik Revue*, which usually contains more job vacancies than the *Hotel & Gastro Union* newspaper. It's also available from news kiosks (Thursdays) or on subscription from *Hotel + Touristik Revue*, Monbijoustr. 130, Postfach 3001, CH-3001 Berne (☎ 031 370 42 22). Both the *Hotel & Gastro Union* and *Hotel + Touristik Revue* newspapers contain articles in French and German. Like Union Helvetia, the Swiss Hotel Association has its own employment agency and publishes a standard employment contract for hotel and restaurant staff, which is in wide use throughout Switzerland. Other weekly newspapers advertising job vacancies for hotel and restaurant staff include *Schweizer Gastronome* and *Expresso*. Besides answering advertisements and visiting agencies, you could also try contacting Swiss hotel and restaurant chains directly.

Bars & Clubs

Jobs in bars and clubs are available throughout Switzerland. English-style pubs in many towns often hire English-speaking bartenders and waiters to add an additional touch of authenticity. Winter resorts have many clubs and discotheques requiring disc jockeys, particularly those with their own collection of up-to-date pop music. Jobs for disc jockeys are also advertised in British music newspapers. Staff, including croupiers, are also required by casinos in many areas of Switzerland (see page 313).

Couriers & Resort Representatives

A courier's or resort representative's duties include ferrying tourist groups back and forth from airports, organising excursions and social events, arranging ski passes and equipment rental, and generally playing the role of Jack or Jill of all trades. A job as a courier is tough and demanding, and requires resilience and resourcefulness to deal with the chaos associated with the package holiday business. The necessary requirements include the ability to answer many questions simultaneously (often in different languages), to remain calm and charming under extreme pressure, and above all, to maintain a keen sense of humour. Lost passengers, lost tickets and passports, and lost tempers are everyday occurrences. It's an excellent training ground for managerial and leadership skills, pays well and often provides opportunities to supplement your earnings.

Couriers are required by many local and foreign tour companies in both winter and summer resorts. Competition for jobs is fierce and local language ability is always required, even for employment with British tour operators. Most companies have age requirements, the minimum usually being 21, although many companies prefer employees to be a few years older. The majority of courier jobs in Switzerland are available during the winter ski season with British ski-tour companies and school ski-party organisers. A good source of information is ski magazines, which contain regular listings of tour companies showing who goes to which resorts. It's wise to find out the type of clients you're likely to be dealing with, particularly if you're allergic to children or yuppies (young urban professionals – similar to children but more immature). To survive a winter in a ski resort, it helps to be a keen skier or a dedicated learner, otherwise you risk being bored to death by ski bums.

Some companies, such as Club Méditerranée, operate both summer and winter hotels and camps throughout Switzerland. Employees are required to speak good French. For information write to Club Méditerranée, 25 rue Vivienne, F-75002 Paris, France. (⌨ www.clubmed.com) Couriers or counsellors are also required for summer camps, which are organised for both adults and children. See also **Voluntary Workers** on page 27.

Sports Instructors

Instructors are required for a variety of sports including badminton, canoeing, diving, golf, gymnastics, hang-gliding, horse-riding, mountaineering, parachuting, rock- climbing, sailing, squash, subaquatic sports, swimming, tennis and wind-surfing. Whatever the sport, it's probably played and taught somewhere in Switzerland. Most jobs for sports instructors are available in summer, as winter sports vacancies are generally filled by the Swiss (for information regarding **Ski Instructors and Guides** see page 29). However, if you're a qualified winter sports instructor, contact Swiss resorts or sports organisations for information about vacancies. You may require an officially recognised qualification to teach some sports, for example a life-saving certificate to teach swimming or a sailing certificate to teach sailing.

Manual Workers

Jobs for manual workers are usually available throughout Switzerland, mostly in the building, construction and farming industries. The minimum salary in the construction industry is around SFr. 3,500 a month. Jobs are also available for cleaners and general labourers in hospitals, factories, warehouses and large hotels. Farmers often require extra labourers, particularly in the spring and autumn to help with the fruit, vegetable and grape harvests. Farming jobs entail hard physical work, usually for around 12 hours a day, six days a week, for a low salary (see also **Voluntary Workers** below). One of the most popular jobs is grape-picking, e.g. in the cantons of Valais and Vaud, lasting for around 8 to 10 days in early October. The work is hard and the salary is around SFr. 60 per day, although many employers pay more.

Unfortunately the worst abuses of seasonal workers' rights also occur in the farming industry, particularly in the Geneva area, where complaints include low pay, long hours, inadequate living conditions and unpaid social benefits. If you're a seasonal worker from a country with a bilateral insurance agreement with Switzerland, the Swiss government doesn't repay federal social security payments (OASI/DI) when you leave Switzerland (see page 257). Therefore there's a temptation for dishonest employers to deduct the

OASI/DI payment from your salary and not declare it, particularly as you're unlikely ever to claim a Swiss pension.

The Swiss are continually digging tunnels; building and repairing bridges and roads; and constructing office blocks and shopping centres (although it's the foreigners who do the manual work). Enquire at building sites in Switzerland – the bigger the site, the better your chances of success. In summer, jobs may be available in ski resorts installing new ski lifts, snow-making pipes and machinery, and building chalets and hotels. Ask at local lift operating companies, estate agents and construction companies. If you have experience or training in the building industry, e.g. as a bricklayer or carpenter, you should be able to command a higher salary, even without local language fluency. Outdoor jobs in the building and construction industries are usually restricted to the warmer months, as trying to find your shovel under two metres of snow can be a handicap in winter.

Voluntary Workers

Voluntary work is primarily to enable students and young people to visit Switzerland for a few weeks or a few months to learn about the country and its people at first hand. Voluntary work is unpaid, although meals and accommodation are normally provided, and a small amount of pocket money may be paid. This, however, may not be sufficient for your out of pocket living expenses (e.g. entertainment and drinks), so make sure that you bring enough money with you. The usual visa regulations apply to voluntary workers and your passport must be valid for at least one year. You will be informed whether you need a visa when you apply (a work or residence permit isn't required). Various kinds of voluntary work are available, including those below.

Farm Work

Voluntary farm work is usually available from March to October (mainly in German-speaking areas) and is organised by the Swiss Farm Work Association. You must be aged between 17 and 30 with a basic knowledge of German or French (depending on the area) and be prepared to work for a minimum of three weeks and a maximum of eight. It's certainly not a holiday, as the work is usually strenuous and the hours long, spread over six days a week (**Sundays are free!**). Officially a maximum of 48 hours a week are worked, although more may be expected. Work may be in the fields, farmyard, farmhouse or in the farm garden. For this you're paid the princely sum of at least SFr. 20 a day (those aged over 18), plus board and lodging, and are insured against illness and accidents. You must pay for your own journey to and from the farm.

Many farms are in remote mountain areas, where living and working conditions may be rather primitive and where there's little social life. If you like a hectic social life (not that many people would have any energy left) and companionship, then this isn't the job for you. Friends applying together aren't usually placed with the same farmer, as only one worker is allocated per farmer due to a lack of applicants. Application forms are available from *Landdienst - Zentralstelle*, Mühlegasse 13, Postfach 728, CH-8025 Zurich (☎ 01 261 44 88, ✉ admin@landdienst.ch). Registration should be made at least four weeks before you wish to start work (a deposit may be payable by overseas applicants and is forfeited if an application is cancelled or a position isn't taken up).

Other farm jobs include work on an organically run farm, in return for which you receive free meals and accommodation (but no expenses). A year's membership and a list of participating farms costs SFr. 20 from WWOOF Switzerland, Postfach 59, CH-8124 Maur (🖳 www.welcome.to/wwoof). You should send an international reply coupon with your letter.

General

Many organisations requiring voluntary workers, mostly for holiday camps for children and the disabled, are listed in a brochure available from *Pro Juventute*, Seehofstr. 15, Postfach, CH-8032 Zurich (☎ 01 256 77 77, 🖳 www.147.ch). The *International Directory of Voluntary Work* (Vacation Work) also contains a wealth of information for prospective voluntary workers.

Winter Jobs

A seasonal job in a ski resort can be a lot of fun and very satisfying. You will get fit, learn or improve a language, make some good friends and may even save some money; all in addition to living in one of the most beautiful countries in the world. **Although a winter job might be a working holiday to you (with lots of skiing and little work), to your employer it means exactly the opposite.** In general, hotel and restaurant staff work much harder in ski resorts during winter than in summer, when life is more relaxed. Some hotel and restaurant employers even forbid employees to ski (although this is rare), particularly key personnel (e.g. chefs) over the Christmas and New Year period. Fortunately, there's a great sense of camaraderie among seasonal workers, which goes a long way towards compensating for the often boring and hard work (the Swiss francs also help).

Ski resorts require an army of temporary workers to cater for the annual invasion of winter sports enthusiasts. Besides jobs in the hotel and restaurant trades already described on page 23, a variety of generally well-paid winter jobs are available, some of which are described below. Usually the better paid the job, the longer the working hours and the less time off there is for skiing. Employment in a winter resort may entitle employees to reduced public transport fares and a discounted ski-pass. An invaluable book for anyone looking for a job in a ski resort is *Working in Ski Resorts – Europe*, by Victoria Pybus & Charles James (Vacation Work).

Note that in a bad season with little or no snow, seasonal workers in the tourist industry aren't covered by unemployment insurance, unlike, for example, workers in the construction industry. Ski-lift operators and others directly dependent on snow conditions for a living, should watch the weather forecast closely and pray for lots of snow. Even if you work in a hotel or restaurant, your contract could be cancelled or cut short when bookings are low or business is bad.

Chalet Girls

Hundreds of chalet girls (chalet boys?) are required each winter to look after the everyday creature comforts of guests in holiday chalets and private hotels, many run by British and other foreign tour operators. The job of a chalet girl or hostess requires hard work, generally offers low pay (as little as half the rate paid by Swiss hotels) and requires a variety of skills and experience. You must usually be able to cook food to cordon bleu standards or have experience catering for parties; do shopping, housekeeping and laundry; deal with obstreperous clients; and generally be a Jill of all trades. Nevertheless, once you get over the initial shock, you will probably find the job satisfying and challenging, and it allows plenty of time off for skiing. One thing for sure, you won't have time to be bored. You will also have to fight off the attentions of hordes of men and survive numerous late night parties – it's a tough life but someone has to do it! A limited number of chalet girls are also required in summer.

Ski Technicians

A ski technician or ski maintenance and repair job entails fitting and maintaining skis, bindings and boots. Although some employers may require previous experience, many ski rental shops provide training and courses are available in some countries, e.g. the UK. Besides doing the round of resort shops, contact tour companies and large luxury hotels, as they often operate their own ski rental and service shops. Local language ability is usually required, although it may depend on the employer and his clientele.

Ski Instructors & Guides

Jobs as ski instructors in Switzerland are almost impossible to obtain unless you've passed the Swiss ski instructors' examinations, although some resorts accept foreign qualifications, e.g. the advanced British Association of Ski Instructors (BASI) qualification or equivalent. Experience and local language fluency are also required. However, jobs can be found as ski companions, ski instructors for children and ski guides with foreign tour operators. Unfortunately in some resorts local ski instructors are hostile towards ski guides, particularly as there's often only a thin dividing line between guiding and instructing, and as a result guide jobs are being reduced. The Ski Club of Great Britain (SCGB) has representatives in many resorts, whose job is to take members on skiing excursions, but not to teach. Swiss resorts (wisely) usually allow British and other foreign school parties to be taught by qualified foreign ski instructors. To teach children, the lowest BASI qualification or equivalent may be sufficient.

Working as an unofficial instructor without a permit or qualifications is strictly illegal. If you work as a ski guide or instructor and an accident occurs through your negligence (for example one of your customers falls down a precipice), you may be liable for damages.

PERMANENT POSITIONS

Permanent positions in Switzerland require an annual residence permit, quotas for which are much lower than for short term permits (see **B Permit** on page 64). Most permanent positions open to foreigners require special skills, qualifications and experience, which are usually more important than the ability to speak fluent French, German or Italian (see **Languages** on page 39). In fact, you may not even be expected to speak the local language at all if your mother-tongue is English. This is often the case when you're employed by an American or British company, or work in a high-tech field where English is an important language spoken fluently by your colleagues. If you need to speak (or learn) the local language, you will be informed at your interview. When necessary, language tuition may be subsidised or paid for by your employer.

There's often a big difference between working for a Swiss or foreign company employing many other English-speaking foreigners, and working for a company where you have few or no non-Swiss or English-speaking colleagues. You will, of course, learn the local language much quicker working with colleagues who don't speak English. However, you may find, as many other foreigners do, that the working environment and general lack of camaraderie, warmth and friendliness, isn't to your liking. The Swiss don't generally mix socially with their colleagues and this may even exclude the occasional after work drink at a local bar.

Foreign qualifications are recognised in many trades and professions, provided the length of training and syllabus was similar to the equivalent Swiss qualification. Under the Bilateral Treaties between Switzerland and the EU Switzerland now recognises most EU-based diplomas and qualifications even for the formerly excluded professions such as teachers, barristers, lawyers and the 'medical professions' such as doctors, dentists, pharmacists and veterinarians. For non-EU citizens the restrictions are still valid but a non-EU foreigner entitled to live in Switzerland, for example as a result of long-term residence or marriage to a Swiss citizen, may be able to study or sit a Swiss examination entitling him to work in a restricted field. Regulations may also be relaxed by individual cantons when there's a shortage of qualified Swiss staff.

When applying for a job, always provide copies of all qualifications and references, as these tend to impress Swiss employers and may also influence the authorities when they're deciding whether to grant a permit.

JOB APPLICATIONS

Seasonal Jobs – Written Applications

Apply for jobs as early as possible, for example January for summer jobs and June or July for winter jobs. For summer jobs in mountain resorts, you should apply in March or April. If you apply too early the worst that can happen is that you will be told to apply again later. The latest dates for applications are usually the end of September for winter jobs and the end of April for summer jobs. In some resorts the season starts in Spring (April), with staff being recruited in January. Don't put all your eggs in one basket – the more job applications you make, the better your chances of success.

Many jobs require local language fluency (see **Languages** on page 39), therefore if you apply for a job in writing, it's best to write in the local language – but obtain help if you aren't fluent. You can brush up your language ability after you've secured a job, however, it's inadvisable to exaggerate your language abilities, experience or qualifications too wildly in a letter. If you're offered a job on the basis of non-existent qualifications, you will soon be found out and risk being fired. A good knowledge of the local language helps when dealing with local officials. For seasonal jobs, German is more advantageous than French, as the majority of jobs are in German-speaking resorts.

When applying for a job requiring experience, don't forget to provide your **curriculum vitae** and copies of qualifications and references. **Always** ask for a job offer in writing and a contract, and steer clear of employers who won't supply them. An official job entitles you to accident insurance, unemployment benefits, and in particular, official protection from exploitation (see also **Illegal Working** on page 34).

Note that writing unsolicited letters for jobs is a hit and miss affair, and is usually the least successful method of securing employment. An employer who doesn't know you from Adam or Eve may be unwilling to risk employing you – if you don't turn up he is left in the lurch. If you're really serious and can afford the journey, it may be worthwhile visiting prospective employers for an interview before the season starts.

Seasonal Jobs – Personal Applications

Your best chance of obtaining a seasonal job may be to apply in person, particularly when looking for a winter job close to the start of the ski season. Success is often simply a matter of being in the right place at the right time, although you can give lady luck a helping hand by your persistence and enterprise. Make an effort to look presentable, as Swiss employers expect a high standard of dress and cleanliness; hair must usually be short (except for women) and tidy, and beards aren't usually permitted (except for women). When looking for a job in person, try the following sources:

- Call on prospective employers and check wanted boards, but avoid calling at hotels and restaurants during meal times;
- Look in local newspapers;
- Ask at tourist offices;
- Check notice and bulletin boards;
- Ask other foreign workers.

Ask prospective employers if they know of anyone looking for staff and leave your name and an address and telephone number (if possible) where you can be contacted. Many tourist offices keep lists of job vacancies from September onwards for the coming winter season. Lists are regularly updated and the service is free. You can place your own advertisement in a local newspaper or on local notice boards, for example in a Migros or Coop supermarket, or on the notice boards of expatriate clubs, churches and other organisations.

In you're an English speaker, the best winter resorts to try are those with a large number of American and British skiers. These include Arosa, Champéry, Crans-Montana, Davos, Engelberg, Grindelwald, Gstaad, Klosters, Les Diablerets, Leysin, Saas Fee, St. Moritz, Verbier, Wengen and Zermatt. However, don't neglect the many smaller resorts, as although jobs may be scarcer, there's less competition from other job hunters (who haven't read this book). **In recent years jobs have been harder to find in Valais and Vaud, where there's higher unemployment, than (for example) in Graubunden and Berne.**

Don't worry if you miss the start of the season, as jobs often become vacant at short notice to replace those who become sick or home sick, injured, sacked, or who run off with the ski instructor (or instructress). However, employers may have difficulty obtaining a permit during the season as allocated permits cannot be transferred to new employees. Don't forget to take sufficient money to see you through the job hunting period. Allow at least two weeks and bear in mind that the cost of living (see page 298) is high in Switzerland.

Depending on your nationality, after you've found a job you may need to return to the nearest border point with your **assurance of a residence permit** paper for a health check (see page 76). When leaving a job at the end of the season, it's advisable to ask for a reference if one isn't provided automatically, particularly if you intend to look for further seasonal work.

If you need a visa to enter Switzerland to take up employment (see page 72), then you will be unable to find a job on the spot, as the visa must be issued by an embassy abroad.

Permanent Positions

There are various ways to find a permanent position in Switzerland, including the following:

- Obtain copies of Swiss newspapers, most of which contain a positions vacant (*Stellenanzeiger/Stellenmarkt*, *offres d'emploi*) section on certain days. When the ability to speak English is paramount, a position may be advertised in English. Swiss companies sometimes advertise for C permit holders (see page 70) or Swiss nationals only. Outside Switzerland, Swiss newspapers are usually available from international news agencies, Swiss embassies and consulates, Swiss trade and commercial centres, and Swiss social clubs. However, they don't always contain the positions vacant sections.

- Apply to American, British and other multinational companies who have offices or subsidiaries in Switzerland, and make written applications directly to Swiss companies. The 2000 largest Swiss companies are listed in *Top 2000* (also available on CD-ROM), a book published by HandelsZeitung Fachverlag AG, Abo-Service, Postfach, CH-8027 Zurich (☎ 01 288 35 45). Many of these companies advertise jobs on their websites. When writing letters for jobs, address them to the personnel department manager (*Personalabteilungs-leiter*, *Chef de Service du Personnel*). Include your curriculum vitae and copies of references and qualifications with your letter. If possible, offer to attend an interview in Switzerland and state when you're available.

- Apply to international recruiting agencies acting for Swiss companies. These companies chiefly recruit executives and key personnel, and many have offices world-wide, including Switzerland. A Swiss company may appoint a sole agent to handle recruitment in a particular country.

- Contact employment agencies in Switzerland. **Note that many Swiss agencies find positions for Swiss citizens only or for foreigners holding a B or C residence permit (see Chapter 3).** Some agencies specialise only in certain fields, for example the computer or catering industries. The Swiss labour exchange doesn't help foreigners find employment unless they're already resident in Switzerland. Swiss employment agencies are unable to apply for residence permits on your behalf and only a bona fide Swiss employer can do this.

- If you're a member of a recognised profession, you can place a 'position wanted' advertisement in a Swiss professional or trade newspaper or magazine. Publicitas SA, Département étranger, Rue Etraz 4, CH-1000 Lausanne (☎ 021 317 81 11) can help you select the most appropriate publication.

- Apply in person to Swiss companies. This method is often successful but doesn't usually shorten the time required to process a job application and obtain a residence permit, which can take up to three months.

- Ask friends or acquaintances working in Switzerland if they know of an employer seeking someone with your experience and qualifications.

WORKING ILLEGALLY

It isn't uncommon in Switzerland for foreigners to work without an official residence permit. The illegal labour market (termed the black economy) thrives because employers are often unable to obtain permits and many foreigners are willing to risk the consequences for the comparatively high wages on offer. In the past it was estimated that the number of illegal workers in Switzerland was as high as 150,000, the majority of whom worked in hotels, restaurants, farming, construction and cleaning jobs. This figure is now much lower since measures were taken to address the problem. Some unscrupulous employers use illegal labour simply to pay low wages for long hours and poor working conditions (Geneva is the black economy's black spot). An employer may also be reluctant to pay for an employee's permit, particularly when he may need him for a few weeks only, e.g. to help with the grape harvest.

It's strictly illegal to work in Switzerland without a permit. If you're tempted to take a job without one you should be aware of the consequences, as the black economy is a risky business for both employers and employees. An employer faces a fine of up to SFr. 5,000 per employee and those who organise or help illegal aliens enter Switzerland can be imprisoned and fined up to SFr. 100,000. There can also be serious consequences for employees. Anyone caught working without a permit is usually fined and deported, and may be refused a permit in future. You can even be black-listed (this also applies to those sacked for serious offences) or deported and your passport stamped so that you're unable to re-enter Switzerland. If you're caught working illegally, even for a few days while waiting for a permit to be issued, you can be fined or your permit application may even be cancelled. **Employees without permits have no entitlement to federal or company pensions, unemployment pay, health or accident insurance (e.g. when skiing), and no legal job protection.**

SALARIES

It can be difficult to determine the level of salary you should receive in Switzerland, as salaries aren't quoted in job advertisements and are kept strictly confidential – the Swiss don't like to discuss money, which simply confirms that they've got loads of it! Usually salaries are negotiable and it's up to you to ensure that you receive the level of salary and benefits commensurate with your qualifications and experience. Minimum salaries exist in all trades and professions. Age is usually a major consideration with many Swiss companies and seniority and experience are favoured by most Swiss employers (unless you're over 50). Many employers, particularly larger companies, are reluctant to pay a young person (e.g. aged below 30) a top salary, irrespective of his qualifications and experience. If you have friends or acquaintances working in Switzerland or who have worked there, ask them what an average or good salary is for your particular trade or profession.

Surveys consistently show that Swiss salaries are among the highest in the world, particularly those of managers and executives, and the Swiss also have the highest net pay after the deduction of taxes and social security contributions. An executive or top manager earns over SFr. 100,000 and top executives around SFr. 250,000 or more, although management salaries have fallen in recent years. A top executive can earn at least 40 times that of the lowest paid worker, the highest differential in the world. Salaries of both skilled and unskilled workers are generally **up to two or three times higher in Switzerland than in most other European countries.** The down side is that Switzerland has among the highest manufacturing labour costs in the world.

Starting salaries with many large Swiss companies may, however, be lower than the national average. Small companies often pay higher salaries, but have fewer permit allocations. Salaries paid by some foreign companies (e.g. American) tend to be, on average, higher than those paid by Swiss companies, partly because many staff are specialists, managers and executives imported from abroad. Your working hours (see page 50) may be longer than in other countries and should be taken into account when negotiating your salary (an extra two hours a week adds up to around two and a half weeks a year). In recent years, salary increases have been low and often below the rate of inflation (salaries have largely stagnated for the last decade).

Some employers may underestimate the cost of living in Switzerland, particularly the cost of housing, which can be astronomical. On average the cost of living (see page 298) is much higher than in other western countries, although the gross earnings and purchasing power of the Swiss are among the highest in the world. Income tax and pension contributions are progressive; the higher your income, the higher your pension and income tax payments (see **Chapters 13 & 14** respectively). They are, however, lower than in most other countries.

Women make up 40 per cent of the Swiss workforce and around 60 per cent of Swiss women aged between 15 and 62 are employed, one of the highest proportions in Europe. However, over 50 per cent of women work part-time compared with just 10 per cent of men. Since 1981, employers in Switzerland have been legally required to pay equal wages to men and women doing the same job. Nevertheless, women's salary levels are (on average) around a third lower than men's, an inequality not entirely accounted for by their different occupations, and foreign women usually earn even less than Swiss women.

As in most countries, although there may be no official discrimination, in practice this isn't always so. Professional women are rarer in Switzerland than in many other western countries and a woman often finds it difficult to reach the top ranks of her profession and only a small proportion are managers or executives – Switzerland has a concrete rather than a glass ceiling where career women are concerned! Although 'the best man for the job is often a woman', this is rarely acknowledged in Switzerland (and in many other countries). Swiss women have held a few one-day strikes to highlight salary inequalities, although they weren't well supported (wherein lies one of the main problems women face in obtaining equality – their own apathy).

Although illegal, married women usually face more discrimination in the workplace than single women, although it's no worse than in most other western countries. Swiss employers must pay the salary of a female employee during pregnancy when she is absent from work, provided she intends to return to the employer after giving birth (see **Pregnancy & Confinement** on page 56). However, as no crèche service is provided by companies, this is often difficult (in Switzerland, a woman is usually either a mother or an employee, seldom both).

A useful guide to salaries and the cost of living is contained in a booklet entitled simply *Switzerland*, published in English by the Federal Office for Industry, Crafts and Labour, Manpower and Emigration Division, Bundesgasse 8, CH-3003 Berne (☎ 031 322 21 11). The United Bank of Switzerland publishes a free booklet (in English) entitled *Prices and Earnings Around the World*, which compares Swiss salaries with those of many other countries (it can be ordered from 💻 www.ubs.ch).

CONTRACT JOBS

Contract jobs, usually for a limited period only, are available through many foreign and Swiss employment agencies specialising in freelance work. Most contract positions are for specialists in the computer, engineering and electronics fields. A number of consulting companies (body shops) in Switzerland specialise in supplying contract staff to major companies. Foreign employees of a foreign company who are living in Switzerland and working temporarily for a Swiss employer, require a work permit. This must be obtained by the Swiss employer, unless the employment is for only a brief period. Employees of most Swiss consulting companies are permanent company employees, although in effect they're often working full-time for another company on a contract basis.

SELF-EMPLOYMENT

Non-EU citizens require a C permit (*Niederlassungsbewilligung, permis d'etablissement*) before they're permitted to be self-employed (see page 70). For them, it's therefore virtually impossible to emigrate to Switzerland to become self-employed or to start a business (unless you have millions of francs and are going to create jobs and exports). There are sometimes exceptions in the fields of music and art, and in professions where Swiss nationals don't usually qualify, for example translating or writing in a non-Swiss language. Foreigners married to Swiss nationals with a B permit may be permitted to be self-employed, although this is usually only allowed if you have a C permit. EU citizens can start self-employment in Switzerland but will have to register with the authorities and get a work permit. This is usually granted if the self-employed person can prove they've set up successfully and can make a living from their trade.

Freedom of trade and commerce is a constitutional right in Switzerland and anyone, including a foreigner with a C permit, has the right to establish a business (provided you don't die of old age while waiting for your C permit). Foreign non-residents who wish to establish a business in Switzerland may be able to negotiate a favourable tax deal with the canton authorities, e.g. in the canton of Vaud a 10-year tax exemption is possible, plus resident permits for the owner and his family.

TRAINEES

Switzerland is a participant in an international trainee (*Praktikant, stagiaire*) programme designed to give young people the opportunity for further education and occupational training, and to enlarge their professional experience and knowledge of languages. The programme has exchange agreements with Argentina, Australia, Austria, Belgium, Bulgaria, Canada, Czech Republic, Denmark, Finland, France, Germany, Hungary, Ireland (Eire), Italy, Luxembourg, Monaco, the Netherlands, New Zealand, Norway, Poland, Portugal, Romania. Russia, Slovakia, South Africa, Spain, Sweden, the UK and the US. If you're aged between 18 and 30 (Argentina, Bulgaria, Czech Republic, France, Germany, Monaco, Romania, Slovakia, South Africa, the US 18 to 35) and have completed your vocational training (minimum of two years), you may be eligible for a position as a trainee in Switzerland. The trainee agreement covers all occupations except those normally barred to foreigners (e.g. lawyers and doctors), and employment must be in the occupation in which you were trained.

Permits are granted for one year and can, in exceptional circumstances, be extended for a further six months. Under the trainee agreement, the granting of a residence permit doesn't depend on quotas or the employment situation. After a training period in Switzerland, a non-EU trainee cannot be re-employed by the same or another employer in Switzerland for a period of 2 to 12 months. This is to prevent people using the trainee programme as a back door for securing a permanent job in Switzerland. Information about the trainee programme can be obtained from the *Bundesamt für Ausländerfragen (BFA)*, Abteilung Arbeitsmarkt, Sektion Auswanderung und Stagiares, Quellenweg 9+15, CH-3003 Berne (☎ 031 325 9511).

AU PAIRS

If you're between 17 and 30 (male or female) you're eligible for a job as an au pair in Switzerland. The au pair system provides you with an excellent opportunity to travel, learn a language and generally broaden your education by living and working abroad. The main aim of the au pair system is to give you the opportunity to learn a foreign language in a typical family environment. The au pair employment conditions state that you must attend language classes for a minimum number of hours a week (around four) and be given sufficient time off to study at home. Evidence of attendance at a language course may be required by the authorities. Foreign au pairs are contracted to work for up to 18 months. Most au pairs in Switzerland come from Europe (particularly Scandinavian countries). British girls are popular, but you should make sure that a family isn't just looking for a low-paid English teacher. Young people from Australia, Canada, Europe, New Zealand and the US **are** permitted to work as au pairs in Switzerland.

You must be prepared to do most kinds of housework and various duties associated with children, including the preparation of their meals, washing and ironing their clothes, cleaning and baby-sitting. You aren't, however, a general servant or cook, although extra services are often taken for granted. You also shouldn't be expected to look after physically or mentally disabled children. Working hours are officially limited to 30 a week (five hours a day, six days a week) plus a few evening's baby-sitting, and include at least one full day and one half day free each week. You're paid between around SFr. 600 and 900 a month, depending on your age, experience, working hours and the canton of employment (you may have fun as an au pair, but you're unlikely to get rich unless you marry a wealthy Swiss).

All meals and accommodation are provided and you have your own room with a lockable door. Your employer pays for your residence permit and may pay part of your language study costs and your journey to and from Switzerland, although this isn't usual. He may deduct compulsory insurance contributions and a share of your health and accident insurance contributions (see **Chapter 13**). If you're under 20, you have five weeks paid holiday a year and four weeks if over 20. On days off, you're paid around SFr. 20 in lieu of board. You should obtain a statement of your precise duties, time off and salary in writing, before your arrival in Switzerland.

You can find a position as an au pair through agencies both in Switzerland and abroad. The major au pair agencies in Switzerland include Pro Filia and the Girls' Friendly Society (*Verein der Freundinnen junger Mädchen, Association des Amis de la Jeune Fille*), who share offices in most major Swiss cities with a number of other (mainly religious) au pair placement organisations. These agencies charge registration and placement fees when a position is found. There are also specialist au pair agencies in most European countries and in North America that can help you find a job as an au pair in Switzerland. It's also possible to advertise for an au pair position in a local newspaper. When you find a suitable job, the family is required to make the formal arrangements. Au pair jobs are also available in many winter and summer holiday areas and are often advertised in tourist offices. **Be wary if someone offers you an illegal au pair job, as this provides no state benefits or protection from exploitation** (see **Illegal Working** on page 34). The *Au Pair and Nanny's Guide to Working Abroad* (Vacation Work) may also be of interest.

The au pair system has been uncharitably referred to as a mine-field of guilt-ridden mothers, lecherous fathers and spoilt brats (probably by an ex-au pair who was bitten by a child!). Your experience as an au pair will depend entirely on your family. If you're fortunate enough to work for a warm and friendly host family, you will have a wonderful experience, lots of free time, and possibly holidays in both Switzerland and abroad. Many au pairs grow to love their children and families, and form lifelong friendships. On the other hand, abuses of the au pair system are common in all countries and you may be treated as a servant or slave rather than a member of the family, and be expected to work long hours and spend most evenings baby-sitting. Many families employ an au pair simply because it costs only a fraction of the salary of the lowest-paid nanny. If you have any questions or complaints about your duties, you should refer them to the agency that found you your position (if applicable). **There are many families to choose from and you should never remain with a family if you're unhappy at the way you're treated.**

LANGUAGES

An important consideration for anyone seeking employment in Switzerland is the local language, which varies depending on the area. Switzerland has four official languages: German, spoken by around 64 per cent of the population, French (19 per cent), Italian (8 per cent) and Romansch (Rhaeto-Roman), which is spoken by around 60,000 people (1 per cent of the population) in the canton of Graubünden. The remaining 8 per cent are foreigners whose mother-tongue isn't one of the Swiss national languages. Although all official languages are equal in principle, this is often not the case in practice, and the German language and German speakers dominate many areas of public life, to the displeasure of the French-speaking Swiss. The cultural and linguistic division between the German and French-speaking Swiss cantons is referred to as the *röstigraben* (the 'fried potato cake' divide). Italian is usually relegated to a distant third place (except in Ticino).

Although English could be called the *lingua franca* of Switzerland, most official publications, forms, warning signs, etc., are printed in French, German and Italian, and seldom in English. English **isn't** taught as a mandatory subject in all Swiss state schools and therefore it isn't as widely spoken as in many other European countries, particularly not by the older generations. However, changes may be afoot. Canton Zurich launched a debate in 2000 regarding the introduction of English as a mandatory subject in primary schools in place of French. If this is adopted in future a Swiss from Zurich and Geneva may have to converse in English – if they talk at all!

Nevertheless, many Swiss do speak good English and it's an important business and commercial language, even **within** Switzerland. Some 15 per cent of all Switzerland's workforce uses English at work, although the German-speaking Swiss are more likely to use it than French or Italian speakers. Wherever you work, you will be inundated with forms, documents, memos and other communications written in the local language. Don't ignore them as some will be important. The same applies to private post – don't throw it away unless you're sure it's junk post.

Berne, Fribourg and Valais are officially bi-lingual and have both French and German-speaking areas. Graubünden is tri-lingual, where (some) people speak German, Italian and Romansch. Some Swiss towns are totally bi-lingual and languages are even alternated during conversation (the Swiss are **very** democratic). In parliament, members are free to speak their mother tongue, which may explain why governmental decisions take so long in Switzerland (it's said that the Swiss get on so well together because they don't understand each other). The problem of which language to use on stamps and currency is solved by using the Latin name for Switzerland, *Helvetia*. A useful phrasebook is published by Dynamicha (ISBN 3-9521323-1-4) combining the four Swiss languages (but not English).

Probably nothing will affect your lifestyle (and possibly your career prospects) in Switzerland more than your ability to speak the local language(s). **In an emergency, being able to make yourself understood in a foreign language could make the difference between life and death.** See also **Language** on page 153 and **Language Schools** on page 169.

German

The language spoken in German-speaking areas of Switzerland is Swiss German (*Schwyzertüütsch, suisse allemand*). It bears little resemblance to the High German (*Schriftdeutsch/Hochdeutsch, bon allemand*) of Germany, which is a foreign language to the Swiss – although not half as foreign as Swiss German is to the French and Italian-speaking Swiss! Most Swiss German speakers do, however, speak High German (fairly) fluently. To the casual listener Swiss German sounds like someone trying to speak while gargling and is often described as 'not so much a language as a throat disease'. There are many dialects of Swiss German and sometimes inhabitants of neighbouring villages, let alone cantons, even have trouble understanding one another.

There are over 100,000 recorded Swiss German words and although many have their origin in High German, the Swiss have successfully managed to make them unrecognisable to anyone but themselves. Most native High German speakers are initially just as confused as other foreigners. When talking to foreigners, many Swiss German speakers attempt to speak High German, or at least will do so when asked. **The Swiss don't like speaking High German and most Germans don't like the way that the Swiss speak their language.**

Even if you don't understand what the locals are saying, the written language in Switzerland is High German, therefore if you understand High German you will at least be able to read the newspapers. Strictly speaking, Swiss German isn't a written language and it's never used in official communications (the most common usage is in advertising). Most people write Swiss German using completely arbitrary phonetic spelling and the Swiss cannot even decide how to spell *Schwyzertüütsch* (Swiss German). Nevertheless there are a few children's books in Swiss German dialects and some poets and authors use it. (It's all a fiendish plot to prevent foreigners from understanding what's going on.) All cantons except those listed under French (below) and Ticino (Italian) are Swiss German-speaking (some are bi-lingual with French or Italian).

There's a useful little book of Swiss German swear words entitled *Lappi, Lööli, Blööde Siech* (untranslatable in polite society) written by Andreas Lötscher. It might come in handy when motoring or repelling ski-lift queue-jumpers – that's if you can get your tongue around any of the words. See also **Swiss German** on page 172.

French

French is spoken in the cantons of Geneva, Jura, Neuchâtel and Vaud, in addition to the bi-lingual cantons of Berne, Fribourg and Valais. In French-speaking Switzerland (*Westschweiz, suisse romande*) the language is almost the same as in France, with few Swiss idiosyncrasies added. The accent is clear and good French is spoken, the purest in Neuchâtel, although the same claim is often made for the French of Geneva and Lausanne. Dialect (*Dialekt/Mundart, patois*) is often spoken in rural villages.

If you work in a French-speaking region, it's usually necessary to speak French at work. Social life in French-speaking areas of Switzerland can also be difficult without at least basic French, although in cities such as Geneva and Lausanne, English is widely spoken.

Italian

Standard Italian with an everyday Lombardy accent is spoken in the canton of Ticino and parts of Graubünden (besides 'High Italian' and some local dialects). It would be almost impossible to work in Ticino without speaking Italian. Socially the language isn't such a problem (nobody can understand you in any case when you're drunk), as Ticino is a popular tourist area where people are used to dealing with foreigners. German is widely spoken in Ticino, mainly due to the influx of German and Swiss German tourists and retirees. The ability to communicate in Italian increases in direct proportion to your number of hands.

2.

EMPLOYMENT CONDITIONS

Working conditions in Switzerland are largely dependent on local canton laws, an employee's individual employment contract, and an employer's employment conditions. In general, foreigners are employed under the same working conditions as Swiss citizens. This usually means that salaries, fringe benefits and employment conditions are among the best in the world. Employees hired to work in Switzerland by foreign (non-Swiss) companies and organisations may be offered even better terms and conditions (including higher salaries) than those provided by Swiss employers.

TERMS OF EMPLOYMENT

Negotiating an appropriate salary is only one aspect of your working conditions. When negotiating your terms of employment for a job in Switzerland, the checklists on the following pages will prove useful. The points listed under **General Positions** (below) apply to most jobs, while those listed under **Executive Positions** (on page 47) usually apply to executive and top managerial appointments only.

General Positions

Salary

- Is the total salary (including expenses) paid in Swiss francs or will it be paid in another country (in a another currency) with expenses for living in Switzerland?
- Is the total adequate, taking into account the high cost of living in Switzerland (see page 298)? Is the salary index-linked?
- When and how often is the salary reviewed?
- Does the salary include a 13th month's salary and annual or end-of-contract bonuses (see page 50)?
- Is overtime paid or time off given in lieu of extra hours worked?

Relocation Expenses

- Are removal expenses or a relocation allowance paid?
- Does the allowance include travelling expenses for all family members?
- Is there a limit and is it adequate?
- Are you required to repay relocation expenses (or a percentage) if you resign before a certain period has elapsed?
- Are you required to pay for your relocation in advance? This can run into many thousands of francs for normal house contents.

- If employment is for a limited period, will your relocation costs be paid by the employer when you leave Switzerland?
- If you aren't shipping household goods and furniture to Switzerland, is there an allowance for buying furnishings locally?
- Do relocation expenses include the legal and estate agent's fees incurred when moving home?
- Does the employer use the services of a relocation consultant?

Accommodation

- Will the employer pay for a hotel (or pay a lodging allowance) until you find permanent accommodation?
- Is subsidised or free (temporary or permanent) accommodation provided? If so, is it furnished or unfurnished?
- Must you pay for utilities such as electricity, gas and water?
- If accommodation isn't provided by the employer, is assistance provided to find accommodation? What does it consist of?
- What will accommodation cost?
- Are your expenses paid while looking for accommodation?

Working Hours

- What are the weekly working hours?
- Does the employer operate a flexi-time system (see page 51)? If so, what are the fixed working hours? How early must you start? Can you carry forward extra hours worked and take time off at a later date or carry forward a deficit and make it up later?
- Are you required to clock in and out of work?
- Can you choose to take time off in lieu of overtime or be paid for it?
- Are you required to work additional hours each week to compensate for extra official company holidays (see **Working Hours** on page 50)?

Leave Entitlement

- What is the annual leave entitlement? Does it increase with age?
- What are the paid public holidays? Is Monday or Friday a free day when a public - holiday falls on a Tuesday or Thursday respectively?

- Is free air travel to your home country or elsewhere provided for you and your family, and if so, how often?

Insurance

- Is extra insurance cover provided besides obligatory insurance (see page 258)?
- Is free life insurance provided?
- Is health insurance provided for you **and** your family? What does it include (see page 266)?
- For how long will your salary be paid if you're ill or have an accident (see **Salary Insurance** on page 264)?

Company Pension

- What percentage of your salary must you pay (see page 261)?
- Are you able to pay a lump sum into the pension fund in order to receive a full or higher pension?

Employer

- What are the employer's future prospects?
- Is his profitability and growth rate favourable?
- Does he have a good reputation as an employer?
- Does he have a high staff turnover? If so, why?

Miscellaneous

- Are free or subsidised language lessons provided for you and your spouse?
- Is a travelling allowance paid from your Swiss residence to your place of work?
- Is free or subsidised parking provided at your place of work?
- Is a free or subsidised company restaurant provided? If not, is a lunch allowance paid? Some Swiss companies provide excellent staff restaurants, which save you both money and time.
- Will the employer provide or pay for any professional training or education required, if necessary abroad? Will he pay for a part or the total cost of non-essential education, e.g. a computer or language course?

- Are free work clothes or overalls provided? Does the employer pay for the cleaning of work clothes (both workshop and office)?

- Does the employer provide any fringe benefits, such as subsidised in-house banking services, low-interest loans, inexpensive petrol, employee's shop or product discounts, sports and social facilities, and subsidised tickets, e.g. for local theatres or sports events?

- Do you have a written list of your job responsibilities?

- Have your employment conditions been confirmed in writing? For a list of the possible contents of your employment conditions, see page 49.

- If a dispute arises over your salary or working conditions, under the law of which country will your employment contract be interpreted?

Executive Positions

- Is private schooling for your children paid for or subsidised? Will the employer pay for a boarding school in Switzerland or abroad?

- Is the salary index-linked or protected against devaluation and cost of living increases? This is particularly important if you're paid in a foreign currency that fluctuates wildly or could be devalued (many currencies have lost ground against the Swiss franc in recent years). Are you paid an overseas allowance for working in Switzerland?

- Is there a non-contributory pension fund besides the compulsory company scheme? Is it transferable, and if so, what are the conditions?

- Are the costs incurred by a move to Switzerland reimbursed? For example, the cost of selling your home, employing an agent to let it for you or storing household effects.

- Will the employer pay for domestic help or a contribution towards the cost of a servant or cook?

- Is a car provided? With a chauffeur?

- Are you entitled to any miscellaneous benefits, such as membership of a club or free credit cards?

- Is there an entertainment allowance?

- Is a clothing allowance available? For example, if you arrive in Switzerland in the middle of winter from the tropics, you will probably need to buy some winter clothes.

- Is compensation paid if you're made redundant or fired? Redundancy or severance pay (or a golden handshake) is unusual in Switzerland and when applicable it should be noted in your employment contract.

EMPLOYMENT CONTRACT

Under Swiss law a contract exists as soon as you undertake a job for which you expect to be paid. For many Swiss, their word is their bond (in mountain areas, contracts are often verbal and sealed by a handshake); however, even if you're employed only part-time, you should insist on a written contract. You and your employer are obliged to abide by the rules and regulations set out in the Swiss law of obligation, a copy of which can be purchased in most bookshops.

There are usually no hidden surprises or traps for the unwary in a Swiss employment contract (*Arbeitsvertrag, contrat de travail*). Nevertheless, as with any contract, you should know exactly what it contains before signing it. If you aren't fluent in the local language, you should try to obtain an English translation of your contract (your language ability would need to be excellent to understand the legal jargon that goes into some contracts). Swiss employers seldom provide foreigners with contracts in English, irrespective of the number of English-speaking foreigners employed. If you cannot obtain a written English translation of your contract, you should at least have it translated verbally so that you don't receive any nasty surprises later – like discovering that you're required to give six month's notice.

In some trades or fields of employment (e.g. agriculture, domestic, and hotel and restaurant jobs) standard employment contracts are drafted by canton governments or a professional body, based on collective labour contracts or legislation (covering around half the workforce). These are usually applicable unless both employer and employee agree otherwise in writing. Employment contract disputes can be easily and inexpensively resolved by a court. For more information contact the Federal Aliens' Committee (*Eidgenössische Ausländerkommission/EKA, Comission fédérale des étrangers/CFE*), Quellenweg 9, CH-3003 Berne-Wabern (☎ 031 325 91 16, 🖥www.eka-cfe.ch). EKA also publish information (both in French and German, **unfortunately not yet in English**) on a wide range of subjects.

Your employment contract may contain the following:

- Job title;
- Department name and manager;
- Main duties;
- Relationships with other departments;
- Responsibility to the employer;
- Place(s) of work;
- Salary details, including 13th month's salary and any agreed increases;
- Confidentiality and restrictions on private work;
- Membership of compulsory health fund (if applicable);

- Medical examination (if necessary);
- A clause stating that the contract is subject to a residence permit or permission to change jobs being granted by the canton authorities;
- The date employment starts;
- Probationary and notice periods;
- Agreement with employment conditions. When you sign your contract, you're also signing agreement with your prospective employer's general employment conditions. Before signing your contract you should obtain a copy of your employment conditions and ensure that you understand them (see below).

WORKING CONDITIONS

Employment conditions (*Arbeitreglement, règlement de travail*) contain an employer's general rules and regulations regarding working conditions and benefits that are applicable to all employees, unless stated otherwise in your employment contract. Employment conditions may include the validity and applicability (of employment conditions); salary and benefits; 13th month's salary and bonuses; working hours; flexi-time rules; overtime and compensation; travel and relocation expenses; federal social security; company pension fund; accident insurance; unemployment insurance; salary insurance; miscellaneous insurance; notification of sickness or accident; annual holidays; public holidays; compassionate and special leave of absence; paid expenses; child allowance; area allowance; probationary and notice periods; education and training; pregnancy and confinement; part-time job restrictions; changing jobs and confidentiality; acceptance of gifts; retirement; military service; and dismissal. All the these points are explained in this chapter or a reference is given to the chapter where the subject is covered in more detail.

Validity & Applicability

Employment conditions usually contain a paragraph stating the date from which they take effect and to whom they're applicable.

Salary & Benefits

Your salary (*Salär/Gehalt, salaire*) is stated in your contract and salary reviews, planned increases and cost of living rises may be included. Only general points, such as the payment of your salary into a bank or post office account and the date of salary payments, are usually included in employment conditions. If the salary payment day varies each month, your employer may provide you with a list of payment dates. Salaries are usually paid earlier in December.

Salaries in Switzerland are generally reviewed once a year around November/December, with pay rises taking effect from 1st January of the following year. Annual increases include a percentage to cover a rise in the cost of living, although if there's a decrease in the cost of living (which can happen in Switzerland), your salary may be **reduced**.

13th Month's Salary & Bonuses

Most employers in Switzerland pay their employees' annual salary in 13 instalments and not 12. This means that in December you receive, in effect, two months' salary (which helps pay your end of year bills), although sometimes you receive half in July and half in December. When a 13th month's salary (*13. Salär, 13ième salaire*) is paid it's stated in your employment contract and is usually obligatory unless your employer declares otherwise. Some companies don't pay a 13th month's salary, but compensate by paying a higher monthly salary. When negotiating your salary with a prospective employer, ask whether a 13th month's salary is paid, although what's more important is the total annual salary. In your first and last year of employment, your 13th month's salary is paid pro rata if you don't work a full calendar year.

Some employers operate an additional annual voluntary bonus (*Gratifikation, gratification*) scheme, based on an employee's individual performance or the employer's profits. If you're employed on a contract basis for a fixed period, you may also be paid an end-of-contract bonus. **If you pay direct income tax, then you will pay a higher overall rate of tax if your 13th month's salary and bonus are paid in the same month.**

Working Hours

Working hours (*Arbeitsstunden, heures de travail*) in Switzerland vary depending on your employer, your position and the kind of industry in which you're employed, with the average around 41. Employees in industry work around 40 hours per week, while workers in the service sector, such as banking, generally work slightly longer hours (around 42 per week). At the other end of the scale, employees in hospitals, catering and hotels may work up to 60 hours a week, although the average is between 45 and 48. Under Swiss employment law, normal working hours should be a maximum of 45 per week. In 2002 an initiative to reduce the normal working week to 36 hours was refused by 74.6 per cent of the voters. Whatever your working hours are in Switzerland, they may be longer than you're used to working. Of the leading industrial nations, only the Japanese and Americans work longer hours than the Swiss.

The Swiss have voted against shorter working hours on a number of occasions. Many Swiss believe their long working hours are partly responsible for their economic success, although most analysts reckon that although the Swiss work longer hours, they don't actually do more work. During the recession in the early 1990s, many companies switched to short-time working rather than make employees redundant, with a proportionate reduction in salary. Some people (especially wives and mothers) choose to work reduced hours, such as 80 per cent, which is four days a week (usually Friday is the free day).

If a company closes between Christmas and New Year or on other unofficial holidays, employees must usually compensate by working around one hour extra each week. If applicable, this will be stated in your employment conditions. Your working hours may not be increased above the hours stated in your employment conditions without compensation or overtime being paid. It may come as a nasty surprise to some foreigners to discover that many Swiss employers (including most large companies) require all employees to clock in and out of work. Anyone caught cheating is liable to instant dismissal.

Flexi-Time Rules

Most Swiss companies operate flexi-time (*Gleitzeit, horaire mobile/horaire flexible*) working hours. A flexi-time system requires all employees to be present between certain hours, known as the block time (*Blockzeit, temps bloqué/heures de présence obligatoire*). For example, from 8.30 to 11.30am and from 1.30 to 4pm. Block time can start as early as 7.30 or 8am, which isn't early by Swiss standards. Employees may make up their required working hours by starting earlier than the required block time, reducing their lunch break (a minimum 30-minute lunch break is a legal requirement) or by working later. Most business premises are open between around 6.30am and 7pm. Smaller companies may allow employees to work as late as they wish, provided they don't exceed the maximum permitted daily working hours stipulated by canton or federal governments. Because flexi-time rules are often quite complicated, they may be contained in a separate set of regulations (it sometimes takes months to understand them).

Overtime & Compensation

Working hours for employees who work a flexi-time system (see above) are usually calculated on a monthly basis, during which time they may run up a credit or deficit, e.g. 15 or 25 hours. Hours can be compensated or increased in the following month(s) by working fewer or extra hours. **Some companies automatically cancel hours worked in excess of 15 or 25 hours if an employee doesn't take time off in lieu of hours worked (*Kompensation, compensation*) within a certain time limit** (they never, however, forget about the hours you owe the company!). Employees who work a flexi-time system may usually take a day or a half-day off work each month in lieu of hours worked or to be worked, without official permission.

Overtime (*Überstunden, heures supplémentaires*) payments may be made for extra hours worked, depending on company policy or your employment conditions. Most companies pay overtime only for work that's urgent and officially approved. Overtime is generally paid at the normal rate plus 25 per cent on weekdays and Saturdays, and plus 50 per cent on Sundays and public holidays. Companies must generally obtain special permission from the canton authorities for employees to work on Sundays and official holidays (see **Sunday Working** on page 58).

Travel & Relocation Expenses

Travel (*Reisespesen, frais de voyage*) and relocation expenses to Switzerland depend on your agreement with your employer, and are usually included in your employment contract or conditions. If you're hired from outside Switzerland, your air ticket (or other travel costs) are usually booked and paid for by your employer or his local agent abroad. In addition, you can usually claim any extra travel costs, for example the cost of transport to and from airports. If you travel by car to Switzerland, you can usually claim a mileage rate or the equivalent air fare cost. Most Swiss employers pay your relocation costs up to a specified amount, although you may be required to sign a special contract which stipulates that if you leave the employer before a certain period elapses (e.g. five years), you must repay a percentage of your removal costs, depending on your length of service.

An employer may pay a fixed relocation allowance based on your salary, position and size of family or may pay the total cost of removal. The allowance should be sufficient to move the contents of an average house (castles aren't usually catered for) and you must normally pay any excess costs yourself. If you don't want to bring your furniture to Switzerland or have only a few belongings to ship, it may be possible to purchase furniture locally up to the limit of your allowance. Check with your employer. A company may ask you to obtain two or three removal estimates when they're liable for the total cost of removal.

Generally you're required to organise and pay for the removal yourself. Your employer usually reimburses the equivalent amount in Swiss francs **after** you've paid the bill, although it may be possible to get him to pay the bill directly or provide a cash advance. If you change jobs within Switzerland, your new employer may pay your relocation expenses when it's necessary for you to move house. Don't forget to ask, as they may not offer to pay (it may depend on how desperate they are to employ you).

Federal Social Security

Swiss federal social security consists of Old Age and Survivors Insurance (OASI) (*Eidgenössische Alters- und Hinterlassenversicherung/AHV, Assurance-vieillesse et survivants fédérale/AVS*)) and Disability Insurance (*Invalidenversicherung/IV, Assurance d'invalidité/AI*), and is obligatory for most residents of Switzerland. A flat rate of 5.05 per cent of your gross salary is deducted at source by your employer. For details see page 258.

Company Pension Fund

Membership of a company pension fund (*Berufliche Vorsorge/BVG, Prévoyance Professionelle/LPP*) is compulsory for all employees earning over SFr. 25,320 a year. The amount you pay varies from around 6 to 15 per cent of your gross monthly salary, depending on your age and your employer's pension fund. See page 261 for information.

Accident Insurance

Accident insurance (*Unfallversicherung, assurance accidents*) is mandatory for all employees in Switzerland. Occupational accident insurance is paid by your employer and covers accidents or illness at work, and accidents that occur when travelling to and from work, or when travelling on company business.

Private accident insurance contributions vary depending on your employer from non-contributory to around 1.5 per cent of your gross monthly salary. For information see page 263.

Unemployment Insurance

Unemployment insurance (*Arbeitslosenversicherung, assurance chômage*) is compulsory for all employees of Swiss companies. You pay 1.25 per cent of your gross monthly salary, which is deducted by your employer. Payment may be included with your OASI/DI payments on your pay slip (total 6.55 per cent). For details see page 257.

Salary Insurance

Salary insurance (*Salärausfallversicherung/Salärlosenversicherung, assurance salaire*) for sickness or accidents varies from non-contributory to around 1 per cent of your gross monthly salary. For information see page 264.

Miscellaneous Insurance

Other insurance provided by your employer is listed in your employment conditions. It may include free life and health insurance when travelling outside Switzerland on company business. Some companies have their own compulsory health insurance schemes.

Notification Of Sickness Or Accident

You're usually required to notify your employer of sickness or an accident that prevents you from working as soon as possible. If you're away from work for longer than two or three days, you may be required to produce a doctor's certificate. The actual period is stated in your employment conditions.

Annual Holidays

Your annual holiday (*Ferien, congé/vacances*) entitlement depends on your profession, position and employer. Most Swiss companies allow four weeks annual holiday up to the age of 50 and five weeks over 50. Some companies may allow a fifth week's holiday at an earlier age, e.g. 45. Top managerial positions may also offer additional annual holidays (but no time to take them!). The average number of paid holidays a year is around 23 days.

Before starting a job, check that your new employer will approve any planned holidays. This is particularly important if they fall within your probationary period (usually three months), when holidays aren't usually permitted.

Public Holidays

Public holidays (*Feiertage, jours fériés*) vary from canton to canton, depending on whether the predominant local religion is Catholic or Protestant. The following dates or days are public holidays in most Swiss cantons:

* 1st January	New Year's Day (*Neujahr, nouvel An*)
2nd January	St. Berchtold's Day (*Berchtoldstag, le 2 janvier*)
* March or	Good Friday (*Karfreitag, Vendredi Saint*)
* April	Easter Monday (*Ostermontag, Lundi de Pâques*)
1st May	May Day (*Tag der Arbeit, Féte du Travail*)
* May	Ascension Day (*Auffahrt, Ascension*) – Thursday 40 days after Easter
* June	Whitsuntide (*Pfingsten, Pentcôte*) – ten days after Ascension
* 1st August	Swiss National Day (*Bundesfeiertag, Fête Nationale*)
* 25th December	Christmas Day (*Weihnachtstag, Noël*)
* 26th December	Boxing Day (*Stefanstag, 26 décembre*)
* Swiss National Holidays.	

If a public holiday falls on a weekend day, there's no substitute weekday holiday unless the number of public holidays in a particular year falls below a minimum number.

Many Swiss companies close down during Christmas and New Year, e.g. from midday or 4pm on 24th December until the 2nd or 3rd of January. To compensate for this shutdown and perhaps other extra holidays, employees are required to work around one hour per week extra, throughout the year. There are also half-day public holidays in some cantons, e.g. Zurich.

Compassionate & Special Leave of Absence

Most Swiss companies provide additional days off for moving house, your own or a family marriage, birth of a child, death of a family member or close relative, and other compassionate reasons. Grounds for compassionate leave (*Sonderurlaub, congé spécial*) are listed in employment conditions.

Paid Expenses

Expenses (*Spesen, frais*) paid by your employer are usually listed in your employment conditions. These may include travel costs from your home to your place of work, usually consisting of a second class rail season ticket or the equivalent cost, paid monthly with your salary. Companies without an employee restaurant or canteen may pay a lunch allowance or provide luncheon vouchers. Expenses paid for travel on company business or for training and education may be detailed in your employment conditions or listed in a separate document.

Child Allowance

In Switzerland parents receive a monthly child allowance (*Kinderzulage, allocations familiales*) of between around SFr. 100 and 250 per child, per month. Child allowance is paid by your employer and varies from canton to canton. The majority of cantons pay a fixed allowance for each child, while some cantons pay an increased allowance for the third and subsequent children (to encourage the Swiss to have more children). The cantons with the smallest population or lowest birth rates, usually pay the highest child allowances. The allowance is usually paid up to a child's 16th birthday (15 in Fribourg and Geneva) or until the age of between 18 and 25 when he remains in full-time education or occupational training. Registration is made by your employer and the allowance is usually paid to the family's main breadwinner (you can choose) in his or her monthly salary payment. Around ten cantons pay a birth allowance of from SFr. 500 to 1,200.

Area Allowance

If you're a civil servant employed by the federal government or a canton or community, you may receive an area allowance or weighting (*Ortzuschlag, allocation locale*), depending on the region where you work. The allowance, which may total a few thousand francs a year, is paid in monthly instalments with your salary.

Probationary & Notice Periods

For most jobs there's a probationary period (*Probezeit, période d'essai*), ranging from two weeks for seasonal workers to three months for permanent employees. Seasonal workers or their employer can usually terminate their contract with a notice period (*Kündigungsfrist, délai de résiliation*) of three days during the probationary period. For permanent employees, notice can be given at the end of any week, with a notice period of one or two weeks. After the probationary period, an employment contract may be terminated by either party at the end of any month, when the contract notice period (e.g. one to three months) applies.

Your notice period depends on your employer, profession and length of service, and is usually noted in your employment contract and employment conditions. If it isn't stated, then the notice period is usually one month during the first year, two months during the second to ninth years, and three months from the tenth year of service. The notice period for many professions is three months and may be longer for executive or key employees, e.g. six months. Your notice period may be extended after a number of years' service, in which case it will be noted in your employment conditions. If an employer goes bankrupt and cannot pay you, you can terminate your employment without notice. Other valid reasons for an employee not giving notice are assault or abuse of you or a colleague by your employer, and failure to pay (or persistent delay in paying) your salary.

Education & Training

Education and training (*Schulung und Ausbildung, enseignement et formation*) provided by your employer should be stated in your employment conditions. This may include training abroad, provided it's essential to your job (although you may need to convince your employer). In addition to relevant education and training, employers must provide the essential tools and equipment for a job, which is, however, open to interpretation.

If you need to learn a language or improve your language knowledge to perform your job, the cost of language study is usually paid by your employer. If it isn't essential, some employers will pay only a part of the cost or nothing at all (one of the penalties of being an English speaker). Employees who aren't of English mother-tongue may be paid to learn or improve their English if it's necessary for their job. An allowance may be paid for personal education or hobbies such as flower arranging, kite flying or break dancing, which aren't work related or of any direct benefit to your employer.

Pregnancy & Confinement

Time off for sickness that is in connection with a pregnancy (*Schwangerschaft, grossesse*) is usually given without question, but may not be paid unless authorised by a doctor.

In early 2003, the parliament discussed a new initiative on a state maternity insurance from which working mothers would be paid 80 per cent of their insurable salary for 14 weeks after giving birth. The benefits shall be paid by the Erwerbsersatzordnung – the same pot that Swiss men get their salaries from whilst on military service. Already now, large companies usually pay salaries up to 80 per cent of the insured sum for a maximum of 14 weeks (two weeks prior to delivery and 12 weeks after), depending on the employee's length of service and whether she was pregnant on joining the company. Pregnant and nursing mothers cannot be required to work overtime and cannot be given notice in the eight weeks before a baby is due or the eight weeks after a birth. You cannot (by law) return to work during the first eight weeks after delivery and you can choose to stay at home for another eight weeks.

Some companies pay a monthly allowance to pregnant mothers-to-be (pregnant fathers receive the Nobel Prize for medicine!). Around ten cantons pay a birth allowance of from SFr. 500 to 1,200.

Part-Time Job Restrictions

Restrictions on part-time employment (*Nebenarbeit, travail accessoire*) are usually detailed in your employment conditions. Most Swiss companies don't allow full-time employees to work part-time (i.e. moonlight) for another employer, particularly one in the same line of business. You may, however, be permitted to take a part-time teaching job or similar part-time employment (or you can write a book!).

Changing Jobs & Confidentiality

Companies in a high-tech or highly confidential (*vertraulich, confidentiel*) business may have restrictions (*Konkurrenzklausel/Konkurrenzverbot, clause de non- concurrence*) regarding employees working for a competitor in Switzerland or elsewhere. You should be aware of these restrictions, as they're enforceable by Swiss law, although it's a complicated subject and disputes must often be resolved by a court of law.

Swiss laws regarding industrial secrets and general employer confidentiality are **very** strict (on a par with murder – no joke!). If you breach this confidentiality, it may not be simply a matter of dismissal and perhaps subsequently having to leave Switzerland. You may also find yourself subject to criminal proceedings, resulting in a fine or even imprisonment. Keep our secrets **SECRET** is the byword of **all** Swiss companies – not just Swiss banks.

Acceptance Of Gifts

Employees are normally forbidden to accept gifts (*Geschenkannahme, accepter des dons*) of more than a certain value (e.g. SFr. 50) from customers or suppliers.

Many suppliers give bottles of wine or small gifts at Christmas that don't breach this rule. (If you accept a bribe, make sure it's a big one and that your bank account is covered by the Swiss secrecy laws.)

Retirement

Your employment conditions may be valid only until the official Swiss retirement age (*Ruhestand, retraite*), 64 for women and 65 for men. If you wish to continue working after you've reached retirement age, you may be required to negotiate a new employment contract (you should also seek psychiatric help!).

Military Service

Salary payment during Swiss military service (*Militärdienst, service militaire*) and time off for military and civil defence duties are included in your employment conditions. These are of no interest to foreigners, as they're liable for Swiss military service only if they become Swiss citizens or have dual nationality, haven't already served in a foreign army, and are young enough to be eligible (see **Military Service** on page 379).

Dismissal

Dismissal is usually permissible in exceptional circumstances only, depending on your contract (although an employer can make you redundant for any number of reasons). For example, refusing to work, cheating or stealing from your employer, competing with your employer, insulting your employer or colleagues, assault on your employer or a colleague, and drunkenness during working hours on your employer's premises (office parties excepted). Under normal circumstances, you cannot be fired in the first four weeks of an illness, in the eight weeks before you're due to give birth or the eight weeks after giving birth, or during compulsory military service.

SUNDAY WORKING

In Switzerland there's a law against working on Sundays and official holidays unless absolutely necessary (some people would like it extended to the other six days of the week!). When necessary, an official form must be completed by your employer and approved by the canton authorities. The general Sunday working law even prohibits the glorious Sunday pastimes of car washing and gardening. If you're fortunate enough to have a garden, you may sit, but not work in it on a Sunday. Washing your clothes on a Sunday is also forbidden, at least in a communal washing machine, as is hanging out clothes to dry.

Sunday is a day of peace when the Swiss won't tolerate noise, e.g. electric drills, hammering or loud music (somebody ought to inform the church bellringers and shooting ranges). Sunday working laws may be less strict or less strictly observed in country areas, where farmers are permitted to work on most Sundays. Fines can be imposed for ignoring the Sunday working law, although as a foreigner you may just be given a warning (besides which, your upstanding Swiss neighbours will probably inform you long before anyone calls the police).

3.

PERMITS & VISAS

With the Bilateral Treaties between Switzerland and the EU coming into force, the laws on work and residency permits have changed considerably and you will find two distinct categories of foreigners living and working in Switzerland: EU citizens who in many ways have similar rights to Swiss citizens and non-EU citizens for whom it has become more difficult to get a work and/or residency permit.

Before making any plans to live or work in Switzerland, you must ensure that you have a valid passport (with a visa if necessary) and the appropriate documentation to obtain a residence permit. Foreigners are issued with a residence permit (*Aufenthalts-bewilligung, autorisation de séjour*) entitling them to live or work (or both) in Switzerland, issued in a plastic cover entitled 'foreigner's permit' (*Ausländerausweis, livret pour étrangers*). EU citizens are allowed to come to Switzerland for up to three months to look for employment. Non-EU citizens must obtain an 'assurance of a residence permit' (*Zusicherung der Aufenthaltsbewilligung, assurance d'autorisation de séjour*) before entering Switzerland. This is an official document issued by the Swiss federal government stating that you've been offered a position with a Swiss employer or have been given permission to live in Switzerland, and that you will be granted a residence permit after arrival. The assurance must be obtained **before** arrival in Switzerland to take up residence. Some foreigners also require a visa to enter Switzerland, even when coming to take up employment or residence (see **Visas** on page 72).

A leaflet issued by Swiss embassies states: 'Anyone entering Switzerland as a tourist will not be able to obtain a residence permit. An application will be considered only after his departure from Switzerland.' In practice, however, this isn't always true. Many employers of seasonal workers rely on hiring workers on the spot. If you apply in person for a seasonal job, an employer may be able to get a permit issued within a few weeks. Before applying for an annual permit for a foreign worker, a Swiss employer must have previously advertised the job vacancy in Switzerland. There are strict annual permit quotas in each canton, plus a federal government quota that can be used in exceptional circumstances. Each canton is granted an annual quota of residence permits based on economic factors and manpower requirements in the canton. In deciding whether to grant a permit, the authorities consider the provision of essential services and supplies, economic necessity due to lack of personnel, and the promotion of commercial development. The authorities can usually exercise their discretion within the bounds of the law.

Most Swiss companies and many foreigners in Switzerland, sooner or later become entangled in the complex and bureaucratic nightmare of the Swiss permit system (do Swiss officials **really** understand it?). You may hear a variety of stories about how foreigners can obtain residence permits, many of which appear contradictory. Although a prospective employer may tell you in good faith that he can obtain a permit, he cannot guarantee that approval will be granted. It's impossible to state absolute rules as the criteria for the granting of permits are many and varied, and include qualifications, experience, profession, quotas, canton and federal government approval, the nationality of the applicant (priority is given to nationals from EEA countries) and the spouse, and the area of Switzerland. Ultimately permit approval may simply be decided on the whim of a government official. If a permit application is denied, your prospective employer may be able to appeal.

Foreigners working for international organisations located in Switzerland are issued with an identity card (*Identitätskarte, carte de légitimation*) and not a residence permit, and aren't subject to quotas or the same regulations as people working for Swiss employers, as described in this chapter.

PERMIT CLASSES

EU Citizens

On 1st July 2002 a new system was implemented based on a bilateral agreement between Switzerland and the EU countries. This will eventually culminate in EU citizens having freedom of movement within Switzerland and Swiss citizens within EU countries. The agreement will be phased in over 12 years and access to the Swiss labour market will be regulated during the first five years after the agreement comes into force. From the start it allowed for immediate annual preferential quotas for EU citizens of 115,000 short-term 'L' permits and 15,000 annual 'B' residence permits. Quotas for EU workers will be abolished after five years, along with the border zone for border crossing workers (G permits).

For stays up to one year a L-EG/EFTA permit is issued. This can be transferred between employers and can be renewed if the employment continues or a new job has been found after the first year. L-EG permit holders can bring their family to Switzerland.

EU citizens with an employment contract for an unlimited term get a B-EG/EFTA permit that is valid for five years. The permit allows the employee to move job or canton without any restrictions. If a B-EG permit holder loses his or her job, he or she can stay in Switzerland for the duration of the permit as long as they have sufficient funds to survive and do not become dependent on Social Welfare. They can claim unemployment benefits under the same conditions as a Swiss citizen, look for a new job or become self-employed.

After five years the B-EG permit is converted into a C permit (*Niederlassungs bewilligung*) automatically.

EU-citizens wanting to work but not become resident in Switzerland can get a G-EG-crossborder permit.

Non-EU Citizens

Under the new system non-EU citizens can only get a work permit for a job in Switzerland if the employer can prove they couldn't find a Swiss nor an EU citizen for the job. This restriction does not apply to highly qualified specialists (university degree usually required) and top executives. The cantonal offices are not allowed to decide on granting a permit on their own anymore but have to have each work permit approved by a federal authority in Berne. Not only has this new practice prolonged the waiting period for a permit considerably but some cantons who traditionally were more generous on giving permits to certain categories of employees had to accept quite a few refusals from the supervisory authority in Berne.

Limited Validity 'L' Permits

An L permit (*Aufenthaltsbewilligung L, permis de séjour L*) is a short-term residence permit, issued (in a purple cover) for a limited period (*begrenzte Gültigkeit/limitierte Gültigkeit, durée limitée*) up to a maximum of 12 months. It's generally granted to students, trainees and au pairs, Specialists employed by foreign companies and sent as consultants to a Swiss-based company, usually also receive an L permit. It's closely linked to the employment it has been granted for, and should this be terminated early, the permit will be revoked and the employee has to leave Switzerland. Changes of employment may be allowed by the authorities if the employee for example can prove that they were made redundant without any fault of their own. The permit automatically ends after one year and an extension is only granted if the employer can claim special circumstances. After 24 months the permit ends irrevocably and a new permit can only obtained after a stay outside Switzerland of a year (in most cases).

Annual 'B' Residence Permits

A B permit (*Aufenthaltsbewilligung, permis de séjour/permis B*) is usually valid for one year and is renewable. It's generally issued only to qualified and experienced people in professions where there's a shortage of skilled labour, and to spouses of Swiss citizens. However, there are special B permits for those who set up companies in Switzerland and invest at least SFr. 60,000 and the so called 'Fiscal Deal' permits for people wishing to live but not work in Switzerland (who usually require a certified net wealth of at least SFr. 2 million and need to spend at least 180 days a year in the country).

B permits (enclosed in a grey cover) are normally renewed annually on application (although this isn't an automatic entitlement). There are fees for the renewal of annual permits, usually paid by the permit holder. Each canton has an annual quota for new B permits, which doesn't include the renewals of existing B permits. Holders of B permits are usually discouraged from changing employment or profession in their first few years in Switzerland (see **Changing Jobs** on page 71).

Work permit application procedures for intra-company transfers, executives and highly skilled specialists were streamlined in 1993, and employers are no longer required to prove that an adequate domestic worker couldn't be found to do a job. At the end of 2002 there were 356,000 B permit holders and 8,800 L permit holders (both EU and non-EU) in Switzerland.

Settlement 'C' Permits

A C permit (*Niederlassungsbewilligung, permis d'etablissement/permis C*) signifies permanent residence and although it may be reviewed from time to time, it can be renewed indefinitely as long as the holder resides in Switzerland. C permits are issued (in a green cover) automatically to B permit holders after five or ten consecutive years as a resident in Switzerland. Citizens of Andorra, Belgium, Denmark, Finland, France, Germany, Greece, Iceland, Ireland, Italy, Liechtenstein, Luxembourg, Monaco, the Netherlands, Norway, Portugal, San Marino, Spain, Sweden, the United Kingdom, the US (since 1995) and the Vatican City, qualify for a C permit after five years. The qualification period for citizens of all other countries is ten years. On special application a C permit can be granted after 5 years if the foreigner claims to be well integrated in Switzerland – the 'test' for this usually being that he masters the relevant language(s) – see pages 153 and 39. The 10-year qualification period is also reduced to five years for a foreigner married to a Swiss, who doesn't qualify for a C permit after five years. C permits are also issued to stateless people and official refugees after five years and to the families of C permit holders. Holders of C permits don't require permission to change jobs, change their cantons of residence or work, or become self-employed. At the end of 2002, there were some 1,082,000 C permit holders.

Border Crossing 'G' Permits

A G permit (*Grenzgängerbewilligung, permis frontalier*) gives a person living in a neighbouring country the right to work in Switzerland (many people choose to live in a neighbouring country, where the cost of living is significantly lower, and commute to their jobs in Switzerland). Unlike L, B and C permits, a G permit doesn't include residential rights in Switzerland. To qualify you must usually have been resident in the border area for at least six months. A G permit is renewed annually and cannot be converted into a B permit. There's no quota for G permits but positions must be advertised in Switzerland and companies must still satisfy the authorities that no equally qualified unemployed Swiss resident is available to fill a vacancy. Permits are usually initially valid for one year. When changing employers or even jobs within the same company, a new permit application is necessary. The total number of G permit holders in 2002 was around 175,000.

Under the new permit system introduced on 1st July 2002, G permits will be split into G-EC permits for EU citizens (over 99 per cent of holders), and G permits for non-EU citizens. The border zone restrictions will be abolished after five years. G permit holders do not have to leave Switzerland every day anymore but only once a week. This makes it possible to stay in Switzerland for example from Monday to Friday but still keep a main residence outside the country although effectively only spending the weekends there.

Employees Of International Organisations

Foreigners employed in Switzerland by international organisations, e.g. the United Nations in Geneva, have a special status. They don't require a normal residence permit, but are issued with an identity card (*Identitätskarte, carte de légitimation*) obtained by their employer. Customs, immigration and housing regulations for employees of international organisations differ considerably from those of 'normal' permit holders (if they had to put up with the usual Swiss red tape, the UN would have gone elsewhere!).

Spouses

The change of legislation has improved the situation for the families of B permit holders. Within 5 years from the permit holder starting work in Switzerland, the spouse and children up to 18 years can move to Switzerland as well. The spouse and children from age 14 automatically are entitled to a work permit in Switzerland. This also applies to spouses of international civil servants and members of diplomatic missions.

The families of L permit holders (including students and trainees) may now be granted residence permits although they don't have an enforceable entitlement. If the permit isn't granted, visits might be a solution but are limited to six months a year and shouldn't exceed three months at any time, with a month between visits. The 'visit only' rule isn't, however, always strictly enforced.

There are no restrictions on the employment of a spouse of a C permit holder.

If you have a live-in partner, it may be possible for him or her if you can prove that you've been living together for at least 5 years and will be living at the same address in Switzerland as well. It's usually easier if you have children and/or have good reasons why getting married is not a viable option for you. This can also apply to partners of the same sex. The foreign spouse of a Swiss citizen must have lived in Switzerland for five years and been married three years before he or she can apply for Swiss citizenship, or have been married for six years and show 'a close relationship with Switzerland'.

Children

From the age of 13 children may work a maximum of three hours a day up to a total of 15 hours per week. At the age of 15 they may work eight hours a day and a total of 40 hours a week. Students (under the age of 18) whose parents are working in Switzerland may apply for a permit once they've found a prospective employer.

Non-Swiss children who have one Swiss parent must follow the normal immigration procedures for foreigners. They aren't, however, subject to quota restrictions and there are no limitations on their freedom to live and work in Switzerland.

Part-Time Employment

Permits are required for all part-time occupations with the exception of voluntary work, which comes under special regulations. This applies to all members of a foreigner's family living in Switzerland. A permit is required even when a part-time job is for a few weeks only, for example temporary work in the farming industry. If you work part-time, your rights as an employee depend on the number of hours you work each week. If you work more than 12 hours a week for one employer, you're entitled to much the same benefits (pro rata) as a full-time employee (see **Chapter 2**).

Students

Foreign students in Switzerland require a B permit. The educational establishment provides the student with a certificate stating that he is a full-time student. After finding accommodation he must take this to the local community office of the local town or area and apply for a residence permit in the normal way (see **Resident's Control** on page 78). Foreign students must be able to satisfy the authorities that they can support themselves financially and may check that students are attending classes. With the student B permit you're allowed to get a job and work up to a maximum of 15 hours a week. There are special regulations for students or trainees studying with international organisations.

Non-Employed Foreign Residents

Foreigners wishing to live but not work in Switzerland (euphemistically called 'leisured foreigners' by the Swiss authorities), must apply for a residence permit from a Swiss embassy or consulate before arriving in Switzerland. Permits are normally issued only to those aged over 55 (i.e. pensioners) or people of independent means, particularly the **very** rich and famous. You're required to furnish proof that you have sufficient assets or income to live in Switzerland, usually via a statement from your bank.

Other information required may be a curriculum vitae; a statement of why you want to live in Switzerland; and the name of someone in Switzerland who can guarantee to look after you in an emergency. If you're a pensioner, you must have retired from all gainful employment. Regulations vary from canton to canton (contact the canton authorities in Switzerland for local residence qualifications).

Visitors

Foreigners who visit Switzerland for under three months without taking up employment, don't require a permit, although some foreigners need a visa (see page 72) to enter Switzerland. Nationals of certain countries including Austria, Belgium, France, Germany, Liechtenstein, Luxembourg, Monaco, the Netherlands, Portugal, San Marino and Spain, can enter Switzerland using an identity card or passport that expired no longer than five years previously. All other foreigners require a full and current passport to enter Switzerland.

Visitors from some countries, e.g. some eastern European countries, may need to explain how they intend to finance their stay in Switzerland when making a visa application. Permit-free visitors may not exceed a total of six months' residence a year. According to federal regulations, foreign visitors must be registered by their landlord with their local community if their stay exceeds three months (this period can be reduced by some cantons). To extend a stay beyond three months without leaving Switzerland, you should apply to the local canton alien's police. If you want to establish temporary residence for longer than six months, you must apply at a Swiss embassy or consulate **before** coming to Switzerland.

Non-EU citizens entering Switzerland as a tourist are generally unable to obtain an annual residence B permit (although an L permit may be issued within a few weeks under certain conditions). Applications for a B permit are officially considered only after the departure of the applicant from Switzerland.

Refugees

On arrival in Switzerland, a refugee (*Fluchtling/Asylant, réfugié*) must submit an application for asylum. While the application is being processed, the 'refugee' is given a document identifying him as such. Refugees aren't permitted to work during their first three-months while their status is being assessed. It's now much more difficult for bogus refugees to obtain a permit and only a small percentage of applicants are successful. If a refugee hasn't been assessed after three months, a permit is issued allowing him to work in a limited number of fields, e.g. hotels, catering, cleaning, agriculture and construction. If a request for asylum is rejected, the applicant must leave Switzerland by the date specified, usually immediately. If the request is approved, a special 'F' or 'N' 'asylum' permit is issued. In exceptional circumstance, e.g. after a review period of many years, a C permit may be issued.

After 'fugitives' file an application for asylum, the canton to which they're assigned has a legal obligation to house and support them. Accommodation is usually in 'barracks' type buildings for single people or furnished apartments for families. Working refugees can borrow money from their local community at low or zero interest. Switzerland has, however, serious problems accommodating asylum-seekers (and its own population) and some towns have resisted accommodating them.

Although there's widespread sympathy in Switzerland with the plight of genuine refugee's, many of Switzerland's asylum-seekers are fleeing economic hardship rather than persecution, evidenced by the small number of applications that are approved. The increase in asylum-seekers has highlighted the xenophobic instincts in some Swiss and there have been a number of racist attacks against refugees. Refugees (and illegal immigrants) are thought to be responsible for much of the sharp increase in drug-associated crime in recent years.

Switzerland has traditionally been a sanctuary for refugees from the world's trouble spots which in the last few decades have included Afghanistan, Cambodia, Chile, Eastern Europe, Lebanon, Sri Lanka, Tibet, Turkey, the former Yugoslavia and Vietnam. However, many Swiss now believe that 'the boat is full' and the flood of asylum-seekers in recent years has forced the Swiss government to change its policy.

PERMIT APPLICATION

The normal procedure for obtaining an annual permit for employment and residence in Switzerland is as follows:

1. An offer of employment is sent to you by your prospective Swiss employer, stating your anticipated starting date.

2. When you accept the offer of employment, your prospective employer applies to the canton alien's police for a residence permit. Only bona fide Swiss companies or employers can apply for a residence permit for a foreigner.

3. On receipt of the permit approval, your prospective employer sends it to you with an employment contract, stating your employment starting date.

4. On arrival in Switzerland, you need to present your 'assurance of a residence permit' paper to the border or airport immigration officials (see page 76).

PERMIT CANCELLATION

B Permits

B permits are cancelled when **any** of the following occurs:

- The permit holder leaves Switzerland.
- The permit holder has lived outside Switzerland for an uninterrupted period of six months, without applying for leave of absence (see page 70).
- The permit expires and isn't renewed.

- When it can be assumed that the permit holder has left Switzerland, for example he has given notice of termination of employment or taken up employment abroad, even if he hasn't notified the Swiss authorities.

C Permits

C permits are cancelled when **any** of the following occurs:

- The permit holder notifies the local authority of his permanent departure.
- The permit holder has lived outside Switzerland for an uninterrupted period of six months, without applying for leave of absence (see below).

Under certain circumstances the B or C permit of the spouse of a permit holder can be cancelled when he or she is widowed or divorced.

LEAVE OF ABSENCE

If you intend to be absent from Switzerland for a period longer than six months and want to be sure of retaining your permit on your return, you can obtain an 'assurance of return' if a B permit holder, or an 'authorisation of absence' if a C permit holder. The assurance of return for a B permit holder must be requested by your employer. It's granted for an absence of up to four years, provided your employer states that you will return to his employment within this period.

If you're a C permit holder, your employer or you personally must request an authorisation of absence from your canton authorities. It's granted for a maximum of three years, provided you can justify the necessity of your absence, for example study abroad, special education or training, or a special assignment for your employer.

IMPORTANT NOTES

- It can take up to three months to obtain a residence permit to live in Switzerland and it's often a protracted affair, from the initial job application, interview and written job offer, until receipt of your permit approval.
- You must enter Switzerland within three months of the date of issue of your residence permit approval. If you're unable to take up employment within this period, you should inform your prospective employer so that he can apply for an extension.
- If the alien's registration office rejects an application for a permit, the reason will be given to the prospective employer in writing, who will

inform you of any right of appeal, the relevant appeal authority and any time restrictions that apply.

● Older children without residence permits should carry passports or identity cards to verify their age, for example to purchase reduced price public transport tickets and cinema tickets for age-restricted performances. Secondary school children are often issued with a school identity or student card (*Schülerausweis/Studenten-ausweis, carte d'identité scolaire/carte d'étudiant*).

● You should carry your Swiss residence permit, passport or other official form of identification with you at all times within Switzerland (except when swimming or jogging!).

● It's advisable to keep a copy (not the originals) of all your family's official papers, permits, passports, birth certificates and other important documents in a safe place, e.g. a safety deposit box.

● Any infringements concerning residence permits or registration of foreigners are taken very seriously by the Swiss authorities. There are penalties for breaches of regulations, including fines and even deportation for flagrant abuses.

CHANGING JOBS

The rules regarding changing jobs vary depending on your type of residence permit and whether or not you're married to a Swiss citizen. If you're a non-EU B permit holder, you aren't generally permitted to change jobs without special permission until you've worked five years in Switzerland. It's easier to change jobs within the same canton, provided your employment contract was terminated through no fault of your own and the economic situation doesn't prevent the requested change. L permit holders cannot change jobs without special permission.

When you change jobs, you may have to resign from your present position before your prospective new employer can apply for a new residence permit. Your new employer will need a copy of the letter from your current employer confirming your resignation. The authorities may also ask for a statement (*Freigabe, libération*) from your present employer, stating that you've resigned voluntarily and that they don't object to your leaving. This doesn't appear to be mandatory but is usually provided on request. Your former employer must provide (by law) a reference (*Zeugnis, attestation*) in the local language and a salary statement (*Lohnausweis, certificat de salaire*) for tax purposes. Some companies will provide a reference in English on request.

A job offer doesn't guarantee that a residence permit application will be approved. This means, at least in theory, that changing jobs in Switzerland before you have a C permit (a permanent residence permit) can be a risky business. In reality, companies **almost** always know when they can obtain a residence permit for a foreigner and wouldn't expect you to resign unless they were confident of receiving the permit approval, **but take care**. Check the notice period in your employment contract or conditions before resigning (see **Probationary & Notice Periods** on page 56) and whether there are any employment restrictions, e.g. with regard to working for a competitor.

Your resignation letter should be sent by registered post to reach your employer by the last working day of the month at the latest, or it can be presented personally to your employer, when a signed and dated receipt should be provided.

The Swiss don't generally change jobs often and some employers may think that you're unreliable if you change jobs more often than a few times during your lifetime (although this has changed in the last decade, during which redundancies have become commonplace). On the other hand, experienced and qualified foreigners with a C permit may find they can job-hop every few years when there are labour shortages.

Other matters to take into account when changing jobs are:

- If you're a member of a company health fund (*Krankenkasse, caisse de maladie*), you may wish to transfer your family's health insurance (see page 266) to another health fund or health insurance company, as you will no longer benefit from the (usually substantial) company discount.

- If you're moving to another Swiss company, your accrued company pension fund benefits will be transferred to a private pension fund account in your name. If you're leaving Switzerland the accrued benefits will be paid to you in full.

If changing jobs entails moving house within Switzerland, see **Chapter 20**.

VISAS

Some foreigners require a visa to enter Switzerland, either as a visitor or for any other purpose. This includes most people who aren't citizens of a western European country (if in doubt, check with a Swiss embassy or consulate). If you need a visa for employment (*Einreisevisum zum Stellenantritt, visa d'entrée pour prise d'emploi*) the procedure is as follows:

1. An offer of employment is sent to you by your prospective Swiss employer, stating your anticipated start date.
2. Take this with your passport to the Swiss embassy or consulate in your country of residence. You will be asked to complete a number of forms and provide passport photographs, which are sent to Switzerland for processing. The Swiss embassy or consulate will tell you exactly what to provide.

3. On receipt of your acceptance of the job offer, your prospective Swiss employer will apply to the canton alien's police for a residence permit.

4. When the application is approved, authorisation to issue the visa is sent to the Swiss embassy or consulate in your country of residence. They will contact you and ask you to visit them with your passport, in which a visa is stamped permitting you to enter Switzerland to take up employment.

If you require a visa to enter Switzerland, you may also need visas to visit other European countries. Check with your country's embassy or consulate in Switzerland. Applications must be made in advance, visas are usually valid for one to three months only and are often expensive. There may also be restrictions on the number of entries permitted on a single visa.

When you're resident in Switzerland, you may need to obtain a character reference (*Leumundszeugnis, certificat de bonne vie et moeurs*) from your community (fee around SFr. 20) in order to obtain a visa for some countries.

4.

ARRIVAL

On arrival in Switzerland to take up employment or residence, there are a number of formalities that must be completed. These are described in this chapter, plus suggestions for finding local help and information and some useful checklists.

BORDER CONTROL

On arrival in Switzerland present your passport and 'assurance of a residence permit' (*Zusicherung der Aufenthaltsbewilligung, assurance d'autorisation de séjour et de travail*) paper to the immigration authorities at the frontier or airport. If you have an entry visa (see page 72) it will be cancelled by the immigration official. Officially you also require an employment contract, although it's unlikely that anyone will ask to see it.

Ask the immigration official to stamp your 'assurance of a residence permit' paper to verify your date of entry. This isn't obligatory but the following is an extract from the Federal Office of Public Health memorandum: **'To facilitate confirmation of date of entry, aliens are strongly recommended to request on entry the appropriate date stamp from the customs authorities.'** This is primarily for the Swiss frontier health authorities (see below).

FRONTIER HEALTH CONTROL

Foreigners from certain countries planning to work in Switzerland may be required to have a health check (usually consisting of an X-ray only) in order to detect contagious diseases. The health check is no longer required by people from EEA countries, Australia, Canada, New Zealand and the US. When applicable, the health check is carried out by a Swiss doctor of your choice.

CUSTOMS

When you enter Switzerland to take up residence, household or personal effects that you've used for at least six months may be imported without paying duty or VAT. A complete list of the items being imported must be provided at the time of customs clearance, together with a request for duty-free import (a form is provided). VAT (7.6 per cent) must be paid on any articles you've used for less than six months. Itemised purchase invoices should be provided. If your Swiss home is a second home, you must pay usually VAT on all imports except clothes and other exempt items (you may be granted an exemption if your home country grants reciprocal rights to Swiss nationals). You will also require the following:

- An inventory of all goods to be imported; articles which do not fulfil the conditions for duty-free charges should be itemised at the end of the list as 'goods for normal customs clearance';

- Your Swiss residence permit or assurance of a residence permit;
- The official foreign registration certificate for motorcars, motorboats and aeroplanes;
- A contract for the lease or purchase of a property or other proof of accommodation (in the case of a second home);
- A photocopy of the passports of all people taking up residence;
- A completed form 18.44 (declaration/application for clearance of household effects), available from the Federal Administration (Bundesverwaltung) website (💻 www.afd.admin.ch/e/private/rv/form_1844_antrag_de.pdf – in English as well as German).

If you import a car duty-free and sell it in Switzerland within one year of your arrival, you're required to inform the customs authorities at the location where it was imported. Import taxes are calculated on the age, value and sale price of a vehicle.

If you plan to enter Switzerland with a foreign registered car and household effects (for example on a trailer), it's advisable to enter via a major frontier post, as smaller posts may not be equipped to deal with you unless they're informed of your arrival in advance. Note also the following:

- Switzerland has no currency restrictions – everyone loves all currency;
- A licence is required to import any guns and ammunition;
- There are restrictions on the type and quantity of plants and bulbs that may be imported;
- For duty-free allowances (e.g. alcohol and tobacco), see page 364;
- For information regarding the importation of cars into Switzerland, see page 202;
- For information about pets, see page 380;
- Never attempt to import illegal goods.

Information concerning Swiss customs regulations is contained in a leaflet entitled *Customs Regulations for travellers domiciled abroad*. It's available from customs offices, Switzerland Tourism offices or the Head Customs Office, (*Oberzolldirektion, Direction des Douanes*) Monbijoustr. 40, CH-3003 Berne (☎ 031 322 65 11, 💻 www.zoll.admin.ch). The customs office will also provide you with detailed information regarding the importation of special items.

MOTORWAY TAX

If you wish to use the Swiss motorways, you must pay a motorway tax of SFr. 40 a year. This tax is payable in addition to Swiss road tax (see page 215) and is applicable to all motor vehicles (including motorcycles) under 3.5 tonnes using Swiss motorways, whether Swiss or foreign registered. On entering Switzerland you may be asked whether you intend to use Swiss motorways, particularly if you enter via Basle, and if you answer yes you will be expected to pay the tax on the spot. On payment of the motorway tax, you're given a windscreen sticker (*Vignette*) which must be affixed to your windscreen left hand side (top or bottom) or centre top. The vignette isn't transferable between vehicles and will tear to pieces if you attempt to remove it (unless you know how!). The motorway tax is applicable to all vehicles, trailers, caravans and motorcycles with a maximum weight of 3.5 tonnes. If you have a trailer or caravan, it requires an additional vignette (elephant caravans are exempt). Vehicles weighing over 3.5 tonnes are subject to a special 'heavy vehicles' tax which is payable daily, monthly or annually (a 10-day pass is also available for those who visit Switzerland frequently for periods of one or two days).

If you don't buy a vignette and are subsequently stopped by the police on a motorway, you will be fined SFr. 100 and must also pay the road tax on the spot. It is, of course, possible to drive around Switzerland without using motorways, but (very) time consuming. The vignette is valid for a calendar year, with a month's overlap at each end, e.g. December 1st 2002 to January 31st 2004. It can be purchased in advance (although unnecessary) at Switzerland Tourism offices or from automobile associations throughout Europe. In Switzerland it's sold at border crossings, customs offices, post offices, garages, service stations and canton motor registries.

The motorway tax is a small price to pay for the convenience of using some of the finest roads in Europe, particularly when you consider that there are no road tolls in Switzerland. To put it into perspective, the annual Swiss motorway tax is about the same price as a **single day's** motoring on French, Italian or Spanish motorways!

RESIDENTS' CONTROL

Within eight days of arrival in Switzerland and before starting work, you must register (*anmelden, s'inscrire*) your family in the local community (*Gemeinde, commune*) where you're living within eight days, **even if you're in temporary accommodation, e.g. a hotel.** This is done at your local community office (*Gemeindehaus, maison communale*) in country areas or an area office (*Kreisbüro, bureau d'arrondissement*) in cities. Cities and large towns often have a special resident's control department (*Einwohnerkontrolle, contrôle d'habitant*).

New arrivals must register to obtain their annual residence permit (*Aufenthaltsbewilligung, permis de séjour*). Switzerland has strict regulations regarding registration for a number of excellent reasons, the most important of which is that most residents pay taxes levied by their local community from their date of registration. Another reason is that each new resident foreign worker is deducted from his canton's annual permit quota. If applicable, you must have a health check **before** you can register. Registration is obligatory for all residents, both foreigners and Swiss nationals.

At your community registration office you will be asked to produce the following (as applicable):

- Your passport (containing the frontier health control stamp, if applicable) and your spouse's and children's passports (if separate);
- Your 'assurance of a residence permit' paper. This will be retained by your community registration office;
- Your marriage certificate;
- Birth certificates for each member of your family;
- Two passport-size photographs (black and white or colour) for each member of your family up to 18 years of age (family members aged over 18 are considered individually). These are available from photograph machines at most railway stations and in town centres. It's useful to have a supply of passport-size photos for all members of your family, for example for school ID cards, train and bus season tickets, ski passes and Swiss driving licences.

You must complete a form that includes such **vital** information as your mother's and father's Christian names, and your mother's and wife's (or husband's mother's) maiden names. If you're divorced, separated or widowed, you should state this on the registration form, as you may be entitled to a small tax concession.

You're also asked to enter your religion on the registration form. All communities in Switzerland levy a church tax on the members of the three main Swiss churches: Catholic, Old Catholic and Reformed. If you enter either Protestant or Catholic you will be registered as a member of the relevant church and will pay church tax. Members of other religions such as the Church of England, Methodists and Baptists, should clearly indicate their religion on the application. If you aren't a member of any church, just enter 'NONE' as your religion. This is quite legal and will ensure that you're able to reclaim any church tax paid without any formalities. Almost all foreigners pay direct income tax (*Quellensteuer, impôt à la source*) and in most cantons church tax is deducted at source (irrespective of religion) from their gross salaries, **often without their knowledge or permission**. If you aren't registered as a member of a Swiss church, church tax can be reclaimed via a form available from your local community office.

Annual B permit (*Aufenthaltsbewilligung, permis de séjour*) holders receive their permits within a few weeks via their employer or community. The fee for your permit depends on your family size and the period covered by the permit, and may be paid by your employer. It's no longer necessary to obtain a stamp in your passport each time you renew your residence permit. However, you must carry your residence permit or passport with you at all times.

If you're a B permit holder and live and work in different cantons, your residence permit won't be renewed by your canton of residence until your permission to work has been approved by the canton where you're employed. If you're not an EU citizen, applications for the renewal of an annual residence permit must be made by your employer, although it's your responsibility to ensure that your permit is renewed. You're employer usually provides you with a renewal form a few months before your permit's expiry date, although you may need to remind him. EU citizens can obtain the relevant renewal forms directly from the local authority.

If you're moving to a new community or leaving Switzerland permanently, you must de-register (*Abmelden, déclaration de départ*) in your present community up to eight days before your departure, and register in your new community within eight days of taking up residence (if applicable).

CHURCH TAX

When you arrive in Switzerland and register in your local community (see **Resident's Control** on page 78) you must complete a form asking you to state your religion. If you state that you're a member of the Reformed, Roman Catholic or Old Catholic (Protestant) religions, you must pay church tax (*Kirchensteuer, impôt du culte*). (Now you know why Swiss churches are in such excellent repair.) The amount of tax payable depends on your salary, your community (parish) and your religion, and can amount to several thousand francs a year if you earn a high salary. Church tax is calculated as a percentage of your basic tax value, and depends on your community and canton tax rates (see **Income Tax** on page 288) and your church.

It doesn't appear on your pay slip or your annual salary statement (*Lohnausweis, certificat de salaire*) and many foreigners are unaware that they pay it. **Nevertheless, if you pay direct income tax, you automatically pay church tax, even, for example if you're registered as an atheist.** However, if you don't belong to an official Swiss church you can reclaim it. If you don't reclaim it, the Swiss official churches divide the spoils among themselves – the interest alone must be worth a Pope's ransom.

If you're wrongly registered as a member of a taxable religion, you can have your records officially changed and reclaim any tax paid, although you can reclaim church tax for a limited period only, for example the last three years. To de-register, you must complete a certificate, available from your local community office, and get it signed by the local priest or vicar of whatever church is your beneficiary. If you do this you will be unable to get married or buried by the church (without paying a huge fee) and it may affect your children's religious status, for example they may no longer receive religious instruction at school. Nevertheless, there are plenty of other churches only too happy to have you as a tax-free member, e.g. Anglicans, Baptists, Methodists, Pentecostals, the Salvation Army and many others, not to mention any number of religious sects.

If you aren't registered as a member of an official Swiss church, you can reclaim your church tax every one to three years, via a form available from your community. Enter your personal particulars, bank account information and your earnings over the period for which you're reclaiming the tax, or alternatively attach a copy of your salary statement (*Lohnausweis, certificat de salaire*) for the period in question. Send the form to your canton's tax office (*Steueramt, bureau des impôts*), the address of which is printed on the form. You will be advised by letter when **your** money (excluding interest!) has been credited to your account, usually after six to eight weeks.

EMBASSY REGISTRATION

Nationals of some countries are required to register with their local embassy or consulate, as soon as possible after arrival in Switzerland. Registration isn't usually mandatory, although most embassies like to keep a record of their nationals resident in Switzerland (it helps to justify their existence).

FINDING HELP

One of the biggest difficulties facing new arrivals in Switzerland is how and where to obtain help with day-to-day problems. For example, finding a home, schooling, insurance and so on. This book was written in response to this need. However, in addition to the comprehensive information provided herein, you will also require detailed local information. How successful you are in finding help depends on your employer, the town or area where you live (e.g. Geneva's residents are better served than Zurich's), your nationality, language proficiency and your sex (women are better served than men through numerous women's clubs). There's an abundance of general local information available in the Swiss national languages (French, German, Italian), although it usually isn't intended for foreigners and their particular needs, but little in English and other foreign languages. You may find that your friends and colleagues can help, as they're often able to proffer advice based on their own experiences and mistakes. But **beware**, although they mean well, you're likely to receive as much false and conflicting information as accurate (not always wrong, but possibly invalid for your particular area or situation).

Your community is usually an excellent source of reliable information, but you will probably need to speak the local language to benefit from it. Some companies may have a department or staff whose job is to help new arrivals or they may contract this task out to a relocation company. Unfortunately many employers in Switzerland seem totally unaware of (or disinterested in) the problems and difficulties faced by their foreign employees. In some cities, e.g. Geneva and Zurich, there are free advice centres for foreigners.

If a woman lives in or near a major town, she is able to turn to many English-speaking women's clubs and organisations for help. The single foreign male (who of course cannot possibly have any problems) must usually fend for himself, although there are men's expatriate clubs in some areas and mixed social clubs throughout the country (see **Appendix A**). One of the best sources of information and help for women are the American Women's Clubs (AWC) located in Berne, Basle, Geneva, Lausanne and Zurich. AWC clubs provide comprehensive information in English about both local matters and topics of more general interest. They can provide detailed information about all aspects of living in Switzerland including apartment costs, schools, names of English-speaking doctors and dentists, shopping information and much more. AWC clubs produce data sheets and booklets containing a wealth of valuable local information, and they also run libraries open to non-members.

AWC publications can be purchased directly from AWC clubs or from local bookshops. Clubs organise a variety of social events, plus many day and evening classes, ranging from local cooking to language classes. The main disadvantage for many foreigners is that AWC clubs have quotas for non-American associate members, i.e. anyone who isn't an American citizen, married to an American or the daughter or mother of a member. The rules may vary slightly from club to club, although in general, associate members must speak fluent English and have strong active links with the US, e.g. through study, work or a husband who works for a US company or the US government. Anyone can, however, subscribe to their newsletters.

American Women's Clubs run excellent orientation programmes for newcomers to Switzerland, open to both men and women and participants don't need to be AWC members (particularly men). Courses are usually held once a year and consist of a series of meetings over a period of weeks, normally during the day (which can be a problem if you're working). Places are limited, so apply early. Course participants receive a comprehensive resource book, which may be available to non-participants for a fee. AWC clubs are non-profit, charitable organisations and are staffed by volunteers.

A good source of information for both newcomers and long-term residents is the Anglo-Phone English-Language Information Service (Case postale 2024, CH-1227 Carouge). Anglo-Phone (☎ 0900 576 444, SFr. 3.13 a minute) provides information on finding help in emergencies; general help; classes (in English); activities; professionals and their services (such as tax planners, accountants and lawyers); leisure and entertainment; sports activities and facilities; retail outlets; clubs and associations; and myriad other subjects. In fact Anglo-Phone will attempt to answer questions on almost any subject, whether it's related to Switzerland or not. They will also try to find English-speaking tradesmen and professionals for those who don't speak the local language, and provide a message service, e.g. for family, friends, business associates and club members. Anglo-Phone also publish a free newspaper, *Swiss Style*, containing information for both residents and tourists (also available on subscription).

In addition to the above, there are numerous social clubs and other organisations for foreigners in Switzerland, whose members can help you find your way around. Many embassies and consulates provide information, particularly regarding clubs for their nationals, and many businesses (e.g. Swiss banks) produce booklets and leaflets containing useful information (see **Appendix A**). Bookshops may have some useful publications (see **Appendix B**) and a number of Swiss English-language periodicals (see page 356) also provide useful information and contacts. Local tourist and information offices can also be of assistance.

CHECKLISTS

Before Arrival

The following checklist contains a summary of the tasks that should (if possible) be completed before your arrival in Switzerland:

- Obtain a visa, if necessary, for you and all your family members (see **Chapter 3**). Obviously this **must** be done before your arrival in Switzerland.
- If possible visit Switzerland prior to your move to compare communities and schools, and arrange schooling for your children (see **Chapter 9**).
- Find temporary or permanent accommodation and buy a car. If you purchase a car in Switzerland, register it and arrange insurance (see pages 208 and 212 respectively).
- Arrange for shipment of your personal effects to Switzerland (see page 98).
- Arrange health insurance for yourself and your family (see page 266). This is essential if you aren't already covered by a private insurance policy and won't be covered automatically by your Swiss employer.
- Open a bank account in Switzerland and transfer funds (you can open an account with some Swiss banks from abroad). It's best to obtain some Swiss francs before your arrival in Switzerland as this will save you having to spend time changing money on arrival.
- Collect and update personal records including medical, dental, schools, insurance (e.g. car insurance), professional and employment (including job references).
- Obtain an international driver's licence, if necessary.
- Obtain an international credit or charge card, which will prove invaluable during your first few months in Switzerland.

Don't forget to bring all your family's official documents including birth certificates; driver's licences; marriage certificate, divorce papers or death certificate (if a widow or widower); educational diplomas, professional certificates and job references; school records and student ID cards; employment references; medical and dental records; bank account and credit card details;

insurance policies; and receipts for any valuables. You also need the documents necessary to obtain a residence permit (see **Chapter 3**) plus certified copies, official translations and numerous passport-size photographs (students should take at least a dozen).

After Arrival

The following checklist contains a summary of tasks to be completed after arrival in Switzerland (if not done before arrival):

- On arrival at the Swiss border or airport, give your permit approval paper and passport to the official for date stamping.
- If you're importing a car, complete a form for temporary importation (see page 202). If you don't own a car, you may wish to rent one for a week or two until you buy one locally (see page 205).
- Visit a frontier health clinic on arrival or within 72 hours (three days) for a health check if necessary (see page 76).
- In the next few days, complete the following (if not done before arrival):
  - Open a post office or bank account and give the details to your employer (see pages 119 and 281 respectively) in order to get paid;
  - Register at your community registration office within eight days of arrival (see **Resident's Control** on page 78) after you've completed the frontier health control X-ray.
  - Register with your local embassy or consulate (see page 81);
  - Arrange schooling for your children (see **Chapter 9**);
- Arrange whatever insurance is necessary for you and your family (see **Chapter 13**) including: health insurance (see page 266); house contents insurance (see page 270) and private liability insurance (see page 271). See also **Car Insurance** on page 212.

5.

ACCOMMODATION

In many areas of Switzerland, finding accommodation with a reasonable rent is becoming increasingly difficult (if not impossible) and finding accommodation at almost any price isn't easy in major cities. In the cantons of Basle-City, Geneva, Zug and Zurich there's an acute shortage of accommodation due to the lack of building land and the high demand. Rents are linked to the average mortgage rent in Switzerland and therefore decreased considerably between 1999 and 2003. However, in areas where rented accommodation is in high demand and short supply, rents can be astronomical. For those on low incomes including seasonal workers, students, pensioners, the young and single-parent families, rents are very high.

Housing accounts for a significant proportion of the average family's budget. You should budget for around 25 per cent of your net income for rent, although it can easily amount to a third or more in high cost areas. Although the federal government subsidises the construction of low cost housing for low-income families, invalids and pensioners, the growing lack of inexpensive rental accommodation has led to demonstrations in some cities and is one of Switzerland's most urgent needs.

There are restrictions on the purchase of property by foreigners in Switzerland. It isn't simply a matter of depositing a suitcase full of cash with an estate agent and walking off with the house keys.

If you live outside Switzerland and commute to a job in Switzerland, you're usually liable for income tax (and other taxes) in your country of residence, and not in Switzerland.

BUYING PROPERTY

A foreigner living and working in Switzerland can buy property as a main residence without any restrictions. There used to be restrictions for those with a B permit (see page 64), but these were reduced considerably in 1997 and foreigners are now allowed to buy a property as their main residence without permission. They also can acquire property to house a business, office or workshop permanently, or buy land provided construction of a dwelling commences within one year of purchase. You can also continue to own it when you leave Switzerland and use it as a second home or rent it to a third party. There are still restrictions for non-residents buying holiday homes or buy-to-let residential property (see **Holiday Homes** below). Since July 2002 when the bilateral treaties between Switzerland and the EU came into force (see page 21), EU citizens have had the same rights to buy and own property as Swiss citizens, and restrictions do not longer apply to them.

The Swiss don't need to fear that foreign workers will buy up all their property as prices are much too high for most of them and the average Swiss family, most of whom can only dream of owning their own home (it takes longer to save the deposit than it does to obtain a C permit!). In fact many thousands of Swiss live (often illegally) outside Switzerland in what are ostensibly 'second' homes and commute to their jobs in Swiss cities such as Basle and Geneva.

Working foreign residents and their families comprise around 20 per cent of the Swiss population and own less than 1 per cent of real estate (although some 5 per cent of Switzerland's total housing is foreign-owned).

To buy a house costs **BIG, BIG** money due to the phenomenally high land prices, particularly in the cities – properties in Zurich's Bahnhofstrasse have been sold at over SFr. 250,000 per square metre and are among the highest in the world. Prices vary considerably depending on the location and age of a property. On average a two bedroom apartment costs around SFr. 350,000 and a four bedroom semi-detached or detached house costs **at least** SFr. 800,000. These are average prices for new properties within 25 to 50km (15 to 31mi) of a major city; property in major cities and other high priced areas is much more expensive. A parking space or garage isn't usually included in the cost of an apartment and costs from around SFr. 25,000. Not surprisingly, Switzerland has the world's highest per-capita indebtedness in the mortgage sector.

A modern three to four bedroom detached house in a good area can easily cost over a million francs. If you wish to buy a house it may be cheaper, depending on where you work, to move somewhere more remote where houses are cheaper and commute to work by car, train or air. Despite the high prices, in most areas there isn't a lot of property for sale, as people seldom move house (it's too expensive). Many buyers spend many months or even years looking.

Although currently growing, home occupier-ownership in Switzerland is under 35 per cent and the lowest in Europe (compared with around 45 per cent in Germany, 55 per cent in France, 65 per cent in the UK, 70 per cent in Italy and 80 per cent in Spain). Most homeowners never actually own their homes, as the capital on part of the mortgage is never paid off during their lifetime, just the interest. The good news is that buildings in Switzerland are built to last at least a thousand years and the quality of workmanship and materials (triple glazing, etc.) are of the highest standard. Houses, unless new, are usually sold without a guarantee. New houses are guaranteed by the builder or architect against defect, e.g. five years for construction defects and ten years for hidden defects.

Buying a house or apartment in Switzerland is a good investment if you intend to live there permanently or for many (many) years, although you shouldn't expect to make a quick profit. The value of Swiss real estate generally keeps pace with inflation, although there have been big price increases in some areas in recent years. Swiss banks, other financial institutions and some companies, are only too willing to provide a mortgage or two to qualified residents. You must put down a deposit of around 15 to 20 per cent, the actual amount depending on your lender. The larger the deposit, the lower your monthly mortgage payments, although repayments mustn't usually be more than one-third of your gross salary. The balance is financed through a first (60 to 65 per cent) and a second mortgage (15 to 20 per cent) at different interest rates. The first mortgage is usually never paid off as you just pay the interest, while the second mortgage is repaid over 10 to 20 years.

The good news is that Swiss interest rates are the lowest in Europe and among the lowest in the world. The mortgage rate is usually variable, although fixed rate mortgages, which must be re-negotiated every three to five years, are also available. A 1 per cent increase in the mortgage rate translates into a 15 to 20 per cent increase in monthly mortgage payments. There's a fee of around 0.5 per cent of the value of a property to establish a mortgage. In autumn 2003 the variable mortgage rate was 3.25 per cent (fixed for two years was 2.75 per cent and fixed for five years 3.5 per cent, Zürcher Kantonalbank).

Property conveyance must be done by a notary (*Notar, notaire*), whose primary role is to protect the interests of the buyer. Due to the complexities of Swiss property ownership laws, particularly with regard to foreigners, it would in any case be almost impossible to find your way through the paper jungle without a notary. On completion of the purchase and registration of ownership, legal fees, land registry fees and a transfer tax (*Handänderungssteuer, impot sur les transferts*) totalling from 2.5 to 5 per cent of the purchase price, are payable to the notary. VAT at 7.6 per cent may also be levied on the purchase of new property in Switzerland and is included in the sale price.

If you have any alterations made to a new home before taking possession, you should negotiate directly with the company involved, e.g. a kitchen or bathroom manufacturer or installer, rather than the architect or builder, who will add a hefty percentage as their fee. Always carefully scrutinise any bills before paying them, as it isn't unusual for them to be incorrect. **Take care before signing any legal papers in connection with buying property and have your lawyer and lender check contracts.**

Holiday Homes

Due to the high cost and the restrictions on foreign property ownership, there isn't a booming business in holiday homes. Switzerland introduced legislation in 1973 (the 'Lex Furgler' legislation) to restrict foreign home ownership and prevent wealthy foreigners from buying up all the best property, mainly in the French and Italian-speaking areas of Switzerland. The 'Lex Friedrich' laws (1985) added further restrictions and introduced a restrictive quota system, which allowed individual cantons to impose even stricter regulations (often decided by local referendum). There is usually no quota for Basle-City, Geneva or Zurich and it's generally no longer possible for non-resident foreigners to buy property in the major cities. There are fewer opportunities to buy in German-speaking cantons than in French-speaking cantons. Swiss property law demands that where foreigners are permitted to purchase homes, a percentage of every development (e.g. a group of chalets or an apartment chalet) must be acquired by Swiss citizens. In some towns, local laws prevent sales to non-residents.

Under the bilateral treaties between Switzerland and the EU (see page 21), EU citizens have the same rights to buy and own property as Swiss citizens, and the above restrictions do not longer apply to them. Non-Eu-citizens living in Switzerland still need permission to buy a holiday home in most places. The permission can be granted under certain conditions such as the property not being rented out for the whole year.

People who are not resident in Switzerland at all can only buy any property with permission. Many cantons make reservations that are entered in the land register, for example that the property may not be sold at a profit within the first years, that it can only be sold to a Swiss citizen or resident foreigner or that it can only be used by the owner and his family but not rented out. Non-resident buyers should also be wary of changes in exchange rates, as they can prove **very** costly. Due to the resale restrictions, high prices and relatively low profit margins, **buying property in Switzerland should be viewed as a lifetime commitment, rather than a quick way to turn a profit.**

Foreigners and each of their dependent children over 20, who must also be financially independent, may buy one property only. This is generally restricted to no more than 100m^2 in living area (or an absolute maximum of 180m^2) and 1,000m^2 of land (with an absolute maximum of 2000m^2). You aren't permitted to buy a property in the name of a foreign company, although joint-ownership is allowed. Property owned by non-resident foreigners cannot be left empty and the owner or a family member must occupy it for at least three weeks a year (if not, you may be forced to sell). As a non-resident, you're permitted to spend a total of up to six months a year in Switzerland, although each visit mustn't exceed three months. Annual Swiss property taxes are payable to the community, the canton and the federal government, and generally total around 1 to 1.5 per cent of the value of a property.

The restricted property market is reflected in the high prices, usually starting at over SFr. 100,000 for a studio apartment and increasing to SFr. 1 million or more for a self-contained chalet. A two-bedroom chalet apartment costs from SFr. 250,000 to 400,000 and three-bedroom apartments start at around SFr. 400,000. Three-bedroom apartments in exclusive developments cost from SFr. 500,000 to SFr. 800,000. The approximate average price per square metre of new buildings in Switzerland is around SFr. 6,500 (the highest in the world).

Swiss mortgages of from 50 to 75 per cent of the sale price are available to non-residents over a period of from 15 to 50 years. If you have additional security, other than the property that you're buying, you may qualify for a larger mortgage. Mortgage rates for non-residents are usually around 1 per cent higher than those for residents. It's also possible to buy a self-contained apartment in a hotel (aparthotel) in some areas, purchased purely for investment purposes, or a purpose-built retirement home (a growth industry in Switzerland).

A number of foreign agents deal in property in the most expensive areas of Switzerland, where property is often built especially for sale to foreigners. Agents arrange inspection flights to Switzerland and often refund the cost of flights (up to a certain limit) on completion of a sale. Most agents offer rental and management services and will arrange to let your property. **Note, however, that a property cannot be let for long periods, e.g. more than 250 days a year.**

Quotas for the sale of property to foreigners aren't always filled due to the high cost and resale restrictions, although cantons that don't fill their quotas can pass them onto other cantons.

RENTED ACCOMMODATION

Rented accommodation (*Mietwohnung, appartement à louer*) in Switzerland usually consists of an unfurnished apartment. Furnished accommodation isn't easy to find (except in holiday areas) and is generally expensive. Unfurnished apartments, both old and new, are generally available in all areas, the latter usually being easier to find, but more expensive. In some areas there's a glut of apartments to rent, although in major cities such as Geneva and Zurich accommodation is in short supply and **very** expensive. Houses to let (furnished or unfurnished) are usually rare and expensive, and rents range from SFr. 3,000 a month up to SFr. 10,000 or more a month in the best areas. Contracts for house rentals tend to be longer than those for apartments and some landlords rent only to Swiss or C permit holders (see page 70).

In the farming, restaurant and hotel trades, an employee's salary or benefits may include a furnished room or apartment. Seasonal workers in the building trade may be accommodated in barrack type buildings at or near building sites. Furnished rooms can be rented in private houses and apartments in most towns for around SFr. 300 to 600 per month, depending on the size, amenities and location. Sharing accommodation can be a solution to high rents, particularly for seasonal workers, for whom rental costs are prohibitively high.

FINDING AN APARTMENT

The chief sources for finding an apartment are the local newspapers, the best days for advertisements usually being Wednesdays, Fridays and Saturdays. Apartments and houses for rent are also advertised (*Wohnungen zu vermieten, appartements à louer*) in free local newspapers, delivered in most areas along with all the other junk post (Switzerland is a world leader in the production of junk post, a major industry). Some cities have free newspapers devoted solely to accommodation. Advertisers may be private owners, real-estate managers or rental agencies. Sometimes advertisements have a box number (*Chiffre Nr., chiffre No./boîte No.*). Unfortunately advertisers seldom reply to letters and it's often a waste of time writing (in major cities, an advertisement for a desirable apartment for rent may attract over 100 replies).

Most towns have rental and real-estate agencies (*Immobilien, agences immobilièrs/régie*), listed in local telephone directories, which usually have a registration fee of around SFr. 50 that's valid for three months. After signing a contract an additional fee is payable. Fees vary from agency to agency, but are usually equivalent to a month's rent. Real estate agents don't usually have a service charge. **Find out what you're expected to pay before signing a contract.**

Apartments and houses for rent are also advertised on company bulletin boards, in company magazines and newspapers, and in official canton newspapers. Some communities publish a list of vacant accommodation in the community. You can insert a rental wanted (*Mietgesuche, demande de location*) advertisement in most newspapers and on bulletin boards in supermarkets, e.g. Migros and Coop, churches, consulates and clubs (many also have newsletters where you can place a wanted ad). Finally don't forget to ask your friends, relatives and acquaintances to help spread the word, particularly if you're looking in the area where you already live.

Information about property to rent in Switzerland is available via the Internet (🖳 www.immopool.ch), where you can also subscribe to an email newsletter that informs you daily about new property available in you chosen area. There are also free classified ads pages such as 🖳 www.baselexpats.com.

LOCATION

New arrivals in Switzerland must usually live in the canton where they work and which issued their residence permit. The best area in which to live obviously depends on your individual situation and requirements, your marital status and your income. Other considerations may include the proximity to your place of work, schools, pub, country or town, shops, public transport, pub, squash or tennis club, swimming pool, pub, etc. There are numerous beautiful areas to choose from in every canton, all within easy travelling distance of a town or city (and a pub). When looking for an apartment, bear in mind the travelling time (particularly in winter when it can increase significantly) and travel costs, for example to your place of work, shops and schools.

It may be possible for some foreigners to live in one of Switzerland's neighbouring countries. In general, however, if you no longer live in Switzerland you aren't entitled to a Swiss residence permit and your employer must apply for a frontier crossing (*Grenzgänger, frontalier*) G permit (see page 65). Permission may depend on your nationality and whether you work for an international organisation. If you decide to live outside Switzerland, you will be subject to the laws of the country where you're resident, including for example registration with the local police, payment of taxes and car registration. Your rent and general living costs may be cheaper outside Switzerland, but the advantages may not be as clear-cut as they first appear, e.g. higher taxes.

Employees of international organisations aren't subject to the same regulations as employees of Swiss companies and there are generally no restrictions on where they may live in Switzerland.

RENTAL COSTS

The cost of renting an apartment varies considerably depending on its size, age, facilities and location. Rents (*Miete, location/loyer*) are high, particularly when you consider that the cost of renting in Switzerland is much more expensive than buying a house in most countries. Rents have been rising rapidly in the last decade and are particularly high in cities and areas where property is in high demand and short supply. In response to property speculation, a law was passed giving prospective tenants the right to know the previous rental charge, to protect them from unwarranted increases (so don't forget to ask). If your rent is increased sharply, you can usually have it reviewed independently; ask your community for information. Subsidised low-cost housing is available in some areas for low-income families, invalids and pensioners. There is, however, sometimes a problem finding genuine low income tenants and often those with relatively high incomes are subsidised.

The rental cost of an apartment depends on many things, the most important (apart from location) being the size and number of rooms. The number of rooms advertised excludes the kitchen (except in Geneva), bathroom and toilet, although the total area (given in square metres) includes all rooms. Generally, the further a property is from a large city or town, public transport or other facilities, the cheaper it will be. Average rental costs for unfurnished apartments are shown in the table below:

No. Of Rooms	No. Of Bedrooms	Monthly Rent (SFr.)		
		Basle	Zurich	Geneva
1 – 1.5	Bed-Sitter/Studio	700 – 1,200	900 – 1,400	750 – 1,000
2 – 2.5	1	1,000 – 2,700	1,600 – 4,000	800 – 1,200
3 – 3.5	2	1,300 – 2,300	2,200 – 4,000	1,200 – 1,500
4 – 4.5	3	1,400 – 2,800	3,000 – 4,500	1,900 – 3,000
5 – 5.5	4	2,000 – 3,100	4,500 – 6,000	2,900 – 3,300

In the above examples the half (.5) room refers to a separate dining area or a larger than average size living room. The rents shown are for good quality new or recently renovated apartments in most rural and suburban areas, inclusive of extra costs (see page 95), but excluding a garage (see page 96). **They don't include apartments located in the central area of towns or in major cities, exclusive residential areas, houses or furnished accommodation – for which the sky's the limit.** Rents are highest in cantons Zug and Zurich and lowest in Jura, Neuchâtel and Valais.) In some areas you can pay over SFr. 10,000 a month for a furnished three or four bedroom house. It's possible to find cheaper, older apartments, but they're rare, generally smaller and don't usually contain the standard 'fixtures and fittings' of modern apartments, e.g. no central heating or double-glazing. **Heating in old houses can be highly eccentric.**

Apartments normally include an oven (usually without a grill), a refrigerator, fitted kitchen units and sometimes a dishwasher or freezer. Note that kitchens are often tiny, even in many large houses. Apartments may be partly or fully carpeted and parquet (wooden) flooring is also fairly common. Larger apartments (from four rooms) usually have a second toilet and may have an en-suite shower off the main bedroom in addition to a separate bathroom. A storage room is usually provided in an apartment or a lockable storage room in the house cellar, which doubles as the mandatory nuclear shelter. Many apartment blocks also have a bicycle storage room. An apartment with a patio (*Gartensitzplatz, terrasse*) is usually cheaper than a top floor apartment, which may have a small balcony only. Generally the higher the floor, the higher the cost (you pay for the rarified air). Top floor or attic apartments (*Dachwohnung, appartement attique*) are the most expensive and are often fitted with an open fireplace (*Cheminée*), considered a luxury in Switzerland.

Unfurnished apartments usually have light fittings only in bathrooms, kitchens and occasionally hallways (most rooms just have bare wires). Fitted wardrobes in bedrooms are rare and curtain rails aren't provided unless they're built-in. A number of built-in linen cupboards and a cloakroom unit may be provided. Most apartment blocks have communal storage rooms for bicycles and luxury apartment blocks may have a communal sauna or heated swimming pool. The hot water supply is often shared and can run out during times of heavy use, although modern apartments usually have their own boilers(s). A metal frame is often provided in apartment grounds for beating carpets.

Most apartment blocks have a communal laundry room with a washing machine and tumble dryer and a separate drying room. Some apartment blocks have their own outside clothes lines, where tenants may hang their clothes to dry. The sharing of washing machines can be most unsatisfactory for families, particularly in large apartment blocks. Tenants may be allocated the use of the communal washing machine for a few hours a week only, at an inconvenient time. In larger, more expensive apartments, a personal washing machine and drier may be provided, which may be located in a private laundry/drying room. If you wish to buy your own washing machine and wash at your convenience, make sure that you have room to install it in your apartment and an appropriate power point (see **Electricity** on page 103).

EXTRA COSTS

Extra costs (*Nebenkosten/NK, frais immobiliers/charges*), totalling roughly 10 to 15 per cent of the rent, are payable in addition to the monthly rent of an apartment. When a property is advertised for rent, it's usually stated whether extra costs are included in the rent. Extra costs cover central heating, communal electricity, waste collection, caretaker (*Hauswart, concièrge*) and cable television (see page 139). They vary from community to community (*Gemeinde, commune*) and are usually divided between all tenants of a building according to their apartment size. There may be an additional annual charge (or a refund) for the central heating and other general costs incurred by your landlord during the previous year. You will receive an itemised account, usually in the autumn, detailing the amount to be paid or refunded. When you pay your rent via a standing order, refunds are normally paid directly into your bank or post office account.

GARAGE OR PARKING SPACE

A garage or parking space (*Parkplatz, parking*) isn't usually included in the rent of an apartment. A single lock-up garage or a parking space in an underground garage is quite common in modern apartment blocks and costs around SFr. 130 to 200 a month. A covered parking space costs around SFr. 80 to 120 a month and an outside parking space from SFr. 75 to 100 a month. All new developments must have adequate parking for both tenants and visitors.

If you live in a town or city, it's often difficult to find an apartment with a garage or parking space. However, it may be possible to rent a parking space, for example in the underground garage of a hotel or in a private car park. You must sign a separate contract for a garage that isn't rented with your apartment. It's possible to rent a garage for the winter months only, although the contract must usually start and end on fixed dates, for example from the 1st October to the 1st April (see **Contract Termination** on page 101). A garage is useful, particularly in winter – unless of course you enjoy trying to find your car among the snowbanks (there are many banks in Switzerland). A garage also prevents your car from melting in summer.

Free street parking is difficult or impossible to find in most cities and large towns. In many towns, tenants must obtain a resident's parking permit for on-street parking or face a fine. This is to discourage people from using the streets as a public car park, which although it does nothing to alleviate parking problems, does save motorists from having to dodge in and out of parked cars.

SIGNING THE CONTRACT

When you find a suitable apartment, you must sign a contract (*Vertrag, contrat*) with the landlord or owner. Apartment contracts are usually for an unlimited period with a notice period of three or six months. A standard contract form is provided in most cantons, although you should take special note of any added or deleted clauses or passages. Your contract should include details of when your rent and extra costs will be increased, if applicable. An unscheduled rental rise, e.g. due to an interest rate increase, must be notified by registered post at least three months in advance.

Your landlord may ask to see your residence permit and in some cases may let an apartment only to a Swiss national or a foreigner with a C permit (see page 70). Students and others with low or no regular income may need a Swiss guarantor to co-sign their contract. Among the most important considerations are the minimum tenancy period before you can move (e.g. one year) and the official moving dates, which are usually fixed for each canton (see **Contract Termination** on page 101). **Before** signing the contract, you may be interested to find out the following:

- Whether there's a limit on your tenancy period (minimum or maximum period);
- On which dates the contract can be terminated;
- Whether a deposit is required (maximum three months' rent);
- How many people may live in the apartment;
- What laundry facilities are provided and when they're available;
- If cable television is available and what channels (see page 139);
- If satellite television reception is possible (see page 140);
- Whether any telephone sockets are installed (otherwise you must pay for them);
- If pets are allowed (you can be evicted if you keep a pet against your landlord's wishes);
- The income tax rate in the community (see page 288);
- When the rent and extra costs are to be reviewed or increased;
- What the parking facilities are (particularly covered parking in winter);
- When the tenant or landlord is required to redecorate the apartment;
- What the house rules are (see page 99);
- Whether there are any churches or shooting ranges in the neighbourhood. If there's a church within DONGING! distance, you will be woken early on Sundays.
- Any special rules or restrictions;
- Whether there's a lift or a goods lift for furniture. Lifts must be provided in some cantons in all buildings with four or more floors.

If you rent a house, it's **even more** important to check the rules and regulations for tenants. You will probably be responsible for the following:

- The gardens and grounds;
- The heating system maintenance, insulation, ordering fuel, etc.;
- The water supply maintenance;
- Chimney sweeping twice a year, which is compulsory for oil and wood burning systems (this may be paid by your landlord);
- Fire precautions (regular inspections may be required by your insurance company, including checking the chimneys).

Often a deposit (*Kaution, caution*) equal to one to three month's rent must be paid, which is deposited in an interest-bearing account. It's repaid with interest when you leave, provided there are no outstanding claims, e.g. for damages or cleaning (see **Contract Termination** on page 101).

Don't sign the contract (both husband and wife must sign) until you're sure that you fully understand all the small print. Ask one of your Swiss colleagues or friends for help, or obtain legal advice (you can also join an association such as ASLOCA which defends the rights of tenants).

MOVING HOUSE

After finding an apartment, it normally takes just a few weeks to have your belongings shipped from within Europe – from anywhere else it varies considerably. If you're flexible about the date, it's much cheaper to have your move done as a part load, rather than a special delivery. Obtain a number of estimates in writing before committing yourself, as costs vary considerably. However, you should be wary of a company whose estimate is much lower than others. Some removal companies promise anything to get a contract and increase the cost later, and many don't deliver on the planned date. Always use an established removal company with a good reputation. Check that a company uses its own vans and staff, as some companies use sub-contractors, known in the trade as 'cowboys'. For international house moves it's best to use a company specialising in international removals.

Try to use a removal company that's a member of an organisation such as the Federation of International Furniture Removers (FIFR) or the Overseas Moving Network International (OMNI). These and some national removal companies are usually members of an advance payment scheme that provides a guarantee. If a member company fails to fulfil its commitments to a customer, the removal will be completed at the agreed cost by another company or your money will be refunded. Make a complete list of everything to be moved and give a copy to the removal company. Don't include anything illegal (e.g. guns, bombs or drugs) with your belongings as customs checks can be rigorous and penalties severe. Give your removal company a telephone number and address in Switzerland through which you can be contacted, and ask a relative or friend to handle any problems in the country from where your belongings are being shipped.

Be sure to fully insure your household contents during removal with a reputable insurance company. Don't insure with a shipping company that carries its own insurance as they will usually fight every cent of a claim. In some countries, almost all removal companies' insurance policies restrict their liability to a pittance, which also applies to goods held in storage. **Make sure that insurance covers your belongings for their true value and have the policy small print checked by an independent expert.** It's advisable to make a photographic or video record of valuables for insurance purposes. If you need to make a claim, be sure to read the small print, as some companies require you to make claims within three or seven days. Any claims outside this period aren't considered! Send your claim by registered post. If you need to put your household effects into storage, it's imperative to have them fully insured against fire, as warehouses occasionally burn down (often as a result of arson). **Note also that many warehouses have no fire alarms, sprinklers or fire-fighting equipment.** It's better to be safe than sorry!

If you plan to transport your belongings to Switzerland personally, check the customs requirements in the countries you must pass through. To expedite customs formalities, it's advisable to inform Swiss customs of the date and approximate time of your arrival in Switzerland. If your household and personal effects are sent unaccompanied, the receiving freight company will send you a customs form (18.44) to be completed and signed. In addition they will require a photocopy of your residence permit, a copy of the personal details' pages of your passport and proof of accommodation, e.g. a copy of a rental contract.

For removals within Switzerland, vans and trucks can be rented by the hour, half-day, or day (local rental companies are the cheapest). Some companies allow employees the use of company vehicles free of charge. Many removal companies sell packing boxes in numerous sizes and rent or sell removal equipment (e.g. trolleys and straps) for those who feel up to doing their own house moving.

Bear in mind when moving home that everything that can go wrong often does, so allow plenty of time and try not to arrange your move to your new home on the same day as the previous owner is moving out. That's just asking for fate to intervene! **Last but not least, if your Swiss home has poor or impossible access for a large truck you must inform the shipping company (the ground must also be firm enough to support a heavy vehicle).** You can ask the local police to reserve a parking space for a removal truck when moving house (at a cost of around SFr. 50). **If large items of furniture need to be taken in through an upstairs window or balcony, you may need to pay extra.**

The cost of moving your house contents from your previous country of residence to Switzerland may be paid by your Swiss employer (see page 52). You're officially allowed a day off work when moving house, provided that you don't move every month! See also **Customs** on page 76 and **Chapter 20**.

HOUSE RULES

All apartment blocks have house rules (*Hausordnung, règlement d'immeuble*), some of which may be promulgated by your local community and enforceable by law (particularly those regarding noise and siesta periods). You should receive a copy on moving into your apartment; if you don't understand them, have them translated. They may include the following:

- A noise curfew between 8pm and 6am (this may start at 9 or 10pm depending on the time of year). The Swiss generally take this very seriously, as most get up before some foreigners go to bed. This may be a slight exaggeration, but they do tend to go to bed early and rise at the crack of dawn. They're likely to hammer on your door, walls and ceiling, or even call the police if you play music or hold a noisy party after 10pm.

- You may be required to inform your neighbours when you're having a party. Even inviting your Swiss neighbours to your party doesn't always do the trick, as they've been known to call the police and complain about the noise as soon as they're back in their own apartment! Some apartment blocks have a party room for the use of tenants. You can be fined or evicted for persistently making too much noise.

- Absolutely no loud noise (e.g. drilling, banging in nails or playing loud music) on Sundays and public holidays. Sunday is a day of rest, when working is forbidden by law (see **Sunday Working** on page 58).

- There's often a midday siesta (*Mittagsruhe, sieste*) during the day, e.g. from noon to 1 or 2pm, during which period you mustn't make any loud noise. This is to allow young children or pensioners an undisturbed afternoon nap.

- No bathing or showering between 10pm and 7am.

- No pets without special written permission (dogs aren't always permitted, although cats are usually okay).

- Restrictions regarding children, e.g. no ball games or cycling on grass areas.

- No leaving footwear outside the door.

- Hanging net curtains at your windows is compulsory in some apartments.

- Special times for airing bedding, i.e. hanging it from windows, which may be dictated by canton law.

- The use of the laundry room, including cleaning after use.

- Removal of waste (rubbish must be sorted and special bags used – see page 106).

- Last but not least, don't flush the toilet between 10pm and 6am and **'gentlemen please sit down when using the toilet between these hours'** (this is an actual example from an expensive apartment block in Zurich, presumably with **very** thin walls).

Your Swiss neighbours will usually be happy to point out any transgression of house rules. In apartment blocks, problems regarding communal areas are dealt with by your caretaker, whereas problems within your apartment should be reported to your landlord.

INVENTORY

One of the most important tasks on moving into a new apartment is to complete an inventory and report (*Hauszustand/Mängelliste, etat des lieux/liste d'erreurs*) on the state of the apartment. This includes the condition of fixtures and fittings, the cleanliness and state of the decoration, and anything missing or in need of repair. The inventory form is provided by your landlord and must be completed, signed and returned, within 14 days of occupying your apartment. If you're taking over an apartment from the previous tenant, the landlord may arrange for the hand-over to be done when you're both present, so that any problems can be sorted out on the spot.

Note down the reading on your meters (electricity, gas, water) and check that you aren't overcharged on your first bill. **Your apartment should be spotless when you move in, as this is certainly what your landlord will expect when you move out** (the meaning of life in Switzerland is a spotless, highly polished stove). Most landlords in Switzerland are honest and won't try to rob you, nevertheless, it's better to be safe than sorry.

CONTRACT TERMINATION

You must generally give a minimum of three months notice **by registered letter** (*Einschreiben, enregistrer/recommander*) when you wish to terminate the lease on your apartment. This applies to most contracts in Switzerland. Notice letters must be signed by both the husband and wife, where applicable. The contract may usually be terminated only on the dates listed in your contract, normally the end of every month except December, or in older contracts, the 31st March, 30th June and 30th September. If it isn't terminated by either party, a lease is normally automatically extended for a further period, as stated in your contract.

If you wish to terminate your contract outside the official moving dates or at short notice, you must find a replacement tenant who's acceptable to your landlord. For example, a prospective tenant must be able to pay the rent (which must be no more than half of a single person's salary or one-third for someone with a family), and there should be a good reason not to accept him, e.g. a registered drug addict or someone with a police record. If you don't find a replacement tenant before you move, you're liable for the rent due until the next official moving date or until a new tenant is found, if earlier. Contracts often have a minimum duration of one year, although the same rules apply regarding moving within this period or outside the official moving dates provided you find a replacement tenant.

You're expected to leave your apartment **spotlessly clean**, as it was when you took it over. In Switzerland 'godliness is next to cleanliness' and the Swiss have a lot of spotlessly clean churches to prove it. One method of avoiding any comeback is to employ professional cleaners, which many people consider well worth the money. Look in your local newspapers or telephone directory under removal cleaning (*Umzugsreinigung, nettoyage pour remise d'appartement*). Professional cleaning can be expensive, for example SFr. 1,000 or more depending on the size of your apartment. The cost varies from company to company, so shop around and don't pay the bill until the apartment has been cleaned to your landlord's satisfaction (it pays not to move too often in Switzerland as it can be an expensive business).

You must pay for any damage to fixtures and fittings and you may also be required to redecorate the apartment, depending on its condition when you moved in, how long you've lived there and the terms of your contract. Usually the decoration (paintwork, wallpaper) and fixtures and fittings will show signs of 'normal wear and tear,' for which an allowance may **not** be made. Necessary repairs or replacements may depend on the length of your tenancy and if you're a long-term tenant certain things may be overlooked. If you have private liability insurance (see page 271), it may pay for accidental damage caused to a rented apartment, although glass may be excluded. The return of your deposit will depend on the cleanliness and condition of the apartment on leaving. The following checklist may convince you to use a cleaning company:

- The cleaning of your apartment should include **everything**, including, carpets (shampoo), floors, walls, paint work, windows (if double glazed, **between** the glass), oven, cupboards, bath/WC, lamp shades, refrigerator, dishwasher, blinds, pipes and radiators in all rooms, garage, patio, balcony, storeroom, attic, basement and decalcification of your boiler. A cleaning company contract should include all the above. Your landlord may even don white gloves to check that the oven is clean.

- Repair or remove any stains or scratches from floors (e.g. parquet floors, which must also be polished), paintwork and walls. These may require painting, papering or sanding. Fill any holes made in the walls for pictures, mirrors and other fittings.

- The garden and house surrounds must be in good order. Remove all weeds from your patio or balcony.

- Restore any alterations or improvements to their original state, sell them to the next tenant, or give them to the owner to avoid restoration costs. The landlord may insist on professional repairs or restoration, usually stated in your contract, and no do-it-yourself.

- Remove fixtures or fittings that are easily removed and which weren't part of the original inventory, for example light fittings.

You can obtain a written statement from your landlord to the effect that the apartment is in acceptable condition and that no further claims will be made, although usually this is unnecessary. You may wish to make a note of your electricity, water and gas meter readings, and ensure that the telephone is disconnected. Finally, if applicable, ensure that your deposit is repaid with interest. Any deductions from your deposit should be accompanied by an itemised list of repairs and a copy of bills. See also **Chapter 20**.

KEYS

You usually receive two or three keys to an apartment or house and two keys for the post box. If you require extra keys you must pay for them. Your house key may also fit your garage or underground garage door, if applicable. The locks fitted to most apartments and houses are usually of a special high security type. Keys have individual numbers and extra keys cannot be cut at the local hardware store. If you require additional keys, you must ask your landlord, who will arrange for copies to be made and sent to you (along with the bill).

If you lock yourself out of your apartment or car, there's usually a local locksmith on emergency call day and night to help you. Ask the telephone operator for the number on 111. This service is, however, **very** expensive and it may be much cheaper to break a window to gain entry to your apartment (but difficult if you live on the 14th floor!). Whatever you do, don't call the locksmith out at night or at weekends – it could bankrupt you (stay in a hotel). If you're an habitual key loser, there are a number of companies that provide a key-return service. For around SFr. 20 they provide you with a coded key-ring tag which you attach to your key-ring. A note on the key-ring tag asks anyone finding the keys to drop them in the nearest post-box. Return rates of over 90 per cent are claimed, including keys lost outside Switzerland.

If you vacate your apartment for an extended period, it may be obligatory to notify your caretaker and leave a key with him or with a neighbour in case of emergencies. If you don't have all the copies of your keys when you move out of an apartment, the barrel of a lock for which you've lost a key may need to be changed at your expense.

UTILITIES

Electricity

Some 57 per cent of electricity in Switzerland is generated by hydroelectric power, around 39 per cent by nuclear power and 4 per cent by a combination of oil, burning waste products and solar power. The electricity supply in Switzerland is 220 volts AC, 10 amps maximum, with a frequency of 50 hertz (Hz). This is suitable for all electrical equipment with a rated power consumption of up to 2,200 watts. For equipment with a higher power consumption (oven, washing machine, dishwasher), a single or 3-phase, 380 volts AC, 20-amp supply is necessary.

Some electrical appliances (e.g. electric razors and hair dryers) are fitted with a 110/220 volt switch. Check for the switch, which may be inside the casing, and make sure it's switched to 220 volts **before** connecting it to the power supply. Electrical equipment rated at 110 volts AC (for example from the US) without a voltage switch, requires a transformer to convert it to 220 volts AC.

Transformers are available from most electrical retailers and they can also be purchased second-hand from Americans returning home. Total the wattage of the devices you intend to connect to the transformer and make sure that its power rating exceeds this sum. Generally all small high-wattage electrical appliances, such as kettles, toasters, heaters and irons need large transformers. Motors in large appliances such as cookers, refrigerators, washing machines, dryers and dishwashers, will need replacing or fitting with a large transformer. In most cases it's less trouble and expense to buy new appliances in Switzerland. **Note that the dimensions of Swiss cookers, microwave ovens, refrigerators, washing machines, dryers and dishwashers differ from those in most other countries**. Equipment purchased abroad won't fit into a standard Swiss kitchen.

Another problem with some electrical equipment is the frequency rating, which in some countries, e.g. the US (again), is designed to run at 60Hz and not Switzerland's 50Hz. Electrical equipment **without** a motor is generally unaffected by the drop in frequency to 50Hz. Equipment with a motor may run okay with a 20 per cent drop in speed. However, electric clocks, clock radios and record players are unusable in Switzerland if they aren't designed for 50Hz operation. To find out, look at the label on the back of the equipment. If it says 50/60Hz, it should be okay. If it says 60Hz, you might try it anyway, **but first ensure that the voltage is correct as outlined above.** If the equipment runs too slowly, seek advice from the manufacturer or the retailer. For example, you may be able to obtain a special pulley for a tape deck or turntable to compensate for the drop in speed. Bear in mind that the transformers and motors of electrical devices designed to run at 60Hz will run hotter at 50Hz, therefore it's necessary to ensure that equipment has sufficient space around it for cooling.

Most apartments and all houses have their own fuse boxes. Fuses may be of two types. Older houses often have screw fuses with a coloured disk, which **when not displayed**, indicates that the fuse has blown. These fuses, which have different amp ratings, can be purchased in most electrical stores and supermarkets. The other type of fuse, found in newer houses and apartments, consists of a simple switch, which when a circuit is overloaded, trips to the OFF position. After locating and remedying the cause, simply switch it back to the ON position.

Regardless of the country you've come from, all your plugs will require changing or a lot of expensive adapters will be necessary (there are over 20 plug configurations in Europe alone). Switzerland has three different plug configurations with two, three or five contact points (including the earth) and a 16 amp rating. Modern Swiss plugs are of the 2 or 3-pin or 2-pin/earth socket type. Pins are round with a 4mm diameter, with live and neutral pins 2cm point-to-point. **When wiring a Swiss plug, it's advisable to put a drop of glue on the screw threads as screws often work loose after a time.** Electric light bulbs are of the Edison screw type. Bayonet fitting bulbs for British-type lamp fittings aren't available in Switzerland, but can be purchased in France.

A low tariff electricity rate is in operation from around 8pm to 6 or 7am, Monday to Friday, Saturday after noon or 1pm and all day Sundays, depending on the area and the time of year. This is a good time to run your washing machine or dishwasher. When your electricity supply is to be switched off, e.g. for urgent plant repairs, you will be notified by your community. Power cuts, while not unknown, are rare and usually happen around once a year in most areas. The electricity supply to washing machines and dryers (communal and private machines) and to dishwashers may be cut for around two hours during the lunch period (for example noon to 2pm) each day, to conserve electricity for cooking. This may occur only during the winter months (October to March) in some areas.

In many cantons, only a qualified electrician is allowed to install electrical wiring and fittings, particularly in connection with fuse boxes.

Gas

Gas is piped from Holland to the major Swiss cities and isn't generally available in homes in Switzerland. However, the use of gas is steadily rising and now accounts for around 10 per cent of total energy consumption (mainly industrial). If you want to cook by gas, you may be able to find a house or apartment that has it (although difficult). In areas without piped gas and particularly in remote areas, homes may have a cooker that uses bottled gas.

Water

Water rates are calculated by one of two methods. If your apartment has its own water meter, you will be billed for the actual water you use. Otherwise you will pay a fixed rate, depending on the size of your house or apartment and possibly the number of taps. (**Note that in Switzerland the left tap is always the hot water tap.**) Water costs are generally low, e.g. SFr. 1.27 per cubic metre (m³), although there have been large increases in some areas in recent years.

Water in Switzerland is usually hard. This means you will need a copious supply of decalcification liquid to keep your kettle, iron and other equipment and utensils clean. Stainless steel pots and pans will stain quickly when used to boil water, unless they're cleaned soon after use. Tap and shower filters must be decalcified regularly. You can have decalcification equipment installed in your water system, which is rarely fitted as standard equipment in apartments. There are various systems available, most of which are expensive and not always very effective. Distilled water or water melted from ice from your refrigerator or freezer, should be used in some electric steam irons (mineral water is also okay). In times of drought, you will be forbidden by your community to water your lawn or wash your car.

Registration & Billing

You don't always need to apply to your local 'Electricity, Gas and Water' company (*Städtische Werke-Elektrizität, Gas und Wasser, centrale sevices techniques:*

électricité, gaz, eau/service industriel) to have your electricity, gas or water supply connected and/or transferred to your name. This may be done automatically by your landlord or community, although a deposit (e.g. SFr. 250) is required in some areas. You will be billed quarterly and may pay your bills automatically via a bank or post office account. You may receive a single bill for your electricity, gas, water and sewage costs or separate bills. Meters are usually read every six months, so the first bill received in a six-month period (i.e. after three months) is an estimate and the second bill contains an itemised list of your actual consumption and costs. If you think the estimate is wildly inaccurate, you can ask for an adjustment.

CENTRAL HEATING

Most apartments in Switzerland have central heating (*Zentralheizung, chauffage central*), paid for each month in your extra costs (see page 95). Heating is usually switched on in autumn and off in spring by your house caretaker or owner, or it may be automatically temperature (climate) controlled. In most apartments, the cost of heating for the whole apartment building is divided among tenants, according to their apartment size. In others, radiators may be individually metered, so you pay only for the heating you use. Some modern apartments have under-floor heating (so be careful when drilling holes in walls).

The highly effective central heating dries the air and can cause your family to develop coughs. Those who find the dry air unpleasant can buy a humidifier (costing from around SFr. 50 to 200) to add moisture to the air. Humidifiers which don't generate steam should be disinfected occasionally (to prevent nasty diseases) with a special liquid available from drug stores (*Drogerie, droguerie*).

WASTE DISPOSAL

Switzerland produces around 430kg of waste per head of population annually, which is around half that generated in the US (the ultimate throw-away society) and lower than most other Western European countries. The country has one of the highest rates of waste recycling in the world and most Swiss religiously sort their rubbish (where there's muck there's money!), which in many cases is obligatory. Recycling is a way of life in Switzerland where there's a successful national campaign to reduce household waste under the slogan 'reduce, reuse and recycle'. All communities publish a collection plan detailing what should be done with different types of waste from aluminium to alp horns, bottles to bicycles, and where the local collection points are located.

Most apartments have large rubbish disposal bins in which rubbish must be deposited in plastic bags (*Kehrichtsäcke, sacs à ordures*). In most communities you must deposit rubbish in special 'official' bags, usually coloured and printed with the community name, sold in local stores and supermarkets. These bags, which come in various sizes, carry a tax and usually cost from SFr. 2 (35litre) to SFr. 6

(110litre) each, depending on their size and the community. Waste deposited in these bags is usually restricted to materials that can be incinerated. If you use unofficial rubbish bags, usually grey or black in colour, they won't be collected and the local waste 'detective' may be employed to track you down (you've been warned!). There's a fine, e.g. SFr. 100, for using a non-approved (non-taxed) bag. In some cantons you must purchase a stamp to put on each rubbish bag.

The aim is to encourage recycling and avoid the unnecessary use of wrappings and packaging, which has already prompted many people to deposit unwanted packaging in supermarket dustbins. It must be working, because since the tax was introduced waste has been reduced by as much as 50 per cent in some areas. Some communities charge residents a separate annual waste tax, e.g. SFr. 30. Bins are usually emptied once or twice per week. In some communities you may need to buy a dustbin (garbage can). Many kinds of waste are recycled or reused in Switzerland including the following:

- Paper and cardboard should be tied in bundles with string and shouldn't include any plastic or metal, e.g. covers or bindings. Collection used to be organised by schools, scouts and other youth groups (proceeds going to club funds), but it's now usually organised by the cantonal authorities. However, in some communities there are no collections and paper must be deposited in a special container or storage area.

- Large objects (e.g. old furniture, carpets, skis and appliances) are collected periodically (e.g. once a month) in some areas, usually just after the official house moving dates (dates are announced in local newspapers). Second-hand junk and furniture stores, often run in aid of a charity such as the Salvation Army, may collect old furniture free of charge.

- Bottles should be deposited in bottle banks (more banks) provided in all towns and villages. Bottle banks are divided into sections for green, brown and white bottles. Their use may be restricted, for example no deposits between 8pm and 7 or 8am and on Sundays and public holidays (or as listed). There's a returnable deposit of SFr. 0.30 to 0.50 on most glass one-litre wine and soft drink bottles, so don't throw them away. Some bottle banks are reserved for large bottles (0.5l or larger) of all colours, which are washed and reused. Switzerland is the world leader in glass recycling with an 85 per cent recovery rate.

- Tin cans may be taken to collection areas or deposited in can-crunching machines. They should be washed, labels removed, lid and base removed, and squashed flat, and should only be deposited in the container specified.

- Some collection bins have containers for used household cooking oils, which shouldn't be flushed down sinks as they clog the pipes.

- Oil and old tyres can be deposited at a special dump or returned to suppliers.

- Hazardous and toxic waste such as paints and thinners should be taken to special dumps.

- All batteries should be returned to retailers, who must provide containers, or taken to a special dump, **and shouldn't be thrown out with the rubbish** (some are recycled). Car batteries should be returned to a garage.

- Aluminium (e.g. cans, tops and frozen food containers) is collected or can be dumped once or twice a year. There are special machines in some areas and separate containers for aluminium waste. A magnet is built into the container: if it's magnetic it **isn't** aluminium.

- Garden rubbish and vegetable or organic waste may be collected and used as compost (special bins may be provided) or you can make your own compost heap.

- Old clothes are collected by charitable organisations, usually once or twice a year (**note that some commercial collectors masquerade as charitable organisations**). If in doubt, deliver your old clothes directly to a bona fide charity such as the Red Cross or Salvation Army. A women's group in your local community may organise a clothes-exchange once or twice a year and will collect and sell nearly-new clothing for a 10 to 20 per cent commission. Old shoes are collected by local shoe stores in some towns and sent to third world countries (opticians may also collect old prescription spectacles).

- Unused medicines and poisons should be returned to a pharmacy or the store where they were purchased, for disposal.

- In some communities there are collection bins for plastic, e.g. soft PVC, metal (miscellaneous), electrical apparatus, mineral items and various other waste items. Plastic bottles have to be returned to stores.

- Old electronics products must be returned to the seller for recycling. Any shops that sell such items have to take them back without any charge.

All communities publish instructions on what to do with different waste and a list of waste collection times and depots. Many large stores, e.g. Migros and Manor, have collection bins for old glass, aluminium, batteries and tins. **The indiscriminate dumping of rubbish is strictly forbidden in Switzerland.**

HOME HELP

The following pages contain information regarding the various types of home help available in Switzerland, which may be of particular interest to working wives and mothers. See also **Home Nursing Service** on page 252.

Part-Time Domestic Help

If you require part-time domestic help (*Putzfrau, femme de ménage*) there are various ways to find someone:

- Place an advertisement (*Inserat, annonce*) in your local newspaper. This is usually the cheapest way of finding help. Your community may have a notice board (*Notizbrett, tableau d'affichage*) where you can place a free advertisement and many stores and supermarkets have a free or inexpensive notice board, e.g. Migros and the Coop.

- Look under positions wanted (*Stellengesuche, marché du travail*) in your local newspapers.

- Contact employment agencies (*Stellenvermittlungsbüro, bureau de placement*) listed in your local telephone directory. This is the most expensive way to find someone.

Expect to pay a minimum of around SFr. 25 an hour for locally found domestic help and around double for someone from an agency. **You must pay old age and survivor's insurance (see page 259) and accident insurance (see page 263) for your part-time domestic help.**

Many communities provide families with a cleaning and general household service (including cooking) when the mother is ill. The service is cheaper if you're a member of a housekeeping and nursing service association (see page 252).

Full-Time Servants

There are regulations concerning the employment of full-time servants (*Diener/Dienerin, domestique*) in Switzerland. These include minimum salaries, maximum working hours, meal allowances, time off and paid vacation. Regulations are usually specified in a booklet available from canton authorities. Salaries may vary considerably depending on the nationality, age and experience of a servant. If your servant is neither Swiss nor has a C permit, you must apply for work and residence permits and pay his pension and accident insurance. Tax must be deducted at source from his income (including lodging and meals, if part of his salary) and all associated paperwork must be completed. Hiring or bringing a foreign servant with you to Switzerland is usually difficult and may be permitted only in exceptional circumstances upon proof of a special need.

Au Pairs

Regulations regarding the employment of au pairs vary from canton to canton. In some cantons priority is given to working mothers, while in others a mother must spend a minimum number of hours a week with the au pair, thus restricting her ability to work full-time. A permit for an au pair is issued for up to 18 months. Although families may hire a succession of au pairs, parents should take care that young children aren't unsettled by the frequent change of 'minder'. It may be better from your child's point of view to find a local person who will work for you for several years.

English-speaking families in Switzerland are unable to employ a Swiss or foreign au pair who wants to learn English. However, if one parent is a native German, French or Italian speaker, for example a Swiss, and the family speaks that language at home, then they may be given permission to employ an au pair wishing to learn that language. For more information see **Au Pairs** on page 37.

Baby-Sitters

If you don't have an 'au pair', close friends or neighbours with teenage children, then baby-sitting agencies (*Babysitter Vermittlungsbüro, agence de babysitting*) are available in major towns and cities. The hourly rate charged by professional baby-sitting agencies depends on the number of children to be cared for. You must pay for public transportation for your baby-sitter to and from your home. If she must stay late at night, you must provide transport to take her home or pay for a taxi. In rural areas, some communities keep a list of baby-sitters. You can also advertise for a baby-sitter in your local newspaper or on a supermarket notice board.

Many holiday resorts have nurseries where you can leave your children while you ski or hike. Some women's organisations, for example American Women's Clubs, have baby-sitting lists or circles (see **Appendix A**). The Red Cross (🖳 www.srk.ch) run a training and referral service in some areas. It may be worthwhile starting your own baby-sitting circle with other local couples. The cost of a baby-sitter varies from around SFr. 15 an hour for a local person, to more than double for someone from an agency. A qualified nurse can be hired from an agency to look after children with special medical needs.

Playgroups & Day Care Centres

There are playgroups (*Spielgruppe, groupe de jeux/classe enfantine*) for children in all cities, fewer in rural areas. Children are usually required to be aged over three, below which they're generally socially unacceptable, i.e. not toilet trained. Groups usually meet for two to three hours, several times a week. There are English-language pre-schools in some areas and day-care centres (*Kinderhort, crèche*) are also quite common. Children are usually accepted on a part-time basis as often as required, although some insist on full-time care only. Age isn't usually a problem, as most centres have fully equipped nurseries. They provide hot lunches, daytime sleeping facilities and outdoor activities. Fees are usually fixed but are sometimes reduced for low income families.

Many villages and towns run a child minding service (*Kinderhütedienst, garderie d'enfants*) that provides baby-sitting facilities during the day for working mothers. Child minding services are also provided by 'day mothers' (*Tagesmütter, Mamans de jour/gardiennes d'enfants*) whose fees are from around

SFr. 20 for a half-day and SFr. 30 for a full day. Children aged from three to five are usually accepted. Many village women's groups organise one afternoon a week, when they take care of pre-school-age children. All the above organisations are listed in local telephone directories or contact your local community for information. Child-minding centres (*Kinderparadies, paradis des enfants*) are also provided by many shopping centres and large stores.

6.

POSTAL SERVICES

There's a post office in most towns in Switzerland, although many smaller post offices have been closed in recent years. In addition to the usual post office services to be found in most countries, the Swiss post office provides a number of unique services, most of which are described in this chapter. In surveys the Swiss postal service is consistently rated one of the world's best (if not **the** best) and delivers some 5.5 billion letters, 1.5 billion newspapers and magazines, and 225 million parcels a year. Information about post office services is available on the Internet (🖳 www.post.ch).

In autumn 2003, many post office services were in the process of changing and the information contained in the chapter may have changed since then.

BUSINESS HOURS

Post office business hours in Switzerland are usually from 7.30 to noon and 1.30 or 1.45pm to 6pm, Mondays to Fridays, and from 7.30 to 11.30 am on Saturdays. In small post offices in major towns, post offices may open later, e.g. 8 or 8.30am, and close for lunch from 11.30am until 2pm. In small towns and villages, opening hours are often restricted, e.g. 7 to 10.30am, 1.45 to 3.30pm and 4.30 to 6pm from Monday to Friday, and 7 to 11am on Saturdays. Main post offices in major towns don't close for lunch and provide limited services for urgent business outside normal business hours. In major towns and cities an urgent business counter (*Dringlichkeitsschalter, guichet d'urgence*) is usually open from 6.30 to 7.30am, and from the close of normal services at 6.30pm until between 8.30 and 11pm, Monday to Saturday. On Sundays, urgent business counters are open from around 11am to 10.30pm. Many smaller towns also have limited urgent business hours on Saturdays and Sundays. Urgent business counter hours are displayed outside post offices. During extended business hours, post offices handle letters and parcels only, and a surcharge of SFr. 1 is made on each transaction.

LETTER POST

Switzerland introduced a two-tier domestic letter postal service in 1991. 'A' class domestic post is usually (around 97.3 per cent) delivered the day after posting and from 1st January 2004 it will cost SFr. 1. for items up to size B5 (250 x 176mm) and 100g, SFr. 1.30 for items up to B5 and 101–250g, and SFr. 2.20 for items from size B5 to B4 (353 x 250mm) up to 500g. Delivery of 'A' class post takes two to five days in Europe and four to ten days to other countries. Delivery of 'B' class domestic post takes two to three working days and costs SFr. 0.85 for items up to B5 and 100g, SFr. 1.10 up to B5 and 101–250g and SFr. 1.80 for items from B5 to B4 up to 500 g. Delivery of 'B' class (surface) post takes four to ten days in Europe and four to eight weeks to other countries. Both 'A' and 'B' items of post can be up to 20mm thick. 'A' class stamps have a screen printed on them to allow for automatic sorting and an *A Prioritaire* sticker isn't required. 'A' class post to European and overseas addresses is sent by airmail, while 'B' class post goes by land and/or sea (surface). The cost of posting a letter or postcard in Switzerland is as follows:

Size	Weight	Thickness	Price (SFr.)					
			Switz.		Zone 1*		Zone 2**	
			A	B	A	B	A	B
B6/B5	Up to 20g#	20mm	1.00	0.85	1.30	1.20	1.80	1.40
B6/B5	21 – 50g	20mm	1.00	0.85	2.20	1.80	3.20	2.50
B6/B5	51 – 100g	20mm	1.00	0.85	3.30	2.50	4.50	3.00
B6/B5	101 – 250g	20mm	1.30	1.10				
B4	Up to 100g	20mm	2.20	1.80	3.60	3.00	5.00	3.50
B4	101 – 250g	20mm	2.20	1.80	6.20	4.00	8.50	5.50
B4	251 – 500g	20mm	2.20	1.80	11.50	7.00	15.00	8.50
B4	501g – 1kg	20mm	5.00	4.50				
B4/5/6	Up to 500g	20 – 50mm	13.00	8.00	19.00	10.00		
B4/5/6	501g – 1kg	20 – 50mm	21.00	12.00	33.00	18.00		
B4/5/6	1 – 2kg	20 – 50mm	32.00	21.00	45.00	32.00		

* Zone 1 – Europe

** Zone 2 – Rest of the world

Includes Postcards.

Note the following when posting letters in Switzerland:

- Letters up to 50mm thick and up to 250g can be sent within Switzerland for a surcharge of up to SFr. 2.30. Letters that are larger then this must be sent as parcels (see page 117).

- It's necessary to use an *A Prioritaire* or airmail (*Luftpost, par avion, via aerea*) label for 'A' class international post, although all letters to Western European countries are transported by air, including 'B' class post.

- Post for the blind weighing up to 7kg is delivered free.

- If you send a letter with insufficient postage it will usually be delivered (but not by A-Post). You will be sent a card showing the postage due, to which you must affix stamps equal to the amount due and re-post. In some cases a letter will be returned with a request for extra postage, otherwise the addressee is liable to pay double the postage due. If you **receive** a letter with insufficient postage, you're required to pay the postage due, either to the postman or at your local post office (a collection form will be left – see **Post Collection** on page 118).

- Post boxes are yellow and are usually set into (or attached to) a wall.

- There's one post delivery a day in the morning, including Saturdays, which is restricted to 'A' class post only.

- It's possible to send international letters and parcels by express (*Urgent*) to most western European countries. The fee depends on the size and the weight of the letter or parcel (minimum SFr. 39). There are also a number of domestic express post services offering guaranteed delivery taking either two (City-Express) or eight hours (Intercity-Express) or next day (Swiss-Express). If you receive an express letter, an *attention!* (*Achtung!*, *Attention!*) sticker is affixed to your letter box or door, advising you of this. **Note that express post has replaced the telegram service, which has been discontinued.**

- Aerogrammes (*Aerogramm*, *aerogramme*) are available from stationery stores (not post offices) and don't include postage.

- Christmas surface post should be sent by around 1st November for North America and by 25th November for Europe. For other destinations ask at a post office.

- All letters to Swiss addresses sent from outside Switzerland should have 'CH' (Confederatio Helvetica) before the town's postal or zip code (*Postleitzahl/PLZ*, *numéro postal/NPA*), which is the European postal designation for Switzerland. A typical Swiss address is shown below; in German, street (*strasse*) may be abbreviated as *str.* and the house number is listed after the street name:

> Heidi Schweizer
> Hauptstr. 10
> CH-3000 BERNE
> Switzerland

All Swiss postal codes are listed in the pink section of Swiss telephone directories. Postal codes are also available via the Internet (🖳 www.post.ch).

- A brochure showing how post should be addressed is available from post offices. A green sticker may be attached to incorrectly addressed letters, asking you to inform your correspondent of your correct address (*Bitte richtige Adresse dem Absender melden, veuillez communiquer votre adresse exacte à l'expéditeur*).

- Parcels may not be tied with a string (otherwise you will be given scissors and sticky tape to re-seal it) and the address must be in the upper right corner.

- A surcharge of SFr. 5 is made for registered (*lettre signature*) letters within Switzerland and SFr. 4 for destinations outside Switzerland, plus the standard postage cost. The sender's address must be written on the back of registered letters. You receive a receipt for a registered letter or parcel. Proof of receipt (delivery) costs SFr. 3 (a card is returned to the sender). Registered letters and packages can be insured. Insured registered letters and packages over 1kg in weight and with a value of over SFr. 5,000, must be security sealed with wax/lead or special tape. The highest insured value for unsealed packages is SFr. 5,000.

- Stamps (*Briefmarke, timbre*) can be purchased from stamp machines outside most post offices. A change machine for one and two franc coins is provided at larger post offices, plus a machine that dispenses books of stamps. Stamps are also sold by shops and kiosks selling postcards (*Postkarte, carte postale*). Books of five plain postcards with stamps can be purchased from post offices. When post is stamped at a counter, stamps are cancelled by the clerk before your eyes, which is both efficient and safe (not that a Swiss person would ever steal the stamps).

- Special stamps are sold to celebrate Swiss National Day on 1st August (*Bundesfeiermarke, timbre de la fête nationale*) that have a surcharge, proceeds from which support Swiss social and cultural organisations. Other special charitable stamps are also sold occasionally. A magazine and brochures describing special stamps and first day covers are published for philatelists and are available from main post offices. For information about services for philatelists visit ▣ www.post.ch and then click on 'stamps'. This website enables you to look at and order stamps online. In addition the website gives the addresses of the regional philatelist centres (there is one centre for each of the six postal regions).

PARCEL POST

For standard parcels (*Paket, paquet/colis*) of any size the postage depends on their weight. Some examples are shown in the table below.

Weight	Price (SFr.)	
	Economy Class	Priority Class
Up to 2kg	6	8
2 – 5kg	8	10
5 – 10kg	11	13
10 – 20kg	16	19
20 – 30kg	23	26

Priority parcels are delivered on the next working day if posted before 12 noon. Economy parcels are delivered within 2 working days. International parcels may be sent by economy (delivery by rail in Europe and air elsewhere), priority (airmail, e.g. two to three days in Europe) and EMS world-wide (courier). Airmail parcels, regardless of destination, take the same time to be delivered as airmail letters. A form must be completed when sending an international parcel weighing over 2kg.

The post office is very strict on how a parcel should be wrapped (no string!) and how the address has to be written (ask your local post office for labels). For any parcel (too small, too big, too thick, too thin) that is not considered 'standard' a charge of SFr. 2 for manual handling is levied. It's often worthwhile to enquire at the post office before closing the parcel.

The Express Mail Service (EMS) to over 160 countries is available from all Swiss post offices for urgent parcels, usually weighing a maximum of 10 or 20kg, depending on the destination. Parcels sent via EMS take one to two days to be delivered within Europe and from two to four days overseas, depending on the destination. The post office also provides an Expresspost courier service and many international airfreight and courier companies (e.g. DHL, TNT and UPS) also operate in Switzerland.

Parcels sent to addresses outside Switzerland must be accompanied by a customs declaration form. Parcels weighing up to 1kg and not more than 90cm in circumference require an international green customs form CN22 and are sent at a special small parcel postage rate. The value of such a parcel should generally not exceed SFr. 50. When sending an international parcel weighing over 1kg, special customs forms must be completed. Parcels can be insured when they're sent by registered post. Inland parcels can be registered for SFr. 2. Most post offices have scales and special post boxes for parcels – don't put letters in them.

Cardboard boxes, called POST PACs, and padded 'jiffy' bags (*Luftpolster Couvert, enveloppe capitonée*) are available from post offices and most department and stationery stores. POST PACs are available in six sizes (costing from SFr. 2 to 4.50) and include sealing tape. A brochure is available from post offices describing how to pack goods for sending by post.

From 1999, all domestic parcels have had a barcode sticker affixed by the post office to enable them to track stray parcels and check delivery times. The sender receives a receipt with a matching barcode sticker (retain it in case of late delivery, loss or damage). It isn't advisable to post parcels in post collection boxes as you don't receive a receipt.

POST COLLECTION

If the postman calls with post requiring a signature, payment of import duty or excess postage when you aren't at home, he'll leave an orange collection form (*Abholungseinladung, avis de retrait*). Present this form with some identification (for example your Swiss residence permit, passport or driving licence) at your local post office, the address of which is printed on the form. The collection form includes the date when the item can be collected and when it will be returned to the sender if it isn't collected (usually after seven days). This is a good reason to inform the post office if you're going to be away from home for some time (see **Change of Address** below), as they will hold your post for a small fee.

You can receive post via the main post office of any town in Switzerland through the international *poste restante* (*Postlagernd, poste restante*) service. Post sent to a *poste restante* address is returned to the sender if it's unclaimed after 30 days. Identification is necessary for collection (see above).

You may be able to obtain a post office box number at your local post office **free of charge**. If you do, all your post will be stored there and the postman will no longer deliver to your home (it may be quicker to pick it up than wait for the postman). You can arrange to be informed when registered or express post arrives.

CHANGE OF ADDRESS

If you're going to be away from your home for up to two months, you can ask the post office (five days in advance) to hold your post for the sum of SFr. 5. You can either collect it at the end of the period or the postman will deliver it on the date you specify. Your post can be redirected to a new or temporary address in Switzerland or abroad for a nominal fee. All inland post, including parcels, is redirected (excluding circulars, which are returned with your new address to the sender). Only cards and letters are redirected abroad. A temporary forwarding order must be completed at your local post office. The post office provides free (no stamp required) change of address cards in local languages for a move within Switzerland.

Printed matter sent from abroad, e.g. magazines, newspapers and newsletters, won't usually be forwarded and will be returned to the sender, possibly without your new address (it does, however, seem senseless to return post, sometimes halfway round the world, rather than redirect it within Switzerland and charge the addressee for the service). You may be able to request that all post is redirected, including post from abroad, provided you're willing to pay for the extra service. If a letter is unable to be delivered due to the wrong address, the addressee no longer being at the address, or the redirection period having expired, it will be returned with a note stating this, e.g. 'moved; redirection period expired' (*Weggezogen; Nachsendefrist abgelaufen, A déménagé; Délai de réexpedition expiré*).

POST ACCOUNT

Anyone over the age of 16 can open a postcheque account (*Postcheckkonto, compte de cheque postal*) at any post office or by contacting Schweizerische Post, Postfinance, Engehaldenstrasse 37, CH-3030 Berne, ☎ 0800 888 666, 🖳 www.postfinance.ch. The following services are provided:

- The facility to pay bills direct from your account.

- Longer opening hours than banks (the post office is also open on Saturday mornings).

- Two or more people can share the same account (a joint account).

- Standing orders can be paid via the account.

- Monthly statements and payment advices for all debits and deposits for an annual fee of SFr. 36 (the fee is waived if you use Internet banking – 🖥 www. yellownet.ch).

- Cash can be sent via the post office (in other European countries this can be done in local currency).

- Interest is paid on deposits (a higher rate is paid on youth accounts for 14 to 26 year-olds).

- Overdrafts of SFr. 1,000 are allowed for a 28-day period (interest is payable on overdrafts).

- A free cash card, called a 'Postcard', is available to account holders. It allows cash withdrawals of up to SFr. 1000 a day to be made from post office ATMs, called 'Postomats', located at over 400 major post offices. When combined with a debit card, the Postcard also allows holders to pay bills in selected stores up to a total value of SFr. 3,000 per month and to obtain up to SFr. 300 in cash from selected stores. Purchases are automatically deducted from your postcheque account. Postcards can also be used to buy petrol, make telephone calls from payphones and obtain cash from ATMs abroad (fee SFr. 4). The debit Postcard is issued to foreigners only if they have their salary transferred to the post account by their employer or make regular deposits of around SFr. 2000.

- With the Postcard you can obtain cash from ATMs (indicated as Eufiserv) in several countries (see 🖥http://www.eufiserv.com/site/atm_countrypick.asp).

- A Postcard can be combined with an SBB half-fare travel card (see page 181), when a photo is added to the card (the charge is automatically deducted from your account). It can also be combined with an annual rail season ticket (with a photo) and paid in monthly instalments.

- A Postcard Eurocard (Mastercard) or VISA card is available for SFr. 50 a year (SFr. 20 for an additional partner card). (🖥 http://visaatm.infonow.net/bin/findNow?CLIENT_ID=VISA).

When you open a postcheque account, you receive transfer forms and a supply of post-paid envelopes with which to pay bills via the post office. **Note that all postcheques must be written in the local language and not in English.**

PAYING BILLS

In contrast with many other countries, cheques drawn on bank accounts aren't the most important everyday means of payment in Switzerland (in fact cheques are hardly used in Switzerland due to the high fees imposed by banks). Most people in Switzerland pay their bills (except when paying in cash) via the post office giro service. The post office handles over 500 million payment orders a year from which it earns the bulk of its income. A blue or red giro payment form (*Einzahlungsschein, bulletin de versement*) is usually included with every bill you receive by post, with which you can pay the bill at any post office or through your bank. You don't need a giro account to pay bills at the post office or to have money paid into a bank account via a post office, **but note that there's a fee for these services.**

If the payment form was produced by a computer, it will include all the necessary details including your name and address, the payee's name and account number, and the amount. If it wasn't produced via a computer you need to enter these details. Post office payment forms must be completed in blue or black ink and in BLOCK CAPITALS. If you make a mistake you must complete a new form as, unlike personal bank cheques, you **aren't** permitted to make corrections. The left hand stub of the payment form is your receipt and is stamped by the post office clerk and returned to you. Payments may be made at any post office, either in cash or through a girocheque account, as follows:

Payment At A Post Office

The procedure for paying bills at a post office is as follows:

1. Take the payment form(s) to the payments and withdrawals (*Ein- und Auszahlungen, versement et paiements*) window.

2. If you're making a number of payments, the clerk will total the amount due. Add up the total in advance so that you can confirm it (write it down if you don't speak the local language).

3. Payment must be in cash or by cheque from a postcheque account. Cash means **CASH** (the folding stuff) and bank cheques and credit cards aren't accepted.

4. The stamped receipt portion of the payment form will be returned to you (check that it's stamped!).

When you want to make a payment at the post office, it is best to go early in the morning, e.g. on your way to work, to avoid queues.

Payment Through A Girocheque Account

If you have a girocheque account, you can make all your giro payments simply by completing a single form and sending it to the post office with the payment slips that came with your invoices. The procedure is as follows:

1. Complete the form with the name, account number and the amount to be paid for each bill.

2. Sign and date the cover form that shows the total amount of all payment slips and the number.

3. Enclose the form with the blue/red giro payment slips in a pre-addressed envelope and post.

Payment of bills can also be made in the same way through a bank account (see page 282). This is a more secure way of paying large bills than using cash.

Giro payment forms are provided by most companies in Switzerland for regular payments, such as rent, health insurance and credit (time) payments (e.g. one giro form per month, up to the total number of monthly payments due). If you prefer, you can have them paid by standing order (*Dauerauftrag, ordre permanent*) from your bank or girocheque account. Just take them to your bank or a post office and they will complete the formalities.

Books of receipts (*Empfangsscheinbuch, livret de récépissés*) are available for SFr. 2 or 4 from any post office. Complete a receipt for each giro payment you make. All receipts are date stamped, thus providing you with a permanent record of all your giro payments in a single book. (All stubs and receipts should be kept for a period of five years, which is the statute of limitations period in Switzerland.) There's a space provided on giro payment forms for notes (*Mitteilungen, communications*), for example to draw attention to a new address. There are different giro payment forms (*Postanweisung, mandat de Poste*) for transferring money to giro account and non-account holders in Switzerland, account and non-account holders in continental Europe, and internationally.

When sending money abroad, just fill in the name and address of the creditor and the amount in local currency; the post office will calculate the amount due in Swiss francs. You receive the payment advice stub as a receipt and payment is made directly to the payee by the post office.

The Swiss don't appear as anxious to be paid as creditors in most other countries. Don't be surprised if you aren't billed for weeks, or even months after you've purchased something – they haven't forgotten you. You won't normally be required to pay in advance when you order goods and will rarely be asked to pay a deposit. You will, however, be expected to pay all bills when due. The payment date (*Fällig am . . ./Zahlbar bis . . ., payable le . . ./échéance . . .*) is usually stated on the bill accompanying the giro payment form, or the number of days within which you must pay the bill. Payment is usually due immediately or within 10, 30 or 60 days. Some creditors offer a discount for prompt payment of bills or payment in cash. If you don't pay a bill on time, you will be sent a reminder (*Mahnung, rappel/sommation*) and you may be charged interest. Usually only two reminders are sent, after which your creditor may take legal action if you don't pay within the specified period.

Post offices keep a directory of all Swiss postal account holders, which can be used to check account numbers. Cash can be sent to any Swiss bank account holder via a giro transfer. Just enter the bank name and giro number, the account holder's name and account number, and the reason for the payment.

You may receive a giro cheque (*Auszahlungsschein, bulletin de paiement*) as a payment, for example for an income tax or road tax refund. This can be cashed at any post office on production of proof of identification (Swiss residence permit, passport or driving licence). **A giro cheque must usually be cashed within four to six weeks (the validity period is printed on the cheque).** Foreign national girobank postcheques can be cashed at any Swiss post office, provided you have a guarantee card (Postcard).

When writing figures in Switzerland (or anywhere in continental Europe) the number seven should be crossed to avoid confusion with the number one, written with a tail and looks like an uncrossed seven to many foreigners. The date is written in the standard European style, for example 10th September 2002 is written 10.9.02 (not as in the US, 9.10.02).

7.

TELEPHONE

Among the various reasons for Switzerland's economic success are the many unfair advantages that it has have over other countries, one of which is that its telephones always work. In Switzerland you rarely get a bad or crossed line and the quality and range of services are second to none. Switzerland has one of the highest numbers of telephones per head of population in the world (over 600 per 1,000 inhabitants) and nearly every household has a telephone (only hermits and cavemen don't have one).

The Swiss telecommunications market has been open to competition since 1st January 1998, when Telecom PTT became Swisscom (an independent company). You can now choose your long-distance phone operator from a number of companies including Econophone (☎ 0800 188 188), GTN (☎ 0800 222 444), Interoute (☎ 0800 450 460), RSL COM (☎ 0800 100 800) Sunrise (☎ 0800 707 707) Orange (☎ 0800 804 804) and, of course, Swisscom (☎ 0800 800 800). There are also smaller companies operating in certain cantons or cities and direct call (previously call-back) companies offering low cost international calls. Swisscom retain their monopoly on local calls, although this will also eventually be open to competition. Switzerland's mobile phone system, previously operated by Swisscom, has also been opened to competition with the entry of diAx (now Sunrise) and Orange into the market. There are also 'dozens' of Internet providers in the country. As a consequence of deregulation, telephone rates have tumbled in recent years and are set to fall even further.

In autumn 2003 the telephone services provided by Swisscom and its competitors were in a constant state of flux and certain information contained in the chapter may no longer be valid.

A list of emergency numbers is provided on page 133.

INSTALLATION & REGISTRATION

If you move into an old apartment, i.e. any apartment where you aren't the first occupant, a telephone line will usually be installed but there will be no telephone. A new apartment, however, may just have a few holes in the wall in preparation for the installation of telephone sockets. Foreigners without a C permit (see page 70) must pay a deposit of SFr. 1,000 before they can have a telephone line connected or installed. This is returned with interest when you leave the country or obtain a C permit, or may be repaid after two years if you pay your bills regularly (although you must request it).

To have a telephone line installed or connected, contact you nearest Swisscom office or telephone freephone ☎ 0800 800 113. Line installation is usually quick and takes an average of around seven to ten days (where a line is already installed connection takes around three days). When you've paid your deposit, Swisscom will arrange for the connection or installation to be completed at a convenient time. If your apartment doesn't already have a telephone socket(s), then you need to pay installation costs. You can rent a telephone from Swisscom (from around SFr. 5 a month) or buy one from Swisscom (from SFr. 70 for the cheapest pushbutton phone) or an independent supplier, which may be cheaper.

USING THE TELEPHONE

Using a telephone in Switzerland is much the same as in any other country, with the exception of a few Swiss idiosyncrasies. Telephone numbers consist of a two or three-digit area code, e.g. 01 for Zurich and 022 for Geneva, and a seven-digit subscriber number. Numbers are usually written as 01 123 45 67 (as in this book) or 01 123.45.67. An area code may cover a city or a much wider area. **When dialling a number in Switzerland, even a number with the same area code, you must always dial the area code.** When dialling Switzerland from overseas, you dial the local international code (e.g. 00 from the UK), followed by Switzerland's international code (41), the Swiss area code **without** the first 0, e.g. 1 for Zurich, and the subscriber's number. See also **International Calls** on page 129.

Service numbers with the prefix 155 or six-digit 0800 numbers are toll-free numbers provided by companies and organisations. Numbers beginning with 156, 157 and 0900/0901 are service numbers (or information lines) where calls cost from SFr. 0.36 to 4.23 per minute (they include 'sex lines'). There's also a wide range of new business numbers which are listed in telephone directories. **There are many new service numbers and it's becoming increasingly difficult to know what are service numbers and how much calls cost.**

Standard telephone tones, i.e. the strange noises you hear when you aren't connected to a subscriber, are provided to indicate the progress of calls. The following standard tones are used in Switzerland and are different from those used in some other countries:

- **Dialling Tone** – A steady note is heard after you lift the receiver, indicating that the telephone is working and that you can start dialling.

- **Ringing Tone** –A single note repeated at long intervals means that the call has been switched through and the number is ringing.

- **Engaged Tone** – A short single note repeated at short intervals means that the number or all lines are busy.

- **Information Tone** – A repeated sequence of three notes in rising pitch means that the party called cannot be reached on the dialled number. If you don't understand the recorded announcement following the tone, call the operator on 111 for an inland call or 1141 for an international call. If you dial a non-existent number, you will receive a message informing you of this and telling you to refer to your telephone directory. If you dial a number that has been changed, you will hear a message stating the new number or that the number no longer exists. Call 111 and ask for the subscriber's new number.

MOBILE PHONES

Mobile phones – which the Swiss call a 'Natel' or a 'Handy' – can be bought in department stores or specialised shops. If linked to a certain provider, the telephone itself is subsidised by the provider (Swisscom, Orange or Sunrise) and can be bought for a small price. However, there usually is a tie-in of 12 to 24 months which can make the telephone quite expensive particularly if you don't use it very often.

With 'Natel Easy' from Swisscom you don't have to have a subscription but instead you need to buy rechargeable cards. Whilst the Swisscom charges are highest, they also have the best net and with both Sunrise and Orange you still find yourself without connection in less populated places – particularly annoying if you rely on your mobile when going hiking or skiing.

CHARGES

Since the deregulation of the Swiss telecoms market and the influx of new companies, it has been difficult to compare rates, although you can do so on the Swiss Union of Telecommunications Users' Internet site (🖳 www.frc.ch) or Comparis (🖳 www.comparis.ch). Some companies have one flat rate (Globacom, Global Access Direct) 24 hours a day, every day, while others such as Swisscom have two or three tariff periods. Sunrise has a graduated system of discounts where the more you spend the more you save. It's important to compare rates, particularly when making international calls, when huge saving can be made by choosing the cheapest carrier.

Swisscom (☎ freephone 0800 800 800) divides national calls into just two zones: local zone and long-distance (over 10km). It also has three tariff periods: peak (from 8am to 5pm Monday to Friday), off-peak (from 6 to 8 am, 5 to 10pm Monday to Friday; 6 am to 10pm on Saturdays, Sundays and public holidays) and night-time (from 10pm to 6am), when calls are charged at a reduced rate. Swisscom provides discounts on frequently called numbers (☎ 0800 86 87 88 for information). A 'Hello People' scheme provides a 35 per cent discount on the number with the highest charge and a 25 per cent discount on six other numbers for a monthly fee of SFr. 3 (applies to both long-distance national and international calls). The fees of most companies are now similar, although all have different special offers and 'discount days' that they announce in the media.

When using a company other than Swisscom, the company will obtain your authorisation to inform Swisscom and have you connected to their network directly (a prefix is no longer required). However, Swisscom will take every opportunity to conclude that you don't want another company's pre-selection anymore, therefore you need to check your bills to see that your connected to the correct company. Despite offering lower rates than Swisscom, new companies are held back by the high interconnection fees they must pay Swisscom (to access their network).

Swisscom bill you for your monthly line rental, calls and telephone rental, as applicable. Your telephone bill doesn't contain an itemised list of calls, which is available for an extra charge if you have a tone phone. It does, however, separate domestic and international calls (subdivided into Europe and overseas), and calls made during different tariff periods. VAT at 7.6 per cent is levied on all telephone charges. Bills must be paid by the date indicated on them.

INTERNATIONAL CALLS

The Swiss make more international calls (per capita) than any other nation and all private telephones in Switzerland are on International Direct Dialling (IDD). Dial 1141 for the international operator to make non-IDD calls, person-to-person and reverse charge calls and international enquiries. Information regarding international calls, including a world time-zone map, can be found in your local telephone directory. For calls made via Swisscom, the time (in seconds) purchased for 10 cents is shown in directories and for operator connected calls, the cost per minute. To make an international call, dial 00 followed by the country code, then the area code **without** the first zero and finally the subscriber's number. The area codes for major towns in most countries are listed in telephone directories, with the tariff per minute. International calls can be timed by the operator or you can buy a telephone with a meter to monitor the cost. International call information is provided in English in telephone directories.

If you make a lot of international calls, it's important to shop around and compare rates, as huge saving can be made by choosing the cheapest carrier (see **Charges** above). You can buy or rent a box that automatically selects the lowest cost routing for each call.

For example, in the autumn of 2003, TELE2 (☎ 0800 24 24 24) were charging SFr. 0.07 per minute (inclusive of VAT) at all times to Austria, Canada, France, Germany, Italy, Liechtenstein, Norway, Sweden, the UK and the US, and SFr. 0.12 per minute for calls to Australia and New Zealand compared with the charges of Swisscom. Swisscom were charging SFr. 0.12 per minute (normal tariff) and SFr. 0.10 (low tariff) for European calls and SFr. 0.25 (weekdays) or SFr. 0.20 (weekends) for calls to Australia and New Zealand. Swisscom on the other hand has a special weekend rate (which runs from midnight on Saturday to midnight on Sunday and on public holidays), when international calls to Germany, France, Austria, Italy, Canada, the US and the UK cost only SFr. 1. per minute for 60 minutes, after which the rate changes back to the normal rate of SFr. 3 per minute (this rate is not valid for mobile phones). However, if you end the call before the 61st minute and dial the same number again, the low tariff starts again.

One of the best ways to save money on overseas calls (except to the US) is to use a direct dial company (previously termed call-back companies, as you needed to dial a number and wait for a return call), where you dial a local freephone number to obtain a dial tone and then make your call. No PIN code or waiting for a call-back is necessary, although some companies provide a PIN code that allows calls to be made from any phone in Switzerland. Direct call companies include Econophone (☎ 0800 18 81 88), and Telegroup (☎ 0800 84 04 80). **Some direct dial companies levy a minimum monthly charge, so check in advance.** Companies usually bill monthly, either by direct debit or to a credit card.

Swisscom provide international prepaid cards (for SFr. 10, 20, 50 or 100) that can be used in over 90 countries from any standard telephone (not mobiles) to call Switzerland. If you do a lot of travelling you can obtain a special number (OneNumber) and make calls from almost any telephone, either in Switzerland or abroad, without the need for cash or telephone cards. All calls are charged to your home bill. You can also obtain a Swisscom Calling Card, which is an international telephone credit card with a predetermined credit limit. AT&T and other major US telephone companies also provide credit cards that allow international calls to be made at low US rates and other Swiss companies offer a similar service.

DIRECTORIES

Swiss telephone subscribers are listed in directories (*Telefonbuch, annuaire téléphonique*) divided into cantons (the smaller cantons share directories). If you don't have the latest local directory when you move into an apartment, you can obtain one free from your local post office. Directories for cantons other than your canton of residence cost around SFr. 10 each.

Information in telephone directories is separated into sections, as follows:

1. Publicity and information about entries;

2. International connections;

3. Short numbers;

4. Pink Pages – A list of all Swiss post codes, including the codes by street for large towns and cities;

5. White Pages – Private subscriber listings by town in alphabetical order (businesses and services may be listed under their type of business or service and/or their name).

Private subscribers are usually listed under the husband's name (if applicable) in telephone directories and also include the wife's maiden name (in brackets) and may include the subscriber's profession. If you want to have more than one entry in your local telephone directory, e.g. when a husband and a wife both retain their family names or when two or more people share a telephone, there's a charge each time a new directory is published. Subscribers are listed under their town or village and not alphabetically for the whole of a canton or city. Businesses aren't always listed under their name but under a group heading, for example a restaurant may be listed under restaurants and not under its name.

Calls to directory enquiries (valid for two queries) cost SFr. 1.60 plus SFr. 0.25 per minute for the first 60 seconds and SFr. 0.80 from the 61st second. If you have a personal computer with a CD-ROM drive you can access all 4 million Swiss subscribers on CD or use the Internet phone book (🖳 www.telsearch.ch). New hardcopy directories are published every two years, although not all at the same time, while new CD directories (Twixtel or Swissinfo) are published twice a year. The latter also usually include a train timetable, the most important Swiss laws and other information about Switzerland.

The yellow pages, i.e. a directory containing business telephone numbers only, is available for most areas. Yellow pages for major areas are produced by Swisscom Directories AG, Die Gelben Seiten, Morgenstrasse 113b, CH-3050 Berne (☎ 031 892 90 90, 🖳 www.directories.ch). They are, however, expensive. Unlike Swisscom directories, subscribers in yellow pages are listed under a business or service heading for the whole area covered by the directory. Yellow pages in Switzerland aren't as widely used as those produced in North America or the UK, where they're indispensable (and free!). Free local telephone directories are produced by council boroughs (*Bezirk, district*) and contain both private and business numbers. Yellow pages are available on the Internet (🖳 www.gelbeseiten.ch).

Swisscom has pioneered a new electronic telephone directory (Teleguide) that enables users of payphones to obtain all Swiss telephone numbers and addresses at the touch of a button. Teleguides are gradually replacing paper telephone directories in public call boxes. You can look up several addresses and numbers for a charge of SFr. 0.50.

PUBLIC TELEPHONES

Most public telephones (*öffentliche Sprechstelle, téléphone publique*) or payphones have International Direct Dialling (IDD). International calls can also be made via the operator. Payphones in Switzerland are owned and operated by Swisscom and most now accept pre-paid cards, called **Taxcards**, rather than coins. You can buy a taxcard for SFr. 5, 10, 20 or 50 from post offices, Swisscom shops, railway station booking offices, petrol stations, campsites, newsagents, kiosks, hotels, government buildings and hospitals. You need to insert the taxcard into a special slot in the payphone and the cost of calls and the remaining credit on the card will be indicated on a digital display. The SFr. 20 and 50 taxcards have two bands, one on either side of the card. When one band is exhausted, you have 30 seconds to turn the card over and continue on the second band (or alternatively insert a new card), without interrupting your call. Taxcards are produced in a variety of designs and (as in many other countries) have become collectors' items. Some payphones also accept coins, credit cards and Postcards.

Coin Payphones

While most payphones now accept Postcards, you will still come across coin payphones. The coins required for payphones vary; some accept 10 and 20 cent coins and SFr. 1 and 5 coins, while others won't accept SFr. 5 coins, but will accept 50 cent coins. Call charges are the same as for private telephones, plus a 'user charge' of SFr. 0.20 a call. Calls to service numbers (see page 134) cost SFr. 0.60 or 0.90 from payphones. Emergency calls are free, although you must insert SFr. 0.60 to obtain a dial tone. Where applicable your money is returned at the end of the call. Instructions for using payphones are listed in English, French, German and Italian as follows:

1. Lift the handset and wait for the dialling tone (a continuous beep).

2. Insert the minimum call charge of SFr. 0.60 or 0.90 (recorded information calls). For a long distance call insert more money, depending on the cost per minute and the time required. When you've inserted the minimum charge, the credit display, which shows how much money you have in credit, stops flashing.

3. Dial the number required.

4. When your credit is exhausted, the credit display starts flashing again and a warning tone is given on the line. **You have 10 seconds to insert more coins before the call is disconnected**.

5. If you wish to make another call **don't replace the handset**, but press the **red button** located below the handset rest and, if necessary, insert additional coins. This prevents the loss of partly used coins.

6. To retrieve a partly used coin that is still in credit, **don't replace the handset** but press the **red button** and insert some coins until the credit display shows the value of a coin that can be retrieved, rather than an intermediate value.

7. Replace the handset and any unused coins will be returned.

There are special Swisscom telephone offices that can be found at main post offices, airports and main railway stations for international telephone calls. Opening times are usually from 6.30 or 7am until between 8.30 and 10.30pm, Monday through to Saturday. There are usually reduced opening hours on Sundays.

MOVING OR LEAVING SWITZERLAND

When moving house or leaving Switzerland, you must notify Swisscom and other telephone companies (as applicable), preferably 30 days in advance **It's particularly important to notify Swisscom early if you're leaving Switzerland and need to get a deposit refunded.**

If you move within Switzerland you can keep your the same number.

EMERGENCY NUMBERS

The following national emergency numbers (*Notfallnummern, numéros d'appel en cas d'urgence*) are listed on page one of all telephone directories.

Number	Service
117	**Police** (*Polizeinotruf, police secours*)
118	**Fire** (*Feuermeldestelle, feu centrale d'alarme*) – see below
144	**Ambulance** (*Sanitätsnotruf, appel sanitaire d'urgence*)

The above numbers should be used only in emergencies.

1414	**Helicopter Rescue** (REGA – *Rettung mit Helikopter, sauvetage par hélicoptère*)
01 251 51 51	**Poison Emergency Service** (*Vergiftungsnotfall, intoxication en cas d'urgence*) – see below
143	**Samaritans** (*Die dargebotene Hand, La main tendue*) – see below
140	**Vehicle Breakdown** (*Strassenhilfe, secours routier*)

The above telephone numbers are staffed or provide recorded information 24 hours a day and can be dialled from anywhere within Switzerland. Recorded information is given in the local language (French, German or Italian); SFr. 0.50 is required to dial an emergency number from a coin payphone (but this money is returned).

Fire Service

The fire service, besides extinguishing fires, attending traffic accidents and natural disasters, also deals with the victims of accidents such as drowning, asphyxiation (lack of oxygen), choking, electrocution, serious burns and hanging. They're certainly the best people to call when faced with a life or death situation.

Swiss Air Rescue Service

The Swiss air rescue service (*Schweizerische Rettungsflugwacht, Garde Aérienne Suisse de Sauvetage*) which is otherwise known as REGA, has 13 bases from which a helicopter or an air ambulance jet can be dispatched. Everywhere in Switzerland (except the Valais) is within 15 minutes flying time. The service also covers the whole world using jet aircraft.

The cost of the REGA service is covered by Swiss third party car insurance. **If you do happen to fall down a mountain and are rescued by REGA, it will cost you around SFr. 2,000 if you aren't insured.** You can become a member of REGA for SFr. 30 a year for a single person over 16, or SFr. 40 a year for a family (this is for just one parent), including all children under 18. SFr. 70 a year for a family (two parents), including all children under 18. Contact the REGA secretariat, Mainaustr. 21, CH-8008 Zurich (☎ 01 385 85 85, 💻 www.rega.ch). Some towns (e.g. Sion, Zermatt) also have local helicopter rescue services.

Samaritans

The Samaritans (*Die dargebotene Hand, la main tendue* – ☎ 143; SFr. 0.20 per call for an unlimited amount of time) provide a confidential and anonymous counselling service in times of personal crisis and receive over 15,000 calls a year. If the duty counsellor doesn't speak English, he'll ask you to call at a time when an English-speaking counsellor will be present (if necessary).

TeleAlarm

Swisscom provides an emergency TeleAlarm call service (*Telefon-Notruf, téléphone-alarme*) for elderly or disabled people for SFr. 34.50 a month (including the provision of a minisender). In the event of an accident, subscribers can transmit an emergency pre-recorded call for help by simply pressing a button on the minisender worn on a cord around their neck.

SERVICE NUMBERS

The following service numbers (*Dienstnummern, numéros de service*) are described in the blue section at the front of telephone directories and can be called from anywhere in Switzerland. Unless specified, recorded information is given in the local canton language or languages (French, German or Italian). If you dial a service number where no information is available, you will be informed of this via a recorded message.

Number	Service
090077	Automatic Alarm Call Service.
111	Inland Enquiries (the charge depends on the type of enquiry and the duration of the call).
1141	International Operator (non-IDD, person-to-person and reverse charge calls).
1151	International Enquiries for Austria.
1152	International Enquiries for Germany.
1153	International Enquiries for France.
1154	International Enquiries for Italy.
1159	International Enquiries for other countries (not listed above).
117	Police – **EMERGENCIES ONLY**.
118	Fire – **EMERGENCIES ONLY**.
140	Motor Breakdown Service.
1414	Emergency Helicopter Service (REGA).
143	The Samaritans.
144	Ambulance – **EMERGENCIES ONLY**.
1600	*Regional News and information about exhibitions and fairs.
161	*Speaking Clock.
162	*Weather Forecasts.
163	*Road Reports.
164	*Sports News and Lottery Results.
175	Fault Repair Service (*Störungsdienst, Service des dérangements*).
187	*Avalanche Bulletins (winter) and lake wind conditions (summer).

* Recorded information.

8.

TELEVISION & RADIO

Television (TV) and radio services in Switzerland are operated by the Swiss Broadcasting Corporation (SBC), which is a private, non-profit company and a public service financed by advertising and licence fees. The quality of Swiss TV leaves much to be desired, although it's no worse than the fare served up in most other European countries. The German-speaking Swiss reportedly watch less TV than almost anyone in Europe and other Swiss also watch much less TV than the European average. The choice of Swiss TV stations has increased in the last few years with the introduction of a number of local cable TV companies. Cable TV and radio is available throughout the country and some 90 per cent of homes in Switzerland receive their TV programmes via a communal aerial or cable. Due to the wide availability of cable TV, satellite TV isn't common in Switzerland, although it's popular with expatriates. TV and radio programmes are listed in daily and weekly newspapers and published in weekly TV magazines.

Television Standards

The standard for TV reception in Switzerland **isn't the same as in some other countries**. Due to differences in transmission standards, TVs and video recorders from the UK, France and the US won't function in Switzerland or the rest of Europe unless they're dual standard. Most continental countries use the PAL B/G standard except for France, which has its own standard which is called SECAM-L that's different from the SECAM B/G employed in the Middle East and North African countries, and SECAM D/K in eastern European and many African countries. The British use a modified PAL (PAL-I) system and the US use the North American NTSC standard. If you bring a TV to Switzerland from the UK or the US, you will receive either just a picture or just sound – **but not both**. Most modern TVs that are sold in France are multi-standard (e.g. SECAM and PAL B/G) and they can therefore be used in Switzerland. TVs can be converted to work in Switzerland, but it isn't usually worth the expense.

Video cassettes can be played back only on a video cassette recorder (VCR) and a TV operating on the same system (e.g. PAL or NTSC) as that on which they were recorded. So if you bring videos from the US, you must also have a compatible TV and VCR. Videos recorded in the UK can be shown on Swiss VCRs and TVs (and British VCRs can be used to show video tapes on a Swiss TV that were recorded in the UK). You cannot, however, make video recordings from a TV designed for use in Switzerland with an incompatible video machine, for example one designed for use in the UK or the US. If you bring a TV and VCR to Switzerland from the US designed for use on 110 volts, you will need a transformer (see **Electricity** on page 103).

It's possible to buy a multi-standard TV or VCR that can handle PAL, SECAM-L and NTSC standards (or two of these three standards). You can also buy a PAL TV with an NTSC-in jack plug connection, allowing you to play

American videos. Many people buy a stereo TV in order to take advantage of dual-language broadcasts, where films and some sports events are broadcast in French, German or Italian plus the original language, which is often English. If you decide to buy a TV in Switzerland, you will find it advantageous to buy one with teletext, which apart from allowing you to display programme schedules also provides a wealth of useful information.

Television Stations

In most cities and many rural areas, the majority of buildings are wired for cable TV (see below), which enables households to receive up to 70 TV stations (average around 40) and some 30 radio stations. The TV stations available include the six Swiss stations (two French, two German, two Italian), plus Austrian, French, German and Italian stations, and a variety of cable and satellite TV stations. Without cable TV, only five or six stations (including the Swiss stations) can be received, depending on the area.

The Swiss Broadcasting Corporation (SBC) is responsible for producing and relaying programmes in the four Swiss national languages (Swiss TV programmes are listed on teletext). Other stations broadcast in English, French, German or Italian. One advantage of foreign TV is that the advertisements are usually unintelligible (although sometimes they're the only thing that make any sense). Foreign programmes, including films, are usually dubbed in the language of the broadcasting channel, the main exception being the occasional old black and white film (silent movies also aren't dubbed!). Note, however, that many recent films have dual soundtracks (see above).

The amount of advertising permitted on Swiss TV is strictly controlled and is around 8 per cent of air time. Information regarding the Swiss Broadcasting Corporation (*Schweizerische Radio und Fernsehgesellschaft, Société Suisse de Radiodiffusion et Télévision*) is available from the SBC, Postfach 26, CH-3000 Berne 15 (☎ 031 350 91 11). (🖳www.srg.ch)

Cable Television

Cable TV (*Gemeinschaftsantenne, antenne collective*) is available in most areas of Switzerland, but is restricted to towns and buildings wired for cable TV. All you need to do to receive cable TV is to connect your TV aerial to a special wall socket. Around 90 per cent of Swiss households are connected to a communal antenna or to a cable network, making Switzerland third in the world in cable TV availability after Belgium and the Netherlands. Cable TV consists of cable relays of Swiss and foreign national TV stations, dedicated cable-only stations and satellite stations. The average Swiss household can receive around 40 TV channels, although some areas receive many more (e.g. 70 in Geneva). English-language cable TV stations are widely available and include CNN International, Eurosport, MTV Europe and NBC Superchannel. Unfortunately for Britons, apart from BBC World and BBC Prime, BBC1 and BBC2 terrestrial stations aren't usually available via cable in Switzerland.

Cable TV isn't always available in remote areas of Switzerland, in older buildings, and in small towns and villages. If you want to receive English-language cable TV, check that it's available (and which stations) before signing a lease. Cable TV costs from SFr. 23.45 (private user) to SFr. 31.10 (company user) a month depending on the channels provided and is included in your apartment's monthly extra costs (see page 95) or billed annually. If you don't own a TV, you may be able to get the cable TV company to seal the aerial outlet and thus avoid paying the monthly rental charge. This is easy enough if you live in a house, but may be impossible if you live in an apartment, where cable TV costs are shared and are included in your apartment's extra costs.

In addition to unscrambled cable TV channels, scrambled TV channels are available in many areas. Like some satellite TV stations (see below), you require a decoder (which can be installed by most TV shops) to receive them and must pay a monthly subscription.

Satellite Television

Although many people complain endlessly about the poor quality of TV in their home countries, many find they cannot live without it when they're abroad. Fortunately satellite TV means that most people can enjoy TV programmes in English and a variety of other languages almost anywhere in the world. Europe is well served by satellite TV, where some 25 geostationary satellites carry over 200 TV stations broadcasting in a variety of languages. All European satellite TV stations can be received throughout Switzerland, although the size of the dish required varies depending on the location.

Astra

Astra (🖳www.ses-astra.com) offers a huge choice of English and foreign-language stations via their satellites. Although they weren't the first in Europe (Eutelsat were), the European satellite revolution really took off with the launch of the Astra 1A satellite in 1988 (operated by the Luxembourg-based *Société Européenne des Satellites*/SES), positioned 36,000km (22,300mi) above the earth. Since 1988, a number of additional Astra satellites have been launched, increasing the number of available channels to 64 (or over 200 via digital). An added bonus is the availability of foreign radio stations via satellite, including all the main British Broadcasting Corporation (BBC) stations (see **Satellite Radio** on page 145).

Among the many English-language stations available on Astra are Sky One, Movimax, Sky Premier, Sky Cinema, Film Four, Sky News, Sky Sports (three channels), UK Gold, Channel 5, Granada Plus, TNT, Eurosport, CNN, CNBC Europe, UK Style, UK Horizons, The Disney Channel, Astravision, BBC World, God channel, MTV 2, MTV Central Europe, Bloomberg UK and the Discovery

Channel. Other stations broadcast in Dutch, German, Japanese, Swedish and various Indian languages. The signal from many stations is encrypted or scrambled, with the decoder usually built into the receiver, and viewers must pay a monthly subscription fee to receive programmes. You can buy pirate decoders for some channels. The best served by clear (unscrambled) stations are German-speakers (most German stations on Astra are clear).

Eutelsat

Eutelsat (🖳www.eutelsat.com) is owned by a consortium of national telephone operators and was the first company to introduce satellite TV to Europe (in 1983). It now runs a fleet of communications satellites carrying TV stations to over 50 million homes. Until 1995 they had broadcast primarily advertising-based, clear-access cable channels. Following the launch in March 1995 of their Hot Bird satellite, Eutelsat hoped to become a major competitor to Astra, although its stations are mostly non-English. The English-language stations on Eutelsat include British Telecom, AFN (American Forces Network), NOVA (Animal planet Europe), DW TV, BBC Prime, Eurosport, Euronews, BBC World and CNBC Europe. Other channels broadcast in Arabic, Belgian, French, German, Hungarian, Italian, Polish, Portuguese, Spanish, Slovakian, Slovenian, Czech and Turkish.

Sky Television

For sky television you must buy a Videocrypt decoder, an integral part of the receiver in most models, and pay a monthly subscription to receive all Sky stations except Sky News (which isn't scrambled). Various packages are available costing from between around GB£10 and GB£30 per month (for the premium package offering all movie channels plus Sky Sports). To receive scrambled channels such as Movimax and Sky Sports you need an address in the UK or Ireland. Subscribers are sent a coded 'smart' card (similar to a credit card), which must be inserted in the decoder (cards are periodically updated to thwart counterfeiters). Sky won't send smart cards to overseas viewers as they have the copyright only for a British-based audience and overseas homeowners need to obtain a card through a friend or relative in the UK or Ireland. However, a number of companies and retailers in Europe (some of which advertise in the expatriate press in Switzerland) supply genuine Sky cards and pirate cards may also be available.

Digital Television

English-language digital satellite TV was launched on 1st October 1998 by BSkyB in the UK. The benefits include a superior picture, better (CD) quality sound, wide-screen cinema format and access to many more stations (including around ten stations that show nothing but movies). To watch digital TV you require a Digibox and a (digital) dish. In addition to the usual analogue channels (see above), BSkyB digital provides BBC 1, BBC 2, ITV Channel 4 and Channel 5, plus many digital channels (a total of 200 with up to 500 possible later). Ondigital launched a rival digital service on 15th November 1998, which although it's cheaper, provides a total of just 30 channels (15 free and 15 subscription), including BBC 1 and 2, ITV3, Channel 4 and Channel 5. Further information about BSkyB digital is available on the Internet (🖳 www.digiguide.co.uk).

BBC World-Wide Television

The BBC's commercial subsidiary, BBC World-wide Television, broadcasts two 24-hour channels: BBC Prime (general entertainment) and BBC World (24-hour news and information), transmitted via the Eutelsat Hotbird 5 satellite (13° east). BBC World is unencrypted (clear) while BBC Prime is encrypted and requires a D2-MAC decoder and a smartcard, available on subscription from BBC Prime, PO Box 5054, London W12 0ZY, UK (☎ 020-8433 2221, ✉ bbcprime@bbc.co.uk). For further information and a programming guide contact BBC World-wide Television, Woodlands, 80 Wood Lane, London W12 0TT, UK (☎ 020-8433 2000). A programme guide is also available on the Internet (🖳 www.bbc.co.uk/schedules) and both BBC World and BBC Prime have their own websites (🖳 www.bbcworld.com and www.bbcprime. com). When assessing them, you need to enter the name of the country so that schedules are displayed in local time.

Equipment

A satellite receiver should have a built-in Videocrypt decoder (and others such as Eurocrypt, Syster or SECAM if required) and be capable of receiving satellite stereo radio. A 60cm dish is generally adequate in many areas of Switzerland, although an 85cm dish or a signal booster is necessary in some regions. A basic fixed satellite system (which will receive programmes from one satellite only) costs around SFr. 1,000 (digital) to SFr. 1,800 (analogue) and a motorised dish (which will automatically adjust its orientation so that you can receive programmes from other satellites) will set you back three or four times as much.

If you wish to receive satellite stations on two or more TVs, you can buy a satellite system with two or more receptors. To receive stations from two (or more) satellites simultaneously, you need a motorised dish or a dish with a double feed antenna (dual LNBs). There are many satellite sales and installation companies in Switzerland. Shop around and compare prices. Alternatively you can import your own satellite dish and receiver and install it yourself. Before buying a system, ensure that it can receive programmes from all existing and planned satellites.

Location

To be to receive programmes from any satellite, there must be no obstacles between the satellite and your dish, i.e. no large obstacles such as trees, buildings or mountains must obstruct the signal, so check before renting an apartment or buying a home. From Switzerland, the Astra satellite is located about 19.2° east of due south. The elevation angle is around 35° above the horizon. Intelsat V1-F4 is in the south-west, about 332.5° west of due south, with an elevation angle of around 26° above the horizon. Before buying or erecting a dish, check whether you need permission from your landlord or a permit from the local authorities. Dishes can usually be mounted in a variety of unobtrusive positions and can be painted or patterned to blend in with the background. New apartment blocks may be fitted with at least one communal satellite dish.

Programme Guides

Many satellite stations provide teletext information and most broadcast in stereo. Satellite programme listings are provided in a number of British publications, such as *What Satellite*, *Satellite Times* and *Satellite TV* (considered to be the best), which are available on subscription. A number of satellite TV programmes can also be displayed via Swiss TV teletext. The annual *World Radio and TV Handbook* edited by David G. Bobbett (Watson-Guptill Publications) contains over 600 pages of information and the frequencies of all radio and TV stations world-wide, and is available in Switzerland from bookshops such as the English book shop Orell Fuessli in Zurich (🖥 www.books.ch) for around SFr. 62.

Television Licence

A TV licence (*Fernsehempfangskonzession, concession de réception de télévision*) which costs SFr. 281.40 per year (SFr. 23.45 per month) is required by all TV owners. The registration of a TV licence and a radio licence can be done together by contacting Billag (☎ 0844 83 48 34, 🖥 www.billag.ch). The TV licence fee is payable quarterly with your radio licence fee (if applicable). The licence fee covers any number of TVs owned or rented by you, irrespective of where they're located, e.g. holiday homes, motor vehicles or boats. Registration must be made within 14 days of buying or importing a TV. **You will be fined if you have a TV and do not have a licence when an inspector calls** (of course, most people wouldn't dream of not paying their licence fee!). However, if your TV is used only for video playback or as a computer monitor, no licence fee is payable – but you mustn't be able to receive any TV broadcasts.

Videos & DVDs

English-language video cassette films and DVDs can be rented from around SFr. 7 to 10 per day from video shops and postal video clubs throughout Switzerland. Rental costs can often be reduced by paying a monthly membership fee or a lump sum in advance. Unfortunately, most local video shops and clubs don't have a wide selection of English-language videos or the latest English films. Check the conditions before hiring, as some companies levy exorbitant 'fines' if you forget to return videos on time (higher than the value of the video). Since the spring of 2003 video shops in Switzerland have been forbidden by law to import the original UK or US videos and DVDs but can only sell the German, French or Italian versions that are licensed for Switzerland expressively. There is no restriction to individuals ordering their videos from a UK or US website, though.

RADIO

The good news for radio fans is that radios have the same standards the world over, although bandwidths vary. FM (VHF) stereo stations flourish in Switzerland and medium Wave (MW or AM) and Long Wave (LW) bands are also in wide use throughout Europe. A Short Wave (SW) radio is useful for receiving international stations such as the BBC World Service, Voice of America, Radio Canada and Radio Sweden. The BBC World Service and the Voice of America are also available via cable radio in many areas (see below). Portable digital radio receivers are available that provide good reception, particularly on short wave, and expensive 'professional' receivers are capable of receiving stations from almost anywhere (although Radio Mars signal might be a bit weak). If you're interested in receiving radio stations from further afield, obtain a copy of the *World Radio TV Handbook* (see page 143).

Swiss Radio

There are over 40 private local radio stations in Switzerland, some broadcasting in English, e.g. Radio 74 (88.8 MHz FM) and World Radio (88.4 MHz FM) in Geneva. Advertising is forbidden on radio stations run by the Swiss Broadcasting Corporation (SBC), but is permitted on local radio stations. Swiss Radio International (SRI) transmits programmes via short wave, cable and satellite in Arabic, English, French, German, Italian, Portuguese and Spanish. The English language programme (24-hours a day) can be heard via the Astra satellite (see page 145). For more information contact Swiss Satellite Radio, Giacomettistr. 1, CH-3000 Berne 15 (☎ 031 350 92 22). Swiss Radio (DRS) publishes a *Radio Magazin* available on subscription from Radio Magazin, Aboverwaltung, Postfach 75, CH-8024 Zürich.

BBC & Other Foreign Stations

The BBC World Service is broadcast on short wave on several frequencies (e.g. 12095, 9760, 9410, 7325, 6195, 5975 and 3955 Khz) simultaneously and you can usually receive a good signal on one of them. The signal strength varies depending on where you live in Switzerland, the time of day and year, the power and positioning of your receiver, and atmospheric conditions. All BBC radio stations, including the World Service, are also available on the Astra satellite (see below) and BBC World Service is available via cable radio (see below). The BBC publishes a monthly magazine, *BBC On Air*, containing comprehensive information about BBC World Service radio and TV programmes. For a free copy and frequency information write to BBC On Air, Room 205 NW, Bush House, Strand, London WC2B 4PH, UK (☎ 020-7240 3456) Many other foreign stations also publish programme listings and frequency charts for expatriates seeking news from home, including Radio Australia, Radio Canada, Denmark Radio, Radio Nederland, Radio Sweden International and the Voice of America.

Satellite Radio

If you have satellite TV you can also receive many radio stations via your satellite link. For example, BBC Radio 1, 2, 3, 4 and 5, BBC World Service, Sky Radio, Virgin 1215 and many foreign (i.e. non-English) stations are broadcast via the Astra satellites. Satellite radio stations are listed in British satellite TV magazines such as the *Satellite Times*. If you're interested in receiving radio stations from further afield you should obtain a copy of the *World Radio TV Handbook* edited by David G. Bobbett (Watson-Guptill Publications).

Cable Radio

If your apartment is wired for cable TV (see page 139), it will also be wired for cable radio, providing reception of around 30 stereo stations. Many cable networks provide the BBC World Service, BBC Foreign Language Service, Voice of America, Swiss Radio International (English service) and Sky Radio, in addition to a wide selection of FM stereo stations from Switzerland (national and local), France, Germany and Austria. All you need do is connect your radio or hi-fi tuner aerial to a special wall socket (cables are available from TV stores).

Radio Licence

A radio licence (*Radioempfangskonzession, concession de réception radio*), which costs SFr. 169.20 per year (SFr. 14.10 per month), is required by all owners of radios (including car radios). Both radio and TV licence (see page 143) registration can be done together by contacting Billag (☎ 0844 83 48 34, 🖳 www.billag.ch). The radio licence fee is payable quarterly with your TV licence fee (if applicable). It covers any number of radios irrespective of where they're located, e.g. holiday homes, motor vehicles or boats (but not radios in the work-place which should be covered by an employer's radio licence). Registration must be made within 14 days of buying or importing a radio and failure to register can result in a fine.

9.

EDUCATION

Switzerland is renowned for the excellence and diversity of its private schools, and although not so well known abroad, Swiss 'state' (publicly funded) schools also have a good reputation in academic circles. The Swiss have always been in the forefront of educational progress and have produced a number of world-renowned philosophers (e.g. Froebal, Pestalozzi, Piaget and Steiner) whose pedagogical theories and research remain a strong influence throughout the world. Even today, Swiss teaching methods are far in advance of most other countries, many of which send delegations to Swiss schools.

Today, compulsory schooling begins at the age of six or seven, after an optional period at nursery school for four to six year olds, and continues for eight, or more often, nine years (an optional tenth year has been introduced in most cantons).

If you're fortunate enough to be among those who can afford to send your children to a private school, you may be surprised to learn that the vast majority of Swiss parents choose to send their children to a state school, even when the cost of private education isn't an important consideration. There are many things to take into account when choosing an appropriate school for your children in Switzerland, among the most important of which is the language of study. The only schools using English as the teaching language are international private schools. If your children attend any other school, they must study in a foreign language. For most children, studying in a foreign language isn't such a handicap as it may at first appear. The majority adapt quickly and soon become fluent in the local language, assisted by the extra language tuition usually provided for foreign children (if only it were so easy for adults). Naturally all children don't adapt equally well to a change of language and culture, particularly teenage children. Before making any major decisions about your children's future education, it's important to consider their individual ability, character and requirements.

For many children, the experience of going to school and living in a foreign country is a stimulating change and a challenge that they relish, providing invaluable cultural and educational experiences. Your children will become 'world' citizens, less likely to be prejudiced against foreigners and foreign ideas, particularly if they attend an international school which has pupils from many different countries. Swiss state schools also have pupils from a number of different countries, with an average of around 20 per cent being non-Swiss.

In addition to a detailed look at the Swiss state school system and private schools, this chapter also contains information about children's holiday camps, apprenticeships, universities, further education and language schools.

STATE OR PRIVATE SCHOOL

If you're able to choose between state and private education, the following checklist will help you decide:

- How long are you planning to stay in Switzerland? If you're uncertain, then it's probably best to assume a long stay. Due to language and other integration problems, enrolling a child in a Swiss state school is advisable only if you're planning to stay for a minimum of one year, particularly for teenage children.

- Bear in mind that the area where you choose to live may affect your choice of school(s). For example, it may be compulsory to send your children to the state school nearest your home.

- Do you know where you're going after Switzerland? This may be an important consideration with regard to your children's language of tuition and system of education in Switzerland. How old are your children and what age will they be when you plan to leave Switzerland? What future plans do you have for their education and in which country?

- What educational level are your children at now and how will they fit into a private school or the Swiss state school system? The younger they are, the easier it will be to place them in a suitable school.

- How do your children view the thought of studying in a foreign language? What language(s) is best from a long-term point of view? Is schooling available in Switzerland in your children's mother tongue

- Will your children require your help with their studies, and more importantly, will you be able to help them, particularly with the language(s)?

- Is special or extra tutoring available in the local language or other studies, if required?

- What are the school hours? What are the school holiday periods? Many state schools in Switzerland have compulsory Saturday morning classes. How will the school holidays and hours affect your family's work and leisure activities?

- Is religion an important aspect in your choice of school? In Swiss state schools religion is usually taught as a compulsory subject. Parents may, however, request permission for their children not to attend.

- Do you want your children to attend a single sex school? Swiss state schools are usually coeducational (mixed).

- Should you send your children to a boarding school? If so where?

- What are the secondary and further education prospects in Switzerland or another country? Are Swiss examinations or the examinations set by prospective Swiss schools recognised in your home country or the country where you plan to live after leaving Switzerland?

- Does the school have a good academic record? Most schools provide exam pass rate statistics.

- How large are the classes? What is the pupil-teacher ratio?

Obtain the opinions and advice of others who have been faced with the same decisions and problems as you are, and collect as much information from as many different sources as possible before making a decision. Speak to teachers and the parents of children attending schools on your shortlist.

Many cantons provide schools with special facilities for disabled, retarded and mentally disabled children. Switzerland doesn't, however, provide special teaching facilities for gifted children with exceptionally high IQs. See also **Choosing a Private School** on page 164.

STATE SCHOOLS

The term 'state' schools is a misnomer, as there are no state (federal) schools (*öffentliche Schulen*, *écoles publiques*) in Switzerland, education being the jealously-guarded responsibility of the cantons. State is used here in preference to 'public' and refers to non-fee-paying schools funded by the cantons from local taxes. This is to prevent confusion with the term 'public school', used in the US to refer to a state school, but which in England refers to a private fee-paying school (confusing isn't it!). The state school system in Switzerland is quite complicated compared with many other western countries and differs considerably from the school systems in, for example, the UK and the US, particularly regarding secondary and university education.

The Swiss canton education system results in 26 school systems, with many minor and some major differences. The school programmes, schedules, syllabuses and categories of schools may all vary from canton to canton, and even from community to community. It's usually necessary to send your children to a school in your canton of residence where you pay your taxes. Some cantons, however, have bilateral agreements allowing children resident in neighbouring cantons to attend their schools. Although the lack of a standardised national state school system may appear strange, it usually affects children (and their parents) only when they move to another canton. Even then, provided the teaching language remains the same, the differences are usually insignificant.

There are no state pre-school nursery schools in Switzerland, although you can enrol your children in kindergarten from the age of five or six (for information regarding playgroups, see page 158). Officially, state schooling in Switzerland starts at the age of seven and is compulsory for eight or nine years (ten in some cantons) until the age of 15 or 16. On average the Swiss attend school until the age of 17, one of the highest average school-leaving ages in the world. Schooling is free for all foreign children of parents with Swiss annual or permanent residence permits (B or C) and who work in Switzerland, although some school books must be purchased by parents.

Most foreign and over 90 per cent of Swiss parents send their children to a Swiss state school for reasons that aren't entirely financial. Swiss state schools have an excellent academic record, aided by the small average class size of around 20 pupils, and are rated among the best in the world. In international tests, Swiss pupils regularly outperform children in most other countries (particularly in maths and science, where pupils don't usually use calculators until secondary school) and Swiss schools have far fewer low-achieving pupils. Attending a state school helps children integrate into the local community and learn the local language. Pupils usually go to a local primary school, although attending secondary school often entails travelling quite long distances.

Swiss state schools usually impose more discipline than many foreign children are used to, for example regular homework that increases with the age of the child, which may initially cause some stress. Generally, the younger children are when they arrive in Switzerland, the easier they will cope. Conversely the older they are, the more problems they will have adjusting, particularly as the school curriculum is more demanding. Parents should try to empathise with their children's problems. If you aren't fluent in the local language, you will already be aware of how frustrating it is being unable to express yourself adequately. Lack of language ability can easily lead to feelings of inferiority or inadequacy in children (and adults!). State schools may provide supervised homework or extra classes for children who require them. The Swiss state school system is more disciplined and less flexible than schooling in many countries, but the results are generally good, with every child being given the opportunity to study for a trade, diploma or a degree.

Subsidised music lessons are given, although parents must usually provide the instruments. In some cases instruments are loaned by the school for a period, but if they aren't you must buy or rent one. Most state schools have little extracurricular activity, for example there are no school clubs or sports teams. If your children want to do team sports, they must join a local club, which means that parents are required to ferry them back and forth for games and social events.

Having made the decision to send your child to a state school, you should try it for at least a year to give it a fair trial. It may take your child this long to adapt to a new language, the change of environment and the different curriculum. A book may be available from your community explaining the intricacies of your canton's secondary school system. For example, excellent guides are published by the cantons of Zurich, *Volkshochschule wohin* (What Next?) and Vaud, *Present et Avenir des Ecoliers* (Present and Future of School Children).

Language

In French and Italian-speaking areas of Switzerland, the teaching language is the same as the everyday spoken language and therefore foreign children are able to improve their language ability through their constant exposure to it. In German-speaking Switzerland the position isn't so straightforward. In kindergarten and early primary school classes, teachers will speak the local Swiss German dialect. In primary school they will officially begin to teach academic subjects in High German (*Schriftdeutsch/Hochdeutsch, bon allemand*), although this isn't always the case. In later years, generally all non-academic study is in Swiss German, while all academic subjects are taught in High German, particularly when text books are required. One of the problems for both Swiss and foreign children alike, is that because most lessons are conducted in Swiss German, there's little opportunity to practice High German. This has led to all subjects being (officially) taught in High German in secondary schools in some cantons.

The Swiss German dialect isn't formally taught in any schools (nobody would know where to start!). This makes school life more difficult for foreign children, particularly teenagers, although young children (e.g. 5 to 12 years) generally have few problems learning Swiss German. If you prefer your children to be educated in the French language and you live in a German-speaking canton, it may be possible to send your children to a school in a neighbouring French-speaking canton. You may, however, be required to live in the canton where your children go to school and may not be permitted to move cantons if you're a new arrival (catch 22!).

Children who don't speak the local language, particularly children of secondary school age, are usually placed in a 'reception' or special class, depending on the degree of language assistance necessary. This allows them more time to concentrate on learning the language (with extra language tuition), as they will usually have already covered the syllabus. They integrate into the normal stream only when they've learnt the language and can follow the lessons. When the next promotion stage is reached, they must have reached a satisfactory standard in the local language or the year must be repeated. If the average mark is unsatisfactory, a child is graded provisional and two provisional reports means he must automatically repeat the year. Satisfactory marks are graded definitive and the child goes onto the next grade.

Children often repeat a year or even two (the maximum) and there's usually a fairly wide age range in the higher school classes. There's no stigma attached to this repetition of classes (except among some children). Children, like adults, learn at different speeds and the Swiss school system simply recognises this fact. If a child fails to maintain the required standard in a higher grade secondary school, e.g. a high school, he may be required to join another school with a less demanding curriculum. Children are given a school report two or three times a year.

All children must learn a second national language from their seventh school year at the latest. The compulsory second language in secondary schools in German-speaking Switzerland is French and in French-speaking Switzerland it's High German. However, many Swiss German parents would prefer English to be taught as a second language in place of French and this has already been adopted in some cantons, e.g. Zurich (much to the ire of the French Swiss).

If English is your mother tongue or a second or additional language, then you're probably already aware of its importance and growing influence throughout the world. It's a big advantage to your children if they can speak it at home every day, particularly if it isn't taught at school. Children don't usually start learning English in Swiss state schools until the age of 12 to 14 and even then it may be voluntary (although, as mentioned above, some cantons such as Zurich have decided to teach English in primary school). English becomes compulsory only when a child is studying modern languages, for example in a high school (*Gymnasium/Kantonsschule, gymnase/école cantonale*) or when a specialist subject is studied requiring English language proficiency.

English Fun Language Clubs for children aged three to ten are becoming increasingly popular (they also offer French, German and Spanish, but English is the most popular language). Many English-speaking parents organise private English classes for their children or teach them themselves. Also of interest to English-speaking parents is All For Kids (Robin Bognuda, Via Cimitero, CH-6592 S. Antonino (☎ 091 858 30 82, 🖳 www.allforkids.ch), who specialise in providing English-speaking families with educational products from the US and the UK.

For more information about Swiss languages, see **Languages** on page 39 and **Language Schools** on page 169.

Enrolment

When you arrive in Switzerland and register in your local community (*Gemeinde, commune*), you're informed about schooling and told when and where to apply for school entrance for your children. In city areas you must apply to your area school commission (*Kreisschulpflege, commission scolaire du district*). School registration dates are announced in local newspapers. The start of the school year throughout Switzerland is between mid-August and mid-September. For example, in 2003 most German-speaking cantons started school on 11th or 18th August, Geneva and Vaud on 25th August and Ticino on 1st September.

School Hours

Swiss school hours differ considerably from those in most other countries and often vary from school to school, as it's generally left to individual teachers to schedule their own classes. Your children will rarely spend all day at school and if you have children of different ages attending school (even the same school), they will be coming and going at different times. This is particularly true for the youngest children, where classes may be divided into sections with varied hours (school hours are designed to prevent mothers from working!). In some cantons 'block times' (*Blockzeiten*) have been introduced where classes start at 8am and end at noon with a second session from 2 to 4pm in the afternoon. A two-hour lunch break is normal, during which schools are closed (state schools in Switzerland don't usually provide school lunches). Older children who have a long journey to school may take a packed lunch to eat on the school premises, for which a room is provided. Some high schools have canteens.

In secondary schools, hours are generally anywhere between 7 to 11am or noon and 1.30 or 2pm to 6pm. In a higher grade secondary school, e.g. a high school (*Gymnasium/Kantonalschule, gymnase/école cantonale*), the school day can last from 7.30am to 5pm (around 40 hours a week), which is a long day, particularly when travelling time is added. The average travelling time to and from school in German-speaking Switzerland is around 30-50 minutes, which together with the demanding school schedule is blamed for the high stress levels of some children. It's not usual for parents to take their children to school; depending on the distance, children will walk, ride bikes or take the tram, bus or train. This is considered important as part of growing more independent, and in many places parents taking their children to school and picking them up by car are frowned upon. School buses are generally provided only for pupils of state schools for the disabled and some private schools.

One or two afternoons or one day a week (usually Wednesday or Thursday) are free and Saturday morning school is normal in many areas of Switzerland. This creates havoc with the family social life such as weekend and day trips. Some cantons have introduced a trial period without Saturday morning school and many communities make it permanent when they get around to a vote.

Health

All children are required to belong to a health insurance scheme, e.g. a health fund, which must be entered on the school application form. Some aspects of children's health are supervised or carried out by the school authorities. All Swiss state schools have an extensive programme of inoculations against polio, diphtheria, TB, whooping cough, measles, German measles and mumps (Switzerland must be a terribly unhealthy place with all these 'diseases' around!). If your child has already undergone a course of inoculations before arrival in Switzerland, show the vaccination certificates to the school health authorities.

In primary and possibly secondary school, children receive a free annual dental inspection from your family or a school-appointed dentist. An estimate is provided for any dental treatment required and some communities pay a percentage of bills for low income families. Your health insurance company may also pay a percentage, but only if your child is insured for dental treatment (see page 273).

Schools provide insurance cover for accidents at school and on the journey to and from school. For this reason, children are required to go by a direct or approved route to school, and if cycling, must use cycle paths to avoid invalidating their insurance policy. Outside these times your children should be covered against accidents by your family health insurance policy.

Holidays

The typical state school holiday (*Schulferien, vacances scolaires*) periods are shown below, although the dates and length of holidays vary, depending on the canton:

January – March	1 – 2 week skiing holiday
April	2 – 3 week spring break
July/August	5 – 7 week summer break
September/October	1 – 3 week autumn break
December/January	1 – 2 week Christmas and New Year break

Schools are also closed on public holidays, e.g. Easter, Whitsuntide and Ascension Day, if these don't fall within school holiday periods. School holiday dates are published by schools and local communities well in advance, thus allowing you plenty of time to schedule family holidays during official school holidays. Normally you aren't permitted to withdraw your children from classes at anytime during the school term, except for visits to a doctor or dentist, when the teacher should be informed in advance (if possible). In primary school, a note to the teacher is sufficient. In secondary school you must complete an official absence form, get it signed by the teacher concerned and hand it in to the school office. For reasons other than sickness, children are generally allowed only one half day off school each year. Anything longer isn't allowed without special written permission, which is difficult to obtain in some areas.

If you're refused permission and insist on withdrawing your child from school, for example for a special holiday, **you can be prosecuted and fined or even imprisoned on your return**. Unfortunately some school authorities don't make allowances for families who want to make, for example, a 'once in a lifetime' visit to relatives overseas, and are unable to go during official school holidays.

Provisions & Equipment

Primary school children require a school bag or satchel (usually different for boys and girls) or a small bag for a kindergarten snack; a pencil case and pencils, etc.; slippers, gym shoes (plimsoles), shorts and a towel for games and exercise periods; and a sports bag for the above if the satchel is too small. The school bag and pencil case are usually provided by a child's Godparents, who play an important role in a Swiss child's life. At kindergarten, children usually take a snack for both morning and afternoon breaks (hungry work being a kid). Teachers recommend fruit, vegetable or bread, rather than cakes. On their birthdays, children are allowed a treat and it's customary to take a cake for the whole class. This custom is continued throughout adult life in most of the country and you will notice that many adult Swiss provide cakes on their birthdays.

Children require hiking boots for their annual school hike (*Schulreise, course d'ecole*). This day outing entails children getting up in the middle of the night for a 10 to 30km hike (the distance depends on their age) around Switzerland to admire the cows and flowers. Parents are required to supply all sorts of odds and ends for handicraft lessons, from toilet roll tubes to empty boxes. Keep a junk supply handy if you don't want to be caught short.

Kindergarten

Attendance at a kindergarten (*Kindergarten, école enfantine/jardin d'enfant*) is voluntary in all cantons except Geneva, where one year is compulsory. Although it isn't a prerequisite for attending primary school, a community is required to provide a Kindergarten for six year olds and often takes five year olds also, although places may be limited. Around 65 per cent of communities provide kindergartens for five year olds and over 95 per cent for six year olds (facilities may be shared with another community). Kindergarten lasts for two and a half to three hours in the mornings, or two hours both mornings and afternoons. Classes may be held on six days a week, with Wednesday and Saturday afternoons free, or a few mornings only, possibly including Saturdays.

Kindergarten is highly recommended, particularly if your children are going to continue with a state education. After one or two years in kindergarten they will be integrated into the local community and will have learnt the local language in preparation for primary school. Children are given road safety training by policemen and are provided with a reflecting triangle or loop to wear to and from kindergarten.

In major cities, private kindergartens and playgroups are available and take children as young as three or four (see page 158).

Primary School

Children must be six years old before 1st January (or 30th June in some cantons) to start primary school (*Primarschule, école primaire*) the following year. To register your children for primary school, contact your local community in rural areas or your local school commission in cities. This may be unnecessary if your children have attended local kindergarten. Coeducation (mixed classes) is normal and primary classes have an average of around 20 pupils. Primary education lasts from four to six years, depending on the canton, until children are 11 to 13 years old. When primary school is for six years (i.e. in the majority of cantons), classes are split into three grades or steps (*Stufe, degré*). The first two years are termed lower grade (*Unterstufe, première degré*), the next two years middle grade (*Mittelstufe, deuxième degré*) and the final two years upper grade (*Oberstufe, troisième degré*). Unlike in some other countries, primary school pupils in Switzerland are generally taught all subjects by one teacher.

In their first or second year of primary school, children receive bicycle road safety training from local policemen, who may also warn them about the risks of talking to strangers. Pre primary school children aren't allowed to ride their bicycles on public roads. Children must be seven years old **and** attending primary school before they're allowed on public roads (kindergarten doesn't count, even when a child is already seven).

In the Swiss state school system, a child's level of secondary education usually depends on his marks in his last primary school year. Children are normally assessed on the average results of tests set by their teacher throughout the year. The most important primary school subjects are the local language, mathematics, local history and geography (*Heimatkunde, histoire et géographie régional*). It's a big advantage for children if their parents or a tutor is able to help them with these and other subjects. The reason for this selection process is to channel children into an appropriate educational and commercial programme that prepares them for a career or a university education. While it's important for children to do well in their last primary school year, a child's future education isn't, however, fixed on leaving primary school.

Secondary School

Secondary school (*Sekundarschule, école secondaire*) education in Switzerland lasts for three to five years, depending on the type of school and the canton. The Swiss secondary school system allows for promotion and demotion, both within a school and from school to school, up to the age of 15 or even later. If your children receive good marks in their last primary school year, they have a better

chance of going to an advanced secondary school or high school (*Gymnasium/Kantonalschule, lycée/école cantonale*), possibly leading to a university or technical institute. If you think your child has been incorrectly graded, you can apply for him to take an entrance examination to a higher or lower school. In some French-speaking cantons, a so called *cycle d'orientation* has been introduced, where pupils of varying ability share the same class, rather than being streamed into different classes. Some main subjects are, however, divided into courses of different grades.

The different types of secondary schools for thirteen year olds (listed below) are broadly based on the education system in canton Zurich and **aren't the same in all cantons.**

- **Secondary Modern School** (*Oberschule, école supérieure*) – Three year's general education including woodwork, metalwork and home economics, as preparation for an apprenticeship in the manual trades. The secondary modern is for less academically gifted children, usually around 5 per cent of the total.

- **Technical School** (*Realschule, école technique*) – Three years of more demanding academic education than secondary modern school, but also directed towards training in the manual trades. The second largest number of children (around 35 per cent) attend a technical school.

- **Secondary School** (*Sekundarschule, école secondaire*) – Three or more year's education in languages, sciences, geography and history as preparation for entrance to a higher school. Most children (around 50 per cent) go to a secondary school, many going on to apprenticeships. Some parents prefer to send their children to secondary school, at least for a few years, rather than to a more demanding high school. Many will have an opportunity to attend a high school or vocational school later, when they may be better equipped to handle the curriculum.

- **Pre-High School** (*Progymnasium/Untergymnasium/Bezirks-schule, prégymnasium/lycée inferieur*) – Pre-high school, as the name implies, prepares children for high school in some cantons.

- **High School** (*Gymnasium/Kantonsschule, lycée/école cantonale*) – High school education prepares students for a university or technical college and lasts for six to seven years, when the maturity examination is taken (see below). A written entrance examination in French, German and mathematics is necessary, and only the top students (around 10 per cent of them) are admitted. Children are on probation for the first three to six months to see how they progress. A Swiss high school provides roughly the same standard of education as an English grammar or high school, but is higher than that provided by an American high school or two-year college. It provides an excellent secondary education, the equal of any school system anywhere.

Vocational Schools

The following schools are special higher education secondary level schools, attended after two or three years in secondary school from the age of 15 or 16. All require students to pass an entrance examination.

- **Commercial or Business School** (*Handelsmittelschule, école de commerce*) – Three years training (federally recognised) for a commercial diploma. A good basic grounding for a business career, but also useful for a career in social work, nursing or as an interpreter.

- **Teacher Training School** (*Lehramtschule/Unterseminar, seminar/séminaire inférieur*) – The course lasts four to five years for primary school teachers. Entrance qualifications vary and training may include a two to three-year practical period. Secondary (two to three years) and higher school (four to five years) teacher training is undertaken at university.

- **Diploma Middle School** (*Diplommittelschule, école professionelle*) – A three-year preparatory school for kindergarten teachers, nurses and medical technicians.

Maturity Examination

Students at a high school study for the maturity (*Matura, maturité*) examination, usually consisting of six different syllabuses. All students generally study French, German, mathematics, geography, history, biology, physics, chemistry and music or art. Other subjects depend on the syllabus chosen and are typically as follows:

- **Syllabus A** – Classical languages. Latin and Greek compulsory;
- **Syllabus B** – Latin as basic language, plus English or Italian;
- **Syllabus C** – Scientific. Mathematics, sciences and descriptive geometry. English or Italian are compulsory;
- **Syllabus D** – Modern languages. German, French and English are compulsory, plus Italian, Spanish or Russian;
- **Syllabus E** – Economics. Science of industrial management and political economy and social sciences. English or Italian are compulsory.
- **Syllabus M** – Music and art. Preparation for the academies of music and arts

Some cantons have given up the traditional syllabus system and now allow the students to choose their own subjects within a certain range. However, in most cases subjects such as German, French, mathematics and sciences are still compulsory.

**Bilingual English/German
Kindergarten, Primary & Secondary School**

A Unique Opportunity for your Child

The Lakeside School offers your child (age range 4 – 13) the very special chance to integrate into life in Switzerland quickly and painlessly. After Lakeside School the children can continue their Bilingual education at the Bilingual Middle School Zurich (age range 13 – 16).

We offer a bilingual immersion programme (English/German) which combines the advantages of the best in English education with the thoroughness of the Swiss approach, taught by only mother tongue teachers.

For further information please contact
Ms. Aebi on 01/914 20 50 or www.lakesideschool.ch

Lakeside School

Lakeside Bilingual Dayschool
Seestrasse. 5
8700 Küsnacht
Telephone 01/914 20 50
Fax 01/914 20 59
E-Mail:
office@lakesideschool.ch

Member of ECIS, SGIS, Association of Zurich Private Schools

All European universities and most American colleges recognise the Swiss maturity diploma as an entrance qualification, although foreign students must provide proof of their English language ability to study in the UK or the US.

PRIVATE SCHOOLS

Switzerland is famous for the quality and variety of its some 600 private day and boarding schools (*Privatschulen, écoles privées*). Individual schools cater for as few as 20 to as many as 2,000 pupils, a total of around 100,000, two-thirds of whom are Swiss. One in seven children in Switzerland attends a private school, one of the highest ratios in the world. Fees vary considerably depending on (among other things) the quality, reputation and location of the school. International day school fees vary from around SFr. 5,000 to 25,000 (e.g. the International School of Basle) a year, while annual boarding school fees are anywhere between SFr. 25,000 and 65,000. Fees aren't all inclusive and extra obligatory charges are made in addition to optional extra services. Some schools will even arrange to have little Sam or Samantha met at Geneva or Zurich airport and conducted by private plane and chauffeured limousine to school (for a price).

There are international primary and secondary day schools in or close to all major cities in Switzerland, where demand exceeds supply. One of the main advantages of an international school is that all lessons are generally conducted in English. There are also French-speaking international schools in Geneva. In recent years, bilingual primary schools teaching in English/French or English/German have become more widespread and popular. International schools have smaller classes and a more relaxed, less rigid regime and curriculum than Swiss state schools. They provide a more varied and international approach to sport, culture and art, and a wider choice of academic subjects. Their aim is the development of the child as an individual and the encouragement of his unique talents, rather than teaching on a production line system. This is made possible by small classes that allow teachers to provide pupils with individually tailored lessons and tuition.

The results speak for themselves and many private secondary schools have a near 100 per cent postgraduate university placement rate. Private school pupils are more likely to question rules and regulations (no wonder most Swiss prefer to send their children to state schools!), be open-minded, express themselves more spontaneously, and be more aware of world problems and politics. If international schools have a negative side, apart from the high fees, it's usually the high pupil turnover. This can have an adverse effect on some children, particularly when close friendships are severed. Some international schools have pupils from as many as 80 countries.

Private schools offer curriculums designed for a wide variety of examinations including the Swiss Maturity examination (see page 161), the American or English systems, the French or International Baccalaureate, the German Arbitur and the Italian Maturita. Many international schools offer curricula tailored to the American college entrance CEEB and British GCSE examinations, and may also offer the International Bacclaureate (*Bakkalaureat*, *baccalauréat*) school leaving certificate, an internationally recognised university entrance qualification. Most international schools offer students the choice of sitting the Swiss maturity (*Matura, maturité*) or the French *baccalauréat* examinations, thus providing children with a bilingual education in an English-speaking environment. Most private schools have an entrance examination, e.g. in English and mathematics, plus an IQ test. **Some Swiss private schools have examinations that are recognised everywhere except in Switzerland, where they aren't accepted for entry to Swiss universities.**

You may prefer to send your children to a private day school across the border, for example in France. Alternatively you can send them to a boarding school in Switzerland or abroad, e.g. in the UK or the US. There are also private schools in Switzerland for children with special language requirements other than English, for example the Japanese School in Zurich.

Make applications to private schools as far in advance as possible. You're usually asked to send previous school reports, exam results and records. Before enrolling your child in a private school, make sure that you understand the withdrawal conditions in the school contract. **Not all Swiss private schools live up to the reputed high standards and there are a number of schools that simply cash in on the good reputation of the best schools.** Always use the utmost caution when selecting a school and don't accept what's stated in the school brochure or prospectus at face value. The checklist below will help you choose an appropriate private school and avoid the charlatans.

A booklet entitled *Private Schools in Switzerland*, containing a complete list of private day and boarding schools in Switzerland, is available for free from the Swiss Federation of Private Schools (SFPS) Hotelgasse 1, Postfach 245, 3000 Bern 7 (☎ 031 328 4050, 💻 www.swiss-schools.ch).

Choosing a Private School

The following checklist is designed to help you choose an appropriate and reputable private school in Switzerland:

- Does the school have a good reputation? How long has it been established? Does it belong to one of the Swiss private school associations?

- Does the school have a good academic record? For example, what percentage of pupils obtain good examination passes or go onto good universities? All the best schools provide exam pass rate statistics.

- How large are the classes and what is the student/teacher ratio? Does the class size tally with the number of desks in the classrooms?

- What are the qualification requirements for teachers? What nationality are the majority of teachers? Ask for a list of the teaching staff and their qualifications.

- What are the classrooms like? For example, their size, space, cleanliness, lighting, furniture and furnishings. Are there signs of creative teaching, e.g. wall charts, maps, posters and students' work on display.

- What is the teacher turnover? A high teacher turn-over is a bad sign and may suggest underpaid and poorly motivated teachers and poor working conditions.

- What extras must you pay? For example, art supplies, sports equipment, outings, clothing, health and accident insurance, text books and stationary. Some schools charge parents for every little thing.

- Which countries do most students come from?

- Is religion an important consideration in your choice of school?

- Are special English classes provided for children whose English (or other language) doesn't meet the required standard?

- What standard and type of accommodation is provided? What is the quality and variety of food provided? What is the dining room like? Does the school have a dietician?

- What languages does the school teach as obligatory or optional subjects? Does the school have a language laboratory?

- What is the student turnover?

- What are the school terms and holiday periods? Private school holidays are usually much longer than state schools, e.g. four weeks at Easter and Christmas and ten weeks in the summer, and often don't coincide with state school holiday periods.

- If you're considering a day school, what are the school hours?

- What are the withdrawal conditions, should you need or wish to remove your child? A term's notice is usual.

- What does the curriculum include? What examinations are set? Are examinations recognised both in Switzerland and internationally? Do they fit in with future education plans? Ask to see a typical pupil timetable to check the ratio of academic/non-academic subjects. Check the number of free study periods and whether they're supervised.

- What sports instruction and facilities are provided? Where are the sports facilities located?

- What are the facilities for art and science subjects, for example arts and crafts, music, computer studies, biology, science, hobbies, drama, cookery and photography? Ask to see the classrooms, facilities, equipment and some of the students' projects.

- What sort of outings and holidays does the school organise?

- What medical facilities does the school provide, e.g. infirmary, resident doctor or nurse? Is medical and accident insurance included in the fees?

- What sort of punishments are applied and for what offenses?
- What reports are provided for parents and how often?
- Last but not least, unless someone else is paying, what are the fees?

Before making a final choice, it's important to visit the schools on your shortlist during term time and talk to teachers and students, and if possible, former students and their parents. **Where possible, check the answers to the above questions in person and don't rely on the school's prospectus to provide the information.** If you're unhappy with the answers, look elsewhere. Finally, having made your choice, keep a check on your child's progress and listen to his complaints. Compare notes with other parents. If something doesn't seem right, try to establish whether the complaint is founded or not, and if it is, take action to have the problem resolved. Don't forget that you or your employer is paying a lot of money for your child's education and you should demand value for money. See also **State or Private School?** on page 150.

CHILDREN'S HOLIDAYS

Holiday camps (*Ferienlager, camps de vacances*) for children are organised during school holidays throughout the year. These include both day and residential camps run by private and state schools, clubs and organisations (e.g. youth organisations, scouts and brownies), churches and private organisations. Activities include skiing, swimming and various other sports; excursions; arts and crafts; and academic subjects. Most camps are reasonably priced. Migros club schools (*Klubschule Migros, école club Migros*) offer an extensive daily activity programme during school holidays (see **Day & Evening Classes** on page 316) and also have their own summer and autumn holiday centre: Freizeit & Sportzentrum Migros, Postfach, CH-8606 Greifensee (☎ 01 941 79 79, 🖥 www.szmg.ch). Most cantons also organise a variety of sports courses during summer holidays. Village Camps (rue de la Morâche 14, CH-1260 Nyon, ☎ 022 990 94 00, 🖥 www.villagecamps.com) are one of the largest Swiss operators of summer and winter camps (both in Switzerland and in other European countries) for boys and girls aged 8 to 18. Eurocamp (Bahnhofstr. 15, CH-8253 Diessenhofen, ☎ 052 646 01 01) operates family holiday camps throughout Europe.

Ask your local school or community office for information about holiday camps. A list of children's camps is available from your local Pro Juventute office (in the telephone directory), who also run holiday camps for the disabled.

APPRENTICESHIPS

Many students look forward to starting work and learning a trade and around 70 per cent of young people in Switzerland undertake an apprenticeship or vocational training. A Swiss apprenticeship (*Lehre*, *apprentissage*) is a combination of on-the-job training and further education, where one or two days a week are spent at a training college and the remainder in the workplace. The syllabus for both schoolwork and practical training is co-ordinated by the Federal Office for Education and Technology. There are plans to introduce a new scheme where apprentices do a year of theoretical education in school followed by two years of practical work. An apprenticeship lasts from two to four years and can be in almost any vocation, for example waitress, secretary, cook, plumber and chimney sweep (three years training in climbing and extricating yourself from chimneys). The employer pays a small salary that increases with age and experience, and he may pay for apprenticeship schooling and the cost of travel to and from school. An apprentice has five weeks holiday a year. School careers officers are available to advise parents and students on a choice of career.

The Swiss apprenticeship system is one of the best in the world. It isn't for failures or students who aren't sufficiently academically gifted to go to high school or university (many successful businessmen and politicians in Switzerland were apprentices). If desired, it's possible to go onto higher education later, for example at a college of technology or a university, after completion of, or even during an apprenticeship. Around 12 cantons pay a vocational training allowance of between SFr. 150 and 300 for children who are in full-time education or training.

You may also be interested in the activities of Intermundo, the Swiss umbrella association for many international youth exchange organisations. There are 11 member organisations and 14 contact members, all of which are non-profit and have no political or religious ties. Exchanges are organised world-wide to further cultural understanding, provide work and practical experience, and learn languages. The ages of participants are from 12 to over 30, depending on the particular exchange programme. Exchanges can last from one week to one year. For further information contact Intermundo (Postgasse 21, CH-3011, ☎ 031 326 29 20, 🖳 www. intermundo.ch)

Many books are published in Switzerland detailing career possibilities for school leavers. One such book is *Study and then?* (*Studieren und dann?*, *Carrefour Uni*) published in both French and German by the Crédit Suisse bank. It's available for SFr. 10 from ESPAS Frau Berweger, Naglerwiesenstrasse 4, 8049 Zürich (☎ 01 344 31 31).

HIGHER EDUCATION

Around 20 per cent of Swiss students attend one of Switzerland's higher educational establishments, which is well below the average for OECD countries. Switzerland also has the lowest number of women (per capita) attending university in Western Europe (around 45 per cent of the total). The country has ten universities (*Universität*, *université*) located in Basle, Berne, Fribourg, Geneva, Lausanne, Lucerne, Neuchâtel, St. Gallen, Ticino and Zurich, plus two tertiary-level Federal Institutes of Technology in Lausanne (EPFL) and Zurich (ETHZ). Other higher education facilities include the Higher Teacher Training Institute in St. Gallen, the School for Design in Basle, and several technical and business colleges throughout Switzerland.

The minimum age for enrolment is 18 and university education lasts for at least four years, although students often take as long as seven to nine years to complete a degree. This is a long time, particularly when compared, for example, with just three years in the UK for a similar degree. There's no fixed study period for a degree and students may take as long as they like. All Swiss higher education facilities, including several technical colleges, are open to foreign students, who comprise around 20 per cent of the total intake. There are usually quotas for foreign students and the number of places available is strictly limited at some universities and for particular courses, e.g. medicine. Fees are payable each term and scholarships and student low-interest loans may be available to foreigners after completion of four semesters. Fees may be reduced after the 10th semester.

There's usually a higher semester fee rate for foreign students, although students (or their parents) who have been residents and tax payers for at least two years in the canton where the university is located pay the Swiss rate. However, cantons without their own universities must pay fees for students studying in another canton, which have been sharply increased in recent years. It isn't the fees, which are between SFr. 700 to 1,400 a year, which make the cost of study in Switzerland expensive, but the high cost of living. For example, in Geneva the authorities recommend a minimum of around SFr. 1,500 to 2,000 per month for accommodation and food, plus university and local taxes, and health insurance (compulsory for university students). **Parents are legally obliged to support their children during their full-time education in Switzerland.** Student accommodation is available in university cities but many students go on living with their parents until they've got their degree.

Foreigners with a C permit (see page 70) are usually accepted on the same terms as Swiss citizens, only if they've attended a Swiss state school for a number of years. Foreigners with a B permit (see page 64) are always subject to the quotas for foreign students. The maturity examination is the usual entrance examination for Swiss nationals and foreigners who have studied in Switzerland. A Swiss university may accept three British A-level passes as an entrance qualification, but an American high school diploma isn't usually accepted. American students usually require a minimum of a BA, BBA or BSc degree. All foreign students require a thorough knowledge of the language of study (French or German), which will usually be examined unless a certificate is provided. A Swiss university degree is called a licence (*Lizenziat, license*), which on a academic scale is somewhere between a British BA or MA (or an American MA) and a doctorate (Ph.D). The Swiss universities are currently adapting their curricula to the Bologna system and therefore will switch from the license to a BA and MA.

FURTHER EDUCATION

Switzerland has over 50 private colleges and university level institutions, many affiliated to foreign (often American) universities. These include business and commercial colleges, hotel and tourism schools, and the world-famous Swiss finishing schools for young ladies. Fees at finishing schools are around SFr. 50,000 a year for students usually aged from 16 to around 24. The traditional training in French cooking, domestic science, floral art, etiquette and savoir vivre, is nowadays supplemented by courses in commerce, languages and catering.

Study in all further education establishments is in small groups and may be full or part-time, including summer semesters. Many schools offer an American Master of Business Administration (MBA) course and subjects may include banking, business administration, communications, economics, European languages, information systems, management, marketing, public relations, and social and political studies.

Tuition costs are high and study periods strictly organised. Most establishments have a good reputation, particularly in the business world. Switzerland is also renowned for its hotel and restaurant training schools (where classes are often taught in English), widely recognised as the best in the world. These include the world-famous Swiss Hotel School in Lausanne (which celebrated its 100th anniversary in 1993), where parents enrol their children 'at birth' to ensure a place.

The Federation of Swiss Private Schools (*Verband Schweizerischer Privatschulen*, *Fédération Suisse des Écoles Privées*) publishes a booklet entitled *Private Schools in Switzerland* containing the names of many further education establishments in Switzerland. It's available from Switzerland Tourism (ST), Swiss embassies and consulates, or from the *Verband Schweizerischer Privatschulen* (see **Private Schools** on page 163). A list of institutes of higher education and hotel and tourism schools is available from ST. See also **Day & Evening Classes** on page 316 and Intermundo under **Apprenticeships** on page 166.

LANGUAGE SCHOOLS

If you don't speak the local language fluently, you may wish to take a language course. It's possible, even for the most non-linguistic person, to acquire a working knowledge of French, German or Italian. All that's required is a little help and some perseverance – or a lot of perseverance if you're surrounded by English-speaking colleagues and only have English-speaking friends! A big handicap for English speakers is that there's often someone around who speaks English (even on top of a mountain), particularly when you want to practice the local language. Although you can travel the world speaking only English, it can be a distinct disadvantage when you need to learn a foreign language. Don't get caught in the trap of seeking refuge in the English language or allowing others to practice their English at your expense. You must persist in speaking the local

GEMINI BILINGUAL DAY SCHOOL
an international school in the Canton of Lucerne

The Gemini Bilingual Day School is the only bilingual school in central Switzerland teaching in both English and German. The international environment of the school is created by our pupils and teachers who come from all over the world (15 nationalities and 18 different languages).

We guarantee an all-round education for children aged from 3 to 11 (Play School to 6th Grade). The Gemini curriculum, composed of the core part of the British National Curriculum and the Swiss curriculum of the Canton of Lucerne, enables all children to transfer either into a Swiss public school or an equivalent English-speaking school.

The school is situated at the foot of Mount Pilatus in a tranquil environment. Gemini offers your child the unique opportunity of:

- An excellent bilingual education in English and German
- The advantage of small classes with an individual learning profile for each child
- Teachers whose mother-tongue is either English or German
- The opportunity to develop appreciation for other cultures and form a meaningful link with the Swiss community

Gemini Extra Services include:

- School bus service
- Day care before and after school
- Music & Movement for all classes
- Chess classes in Primary school
- Photography classes in Primary school

Gemini

You are welcome to visit us any time or to refer to our website:
www.gemini-school.ch
We look forward to hearing from you, either by telephone or e-mail:
+41-41-310 43 53 / gemini.school@tic.ch

language; give in too easily and you will never learn. One of the penalties of being a native English speaker is that you may receive little or no encouragement to learn the local language, but will be condemned as a lazy foreigner if you don't learn it. **Most foreigners in Switzerland find that their business and social enjoyment and success is directly related to the degree to which they master the local language(s).**

There are language schools (*Sprachschule, école des langues*) in all cities and large towns. Most schools run various classes depending on language ability, how many hours you wish to study a week, how much money you want to invest, and how quickly you wish to learn. Some Swiss employers provide free in-house language classes or may pay their employees' course fees (corporate courses for executives and managers are particularly big business). For those for whom money is no object (hopefully your employer), there are total immersion courses for two to six weeks, where you study from 8am to 5pm, five days a week. The cost for a Berlitz two-week total immersion course is around SFr. 13,000. At the other end of the scale, free language courses are available in some cities, e.g. at the Worker's and Popular universities in Geneva. Language classes generally fall into the following categories:

Type Of Course	Hours Per Week
Extensive	4 – 15 hours
Intensive	15 – 30 hours
Total Immersion	30 – 40 hours

Don't expect to become fluent in a short period unless you have a particular flair for languages or already have a good command of a language. Unless you need to learn a language quickly, it's better to arrange your lessons over a long period. However, don't commit yourself to a long course of study (particularly an expensive one) before ensuring that it's the right course. Most schools offer free tests to help you find your correct level, a free introductory lesson and small classes or private lessons.

Among the cheapest is Migros Club School (🖥 www.klubschule.ch – see also **Day & Evening Classes** on page 316), a subsidiary of the Migros supermarket chain. Migros offers inexpensive evening courses at all levels, usually consisting of two, two-hour sessions a week. The people's high school (*Volkshochschule, université populaire* – 🖥 www.vhs.ch), Coop leisure centres (*Coop Freizeit Center, centre de loisirs Coop*) and various voluntary organisations (e.g. American Women's Clubs – 🖥 www.fawco.org) also run inexpensive classes. Many language schools run special classes for au pairs costing around SFr. 150 a month for four hours per week. **However, the quality of language teaching is extremely variable and many schools hire 'teachers' without formal teacher training.**

You may prefer to have private lessons, which are a quicker but more expensive way of learning a language. The main advantage of private lessons is that you learn at your own speed and aren't held back by slow learners or dragged along in the wake of the class genius. You can advertise for a teacher in your local newspapers, on shopping centre bulletin boards, university notice boards, and through your or your spouse's employer. Your friends or colleagues may also be able to help you find a suitable private teacher or choose a language school.

Swiss universities hold summer language courses and many holiday language courses are organised (summer and winter) throughout Switzerland for children and young adults aged up to 25. Switzerland Tourism (ST) publish a brochure entitled *Holidays and Language Courses* listing summer language courses in English, French, German, Italian, Romansch and Spanish. Eurocentres (passage Saint-Francois 12, Case Postale 313, CH-1000 Lausanne 17, ☎ 021 312 47 45, 💻 www. eurocenters.com), operated by a Swiss charitable foundation, offer reasonably priced intensive language courses both in Switzerland and other countries, inclusive of accommodation with a local family. If you already speak the local language(s) but need conversational practice, you may wish to enrol in a course at an institute or local club, for example pottery, painting or photography (see **Day & Evening Classes** on page 316). For further information about languages in Switzerland, see **Languages** on page 39 and on page 153.

Swiss German

It's rarely absolutely necessary for foreigners to master Swiss German (*Schwyzertüütsch, suisse allemand*), although you may find yourself excluded from everyday life in German-speaking Switzerland if you don't understand it. You will find that speaking Swiss German opens doors, both in business and socially, and is particularly important if you plan to settle permanently in a German-speaking area of Switzerland or are thinking of applying for Swiss citizenship.

Opinion is divided over whether it's an advantage to speak High German before attempting to learn Swiss German. If your High German is poor, learning Swiss German won't help you speak, read or write High German and may even be a hindrance. There are a significant number of foreigners in Switzerland who can speak Swiss German reasonably fluently, but are unable to speak, read or write High German properly.

The Federation for Swiss German (*Verein Schweizerdeutsch*) organises Swiss German classes in local dialects in Basle, Winterthur, Zurich and occasionally Zug. They insist that all students have a good command of High German before enrolling in Swiss German courses. For information contact Dr. Alfred Egli, Unt. Heslibachstr. 1, CH-8700 Küsnacht (☎ 01 910 73 78). The Migros Club School (*Klubschule Migros, école club Migros*) and People's High School (*Volkshochschule, université populaire*) also run Swiss German classes in many areas (see **Day & Evening Classes** on page 316).

Various books are available for students of Swiss German including *Schwyzertüütsch* by Arthur Baur (Gemsberg Verlag, Winterthur) and *Dialect and High German in German Speaking Switzerland* by Alfred Wyler (Pro Helvetia).

10.

PUBLIC TRANSPORT

Public transport services (*öffentlicher Verkehr, transport publique*) in Switzerland are excellent and provide a frequent, convenient and inexpensive service to every corner of the land. All modes of public transport are highly efficient, completely integrated, clean and usually punctual to the minute (among the most accurate clocks in Switzerland are those at railway stations). With some 6,300km (around 3,900mi) of fixed transport lines (trains, trams, trolley-buses and cableways), Switzerland has the densest public transport network in the world.

On first acquaintance, Swiss public transport may seem expensive to some foreigners. However, if you take advantage of the often bewildering range of discounts and season tickets available, public transport provides excellent value for money and is often a bargain (particularly when high Swiss salaries are taken into consideration). Even greater savings can be made with tickets combining travel on different public transport systems, e.g. railways, buses and trams. It isn't essential to own a car in Switzerland, particularly if you live in or near a large town or city. For example, Zurich has one of the world's best public transport systems, which even includes the loan of free bicycles. This is verified by the frequency of use by its citizens, which is double the average in other major European cities. However, if you live in a remote village or a town off the main train and bus routes, you will find it more convenient or even mandatory to have your own transport.

The Swiss have a simple and 'ingenious' method of encouraging people to use public transport. Instead of slashing services and increasing costs and thus driving more people onto the roads, they do the opposite, and invest vast sums to improve services and provide better value for money. The government firmly believes that the benefits of a first class public transport system far outweigh the cost, even if it means increased public subsidies (although costs are causing concern). The Swiss people are justly proud of their public transport and could claim to have the best system in the world (but are much too modest to do so).

TRAINS

The Swiss railway network is one of the most extensive in Europe, with around 10,246km of track (almost all electrified), 1,800 stations and 623 tunnels. It includes 2,861km of private lines operated by some 100 'private' companies – although they aren't strictly private as many are run by canton governments. The Swiss federal railways are usually referred to by their initials, which vary according to the local language: SBB (Schweizerische Bundesbahnen) in German, henceforth used to refer to the Swiss federal railways, CFF (Chemins de Fer Fédéraux) in French and FFS (Ferrovie Federali Svizzere) in Italian. The SBB celebrated its 150th anniversary in 1997 and became a private company in 1999. It's renowned for its punctuality (although building or maintenance work and bad weather occasionally delay trains), comfort and speed, the only disadvantage being that the speed of some trains doesn't allow time to admire Switzerland's beauty (if you're sightseeing, make sure you catch a slow train).

Despite frequent fare increases in recent years to try to reduce SBB's deficit, Swiss trains remain relatively inexpensive if you take advantage of special tickets, excursion fares, family reductions and holiday package deals. Over long distances trains are cheaper than buses. The Swiss are Europe's most frequent train travellers and average around 1,798km a year, per head of population. Most Swiss trains consist of 1st class, usually denoted by a yellow stripe along the top, and 2nd class carriages.

Trains are categorised as local trains (*Regionalzug/Lokalzug, train régional*), fast trains (*Schnellzug, train direct*), Intercity (IC), InterCity Express (ICE) and Eurocity (EC), depending on the number of stops made. Intercity and InterCity Express trains are fast trains serving the main Swiss cities. Eurocity trains are fast international trains, providing regular services between major Swiss towns and over 200 European cities. They're air-conditioned and provide both a restaurant and a mini-bar trolley service. A supplement is payable by all passengers on EC trains and a seat reservation is obligatory for international travel (optional on Intercity and many domestic fast trains). The reservation fee is SFr. 5 and bookings can be made from 24-hours to two months in advance (up to three months for compartments in sleeping cars). Sleeping cars and cars with seats that convert into berths (*couchettes*) are available on most Eurocity trains. A private CityNightLine (CNL) sleeper train service (a joint venture with Austria and Germany) was introduced in 1995 and CNL plans to make Zurich the sleeper capital of Europe. International car trains also operate from Switzerland to a number of countries. It's advisable to reserve seats in advance, particularly when travelling during holiday periods or over weekends.

In recent years, the SBB has invested heavily in expanding and modernising its rail network, introducing new rolling stock and improving services. The latest examples are new S-Bahn (S is short for *schnell* or fast) suburban train services in Zurich with new double-decker trains, as well as in many other areas of Switzerland. Fast regional trains, called RegioExpress, have also been introduced in some areas, e.g. between St. Gallen and Chur. The *TGV* (*Hochgeschwindigkeitsbahn, Train à Grand Vitesse*) French high speed trains run daily from Berne, Geneva, Lausanne/Neuchâtel and Zurich to Paris and southern France, at speeds of up to 300kph. Geneva to Paris takes around three-and-a-half hours. From spring 1996, 200kph (120mph) Cisalpino (CIS), Pendolino tilt-body trains have connected major Swiss towns with Milan, and German ICE high speed trains link Interlaken and Zurich with cities throughout Germany. Switzerland is building two new high-speed rail tunnels through the Alps to carry heavy goods and passengers, the New Transalpine Railway Project (*Neue Eisenbahnalpentransversalen/NEAT*), which is expected to be operational in 2016 at an estimated cost of SFr. 14.7 billion.

In addition to the SBB, there are many small private railways in Switzerland. Among the most interesting, for both train enthusiasts and tourists alike, is the Glacier Express, the slowest express in the world (average speed 20mph). It runs from St. Moritz to Zermatt and negotiates 291 bridges and 91 tunnels during its 7.5 hour journey (the Swiss make holes in both their mountains and their cheese). The Montreux Oberland Bernese (MOB) railway from Montreux to Zweisimmen/Lenk/Lucerne is 1st class only, with ultra-modern panoramic or superpanoramic (sounds like a cinema screen) express coaches and a saloon bar coach with hostess. The Bernina express from Chur to Tirano in Italy, has the highest (2,253m/7,390ft) railway traverse in the Alps and provides a unique and beautiful experience. Switzerland Tourism (ST) publish several brochures for steam train fans, including *Dampf 2001* and *Finest Alpine Railways*.

Most public and private trains and carriages can be chartered for special occasions. You can also charter a special Panorama 'Vista Dome Car' and have it hooked onto most scheduled trains or alternatively charter a whole train. You can even charter the Orient Express! An excellent book for train buffs is *Switzerland-Rail-Road-Lake* by Anthony Lambert (Bradt Publications).

Information about Swiss rail services is available via telephone (☎ 0900 30 03 00 (calls cost SFr. 1.19 per minute) and the Internet (🖳 www.rail.ch **or** www.sbb.ch).

General Information

- All Swiss Intercity and long-distance trains provide a mini-bar trolley drinks and snacks service at your seat, and most have a snack and/or restaurant car (some self-service). Restaurant cars are denoted by a crossed fork and knife on time-tables.

- Many main railway stations offer a choice of restaurants and snack bars, generally providing good food and value for money.

- Shops in the vicinity of most train stations (approx. 200m) have extended opening times, including opening on Sunday and on public holidays (6am to 10pm).

- Many large railway stations provide wash, shower and brush-up 'McClean' facilities, including hair dryers (there's a fee). Some provide nappy (diaper) changing rooms.

- There are instant passport photograph machines at most stations.

- The SBB has a 'silent carriage' on each train where mobile phones and noisy conversations are banned!

- Park and Ride (P+R) car parks are provided at many railway stations, where you can park from around SFr. 5 per day, depending on the station.

- Wheelchairs for disabled passengers are provided at many railway stations. Most trains have facilities for the storage of wheelchairs and new trains have special carriages to accommodate wheelchairs. The SBB publish a brochure entitled *Information and Tips for Handicapped Train Travellers* (🖳 www. rail.ch/pv/behserv_e. htm). There's also a special hotline for disabled travellers (☎ 0800 00 71 02).

- Main railway stations have banks with extended opening hours and many smaller stations provide money changing facilities (see **Foreign Currency** on page 279). At many stations you can buy and sell foreign currencies, buy Swiss franc traveller's cheques and cash traveller's cheques.

- Bicycles can be rented from many railway stations and transported on trains (see **Bicycle Rental & Transportation** on page 323). Bicycle and moped parking, both covered and uncovered, is provided at most stations.

- A person or guide dog accompanying a disabled or blind person travels free of charge with a special SBB pass. The disabled or blind person must be a Swiss resident and have a medical certificate and an official ID card for disabled passengers issued by the cantonal authorities.

- Most information regarding the SBB is available in French, German, and Italian at railway stations.

- The SBB runs a Junior-Club SBB (🖳 www.magicticket.ch) for children aged 6 to 16, which offers members special reductions on excursions and a bi-annual magazine.

Buying Tickets

Tickets (*Fahrkarte, billets*) should be purchased from ticket offices or ticket machines (provided at most stations), before boarding a train. However, if you don't get the chance to buy a ticket, it's possible to purchase your ticket on the train from the conductor for a 10 per cent surcharge (with a SFr. 5 minimum).

Most ticket offices are open from around 6am until 7.30pm (even later at major stations). Single (*einfach, simple*) and return (*Retour/hin und zürück, aller-retour*) tickets for local destinations can be purchased from ticket machines.

The SBB has introduced new touch-screen ticket machines in many stations, which are easy to use in a number of languages:

1. If you wish to pay with cash, make sure that the machine you choose accepts bills and coins, as some only accept cards (machines are clearly marked).

2. Touch the button for the desired language.

3. Choose your destination from the list shown. If your destination isn't shown, type it in after pressing the 'Other Destinations' button.

4. Touch the screen button for a one-way (indicated by a single arrow) or return ticket (indicated by two arrows pointing in different directions).

5. Touch the screen button for a first or second class ticket.

6. Touch the screen button for a full or half-fare ticket. Half-fare is applicable to children aged 6-16 or holders of a half-fare travel card (see **Season & Special Tickets** on page 181) Children under six travel free when travelling with an adult, otherwise they pay half-fare until their 16th birthday.

7. Choose whether you wish the ticket to be valid from today or from a later date.

8. Touch the screen button for the desired number of tickets.

9. Insert the amount displayed on the screen. All coins except 5 cents are accepted, as well as SFr. 10, 20 and 50 bills. Other methods of payment include REKA cheques, Postcard, American Express, Diner's Club, Visa, Eurocard, Maestro, and EC cards.

10. Take your ticket and change from the tray at the bottom.

It's recommended that you use the ticket counter for anything remotely complicated, which will prevent money being wasted on useless tickets! (You can also take a ticket bought in error to the counter for a replacement.)

Some stations have old-style ticket machines, which aren't touch screen and don't look as modern. The instructions for the older machines are as follows:

1. Choose your destination from the list and press the corresponding button.

2. Choose your class, whether you're paying full fare and whether you want a return ticket. Press the buttons next to the correct combination.

3. Pay the amount displayed using coins (except for 5 cents) and SFr. 20 notes.

4. Don't forget to retrieve your ticket and change from the tray at the bottom!

If you make a mistake, press the *Korrektur/Annulation* button. As above, it's recommended that you use the ticket counter if you're making a 'complicated' journey, it's a lot easier.

You must buy a half-fare 2nd class ticket for a dog, which is also valid in 2nd class. In some regions, e.g. Zurich, it's **mandatory** for passengers to buy a ticket or validate a multiple-ride ticket in a special machine (*Entwerter, oblitérateur*), indicated by an eye symbol, before boarding a train. All trains requiring passengers to have a validated ticket before boarding are denoted by the eye symbol on the side, which is also shown on departure boards (there's no conductor on these trains).

Failure to buy or validate a ticket can result in a SFr. 60 minimum fine if you're discovered during a spot-check, in addition to which you must pay the correct fare. If you forget to buy a ticket or forget to date stamp your ticket and notify the conductor **before** makes a spot-check, you must pay a 10 per cent surcharge. Make sure you don't accidentally travel in a first class coach with a second class ticket, which also incurs a SFr. 60 fine Any journey by rail, boat or postbus may be broken without extra cost or formality, provided your ticket remains valid. It's advisable to notify the conductor when planning to do so, otherwise he may retain or cancel your ticket. A 2nd class ticket can be upgraded to 1st class on payment of the fare difference.

Tickets may be purchased with a Eurocard, American Express, Diners Club, Mastercard, Visa, Rekacheques and traveller's cheques in Swiss francs.

The validity of a ticket depends on the journey distance and whether the ticket is for a single or return journey, as shown below:

Type of Ticket	Distance (km)	Validity
One Way (Single)	Up to 115	Day Of Issue
One Way (Single)	116+	Day Of Issue
Return	Up to 115	Day Of Issue
Return	116+	1 Month

Seat reservations can be made for SFr. 5 on all IC, ICE, CIS, EC and *TGV* trains. Reservations are obligatory for CIS Cisalpino trains. Information regarding trains and tickets is available from information offices (denoted by a blue letter 'i' in a white circle on a blue background) at major stations or the ticket office at smaller stations. Rail journeys can be combined with travel on local buses, postbuses and boats. Dogs are permitted to travel in passenger carriages and require a 2nd class ticket (season tickets are also available). Small dogs up to 30cm (12in) in length carried in baskets travel free.

Season & Special Tickets

Many season tickets (*Abonnement*) and special discount tickets are available in Switzerland. These include family tickets; discounts for the young (16 to 25) and senior citizens; reduced price tickets for commuters and groups of ten or more; ski-day, hiking and cycling tickets; and special holiday and excursion tickets. Information is available from the information or ticket office at any railway station (staff usually speak English).

The best rail offer **of all time** is the annual half-fare travel card (*Halbtax-Abo, Abonnement demi-tarif*), a joint venture of the Swiss transport enterprises, costing SFr. 150 for one year or SFr. 250 for two years or SFr. 350 for three years. The half-fare travel card is also available with a Eurocard/Mastercard, Postcard, M-Card (Migros bank) or Visa card (cards contain a photograph and double as credit/bank cards and half-fare travel cards). A special half-fare travel card for 16-year-olds (who usually pay full price) is available for SFr. 87. The card entitles the holder to half-fare travel on all SBB trains, postbuses, selected city buses and trams, and many ferries and cable cars – for a whole year, a total network of around 18,000km (over 11,000mi). The half-fare travel card is available from any railway station and many postbus depots and travel agents, on production of a passport photo and the fee. You must sign your half-fare travel card below your photograph. The half-fare travel card can also be used with a Family Card (see page 181). Youths aged under 25 can purchase a half-fare travel card for SFr. 249 that provides half-fare travel before 7pm and free travel after 7pm until services end.

Holders of a half-fare travel card may purchase day cards, providing unlimited travel for a whole day on all SBB trains and postbuses. Day cards cost SFr. 52 each for 2nd class (SFr. 86 1st class) or SFr. 260 for a multiple day card providing six days travel (SFr. 430 1st class). A personal monthly travel card is also available to half-fare travel card holders which converts your half-fare travel card into a general season ticket (see below) for one month. As with any other ticket, day cards must be stamped before use. A child's day card is also available.

If you're a regular train commuter, you can buy a weekly, monthly or annual point-to-point season ticket (*Streckenabonnement, abonnement de parcours*). An annual point-to-point season ticket costs around the same as nine monthly tickets. In some cantons the rail network is divided into zones and season tickets are available for a number of zones or the whole network. A photograph is required for an annual season ticket. A multiple journey card is also available, allowing you to make 12 one-way trips for the price of five ordinary return tickets. You can make further savings by combining bus (both postbuses and local services) and rail journeys. Ask at any railway station.

The general season ticket (*Generalabonnement, abonnement général* or *GA*), which is held by more than 250,000 people, provides unlimited travel on all SBB trains, postbuses, tram/bus companies in some 35 cities and towns, many private railways and lake steamers. It also includes a 50 per cent reduction for one person on other licensed coach operators, mountain railways and aerial cableways. Tickets can be extended during a vacation or long period spent outside Switzerland by depositing them at a station. It costs SFr. 2,900 a year (SFr. 4,600 1st class) for an adult first family member and SFr. 2,150 (SFr. 3,400 1st class) for a youth aged 16 to 25, senior citizen or disabled person. Tickets aren't transferable (outside the listed users) and the first family member requires a passport photo. (There are a number of combinations especially for families – ask ticket office staff for information.)

A transferable (impersonal) *GA* is available for companies and organisations for SFr. 4,400 a year (SFr. 7,000 1st class). Although annual season tickets may appear to be expensive, if you do a lot of travelling on public transport they're a real bargain. There is even a GA for dogs, the Dog *GA*, which costs SFr. 650 (both 1st and 2nd class), available without a picture. It cannot be deposited during absences from Switzerland.

There are no special student fares within Switzerland, although youth fares are available for those aged 16 to 25 (30 for full-time students). Discounts are also available on selected international routes, e.g. from BIGT Wasteels (see also **Rail Passes** on page 197). A brochure is available from railway stations describing the various season and special tickets available. Finally, if you want to encourage someone to visit you, you can send them SBB travel gift vouchers (from SFr. 5 to 100), which you can buy at ticket counters (cash only).

Family Services

A special family card (*Familienkarte*, *carte-famille*) is available from railway stations (and postbus depots) for SFr. 20 for the first and second children, with subsequent children free. It's valid for two years and entitles children aged up to 16 to travel free and single children aged from 16 to 25 to travel at half-fare, **when accompanied by a parent**. The parent must have a valid ticket, which includes half-fare tickets or other special rates, but not a commuter ticket. For example, a parent with a half-fare travel card (see page 181) travels for half-fare and any number of his children under 16 travel free. The family card can be used for travel on all SBB trains, private railways, postbuses and lake steamers. It can also be used in around 35 towns to purchase city bus and tram day-cards with the same conditions as for trains. The family card must be signed and dated by the holder.

A special SBB playroom car for children, denoted by an illustration of a boy and a girl wearing sunglasses on the outside of the carriage, is provided on many routes. Simply look for the sign 'FA' next to the time on SBB timetables. The non-smoking playroom cars, currently sponsored by the magazine 'Schweizer Familie', have a nappy-changing room and folding seats to allow room for prams and push chairs. They contain a central play area (reserved free of charge for families with children aged 2 to 12) equipped with a slide, swing, 'fairy-tale' telephones, books and games.

Luggage

A 'normal' amount of luggage (three items) can be carried on a train without charge, officially weighing up to 30kg, but nobody checks or weighs it. The SBB has many ways of lightening your load or taking a load off your mind when travelling by train, including the following:

- Providing you have a valid ticket for the same route, luggage can be sent unaccompanied for SFr. 10 per item (SFr. 8 for groups and family card holders) and collected at your destination station. International luggage can be sent unaccompanied for SFr. 20 per piece (up to a maximum weight of 25kg). Skis and ski boots can be sent for SFr. 20, for which free plastic bags are provided. Luggage can be booked in at postbus depots for delivery to a railway station or airport. Luggage can also be sent unaccompanied to

Switzerland from abroad with a customs declaration form. It's advisable to register your luggage early, preferably the day before departure. There may be a storage charge of around SFr. 1 or 2 per day, per item, depending on the station.

- A special rail freight container (*Alles Schlucker, fourre-tout*) measuring 79 x 44 x 34cm can be purchased from stations for SFr. 10 for bulky or loose items of baggage.

- Bicycles can be sent between any two stations in Switzerland for SFr. 12 with a ticket and SFr. 24 without one. To send bikes internationally, the cost is SFr. 24 for normal bikes and SFr. 40 for tandems (both prices with a ticket).

- Luggage travelling within Switzerland can be insured for around SFr. 5 for each SFr. 1,000 insured value and bicycles SFr. 5 for each SFr. 500 insured value. Luggage travelling internationally can be insured for SFr. 10 per SFr. 1,000 insured value.

- Railway porters are sometimes available at main stations such as Zurich. There's a fixed scale of charges of around SFr. 1 per article and a small tip is customary – one of the few exceptions to the Swiss 'no tipping' rule (see page 387).

- Many stations have luggage lockers in several sizes (e.g. SFr. 5 for a medium-size locker) and luggage trolleys (at major stations you must pay a returnable deposit of SFr. 2).

- Luggage that weighs up to 25kg can be registered for some European countries, which are currently Austria (SFr. 44 for the first piece, SFr. 20 for additional pieces), France (SFr. 30 per item), Germany (SFr. 20) and Luxembourg (SFr. 20).

See also the special **Fly + Rail** baggage service that is available for air travellers on page 193.

BUSES & TRAMS

Two separate bus services are provided throughout most of Switzerland; the postbus service and local city and suburban bus networks. Together they cover **all** towns and villages in Switzerland. There's an extensive tram or trolley bus network in all major cities (trams were reintroduced in Geneva in 1998). Like the SBB, bus companies offer many special day, multi-ride and season tickets. There are also international bus services (e.g. Eurolines) to various countries.

Combined bus (postbus and local buses) and train commuter tickets are available from railway stations, offering large savings compared with the cost of separate bus and train tickets.

Postbus Service

The postbus service (*Postauto, Car Postal*) covers around 10,316km (6,448mi) of Switzerland's principal roads and provides regular services to over 1,600 localities along its 771 routes. Many remote villages are served only by postbuses, which carry over 97 million passengers a year. Postbuses are painted bright yellow and distinguished by a red stripe and the postbus alphorn motif on their sides. They have a distinctive horn to warn motorists of their approach on mountain roads, which plays the first three notes of Rossini's overture to his opera *William Tell*. The postbus service is comfortable, punctual, inexpensive and safe, and employs one of the most modern fleets of buses in the world. Postbus drivers inspire confidence and are among the world's best professional drivers – in the entire history of the service there has hardly been a serious accident (aided by two independent braking systems and a handbrake). It's probably the best national bus service provided anywhere in the world.

The main task of the postbus service is to deliver and collect the post. Around one-third of Swiss homes rely on the postbus service for their post and newspapers, which is one reason why postbuses have the right of way on all roads (postbus drivers can give instructions to other road users). Trailers are often attached to the rear of buses to carry parcels and luggage (in winter a special ski trailer is also used).

Like trains, postbuses also use the eye symbol, although it doesn't have the same meaning. The eye symbol on a bus signifies that a ticket validation machine (*Entwerter, oblitérateur*) is installed on the bus for holders of multi-ride tickets. Passengers without tickets must board at the front of the bus and buy a ticket from the driver. When a bus stop is located outside a post office or railway station, you should buy your ticket there to avoid delays on boarding a bus. Postbuses don't automatically stop at all stops, and it's usually necessary to press the stop button to get the driver to stop when you want to get off. A stopping sign (*hält an, arrêt*) is illuminated at the front of the bus when it's about to stop. You must usually press a button to open the doors. If you're waiting at a 'request' stop, you will need to flag the bus down (wave to the driver) to get it to stop.

Dogs are carried on postbuses for half-fare (small dogs in baskets are carried free). Bicycles may be carried free in the baggage compartment. Children under six travel free and children aged 6 to 16 pay half-fare when they have a Junior Card (available at Postbus depots and train stations). There's a 20 per cent reduction for groups of ten or more. Reservations are necessary on some long distance postbus routes. Journeys may be broken, but tickets must be officially endorsed at the start of each journey. Passengers can take hand luggage (no weight limit), although a charge is made for unaccompanied baggage. Postbuses operate weekly bus tours abroad, which include hotel accommodation, full board (all meals), excursions and entrance tickets. The half-fare travel card (see page 181) allows half-fare travel on all postbuses and some local bus services. Other discounts are offered by the tickets described below.

The following information applies to a multi-journey ticket (*Mehrfahrkarte, carte multicourse*):

- Six return journeys for the price of three;
- Half-fare travel card holders and children under 16 receive a 50 per cent discount;
- Tickets are transferable and can be used by several people travelling together;
- Tickets are available from all postbus depots; or on the Internet ▣ www. shop.sbb.ch.

The following information applies to a route-pass (*Streckenabonnement, abonnement de parcours*):

- The pass is for commuters or anyone who regularly travels the same route (point-to-point);
- A choice of season tickets valid for a week, a month or a year, are available;
- The pass enables you to have an annual pass for 75 per cent of the normal annual fare (pay for nine months and travel for 12);
- Additional savings of around 25 per cent can be gained for those aged from 6 to 25;
- Weekly tickets are offered for 30 per cent of the cost of a monthly ticket;
- Passes aren't transferable, require a photograph and must be signed by the holder;
- Passes can be combined with services operated by other bus companies;
- Passes are available from all postbus depots.

City Buses & Trams

Most towns and cities in Switzerland are served by local bus services, and the main cities also have tram or trolley-bus services, which are usually self-service. Tickets for both single and multiple journeys must normally be purchased before boarding, from ticket machines located at most stops. Tickets are also sold at ticket offices, newspaper kiosks, and railway stations near bus and tram stops. Tickets can **sometimes** be purchased from the driver, but a surcharge may be payable if a ticket machine was provided at the stop where boarding.

Tickets are usually valid for both buses and trams, if applicable, and journeys may combine both, so long as you travel in one direction only. You can break your journey but must complete the overall journey within the time limit shown on your ticket. You aren't permitted to make a return journey on a single ticket, which is valid for a limited period (e.g. one hour), depending on the number of zones selected. You must validate (time and date stamp) a multi-ride ticket in the special 'ticket-validation slot' provided or in a separate ticket validation machine (*Entwerter*, *oblitérateur*), either before boarding or on board a tram or bus (many trams and buses have a machine inside). If there's no validation machine at the stop where boarding or on board, inform the driver. He'll either ask you to pay the fare or to validate your ticket in the next machine.

There are no conductors on buses or trams, but random checks are made by ticket inspectors. If you don't have a valid ticket, you must pay a compulsory on-the-spot fine, e.g. SFr. 60 to 80, in addition to an administration fee if it isn't paid on the spot and possibly also the correct fare, depending on the inspector. If you refuse or are unable to pay the fine, you can be arrested (persistent offenders are put in the stocks!). Journeys on most city bus and tram services can be combined with travel on postbuses and SBB rail services, with large savings. The procedure for buying a ticket from a machine is roughly the same throughout Switzerland:

1. Study the coloured route plan shown on the front or side of the ticket machine. Instructions on the machine and in information leaflets are usually given in English. The stop where you're located may be marked by an arrow or a red spot. Zones are shown in different colours on the route plan. Locate your destination and the route number required. Press the appropriate fare selection button, usually colour coded to match the different zones, for example blue, red and yellow (in some machines you press the button corresponding to the postcode of your town of destination or simply press the button for your destination). If both single and return tickets are dispensed, it's shown by arrows; a single arrow denotes a single ticket and two arrows pointing in opposite directions denote a return ticket.

2. When you've selected the correct fare insert the exact coins, unless you're sure the machine gives change (some don't). Machines usually accept all coins from SFr. 0.10 and some also accept notes.

3. Remove your ticket and change from the tray.

4. If you've purchased a multi-ride ticket, validate it in the ticket validation slot or the separate machine provided.

In some cities, e.g. Zurich, new machines have been installed selling tickets for all city transport, including local trains, trams, buses and boats. The procedure for buying tickets from these machines is virtually identical to buying rail tickets (see page 179). The main difference is that there are coloured buttons for the different zones, e.g. in Zurich a yellow button indicates a short journey and a blue button the entire city zone. If you want a 24-hour day pass, press the button marked with arrows in opposite directions. These machines don't accept banknotes. If you're in doubt about how to use a ticket machine, ask someone to help you; kicking it won't help (but may make you feel better!). In some cities, e.g. Geneva, 'rechargeable' tickets have been introduced, whereby you can recharge your ticket in special machines located at stops. Some ticket machines also accept credit cards.

Transferable and non-transferable, monthly and annual tram and bus season tickets are also available, and are valid in around 35 towns.

Special Tickets

There are a variety of special city bus and tram tickets available in most regions, including the following:

- Single and multi-ride (e.g. 12 single trips) tickets for different zones, with a time limit to reach your destination, e.g. 30 minutes to two hours, depending on the number of zones. You may change buses or trams, but must travel in one direction only.

- Day-cards offering unlimited 24-hour travel on city trams, buses and suburban trains (plus boats and funiculars, if applicable) are available in around 35 towns from around SFr. 7 (the price depends on the number of zones). You must usually sign a day-card and it isn't transferable. In some towns a multiple day pass is available, e.g. in Zurich a six-day multiple pass is available (it must be validated before use each day).

- Special reduced price tickets allowing unlimited travel on city buses and trams are provided for visitors to trade fairs and conventions, as well as guests at some hotels. Ask at the local public transport information office, tourist office or hotel desk.

- Ecology season tickets (*Umweltschutzabonnement/Umweltpass, le billet vert*) are available in some regions. They combine unlimited travel on all local buses, trams and trains (excluding fast, Intercity and Eurocity trains).

- Tickets for students under 30 years of age (with a student ID card), pensioners and the disabled (buses specially-designed for wheelchair-bound passengers are provided in some cities).

- Monthly and annual season tickets are available for adults, under 25s, pensioners and the disabled. A monthly pass is available in most cities, allowing unlimited travel on all city transport.

- Family and day tickets are available and the half-fare travel card (see page 181) is valid on most local bus services, where the same conditions apply as for trains and postbuses.

If you find all the different tickets for buses (and trains) bewildering, it's hardly surprising. With such an abundance of season and special tickets, the only thing you can be sure of is that unless you're travelling free, you may be paying too much! The solution is simply to tell the ticket office clerk where you want to go, when and how often you want to travel, and whether 1st or 2nd class (trains only). You can generally rely on him to provide you with the cheapest ticket available – unless it's his first day on the job, in which case he'll be just as confused as you are!

General Information

- Trams and buses don't usually operate between around midnight and 5.30am, although major cities have a 'Night Bus' system for ferrying night owls home.
- Children under six years of age don't require a ticket when accompanied by an adult. Children from 6 to 16 usually pay a reduced fare. You must generally pay half-fare for dogs and non-collapsible baby carriages; prams usually require an additional full fare.
- School bus and tram passes may be invalid after around 8pm or on Sundays and school holidays.
- A person or guide dog accompanying a disabled or blind person travels free of charge with a special SBB pass. The disabled or blind person must be a Swiss resident with a medical certificate and a special ID card for disabled passengers issued by the cantonal authorities.
- Groups of ten or more people are usually given a discount.
- Ticket machines don't always give change, so check before inserting coins. If in doubt, insert the exact fare.
- When waiting at a 'request' bus stop, you may need to signal the driver to stop (wave to him).
- On many buses and trams you must press a button to open the doors to get on or off (doors are closed by the driver). Trams halt at most stops (some are only request stops, indicated by a hand with the palm face out), although the doors may not open unless you press a button. When on a bus, you must usually request the driver to stop by pressing a stop button when you near your destination.

> ● In many towns, children up to the age of 16 can travel free and children who are aged 16 to 25 travel for half-fare when accompanied by a parent with a family card (for information see **Family Services** on page 183) and a valid ticket.

Finally, check the line number and direction of a tram or bus before boarding. If in doubt ask someone.

SHIPS

Over 140 ships with accommodation for a total of around 60,000 passengers are in service from spring to autumn (April to October) on lakes and rivers throughout Switzerland. Regular car ferry and passenger services operate all year round on the main lakes, although services are reduced in winter and bad weather sometimes causes cancellations. In the summer there are special round trips including breakfast or lunch, folklore, night, and dinner and dance cruises. Paddle steamers are in service on many Swiss lakes (paddles are provided). Reduced fares are usually offered for groups, schools parties and holders of the Swiss Card, while holders of an SBB general season ticket and the Swiss Pass (see page 195) travel free. The Swiss Boat Pass (SFr. 35) provides a 50 per cent discount on all boat cruises and is valid for one year on 14 lakes serviced by the Swiss Shipping Company and its partners. The Swiss Family Boat Pass costs SFr. 50 a year and gives the parents a 50 per cent discount, while the children below 16 years travel free. (🖳 www.vssu.ch). Ships can be chartered for private cruises on most lakes. Ferry passengers may break journeys without formality.

Car ferry services are provided on lakes Constance, Lucerne (*Vierwaldstättersee, lac des Quatre-Cantons*) and Zurich. Passenger ships of the Köln-Düsseldorf (KD) German Rhine Line operate scheduled services between Basle and points in Germany, France and the Netherlands. Free or reduced price steamer services are available for Eurailpass and Eurail youthpass holders (see **Rail Passes** on page 197).

CABLE CARS & MOUNTAIN RAILWAYS

There are over 500 cog or rack railways, funiculars and aerial cableways in Switzerland, which cover a total of around 750km (over 450mi). Most of them operate throughout the year (bad weather excepted) and in winter an additional 2,000 ski-lifts (i.e. chair-lifts and T-bars) are in use. Holders of a half-fare travel card (see page 181) and general season tickets can obtain reductions on many cable cars and mountain railways, so don't forget to ask before buying a ticket.

Cable cars and mountain railways are generally expensive, particularly those that scale the heights, for example Jungfraujoch (3,454m/11,332ft) and the Klein Matterhorn in Zermatt (3,884m/12,743ft). It costs SFr. 167 to travel from Interlaken to Jungfraujoch full fare (but there are many special offers – for details see 🖳 www.jungfraubahn.ch). Note that the view, which **on a clear day** can stretch for hundreds of kilometres in each direction, is often disappointing due to cloudy or bad weather. If you plan to travel to the top of a mountain, don't forget to take sunglasses and a warm pullover.

TIMETABLES

Swiss timetables are truthful and accurate, meaning that a train or bus due at 8.17am will arrive at or very close to this time. (What else would you expect from the country that invented precision?) This is a most pleasant surprise if you come from a country where timetables are largely fictitious and arrival and departure times are usually figments of somebody's wild imagination. Avalanches and landslides do, however, occasionally upset Swiss timetables.

Local bus and train timetables are posted in offices, factories and restaurants, and are also available from post offices. All services run frequently, particularly during rush hours. At major airports and railway stations, arrivals (*Ankunft, arrivée*) and departures (*Abfahrt, départ*) are shown on electronic boards. Regional timetables (*Regionalfahrplan, horaire régional*) for both train and bus services are available free of charge from all stations and bus depots. A special timetable is published for trains with restaurant cars. Local timetables (often sponsored by Swiss banks) for buses and trains are delivered free once or twice a year to households in most areas of Switzerland. An excellent railway map of Switzerland, including 13 city plans, can be purchased at any SBB station for SFr. 19.80. A variety of free local and regional maps are also published.

If you're a frequent traveller on public transport, then the official timetable (*Offizielles Kursbuch, indicateur officiel*), published annually at the end of December is a must. It costs SFr. 16 from any railway information or ticket office (it's also available on CD-ROM for SFr. 16) and includes the following three timetable books:

1. Swiss inland railways, cableways and ships;
2. Inland postbuses;
3. International rail services.

The inland timetables (books 1 and 2) are published annually and the international rail services timetable (book 3) is published in two parts, summer and winter. The international timetable for the second half-year (winter) is sent free on application (a post-free postcard is included in book 3). The inland railways timetable includes many privately operated railways. All timetables contain information in English.

Train information can be obtained from the SBB's Rail Service Number (☎ 0900 30 03 00, costing an expensive SFr. 1.19 a minute!) or from station information offices. An interactive timetable for Swiss trains, ships and post buses is available via the Internet (💻 www.sbb.ch).

TAXIS

Taxis in Switzerland are among the most expensive in the world, with a basic charge of SFr. 6, plus SFr. 3.50 for each kilometre, depending on the area and time of day (rates quoted are for Zurich). There are additional charges for each piece of baggage, e.g. SFr. 5 for a half load and SFr. 10 for a full load, and extra passengers, so it's easy to run up a large bill. Waiting time is charged at around SFr. 63 an hour. Due to an increase in violence, some towns and cities have lowered night taxi rates for women. Taxis sometimes cannot be stopped on the street, but can be hired from taxi ranks at railway stations, airports and hotels, or ordered by telephone. Taxis are usually plentiful, except when it's raining, you have lots of luggage or you're late for an appointment. In most major cities, for example Basle, Berne, Geneva and Zurich, a service charge is included in the fare, although drivers may still expect a tip. Elsewhere you may tip if you wish, but it isn't obligatory.

In winter, many taxis have ski racks, particularly in ski resorts. When travelling with skis or other large objects, mention it when booking by telephone. Special wheelchair taxis are provided by taxi companies in major cities, most of which have a central telephone number, for example in Geneva and Lausanne it's 141.

AIRLINE SERVICES

Switzerland is well served by airline services, both international and domestic. In autumn 2001, Swissair, the Swiss international airline, filed for bankrupty – a major blow to Swiss air transport and Swiss pride! A large number of its employees, aeroplanes and routes have been taken over by its former subsidary Crossair, which was purchased by the Swiss banks when Swissair foundered. Crossair subsequently changed its name to 'Swiss International Airlines' and is now operating under the label 'Swiss'. Since its official launch in April 2002, Swiss has had a turbulent time with its business concept undergoing radical changes several times. In the beginning of 2003, Swiss decided to downsize considerably and has given up many of its former connections to smaller airports in Europe, focusing mainly on the most profitable connections. In September 2002, Swiss became a member of the Oneworld Alliance and hopes to benefit from the co-operation with bigger partners such as British Airways.

Although air fares to and from Switzerland aren't the most competitive in Europe, a range of special fares are available including package tours, APEX, super APEX, PEX, super PEX, Eurobudget, excursion fares and under 12 discounts.The arrival of Easy Jet (Zurich) and Ryan Air (Geneva) has put a lot of pressure on air fares and in the summer of 2003 Swiss introduced a new low-fare booking system for flights in Europe (only available for Internet booking 🖥 www.swiss.com).

When planning an intercontinental flight, it may be cheaper to book your ticket in Frankfurt, London or Luxembourg, as ticket prices are generally much lower there than in Switzerland (even after taking into account the cost of getting to and from the airport concerned). In fact, it's possible to book a European package holiday (e.g. flying out of London) via a British travel agent and save up to 50 per cent on local prices, including the cost of the return flight to London! If you're planning a trip abroad during the school holidays, book **well** in advance, particularly if you're going to a popular destination, e.g. London or Paris (the Swiss book months ahead).

Easy Jet (🖥 www.easyjet.co.uk) has daily flights from Zurich Airport to London-Luton and from Geneva to London-Luton, London-Gatwick and Liverpool. The fare depends on when you book, but usually it's a lot cheaper than with most other airlines.

A Fly + Rail Baggage service is provided by postbuses, SBB and international airports. You can check in your luggage at over 100 railway stations and postbus depots to Basle, Geneva and Zurich airports and onto your final destination. The cost is SFr. 20 per item (up to 32kg or the airline's specification) each way with discounts for Swiss First Class passengers and Travel Club members, provided that you travel by rail to the airport. Baggage book-in times are listed in a leaflet available from railway stations (you must register your luggage up to 24 hours in advance). This service isn't available for flights with all airlines. If you're flying with Swiss you can also do your flight check-in up to 24 hours before your flight departure time and receive your boarding card on the spot.

This service is available at the following railway stations: Aarau, Arosa, Baden, Basle, Bellinzona, Berne, Biel/Bienne, Brig, Buchs (SG), Burgdorf, Chiasso, Chur, Davos Dorf/Platz, Dietikon, Frauenfeld, Fribourg, Geneva, Grenchen, Gstaad, Interlaken Ost/West, Klosters, Konstanz, La Chaux-de-Fonds, Langenthal, Lausanne, Locarno, Lucerne, Lugano, Montreux, Neuchâtel, Olten, Rapperswil, Saas Fee, Sargans, Schaffhausen, Sierre/Siders, Sion, Solothurn, St. Gallen, St.Margrethen, St. Moritz, Thalwil, Thun, Uster, Vevey, Wädenswil, Wil(SG), Winterthur, Zermatt, Zug and Zurich. A valid air ticket with a reservation status of 'OK,' a railway ticket and a valid passport and/or visa must be produced when registering your luggage. Information regarding the latest check-in times is available from SBB stations. Baggage can also be checked-in at foreign airports and collected from an SBB station or postbus depot for SFr. 20 per item (up to 30kg). A special green address label (obtained before your journey) must be attached to each item of baggage for customs' declaration. A welcome surprise at Swiss airports (particularly Zurich) is an ample supply of luggage trolleys, which also allow you to take your baggage up and down escalators.

Airports

Most international airlines provide scheduled services to and from Switzerland via one of the three Swiss international airports (*Flughafen, aéroport*): Basle-Mulhouse EuroAirport, Geneva-Cointrin and Zurich-Kloten. Basle airport is actually located in France around 5km/3mi (25 minutes) from Basle city centre. It's unnecessary to go through French customs or immigration to enter or leave Switzerland via Basle airport, as the road between Basle city and Basle airport is fenced in all the way, which is important if you need a visa to enter France (if you need to travel through France to reach another airport, you may need a visa). The Basel transport company operates a shuttle bus service from Basle airport to Basle railway station.

Zurich is by far the largest and most modern Swiss airport, and is highly rated by international travellers who have consistently rated it one of the best in the world. Zurich airport has a direct rail connection (every 20 minutes) to Zurich main railway station, taking ten minutes. Modems are provided for passengers with personal computers in both first and business class lounges at Geneva and Zurich airports. Geneva airport is relatively small and provincial in comparison with Zurich, although it has been expanded and modernised in recent years. However, its services are stretched to breaking point during the ski season, when it's invaded by thousands of skiers in transit to nearby ski resorts (mostly in France). Geneva airport has a direct rail connection to the main city railway station, taking six minutes.

Besides the three main international airports, there are over 40 smaller airfields in Switzerland. Berne, the capital city of Switzerland, doesn't have an 'official' international airport, although its airport provides scheduled flights to London, Paris and various destinations in Italy. Berne is served by regular domestic flights from many other Swiss airports. A postbus service runs from Berne airport to the city centre. Lugano also has an important regional airport. Note also the following:

- All major Swiss airports have wheelchairs and ambulance staff on hand to help disabled travellers and airlines publish brochures disabled travellers.
- Long and short-term parking is available at all major airports, including reserved parking for the disabled.

- Both Geneva and Zurich airports have shopping centres open from 8am to 8pm, seven days a week.

- Airport authorities claim that X-ray machines used for hand baggage at Swiss international airports, are safe for film. **Note, however, that these metal detectors may not be safe for magnetic storage media such as computer hard and floppy disks.**

For flight information telephone:

Airport	Telephone Number
Basle/Mulhouse	061 325 31 11
Berne	031 960 21 11
Geneva	022 717 71 11
Lugano	091 610 11 11
Zurich	01 816 22 11

Flight information is also available from the Swiss television teletext service. Kuoni Travel publish a comprehensive Air Guide listing the most convenient connections from all Swiss airports to over 260 destinations world-wide. It's available free from Kuoni offices and is also available on the Internet 🖳 www.kuoni.ch.

HOLIDAY & VISITORS' TICKETS

Visitor's to Switzerland and Swiss residents travelling by train within Europe can buy a range of special tickets and passes. A useful brochure for visitors entitled *Discover Switzerland by Train, Bus and Boat*, is published by the SBB. One of the most interesting journeys for visitors is the 'Golden Pass' taking in Lucerne, Interlaken, Zweisimmen and Montreux, while another is the Lake Geneva region Pass which includes railways, funiculars, and boats of the Lake Geneva Shipping Company. **Some tickets are valid only if your permanent residence is outside Switzerland.**

Swiss Pass

Visitors to Switzerland can buy a Swiss Pass (🖳 www.myswitzerland.com) which provides unlimited travel by rail, post buses and ships throughout the country, plus buses and trams in around 36 towns and cities. There are also reductions on many mountain railways and aerial cableways. It's available outside Switzerland at Switzerland Tourism offices, Swissair offices and travel agents, and in Switzerland at international airports and at a few main railway stations, on production of your passport or identity card. There's a 15 per cent discount for two or more people travelling together. The prices are as follows:

	Validity	Cost	
		1st Class	2nd Class
Adults	4 days	SFr. 360	SFr. 240
	8 days	SFr. 510	SFr. 340
	15 days	SFr. 615	SFr. 410
	22 days	SFr. 715	SFr. 475
	1 month	SFr. 790	SFr. 525
	Validity	**Cost**	
		1st class	2nd class
16-26 Year Olds	4 days	SFr. 270	SFr. 180
	8 days	SFr. 383	SFr. 255
	15 days	SFr. 462	SFr. 308
	22 days	SFr. 537	SFr. 357
	1 month	SFr. 593	SFr. 394

A Swiss Flexi Pass is available allowing three to eight days unlimited travel within a period of one month.

	Validity	Cost	
		1st class	2nd class
Flexi Pass For All	3 days	SFr. 345	SFr. 230
	4 days	SFr. 420	SFr. 280
	5 days	SFr. 480	SFr. 320
	6 days	SFr. 540	SFr. 360
	8 days	SFr. 630	SFr. 420

Note that the costs for children are half the adult rates quoted above.

When you arrive in Switzerland with a Swiss Pass, take it to an SBB desk, for example at an international airport terminal. They will enter the validity dates and stamp your pass, without which it's invalid. The Swiss Pass is available only to those with their permanent residence outside Switzerland and Liechtenstein.

Half-fare travel cards are available for senior citizens (men over 65, women over 64), which costs SFr. 90 a month from SBB ticket offices.

Swiss Transfer Ticket

The Swiss Transfer Ticket provides you with return travel from the Swiss border or one of Switzerland's airports to your destination rail station in Switzerland. It's valid for up to one month and costs SFr. 118 2nd class and SFr. 182 1st class.

Swiss Card

The Swiss Card provides return travel from the Swiss border to your hotel in Switzerland, plus unlimited half-fare travel on Swiss federal railways (SBB), postbuses and ships for a period of one month. It can be purchased at the same locations abroad as the Swiss Pass (see above), but not in Switzerland. Costs for one month for an adult are SFr. 170 (2nd class) and SFr. 242 (1st class). Children up to the age of 16 can travel free with a parent with a Swiss Card, when the parent has a family card (see page 183).

Rail Passes

A range of rail passes are available for visitors to Europe and Swiss residents travelling in Europe. Passes include Euro Domino (three to eight-day passes for those aged up to 26), Eurotrain/SSR and BIJ Wasteels (under 26 year olds). For seniors, there's a Swiss Pass for the over 50s offering 50 per cent discounts, as well as the RailPlus for seniors for SFr. 32 per year which provides a 25 per cent reduction. A range of Eurail passes allowing travel in 12 countries are available for those with their permanent residence outside Europe, including the Eurailpass, the Eurail Flexipass, the Eurail Selectpass and the Europass.

The Inter-Rail Pass is valid for 12, 22 days or one month and is available to youths and adults. The Inter-Rail youth card allows 2nd class rail travel in 28 European countries (including the UK and Ireland) plus Morocco, and it also provides discounts of up to 50 per cent in the country where it's purchased. The cost of the pass depends on the countries selected (Europe has been split into eight zones). The Inter-Rail 26+ card no longer covers many western European countries and is therefore of limited interest to most travellers. Inter-Rail passes are better value than Eurail passes and are available to those who have their permanent residence in Europe, but they must be purchased in your country of residence. A free Eurail/Inter Rail timetable is available from offices selling Eurail passes, plus a wide range of brochures and maps.

An excellent book for European rail travellers is *Europe by Train* by Katie Woods (Ebury Press). It covers accommodation, visas, food, sights, customs and even the idiosyncrasies of local transport. *Europe by Eurail* by George and Laverne Ferguson (Globe Pequot) provides tips on how to plan a European tour using a Railpass or other tourist tickets, making day trips from selected base cities. Thomas Cook Publications publish and supply a wide range of books, guides and maps for train travellers including a *Railpass Guide, European Timetable* (includes rail and shipping services), *Rail Map of Europe,* and the *Overseas Timetable* (rail, bus and shipping services outside Europe). Thomas Cook publications are available direct from Thomas Cook Publishing, PO Box 227 Units 19-21 The Thomas Cook Business Park, Peterborough, PE3 8XX, UK (☎ 01733-416477, 💻 www.thomascookpublishing.com).

11.

MOTORING

Swiss motorways and secondary roads are excellent and rate among the best in the world. The total network covers some 70,000km (around 43,500mi), of which around 2,000km (over 1,200mi) are motorways. Switzerland is constantly improving its road system and spends a higher percentage of its motoring tax revenues on its roads than most countries. Almost every second person in Switzerland owns a car, making it one of the most heavily motorised countries in the world. However, despite the heavy traffic, Switzerland has less fatal accidents (per vehicle) than most other European countries. Although the country has an excellent public transport system, most Swiss prefer to travel by car and vigorously protest against any plans to restrict their freedom.

Traffic density in the major Swiss cities is fast approaching the choking levels already experienced in many other European countries, although generally there are fewer traffic jams, and parking, although often a problem, isn't impossible. During rush hours, from around 6.30 to 9am and 4 to 6.30pm Monday to Friday, the flow of traffic is naturally slower and any interruptions (roadworks, breakdowns or accidents) can cause huge traffic jams (*Stau*, *embâcle*). Town centres are to be avoided during rush hours, particularly Geneva and Zurich. Motorway travel is generally fast, although it's occasionally slowed to a crawl by road works and the favourite Swiss motor sport of running into the rear of the car in front. Outside rush hours, motoring is usually trouble-free, and driving on secondary roads in country areas is often enjoyable. In winter, many mountain passes are closed due to heavy snowfall from around November to May (see page 222) and vehicles using pass roads that remain open during winter require snow chains (shown on a sign which also indicates whether a pass is open or closed). Cars are banned in some mountain resorts.

Although Switzerland has the most stringent anti-pollution motoring laws in Europe, traffic pollution is giving rise to concern, particularly in the major cities (38 per cent of Zurich's residents voted to ban most traffic from the city in 1997). Nevertheless, it's generally lower than in most other western countries.

Information regarding closed roads and passes is available from the Swiss motoring organisations (see page 232), the Swiss television teletext road information service, and the road conditions telephone service number (163). Signs on motorways show the local radio frequency on which road and traffic bulletins are broadcast. Emergency SOS telephones are located on mountain passes and motorways at 1.6km (1mi) intervals and every 150m in tunnels, where there are also fire extinguishers. Black arrows on white posts at the roadside show the direction of the nearest SOS telephone. The Swiss Bureau for the Prevention of Accidents (see **Accidents** on page 225) publish safety leaflets for motorists, motorcyclists, cyclists and pedestrians.

CAR IMPORTATION

If you intend to bring a motor vehicle or motorcycle to Switzerland, either temporarily or permanently, first ensure that you're aware of the latest regulations. In order to reduce air pollution, all new cars registered in

Switzerland must be fitted with a catalytic converter or catalyser (*Katalysator, catalyseur*) that meets the US 1983 standards. Check with the manufacturer's export department, the Swiss importers or the local canton vehicle licensing authority in Switzerland, regarding the latest Swiss regulations. If you're tempted to buy a tax-free car prior to coming to Switzerland, make sure that it conforms to Swiss regulations. Previously it could cost thousands of francs to convert a car imported from certain countries to Swiss standards, although the importation of US-made cars was made easier in 1996 and Swiss residents can now import one car a year for their personal use with minimum testing and modifications. Any car sold in the European Union automatically conforms to Swiss standards and can be imported without modifications.

If you wish to import a car (even temporarily), inform the border customs staff on arrival in Switzerland. It's advisable to enter via a major frontier post (e.g. Basle or Geneva) as smaller frontier posts aren't always equipped to deal with car importation without advance notice. Registration can, however, also be done at customs offices in major cities. You're required to complete a form and show your car papers. The amount of tax and import duty payable and when due, depends on how long you've owned your car, as shown below. Before importing a car, check the documents required with your local Swiss embassy or consulate, or contact the Head Customs Office, (*Oberzolldirektion, Direction des Douanes*) Monbijoustr. 40, CH-3003 Berne (☎ 031 322 65 11).

Cars Owned Less Than Six Months

If you've owned your car for less than six months, you must pay import duty and tax on importing it into Switzerland. You need to provide documentation confirming the value of the vehicle, the country of origin and an EUR1 certificate (if applicable). Clearance can either be done on entry into Switzerland at main border posts or inland in major cities, on authorisation from the border customs office. The customs post will issue you with an authorisation (form 15.25) valid for two days, by which time the car must be presented to a customs depot in the interior. Import duty is calculated on the weight and/or engine size of your car, so remove all luggage and non-standard spares before having it weighed. In addition to import duty, you must also pay a 3 per cent statistical charge (expensive things statistics, particularly considering they're usually wrong!). You must also pay VAT at 7.6 per cent on presentation of evidence of the car's cost.

Cars Owned Longer Than Six Months

If you've owned your car for **at least six months** and are importing it as part of your personal effects, it will be exempt from customs duty and VAT for two years. You're allowed to drive your car in Switzerland for a maximum of one year on foreign registration plates or until they expire if they're only temporary. You will be given a permit (*Bewilligung, permis*) that must be produced on demand if you're stopped by the police in Switzerland. The car must be for your personal use only and mustn't be lent, rented or sold to a third party in Switzerland for one year from the date of importation. Ensure that you're legally insured to drive in Switzerland during this period (see **Foreign Registered Vehicles** on page 214).

Around one month after importing a car, you will receive a letter from your canton's motor registration office (*Strassenverkehrsamt, office de la circulation routière*), informing you that in one year's time your car will require an official serviceability control test (*Fahrzeugkontrolle, contrôle des véhicules à moteur*). If your foreign registration plates are only temporary and aren't renewable, you must have your car tested to obtain Swiss registration plates (see **Control Test** on page 207).

There's sometimes a delay in calling up cars for the control test and you may be able to run your car on foreign plates for longer than one year. When your car is called up for the test, it may be expensive to comply with Swiss safety and pollution regulations, and may not be worth the expense. If you have a right-hand drive car or an old car, it's usually advisable to buy a car in Switzerland before your first year is completed or when your car is called up for test. The authorities may give you just a few weeks notice of the test date and if you decide not to have your car tested you must inform them and export it before the test is due.

After your car passes the test it will require Swiss road tax, insurance and registration plates. **However, you aren't required to pay import duty or tax yet.** You can apply to your motor registration office for deferred duty plates, which are valid for one year and usually renewable for a further year. These plates are distinguished by a red stripe on the right hand side, on which the year and month of expiry is shown in white. Swiss registration plates indicate the canton of residence of the owner (e.g. GE = Geneva, ZH = Zurich) and have both a Swiss flag emblem and the canton insignia on the rear number plate.

After running your car on deferred duty plates for one or two years, you must have it weighed for duty payment. The amount payable also depends on the age and value of the car. You may change your car during the deferred-duty period, but proof of export of your old car must be provided.

Tax-Free Importation

If your stay in Switzerland is only temporary and you're domiciled outside Switzerland (e.g. foreign students and businessmen), you may be eligible to buy a duty-free car **in Switzerland** and run it on tax-free 'Z' plates (*Zollschilder, plaques d'immatriculation douanières*) for a maximum of two years. You may need to provide documentary evidence of your status, as most Swiss residence permit holders are considered by the authorities to be domiciled in Switzerland and aren't eligible. Like deferred duty plates, 'Z' plates are initially issued for one year and can be renewed for a second year. They're available from your canton's motor registration office on presentation of a special certificate from a Swiss insurance company. This certificate states that you have valid insurance and that your car has passed the official Swiss serviceability control test (see page 207). Insurance may be more expensive with 'Z' plates.

If you're planning to leave Switzerland and take up domicile abroad, you may be entitled to buy a duty-free car in Switzerland and run it on 'Z' plates for up to three months prior to your departure. An emigrating person who **retains** Swiss domicile may take delivery of a duty-free car ten days before departure, but may not re-import it into Switzerland without paying duty and tax.

BUYING A CAR

Cars are cheaper in Switzerland than in many other European countries. In addition, you can obtain a discount of around 10 per cent off the list price of most new cars, even when leasing. If you aren't offered a discount, ask for one. If you're buying a used car from a garage and aren't trading in another vehicle, try to negotiate a reduction, particularly when paying cash. **In Switzerland a car is insured and not the driver, so if you test-drive a car it must be insured – you cannot drive it on your own insurance (see page 212).** If a car has licence plates it should be insured, as you're unable to obtain them without insurance (garages have special plates which they can fit to any car).

New Cars

Making comparisons between new car prices in different countries is often difficult, due to fluctuating exchange rates and the different levels of standard equipment. The price of new cars in Switzerland was kept unnecessarily high by importers' cartels and the high cost of personally importing a car from abroad, although this is no longer the case. It's often cheaper to buy a new car from the factory of a European manufacturer or from an exporter in countries which levy high car taxes. This option is worth considering, particularly if you're planning to buy an expensive car. In some countries (e.g. the UK) a tax free car can be purchased up to six months prior to being exported. Personally importing a car from the US is usually much cheaper than buying the same car in Switzerland or elsewhere in Europe. However, you must ensure that it conforms to Swiss specifications. Contact manufacturers and exporters directly for information.

Used Cars

Used cars (*Occasionswagen*, *voiture d'occasion*) in Switzerland are usually good value for money, particularly those over five years old (most Swiss wouldn't be seen dead in an old car unless it's a classic), which are usually in good condition. Nevertheless, if you intend to buy a used car in Switzerland, whether privately or from a garage, check the following:

- That it has passed the official control test (see page 207).

- That it hasn't been involved in a major accident and suffered structural damage. A declaration that it's accident free (*Unfallfrei, sans accident/non-accidenté*) should be obtained in writing.

- That the chassis number tallies with the car registration paper (*Fahrzeugausweis, permis de circulation*).

- That the service coupons have been completed and stamped and that servicing has been carried out by an authorised dealer (if under warranty).

- That the price roughly corresponds to that shown in the TCS monthly guide to used car prices issued by the Touring Club of Switzerland (*Touring Club der Schweiz, Touring Club de Suisse*).

- That import tax and duty have been paid (if applicable).

- Whether a written guarantee is provided.

When buying a car from a garage, some protection is afforded if it's a member of the Swiss Motor Trade Association (*Autogewerbeverband Schweiz, Association Suisse des Automobilistes*, 🖥 www.agvs.ch). Most garages give a warranty on used cars, e.g. three months or 4,000km (around 2,500mi). **Second-hand car prices in the more remote parts of Switzerland (e.g. Graubunden or Valais) are generally higher than in the major cities (e.g. Geneva and Zurich).** If you live in a remote area, it's worthwhile comparing prices in national newspapers and used car sites on the Internet.

Leasing

If you don't want to pay cash or a large deposit, you can usually lease a new or used car. You're still eligible for a discount on most new cars, which should be offered automatically (if you aren't offered a discount, ask for one!). Usually there are no leasing restrictions for foreigners with a B permit (see page 64), although you may not be eligible to lease a car during your first three months in Switzerland. **Bear in mind that the reason there are so many leasing companies is that it's a lucrative way to make money and is generally the most expensive way for an individual to own a car (unless the payments are tax deductible, which they aren't for individuals!).**

On the other hand, interest paid on a car loan, e.g. from your employer or from a bank is tax-deductible, the terms are more transparent and it's usually a lot cheaper. Many leasing contracts have high exit costs, i.e. if you want to cancel the contract early you must pay a higher interest on the time you've had the car, which can amount to several thousand francs. Leasing contracts are also often written in such a way as to avoid the strict rules on consumer credit and may be declared illegal by a court. Before signing a leasing contract, obtain advice from a lawyer or a consumer protection organisation and take out insurance for legal assistance (*Rechtsschutz-versicherung, assurance de la protection*) which will pay for a lawyer if there's a problem with the contract.

Most car manufacturers/importers operate their own leasing schemes. Shop around as leasing contracts vary considerably from garage to garage, even between those selling the same models. There are also a number of independent leasing companies, listed in local phonebooks or on the Internet (🖳 www. search.ch is useful for locating them).

CONTROL TEST

All cars are liable for a stringent official serviceability control test (*Motorfahrzeug-kontrolle (MFK), contrôle des véhicules à moteur/expertisé*). New cars are eligible for the test only after they're four years old, unless there's a change of owner or the owner moves to a different canton. The next test is due when the car is seven years old, and from then every two years. In practice tests may be less frequent, as vehicles require testing only when the owner has been officially informed by a test centre. In some cantons there's sometimes a backlog of cars waiting for test and there have been instances of cars not being called up for months after the due date. You can apply to have your car tested earlier than required, for example if you want to sell it.

Many people won't buy a used car that hasn't had a test in the last year, even when it's offered at a bargain price (the Swiss are a suspicious lot!). If the ownership of a used car that is more than ten years old changes after the first year of the test validation period, the new owner must get the car re-tested. However, had the ownership not changed, the test wouldn't have been due until the end of the test period. If you buy an old car that requires testing, it could need expensive repairs. Get the owner or garage to have it tested before you buy it, or failing that, obtain a written undertaking that the owner will pay for any repairs that are necessary.

If you own an old or imported car which is called up for test, it may be advisable to get a garage to take it in for you or take a mechanic with you. Apart from the fact that their local language ability is probably better than yours, they're usually looked upon more favourably than the general public. If you have any questions regarding the test, it's advisable to discuss them with the testing station in advance. If you get a garage to do a pre-test check on your car, don't ask them to repair it to test standard as this could result in unnecessary expense. Get them to take it for the test to find out what (if anything) needs fixing. Essential repairs recommended by a garage may not be the same as those officially required after the test.

You can have the Automobile Club of Switzerland (ACS) or the Touring Club of Switzerland (TCS) check your car before taking it for the test (in some cantons the TCS is authorised to carry out official control tests). This is advisable, particularly if you plan to register an imported car in Switzerland, as they will tell you what modifications (if any) need to be made. It can be expensive to get a car through the test. For example, a windscreen with a tiny stone chip may need replacing (although this is covered by part or fully comprehensive insurance in Switzerland) and tyres must have at least 1.6 mm of tread over their entire surface. A car without a 'CH' sticker on the back or with no breakdown triangle will also fail. The test is normally completed while you wait and takes around 30 minutes.

The canton test centre is usually located at your canton's motor registration office, the address of which is listed on both your driving licence and car registration paper (*Fahrzeugausweis, permis de circulation*). Business hours are usually 7.30am to 4pm, Monday to Friday. The test costs around SFr. 60, while a full retest is usually about half this and a minor retest even less. When you apply for a test, you're sent a form which must be completed and returned with your car registration paper. If your car fails the control test and you wish to have it repaired at a later date, you can have the registration paper stamped 'invalid' and you won't be required to pay road tax or insurance from this date. When you wish to have the car tested again, you can obtain a 'day plate' from the police to take the vehicle to the test centre.

EXHAUST TEST

All Swiss registered cars with a catalytic converter require an exhaust emission test (*Abgastest, test anti-pollution*) every two years, cars without one must be tested annually. The amount of carbon monoxide, carbon dioxide and hydrocarbons emitted by the exhaust mustn't exceed the manufacturer's limits. If they do, adjustments or repairs must be made to the engine, fuel system or exhaust, as necessary. Cars registered in Switzerland before 1st January 1971 are exempt (older cars registered after this date must have the exhaust test).

A green and white sticker is fixed to the rear or a side window of your car, showing the year and month when the test is next due. The test certificate must be kept in your car and be produced when asked by the police. The exhaust emission test costs between SFr. 50 and SFr. 150 and is usually reduced when combined with a service. If you're stopped by the police without a valid exhaust test certificate (*Abgas-Wartungs-dokument, fiche d'entretien du systeme antipollution*), you can be fined up to SFr. 200.Vehicle anti-pollution controls in Switzerland are among the strictest in Europe and police have pollution meters to detect cars exceeding pollution levels.

CAR REGISTRATION

In Switzerland a new or used car doesn't have registration plates (*Polizeinummer/Autoschild, numéro d'immatriculation*) when purchased. Car registration plates are issued to individuals and when a car is sold they're returned to the issuing canton's motor registration office or transferred to a new car. When you apply to register a car in Switzerland for the first time, you must apply to your canton's motor registration office for registration plates. If you're buying a new or used car from a garage, they will usually apply for the registration plates on your behalf and complete the formalities. When applying for Swiss registration plates for the first time, you must provide the following:

- Your Swiss or foreign driving licence (before you've completed one year's residence in Switzerland, you must obtain a Swiss driving licence);
- Your foreigner's permit (*Ausländerausweis, livret pour étrangers*);
- A certificate of residence (*Wohnsitzbescheinigung, carte d'indigène/attestation de domicile*), available for a fee of around SFr. 5 from your community office;
- A certificate from an insurance company confirming that the car has been insured at least for third party liability.

A new car must undergo an official test (*Prüfgebühr, taxe de contrôle/frais d'examen*) at a canton motor registration office to ensure that it meets Swiss specifications. The test fee (for a car purchased from a Swiss dealer) is about SFr. 130 and the cost of the car registration paper (*Fahrzeugausweis, permis de circulation*) is around SFr. 40 to 60 depending on the canton. The test is arranged by the garage. If you already own a Swiss registered car, your canton's motor registration office requires your existing car's registration paper, plus a valid certificate of insurance for the new car from your insurance company.

When changing cantons or leaving Switzerland, registration plates must be returned to your canton's motor registration office (see **Chapter 20**). Notify your canton's motor registration office within 14 days of a change of car or address, a change of canton or when leaving Switzerland. When you register a car or inform your canton's motor registration office of a change, they will send you a bill (or a refund) for road tax and the car registration fee, as applicable.

If you're buying a new car and haven't sold your old car, or intend to run two or more cars, you can obtain interchangeable registration number plates (*Wechselnummer, plaques interchangeables*) from your canton's motor registration office. This allows you to drive two or more cars on the same insurance and to swap one set of registration plates between them (see **Car Insurance** on page 212). **Only the vehicle bearing the interchangeable registration plates can be parked or used on a public road.**

SELLING A CAR

The main points to note when selling a car are:

- If you intend to buy another car, you must retain your registration plates and transfer them to your new car, provided you remain a resident of the same canton. Car registration includes road tax and you're billed for (or reimbursed) the difference when you register a new car. When leaving Switzerland or changing cantons, you must return your licence plates to the issuing canton's motor registration office within 14 days. An application for new plates must be made in your new canton within 14 days of taking up residence.

● Inform your insurance company. Your insurance for a vehicle is cancelled automatically when your registration is cancelled or transferred. It's the responsibility of the new owner of a car to register his ownership with his canton's motor registration office. The seller or buyer is required to have a car's registration paper cancelled at his canton's motor registration office. **It isn't advisable to sell your car and give the registration paper to the new owner before you've cancelled your registration.** You cannot cancel your insurance until the registration in your name has been cancelled, and the new owner may delay doing this.

● If you're selling your car privately, insist on payment in cash, which is normal practice in Switzerland.

● Include in the receipt that you're selling the car in its present condition (as seen) without a guarantee (*ohne Garantie, sans garantie*), the price paid and the car's kilometre reading. The new owner may ask for a declaration in writing that the car is accident free (*Unfallfrei, sans accident/non-accidenté*). This refers to major accidents causing structural damage and not slight knocks.

● The best place to advertise a car for sale is in local newspapers, on free local notice boards, and in the Friday and Saturday editions of major city newspapers. It doesn't matter if you don't live close to a major city, as major city newspapers are distributed throughout Switzerland. Buyers will travel a long way to buy a car that appears to be good value for money (if nobody calls you will know why!).

DRIVING LICENCE

The minimum age for obtaining a driving licence in Switzerland is 18 for a motor car or a motorcycle over 125cc, 16 for a motorcycle of between 50 and 125cc and 14 for a moped (see page 222). Holders of a full foreign driving licence may drive in Switzerland for one year using a foreign or international driving licence. If you or any members of your family hold a foreign driving licence and intend to remain in Switzerland for longer than one year, you must apply for a Swiss driving licence (*Führerschein, permis de conduire*) during your first year in Switzerland. **If you don't apply during your first year, you aren't allowed to drive after this period until you've passed a Swiss driving test.**

You can apply for a Swiss licence at any time after your arrival, provided that you're living in permanent accommodation and not, for example, in a hotel. Holders of licences from Africa (excluding South Africa), Asia (excluding Japan), Central and South America, and Turkey must pass a practical driving test. If you fail the practical driving test, you're required to take a full Swiss driving test, including a written examination. Some foreign licences, for example licences printed in Arabic or Chinese, must be translated into an official Swiss language or an international licence must be obtained. To apply for a Swiss driving licence you need to:

- Obtain an application form from your canton's motor registration office or an approved optician (see next point).

- Arrange a sight test (around SFr. 20) with your doctor or an approved optician (listed on the back of the application form). The optician will complete a section on the back of the form after the test is completed. The sight test is valid for six months. You require some form of official identification, e.g. a passport or identity card.

- Provide one to three colour passport photographs (approximately 35 by 45 mm and not older than 12 months), as requested by the cantonal authority . This can be obtained from photo booths at most railway stations.

- Complete the application form and take it to your canton's motor registration office (the address is listed on the back of the form) with the following:
  - Your foreign driving licence and if applicable, an international driving licence;
  - Your Swiss residence permit;
  - The completed application form, including the eye test report;
  - One to three passport photographs;
  - A police certificate, if applicable. This certificate is required in some cantons and is available from your canton's foreigners' police (*Fremdenpolizei, police des étrangers*) for around SFr. 15.

Your Swiss driving licence will be sent to you around one week later with a bill and is valid for life. The cost varies wildly depending on your canton of residence (e.g. Basel SFr. 140).

If you're required to take a Swiss driving test (see **Learning to Drive** on page 237), you should note that it's more comprehensive than many foreign tests and includes a written examination and the completion of a first-aid course. The written exam may be taken in English and other languages, although according to some reports the English is almost unintelligible and the local language version may be easier – provided of course you can understand it! You're permitted to make just five mistakes in 60 questions. It can take some months to obtain a Swiss driving licence if you fail the written test a few times, **during which period you aren't permitted to drive in Switzerland.**

An international driving licence is required if you intend to drive in some countries. This may vary depending on which driving licence(s) you hold. Check with a Swiss motoring organisation (see page 232). An international driving licence is obtainable from the ACS or TCS and canton motor registration offices for SFr. 40 and is valid for three years in all countries except the US and Canada. You must provide your passport, a Swiss or foreign driving licence, a passport-size photograph and the fee. A translation of your Swiss or foreign driving licence is required for some countries and is obtainable from Swiss motoring organisations or canton motor registration offices for SFr. 25. Holders of a car driving licence can ride a motorcycle of up to 50cc in Switzerland without a special licence. For motorcycles over 50cc, you must have a motorcycle licence (see page 222).

The new credit card size driving licence recently introduced no longer shows your address and therefore does not have to be re-issued every time you move. If you move to a different canton you now only have to inform the cantonal motoring authority in writing of your new address and of the number of the driving licence.

CAR INSURANCE

The following categories of car insurance are available in Switzerland:

- **Third-Party** (*Haftpflicht, responsibilité civile*) – Includes passenger cover and is compulsory in all cantons.

- **Part Comprehensive** (*Teilkasko, casco partielle*) – Known in some countries as third party, fire and theft. Includes cover against fire, natural hazards (e.g. rocks falling on your car), theft, broken glass (e.g. windscreen) and damage caused by a collision with animals (for example a collision with a deer is possible on some country roads, which incidentally, must be reported to the local police). You can usually choose to pay an excess (*Selbstbehalt, franchise*), for example the first SFr. 500 to 2,000 of any claim, in order to reduce your premium. **Part comprehensive insurance is compulsory in some cantons.**

- **Full Comprehensive** (*Vollkasko/Kollisionskasko, casko intégral (complète)/ assurance tous risques*) – Covers all risks including self-inflicted damage to your own car. You can choose to pay an excess (*Selbstbehalt, franchise*) in order to reduce your premium. Also covers high fliers against collisions with aircraft. It's usually compulsory for leasing and credit purchase contracts.

If you take out third party insurance with a Swiss insurance company and wish to increase your cover to full comprehensive later, you aren't required to do this through your third party insurance company, but may shop around for the best deal. Separate passenger insurance is unnecessary as passengers are automatically covered by all Swiss motor insurance policies. However, extra passenger cover (*Insassen Versicherung, assurance passager/accidents des occupants*) is available for a small extra charge, providing higher financial cover for passengers and including the owner-driver, which third party doesn't. Swiss motor insurance always includes a green card (available free on request), which extends your insurance to most European countries.

The cost of motor insurance in Switzerland is high and varies considerably between insurance companies. Full comprehensive insurance includes part comprehensive but not third party, which is calculated separately. Your foreign no-claims bonus is usually valid in Switzerland, but you must provide written evidence from your present or previous insurance company (not just an insurance renewal notice). The no-claims bonus in Switzerland is a maximum of 70 per cent (increased from 55 per cent a few years ago) and is more generous than in many other countries. However, it may vary for third party and full comprehensive insurance and there isn't a no-claims discount on the part comprehensive part of your insurance. No claims are usually 10 per cent after one year (or step), 20 per cent after two years, 25 per cent after three years and an additional 5 per cent a year up to a maximum of 70 per cent after 12 years. After a claim you usually lose four steps (20 per cent) or two years' no-claims. Accident prone drivers can, however, find themselves paying up to 170 per cent (the maximum) **above** the basic premium.

Inexperienced, young or accident prone drivers, must usually pay an extra excess (*franchise*). Drivers under 25 must pay a 20 per cent loading or the first SFr. 1,000 of a claim and inexperienced drivers (holders of a licence for less than two years) must pay the first SFr. 500 of a claim. The extra premium for full comprehensive insurance for young or inexperienced drivers can be from SFr. 300 to 3,000, depending on the car. Your type of permit (see **Chapter 3**) may also influence the cost of car insurance. B and C Permit holders usually pay the standard rate, but A Permit holders and those on short-term contracts may need to pay up to double and **in advance**. Shop around for an insurance policy and ask companies whether they have higher premiums for foreigners – not all do! If you're staying in Switzerland for only a short period, check whether you can take out a fixed period policy or terminate your insurance at short notice without penalty.

Most insurance companies try to tie you into a five or ten-year contract which you cannot cancel unless your premium is increased (which happens frequently) or you change vehicles. You can, however, tell your insurance broker that you want a shorter term or request that the contract can be cancelled at the end of each year (usually with a notice period of three months). If you want to change companies, you must notify your insurance company in writing by registered letter (your new insurance company will be happy to do this for you).

Some employers may have an arrangement with a car insurance company, whereby employees are offered a discount. Ask your colleagues for their advice and shop around. Motor insurance premiums are usually valid for a full calendar year from January to December. If you take out a policy in mid-year, you may be billed to the end of the year only. Many companies send out bills in advance with 30 days to pay, so that payment is received before the start of the new insurance period.

If you own two or more cars, you need only insure the most expensive one, provided you (or your family members) intend to drive only one car at a time. If this is the case, contact your insurance company and ask them for a interchangeable registration number (*Wechselnummer, plaques interchangeables*) for the vehicles involved. There's an extra insurance charge of around SFr. 100 a year. Registration plates can be fitted with a quick release mount, so that they can be easily swapped between cars. This also means that you pay road tax only on the most expensive car, as only one car can be on the road at a time. An interchangeable number cannot be swapped between a car and a motorcycle, although you can obtain a change number for two or more motorcycles. **If you insure two cars in the same name, you can claim a no-claims bonus for one car only. You must pay the full premium for the other.**

If you're going to be out of Switzerland for at least 30 days but less than one year, you can save a proportion of your car insurance and road tax. To qualify you must remove your car plates, return them with the registration paper to your canton's motor registration office, and inform your insurance company. Upon your return, notify your insurance agent, who will authorise you to reclaim your licence plates from your canton's motor registration office. A car mustn't be driven or parked on a public road without registration plates. Some people garage their cars for around three months during winter, preferring to use public transport when road conditions are bad. Due to the fees and effort involved, it isn't worthwhile taking a car off the road (and reclaiming insurance and road tax payments) for a period of less than three months.

For a small extra premium of around SFr. 20 a year, your insurance company will cover your legal costs (*Rechtsschutz, assurance de la protection*) arising from road accidents (it's also available from Swiss motoring organisations, but is more expensive). A special federal insurance (*Bundesversicherung, assurance fédérale*) scheme covers victims of hit-and-run accidents (see page 227).

Foreign Registered Vehicles

It isn't mandatory for cars insured in an EU member country to have an international insurance 'green' card (*Internationale Versicherungskarte für Motorfahrzeuge, carte internationale d'Assurance automobile/carte verte*) for Switzerland. Motorists insured in an EU country are covered for third party insurance in all EU countries, plus the Czech Republic, Hungary, Liechtenstein, Norway, the Slovak Republic and Switzerland. Most insurance companies in Western Europe provide a 'free' green card, which extends your normal domestic insurance cover to other western European countries (although it doesn't always include Switzerland).

This doesn't include the UK, where you can usually obtain a green card for a maximum of three months and it's expensive. A green card must be signed to be valid and in some countries, e.g. the UK, all drivers must sign it, not just the car owner. Your insurance cover may be invalid if you drive in Switzerland with a foreign insurance policy stating that you're a resident of another country, when you're actually resident in Switzerland. Contact your insurance company to find out your legal position.

If you bring a foreign-registered car to Switzerland, you may need a new insurance policy. This can be either a special European insurance policy (expensive) or insurance with a Swiss company. A few Swiss insurance companies (e.g. Zurich-Versicherungen) will insure a foreign registered car, but usually for a limited period only, e.g. one year.

ROAD TAX

Road tax (*Verkehrssteuer, impôt sur la circulation*) rates in Switzerland vary considerably from canton to canton. It's calculated on the engine size (CC), power (DIN-PS) or the weight of your car, depending on your canton of residence. Canton Ticino are the exception, where they charge a basic premium of around SFr. 150 and add the DIN-PS figure, times the weight of the car, divided by 800 (creating these calculations keeps thousands of civil servants in work). This means you can usually expect to pay around SFr. 180 for a car with an engine size of 1 to 1,079cc; SFr. 200 for a car with an engine size of 1,080cc to 1276cc and SFr. 230 for a car with a engine size of 1,277cc to 1,472cc.

When you register a car with your canton's motor registration office, the road tax bill is sent with your car registration paper. A refund is possible if you leave Switzerland, change cantons or take your car off the road for more than 30 days (see **Car Insurance** on page 212). If you have two or more cars using the same registration number, you must pay road tax only on the most expensive one, as only one vehicle can be on a public road at a time.

An additional motorway tax of SFr. 40 applies to all vehicles up to 3.5 tonnes using Swiss motorways (see **Motorway Tax** on page 77).

GENERAL ROAD RULES

The following general road rules may help you adjust to driving in Switzerland:

- You may have already noticed that the Swiss drive on the right-hand side of the road. It saves confusion if you do likewise!

- All motorists must carry a red breakdown triangle. It must be stored inside the car within reach of the drivers seat, not in the boot, as this may be damaged and jammed shut in an accident. If you have an accident or breakdown, the triangle must be placed at the edge of the road at least 50 metres behind the car on secondary roads and at least 150 metres on 'roads with fast traffic', e.g. motorways.

- Swiss traffic regulations state that you **should** carry first-aid equipment and some chalk (to mark the position of vehicles in case of an accident!). In many European countries it's mandatory to carry a fire extinguisher and a first-aid kit (see **Motoring Abroad** on page 237). If you witness an accident, you must stop and render assistance and give evidence if required. Only give medical assistance when absolutely necessary and when qualified (see also **Accidents** on page 243).

- In towns you may be faced with a bewildering array of signs, traffic lights and road markings. If in doubt about who has priority, always give way (yield) to trams, buses plus all traffic coming from your RIGHT. All drivers must give way to police cars, ambulances and fire engines in emergencies (with disco lights and wailing sounds) and trams and buses, e.g. leaving stops. On secondary roads **without** priority signs (a yellow diamond on a white background, used throughout most of continental Europe) you must give way to vehicles coming from your RIGHT. **Failure to observe this rule is the cause of many accidents.** The priority to the right rule usually also applies in car parks. If you're ever in doubt about who has the right of way, it's generally wise to give way. As the Swiss say 'fairness above all' (*Fairness vor allem, fair-play avant tout*) – particularly when confronted by a 28-tonne truck (might is right!).

  In a situation where all motorists at crossroads must give way to the motorist on their right, it isn't necessary for them to stay there 'until hell freezes over'. Drivers may agree among themselves who has priority (when they end up in a heap, the police must sort out the mess).

- On roundabouts (traffic circles), vehicles on the roundabout have priority and not those entering it, who are faced with a give way sign. Traffic flows anti-clockwise around roundabouts and not clockwise as in the UK and other countries driving on the left. Although the British think roundabouts are marvellous (we spend most of our time going round in circles), they aren't so popular on the continent of Europe, although they're becoming more common.

- The wearing of seatbelts is **compulsory** and includes passengers in rear seats when seatbelts are fitted. In the event of an accident, a Swiss insurance company **isn't obliged** to pay the whole cost of damages when it 'appears' those injured weren't using their seatbelts (benefits may be reduced by up to 50 per cent). Children under the age of 12 may ride in the front of a car, but only when it's impossible for them to ride in the back, e.g. it's already full of under 12-year-olds. Children under seven must occupy a special children's seat, even in the rear of a car. If you're caught with a child under seven who isn't in a child's seat, your licence may be confiscated for several months. Although generally extremely law-abiding, around 25 per cent of Swiss drivers don't always fasten their seatbelts, although you can be fined for not doing so. The Swiss Bureau for the Prevention of Accidents (see **Accidents** on page 243) publish a brochure entitled *Children in Cars*, which compares the different types of baby seats and boosters available for babies and children, plus a general brochure regarding seatbelts.

- Don't drive in bus, taxi or cycle lanes unless it's necessary to avoid a stationary vehicle or obstruction and give priority to authorised users. Bus drivers get irate if you drive in their lanes and you can be fined for doing so. Be sure to keep clear of tram lines and outside the restricted area delineated by a line.

- Dipped (low beam) headlights must be used in tunnels, fog, snowstorms, heavy rain and when visibility is reduced to less than 200 metres. Many people drive around with their headlights blazing most of the time (probably cave-dwellers or people who do most of their driving in tunnels). However, joking aside, this practice has proved to be safer and is mandatory in most Scandinavian countries. It's illegal to drive on parking (side) lights at any time, although many people do it. Front fog or spot lights must be fitted in pairs at a regulation height and should be used only when visibility is less than 50 metres. Rear fog lamps are officially permitted on the offside only (to prevent following vehicles mistaking two fog lamps for brake lights) and although many cars have two, only the offside lamp should be fitted with a bulb. Unfortunately, many Swiss drivers don't know what fog lamps are for and use them when visibility is good (or forget to turn them off), but fail to use them in fog.

- **Note that headlight flashing has a different meaning in different countries.** In some countries it means 'after you' (generally also in Switzerland) and in others 'get out of my ******* way. (It may also mean 'I am driving a new car and haven't yet worked out what all the switches are for'.) A vehicle's hazard warning lights (both indicators simultaneously) may be used to warn other drivers of an obstruction, e.g. an accident or a traffic jam.

- The Swiss are obsessed with amber flashing lights, which are usually a warning to proceed with caution, for example for roadworks, non-functioning traffic lights and to indicate special speed restrictions, particularly on motorways. Many crossroads and junctions have flashing amber traffic lights outside rush hours. Flashing amber lights also operate in conjunction with normal traffic lights, as a warning to watch for cyclists and pedestrians when turning right at junctions.

- You may notice that many traffic lights have an uncanny habit of changing to green when you approach them, particularly during off-peak hours. This isn't magic or a result of your magnetic personality, but due to sensors installed in the road that change the lights to green when no other traffic has priority.

- When two vehicles meet on a narrow mountain road, the ascending vehicle has priority – the other must give way or reverse, as necessary. Postbuses always have right of way irrespective of direction and drivers sound their horns to announce their approach to blind corners and narrow turns. When the road is too narrow to pass, postbus drivers have the authority to give other road users instructions regarding reversing or pulling over to one side.

- On-the-spot fines can be imposed for traffic offences such as minor speeding (see page 228); not being in possession of car papers (see page 224); not removing your ignition key when leaving a vehicle unattended; not using dipped (low beam) headlights at night, in tunnels or in poor visibility; and parking infringements (see page 234). Non-resident foreigners must pay fines on the spot. Residents who are unable to pay on the spot are given a giro payment form, payable within ten days. A fine of around SFr. 50 or more (for any offence) is recorded for posterity on your canton register (see **Crime** on page 373). It pays not to contest a fixed fine unless you have a foolproof defence, because if you lose the case the eventual fine will be much higher.

- Many motorists seem to have an aversion to driving in the right-hand lane on a three-lane motorway, which in effect, reduces the motorway to two lanes. Motorists must signal before overtaking **and** when moving back into an inside lane after overtaking, e.g. on a motorway. If you drive a right-hand drive car, take extra care when overtaking – the most dangerous manoeuvre in motoring.

- When stopped at traffic lights and railway crossings, there may be a sign indicating you must switch off your engine. There are mandatory regulations in some cantons and towns requiring motorists to switch off their engines when waiting at traffic lights or railway crossings. Also known as the 'for purer air – switch off engine' or 'cut your motor' (*Für bessere Luft – Motor abstellen, Coupez le Moteur*) campaigns. You can be fined for not switching off your engine. When stopped in tunnels, e.g. due to a breakdown, accident or traffic jam, you **must** switch off your engine (carbon monoxide poisoning can drastically shorten your life expectancy).

- Approach a railway level crossing slowly and **STOP**:
  - as soon as the barrier or half-barrier starts to fall;
  - as soon as the red warning lights are on or are flashing;
  - in any case when a train approaches.

  Your new car may be built like a tank, but it won't look so smart after a scrap with a 70-tonne locomotive. A heavy vehicle that's slowing traffic is required to stop at the '300 metre' sign before closed railway crossings, to allow other vehicles to overtake it.

- Be particularly wary of moped (*Motorfahrrad/Mofa, vélomoteur*) riders and cyclists. It isn't always easy to see them, particularly when they're hidden by the blind spots of a car or are riding at night without lights. Many moped riders seem to have a death wish and tragically many (mostly teenagers) lose their lives annually in Switzerland (maybe 14 years of age is too young to let them loose on the roads?). They constantly pull out into traffic or turn without looking or signalling. **When overtaking mopeds or cyclists, ALWAYS give them a wide. . . WIDE berth.** If you knock them off their bikes, you may have difficulty convincing the police that it wasn't your fault; far better to avoid them (and the police).

- Drive slowly when passing a stationary tram or bus, particularly a school bus. Where passengers must cross a road to reach a pedestrian path, for example from a tram stop in the middle of the road, motorists must stop and give way.

- A 'CH' (from the latin *Confoederatio Helvetica*) nationality plate (sticker) must be affixed to the rear of a Swiss registered car when motoring abroad. Drivers of foreign-registered cars in Switzerland must have the appropriate nationality plate affixed to the rear of their car. You can be fined on the spot for not displaying it, although it isn't often enforced judging by the number of cars without them (maybe German and Italian-registered cars are exempt?). Cars must show only the correct nationality plate and not an assortment.

- If you need to wear glasses or contact lenses when motoring, it will be noted on your Swiss driving licence and you must always wear them. You must also carry a spare pair of glasses or contact lenses when driving.

- **It's illegal to use a car telephone when driving in Switzerland (unless it's a hands-free phone), for which you can be fined SFr. 100!**

- A roof rack load may be a maximum of 50kg (110lb) for vehicles registered from January 1st 1980 and 10 per cent of a vehicle's unladen weight for vehicles registered before this date.

- Trailers registered in Switzerland may be up 2.1m (6.9ft) wide and 6m (19.7ft) long (tow-bar included). Trailers registered abroad may be up to 2.2m (7.2ft) wide and 7m (23ft) long, but aren't permitted to travel over Swiss mountain passes. A special permit must be obtained at Swiss border posts. If a towing vehicle has insufficient power to pull a trailer or caravan up an incline in heavy traffic, a journey over mountain passes mustn't be attempted. When towing a caravan or trailer of up to 1,000kg (2,204lb) in weight, you're restricted to 80kph (50mph) on motorways and 60kph (37mph) on all other roads (except where lower speed restrictions apply).

- A *Handbook of Swiss Traffic Regulations* is available for SFr. 12 from canton motor registration offices and customs offices. It's recommended reading for all motorists and is available in English, French, German, Italian and Spanish.

SWISS DRIVERS

The most popular Swiss motor sport is a public-road variation of stock car racing, commonly referred to as 'tail-gating' or 'shunting'. The rules of tail-gating are relatively simple: drivers are required to get as close as possible to the car in front **without** making contact, e.g. smashing into its rear. Unfortunately (as with all motor 'sports') there's an element of risk involved, which in this case is exacerbated by the low level of skill of the average participant, many of whom have yet to master the art of stopping at 120kph (or often faster) within a few car lengths. This results in quite a few collisions, often in motorway tunnels and always during rush hours.

A tail-gater usually sits a few metres (centimetres?) from your bumper and tries to push you along irrespective of traffic density, road and weather conditions, or the prevailing speed limit. There's no solution, short of moving out of his way, which is often impossible (if you could move out of the way, there would be no 'fun' in doing it). Flashing your rear fog lamp or warning lights usually has no effect and braking can be disastrous – nothing deters the habitual tail-gater. Sudden stopping and braking are allowed only **in an emergency** and motorists have been successfully sued for damages by someone who has run into the back of them, **because they stopped for no apparent reason.** Always try to leave a large gap between your vehicle and the vehicle in front. This isn't just to allow you more time to stop, should the vehicles in front decide to come together, but also to give the inevitable tail-gater behind you more time to stop. **The closer the car behind you, the further you should be from the vehicle in front.**

The majority of motorists in Switzerland (and many other countries) drive much too close to the vehicle in front and have little idea of stopping distances. The *Handbook of Swiss Traffic Regulations* (see above) states that the safe stopping distance (including thinking distance) is **45m (147ft)** at 60kph (37mph), which increases to a massive **144m (472ft)** at 120kph (74mph). These stopping distances are for dry roads with good visibility and are greatly increased on wet or icy roads. Although these distances may be generous, **they aren't stupid.** If further proof is needed of how dangerous and widespread tail-gating is, simply check the statistics on the number of 'concertina' (multiple car) accidents in Switzerland, particularly on motorways and in tunnels.

The Swiss have a few other motoring idiosyncrasies, one of which is an aversion to using their handbrakes, even when stopped on a hill (they would rather burn their clutch out). Don't get too close as they're likely to roll back into you (it's all part of the racing image, as a good getaway is all important). Other common habits are a tendency to drive in the middle of the road on country lanes and sudden braking when approaching a 50kph or other speed restriction (which can be annoying). In general, Swiss drivers are above average (average is bad) and no worse than most other European drivers. However, some foreigners consider Swiss drivers to be more aggressive and impolite than motorists in many other countries (e.g. the UK and the US). They are, for example, often reluctant to give way to a motorist waiting to pull out into traffic, and on motorways many drivers remain in the overtaking lane and cut across at the last moment when they want to take an exit. Swiss motorists are, however, usually law abiding (except with regard to speed limits), observe parking restrictions (more than most other European motorists) and are kind to animals.

Don't be too discouraged by the tail-gaters and road hogs. Driving in Switzerland is often a pleasant experience, particularly when using country roads, which are relatively traffic free outside rush hours. If you come from a country where traffic drives on the left, most people quickly get used to driving on the 'wrong' side of the road. Just take it easy at first, particularly in winter, and bear in mind that there may be other motorists around just as confused as you are.

WINTER DRIVING

Winter driving in Switzerland needn't be a survival course. Most motorists fit snow tyres (*Schneereifen/Winterreifen, pneu neige*), which although not compulsory help make winter driving safer. If you have an accident on snow in a vehicle that isn't fitted with snow tyres, you may be considered to be at fault if the other vehicles involved have snow tyres, irrespective of other circumstances. In some rural areas, roads aren't cleared of snow, in which case snow tyres may be a necessity. In towns, many roads are salted or gritted in winter, although some cantons have cut down on the use of salt because of its corrosive and anti-environmental properties. Due to the risk of corrosion, many motorists change to steel wheels in winter, rather than fit snow tyres to their expensive alloy wheels (assuming you could buy snow tyres in the correct size). Shop around for the best buys in winter tyres and steel wheels as prices vary considerably.

It's necessary or even compulsory to fit snow chains (*Schneeketten, chaîne à neige*) on a vehicle's driving wheels in some areas, particularly on mountains roads and passes (see below). When chains are necessary, it's indicated by a road sign; ignore it at your peril – driving or sliding off a mountain can damage your health, not to mention what it can do to your car. Buy good quality snow chains and practice putting them on and removing them **before** you get stuck in the snow – even getting the container undone can be a trial with cold numb fingers, let alone fitting them. Studded tyres (spikes) may be used on vehicles up to 3.5 tonnes from 1st November to 31st March. Vehicles with studs are restricted to 80kph (50mph) and aren't permitted to use motorways.

Special winter driving courses are held in all areas of Switzerland, where motorists can learn how to drive on snow and ice (don't, however, expect to compete with Scandinavian rally drivers after a day's tuition). The cost is between SFr. 100 and 200 and courses usually last a whole day. It isn't necessary to use your own car, as you can rent one from the centre (better than wrecking your own). If you use your own car, you can take out special insurance cover for around SFr. 15 to 20 a day. Contact your canton's motor registration office or Swiss motoring organisations for more information (see page 232). The Swiss Conference for Road Traffic Safety (*Schweiz. Konferenz für Sicherheit im Strassenverkehr, Conférence Suisse de sécurité dans le Trafic Routier*) subsidises advanced and special driving courses, e.g. anti-skid courses, for both motorists and motorcyclists in many centres throughout Switzerland.

The edges of most rural roads are marked by two-metre high poles, which are necessary in areas where there's heavy snow (without the poles, even a light snowfall can obscure the edges of the road). Skis carried on ski roof racks should have their curved front ends facing towards the rear of the car.

A few final words of warning. **Take it easy in winter.** In bad conditions you will notice that most Swiss slow down considerably and even the habitual tail-gaters leave a larger gap than usual between them and the car in front. Even a light snow fall can be treacherous, particularly on an icy road. When road conditions are bad, allow two to three times longer than usual to reach your destination.

MOUNTAIN PASSES

Snow chains must be fitted to all vehicles crossing mountain passes in winter (even in summer, freak snow storms can make roads treacherous). Always check in advance whether a pass is open, especially if using the pass means making a detour. A sign on the approach road indicates whether a pass is open (*offen, ouvert*) or closed (*geschlossen, fermé*) and whether chains are necessary.

The following mountain passes are open year round, although opening times may be reduced in winter (e.g. from 7am to 6 or 9pm): Bernina, Brünig, Flüela, Forclaz, Julier, Maloja, Mosses, Ofen (Il Fuorn), Pillon and Simplon. The Albula, Furka, Great St. Bernard, Grimsel, Klausen, Oberalp, San Bernadino, Susten and Umbrail passes are open from June to October. The exceptions are Lukmanier (May to November), St. Gotthard and Splügen (May to October) and the Nufenen pass (June to September). The Great St. Bernard, St. Gotthard and San Bernadino passes have alternative road tunnels open all year round. There's a toll of from around SFr. 30 (depending on your car's wheelbase) to use the Great St. Bernard road tunnel between Bourg St. Pierre and Aosta (Etroubles) in Italy. The status (open/closed) of Swiss alpine tunnels and passes is given on Swiss television teletext.

MOTORCYCLES

The Swiss have a passion for motorcycles and only the Japanese own more bikes per head of population. Switzerland is a great country for bike enthusiasts and its clean mountain air, excellent roads, beautiful scenery and generally good weather (from spring to autumn) make it a Mecca for bikers.

Mopeds

The following rules apply to riders of mopeds (*Motorfahrrad (mofa)*, *vélomoteur*):

- They must be at least 14 years old;
- Permission must be obtained from a parent if they're younger than 18;

- They must have an eye test and pass a written road rules test;
- A licence plate (*Kontrollschild, plaque*) be obtained and/or a *vignette* from their community, which includes road tax and third party insurance. The cost varies considerably (e.g. from SFr. 25 to 70 a year) depending on your canton of residence and is renewable annually by 31st May. Insurance is also available from Swiss motoring organisations, e.g. the VCS (see **Motoring Organisations** on page 232).
- A lock must be fitted which blocks a wheel or the steering or a cable or chain lock must be used;
- A crash helmet must be worn.

An application for a licence must be made to your canton's motor registration office with the following:

- Your Swiss residence permit;
- Two photographs;
- A completed application form, available from your community.

The maximum permitted speed for a moped is 30kph (19mph). Motorists with a car driving licence (Swiss or foreign) may ride a moped without passing a test or obtaining a special licence. Theft insurance can be taken out separately and breakdown assistance is available from Swiss motoring organisations for around SFr. 20 a year. Swiss motoring organisations also run motorcycle instruction courses.

Many moped riders are killed each year in Switzerland, mostly teenagers. If you have a child with a moped, it's important to impress upon him the need to take care (particularly in winter) and not take unnecessary risks, e.g. always observe traffic signals, signal before making a manoeuvre and WEAR A CRASH HELMET (some riders don't bother, although it's against the law). Car drivers often cannot see or avoid moped riders, particularly when they're riding at night without lights or when they dart out of a side street without looking. **Mopeds in the wrong hands can and do KILL!**

Motorcycles Up To 50cc

The following rules are applicable to riders of motorcycles (*Motorrad, moto*) up to 50cc:

- They must be at least 16 years old;
- A crash helmet must be worn;

- They must have valid third party insurance;
- They must always carry their insurance certificate and driving licence.

Motorcycles 50 – 125cc

The following rules are applicable to riders of motorcycles (*Motorrad, moto*) which are between 50 and 125cc:

- They must be at least 18 years old;
- They must attend 8 hours of traffic theory and pass a practical test;
- A crash helmet must be worn;
- Dipped (low beam) headlights must be used at all times;
- They must have valid third party insurance;
- They must always carry their insurance certificate and driving licence.

The same application form is used to apply for a motorcycle licence as for a car driving licence (see page 210) and includes an eye test. After you pass the written road rules test, a provisional licence is issued for three months. This can be extended for a further two months, after which a practical test must be taken.

If you already have a car driving licence then no road rules and practical tests are required but you still have to do a traffic theory course of at least 8 hours.

Motorcycles Over 125cc

The same restrictions apply to motorcycles of over 125cc as to motorcycles of between 50 and 125cc (see above). In addition a traffic theory course of at least 12 hours (6 if you've already passed the test for motorcycles up to 125cc) and a practical test must be taken. **You must be 25 years old to drive motorcycles with an engine power exceeding 25kw (33.5hp).**

For all licences you must have had an eye test, attended a first aid course and passed a road rules test before you can apply for a provisional driving licence.

CAR PAPERS

The following papers must be carried when motoring:

- Driving licence (Swiss if held);
- Vehicle registration papers;
- Exhaust test certificate (Swiss-registered cars only);

- Your insurance certificate and green card (international motor insurance certificate) if applicable. Motorists must also carry their insurance certificate or green card when driving outside Switzerland.

- You should have a European accident report form (*Europäisches Unfallprotokoll, rapport européen des accidents routiers*), although it isn't compulsory.

If you're stopped by the police and are unable to produce your car papers, you can be fined on the spot. It's advisable to make a copy of all your car papers and keep the originals on your person or lock them in the glove box of your car.

ACCIDENTS

General

If you're involved in an car accident (*Verkehrsunfall/Autounfall, accident d'auto*) in Switzerland, the procedure is as follows:

1. Stop immediately. Place a warning triangle at the edge of the road at least 50 metres behind your car on secondary roads or 150 metres on fast roads, e.g. motorways. If possible a triangle should be placed in both directions. If necessary, for example when the road is partly or totally blocked, switch on your car's hazard warning lights and dipped (low beam) headlights and direct traffic around the hazard. In bad visibility, at night, or in a blind spot, try to warn oncoming traffic of the danger, e.g. with a torch or by waving a warning triangle. **Motorists who witness an accident are required by law to stop and render assistance.**

2. If anyone is injured, immediately call a doctor or ambulance (dial 144 in most areas), the fire brigade (dial 118) if someone is trapped or oil or chemicals have been spilled, and the police (dial 117). **If someone has been injured more than superficially the police MUST be summoned.** Don't move an injured person unless absolutely necessary to save him from further injury and don't leave him alone except to call an ambulance. Cover him with a blanket or coat to keep him warm. The REGA helicopter service (see page 134) is available for the evacuation of seriously injured people (☎ 1414 in an emergency situation).

3. If there are no injuries and damage to vehicles or property isn't serious, it's unnecessary to call the police to the accident scene. Contacting the police may result in someone being fined for a driving offence. If you and any other driver(s) involved aren't willing to let your insurance companies deal with the matter, then you're at liberty to call the police. For anything other than a minor accident it's advisable to call the police, as it will be too late to try to

sort out who was at fault afterwards. **It's advisable to report any minor accident to the police within 24 hours to avoid any repercussions later (if someone else reports it and you don't, you could find yourself in trouble and can even end up losing your licence for a period!).**

4. If the other driver has obviously been drinking or appears incapable of driving, call the police. In all cases you mustn't say anything that could be interpreted as an admission of guilt (even if you're as guilty as hell!). Apparently admitting responsibility for an accident, either verbally or in writing, **can release your insurance company from responsibility under your policy**. You must say nothing or only that your insurance company will deal with any claims, and let the police and insurance companies decide who was at fault.

5. If either you or the other driver(s) involved decide to call the police, don't move your vehicle or allow other vehicles to be moved. If it's necessary to move vehicles to unblock the road, mark their positions with chalk (have you ever tried writing on snow or ice with chalk?). Alternatively take photographs of the accident scene if a camera is available or make a drawing showing the positions of all vehicles involved before moving them (there's a space for this on the insurance accident report form)

6. Check whether there are any witnesses to the accident and take their names and addresses, particularly noting those who support **your** version of what happened. Note down the registration numbers of all vehicles involved and their drivers' names, addresses and insurance details. Give any other drivers involved your name, address and details of your insurance, if requested.

7. If you're detained by the police, you will have no right to contact anyone or to have legal representation. If you're travelling with a passenger, ask him to contact anyone necessary as soon as you realise you're going to be detained. **Don't sign a statement, particularly one written in a foreign language, unless you're CERTAIN you understand and agree with every word.**

8. If you've caused material damage, you must inform the owner of the damaged property as soon as possible. If you cannot reach him, contact the nearest police station (this also applies to damage caused to other vehicles when parking).

9. Complete the accident report form (*Europäisches Unfallprotokoll, rapport européen des accidents routiers*) provided by your insurance company as soon as possible after the accident and send it to your insurance company, even if you weren't at fault. **Don't forget to sign it.** If you have an accident, obtain another accident form as soon as possible (accidents usually happen in threes!).

Hit-And-Run Accidents

If you're the victim of a hit-and-run accident, report it to the local canton police immediately, preferably before driving your car away (if possible). They will inspect your car and take photographs and paint samples. This isn't just to help them catch the culprit, but to enable you to make a claim on a special federal insurance (*Bundesversicherung, assurance fédérale*) covering hit-and-run accidents. You or your insurance company must pay the first SFr. 1,000 of a claim and the federal insurance will pay the rest. What a civilised country!

DRINKING & DRIVING

As you're no doubt aware, driving and drinking don't mix – an estimated 20 per cent of Swiss road deaths are a result of drunken driving. In Switzerland, you're no longer considered fit to drive when your blood alcohol concentration exceeds 50mg of alcohol per 100ml of blood, although if you cause an accident you can still be fined if you've been drinking, even when below the legal limit. The law regarding drunken driving is strict. If convicted you will lose your licence for a long period (at least a year), receive a heavy fine (several thousand Swiss francs) and may even be imprisoned. To ensure that they have the same impact on everybody, fines are usually calculated as a percentage of the offender's salary. Anything more than two small beers or a couple of glasses of wine may be too much for some people. Random breath tests can be carried out by the police at any time.

If you have an accident while under the influence of alcohol it can be very expensive. Your car, accident and health insurance may all be nullified. This means you must pay your own (and any third party's) car repairs, medical expenses and other damages. **Anyone who holds a driving licence and travels in a car with a drunken driver is held equally responsible under Swiss law.**

CAR THEFT

Car theft is relatively rare in Switzerland, so rare in fact that there were officially no cars stolen at all in 1993. One reflection of the low rate of car theft is that until recently it was unusual for cars to be fitted with an alarm or engine immobiliser in Switzerland. However, thefts of articles from cars is on the increase in Swiss towns (many trusting Swiss make it easy for thieves by leaving their car windows open and the keys in the ignition!). Don't take any unnecessary risks and always lock your car and put any valuables in the boot or out of sight, particularly when parking overnight in a public place.

Outside Switzerland car theft is rife. When visiting some of Switzerland's neighbouring countries (particularly Italy) you'd be well advised to have foolproof theft insurance and have your car fitted with every anti-theft device on the market. This is particularly important if you own a car that's particularly desirable to car thieves (anything in Italy). For complete peace of mind, you're better off using public transport or hiring a car.

PETROL

Unleaded (*Bleifrei, sans plomb*) petrol costs from around SFr. 1.28 a litre, super plus unleaded costs around SFr. 0.10 more and diesel about SFr. 1.32 a litre. Leaded petrol (around SFr. 1.25 a litre) is becoming increasingly difficult to find but many larger petrol stations sell an additive which allows unleaded fuel to be used in older cars. Unleaded petrol is 95 octane and super plus unleaded petrol 98 octane. The price of petrol can vary from week to week, depending on the value of the US$ and the world market price of crude oil (unlike in some countries, the price of petrol in Switzerland goes both up **and** down). The price of petrol varies by up to SFr. 0.10 to 0.20 a litre, with motorway petrol stations the most expensive and supermarkets the cheapest.

Most large petrol stations are open from around 6am until 10 or 12pm. When paying at self-service petrol stations, either tell the cashier your pump number or hand him the receipt issued by the pump (if applicable). Outside normal business hours, many petrol stations have automatic pumps accepting SFr. 10 and 20 notes. Petrol pumps may also accept international credit cards (e.g. Eurocard and American Express), Reka cheques and credit cards issued by oil companies. **Not all petrol stations accept credit cards, and some of them may just accept certain types.**

In Switzerland you're allowed to carry spare petrol in plastic cans, up to a maximum quantity of 25 litres. **Note that many other countries have restrictions on how much petrol you're allowed to carry in your car (other than in the petrol tank) and some ban plastic petrol cans.** For more information check with a motoring organisation (see page 232).

SPEED LIMITS

The following speed limits are in force throughout Switzerland:

Motorways	120kph (75mph)
Dual-Carriageways	100kph (62mph)
Country Roads	80kph (50mph)
Towns	50 or 60kph (31 or 37mph) or 50kph if not signposted
Residential Roads	30kph (18mph) or as signposted (sometimes 30 or 40kph is signposted for sharp bends)

Some cantons have introduced controversial temporary speed limits (coupled with intensified speed checks) of 100kph (62mph) for cars and 70kph for trucks and cars towing caravans on certain stretches of motorways in July and August, in an attempt to reduce 'summer smog'. In some cities, e.g. Zurich and Basle, 'blue' zones have been established where speed limits have been reduced to 30kph (20mph). Roads in blue zones are liberally dotted with 'sleeping policemen' (speed bumps) and other obstacles to slow traffic.

When towing a caravan or trailer, you're restricted to 80kph (50mph) on motorways and 60kph (37mph) on all other roads. Mobile radar traps and laser detectors (more accurate than radar) are regularly set-up around the country, in addition to permanent photographic radar traps. If you're caught speeding, the police may send you a souvenir picture of your car number plate, with the fine (*Busse/Strafe*, *amende*). Cameras are also positioned at major intersections to photograph the registration numbers of cars driving through red lights. Many fines for motoring offences were sharply increased in 1996.

Swiss law requires motorists to adapt their speed to the weather, visibility and road conditions. In particular, you must be able to come to a full stop within the distance you can see. This means that you can be fined for speeding, for example at night or in bad weather, even if you were driving within the speed limit.

Speeding fines depend on the speed above the legal speed limit, and for serious offences, the offender's number of previous motoring convictions. For marginal speeding 1 to 5kmh above the limit the fine is SFr. 40, except on motorways where it's SFr. 20. Fines for driving more than 5kmh above the speed limit depend on where the offence was committed, e.g. town centre, town suburb or country road/motorway. Fines for 6 to 10kmh above the limit are from SFr. 60 to 120, 11 to 15kmh above (SFr. 120 to 250), 16 to 20kmh above (SFr. 180 to 240) and 21 to 25kmh above (SFr. 260 on a motorway). If you're caught doing over 15kmh above the speed limit in a town centre, over 20kmh in a suburb or on a country road or over 25kmh on a motorway, you must appear in court, will be heavily fined (e.g. SFr. 500 to 1,000) and could also lose your licence for a period.

If you're stopped by the police for marginal speeding (where a fixed penalty applies), fines can be paid on the spot or by giro payment within ten days (they **must** be paid on the spot if you're a foreign visitor, although if you're unable to pay they won't usually impound your car). Swiss driving licences aren't 'endorsed' (stamped), where a number of offences (or points) results in an automatic ban. Nevertheless an accumulation of offences (not just for speeding) can result in a driving ban. Fitting and using radar warning devices is illegal in Switzerland and in most other European countries. You're forbidden to drive on motorways in the fast lane unless overtaking, and where signposted, below a minimum speed limit (you can be fined for doing so).

Many Swiss motorists have a complete disregard for speed limits, particularly during rush hours on motorways. The police could have a field day any time they wanted, although police cars are rarely seen on motorways (but they also use unmarked cars), except when attending accidents. Motorists tend to drive faster in southern Switzerland and are generally less disciplined than motorists in the north.

GARAGES

Garages in Switzerland are generally open from 7am to 6.30pm and most close for lunch between noon and 1pm. Servicing and repairs are expensive (particularly in major towns), but the quality of work is generally of a high standard. You may find that smaller garages (not unqualified back street places, but reputable garages who guarantee their work) are cheaper than main dealers. If you require a major repair job or service and are able to drive your car, it may pay you to have it done outside Switzerland. Similarly, if you require new tyres or a new exhaust, they may be cheaper in one of Switzerland's neighbouring countries.

Most garages, including all main dealers, provide a replacement car (*Ersatzwagen, véhicle du remplacement*) for around SFr. 50 a day, while your car is being serviced. Some garages supply a free car when you have a service done and charge for petrol only. If you're a member of a Swiss motoring organisation such as the TCS (see page 232), you can have your car tested for around SFr. 60 and receive an accurate estimate of any repairs necessary.

ROAD MAPS

The following road maps (*Strassenkarte, carte routière*) are among the best available:

- Good free maps of Switzerland are available from city tourist information offices, car rental offices and many Swiss banks. Switzerland Tourism offices sell a good map of Switzerland for SFr. 1.

- An excellent road map of Switzerland is available from offices of the Zurich insurance company.

- A detailed Swiss road map book entitled *Auto Schweiz* (*Suisse*) is published by Kümmerly + Frey, containing 35 town plans (it's also available without the town plans).

- The ACS and TCS Swiss motoring organisations produce many Swiss road maps (see page 230).

- Free local town maps are available from many tourist information offices. More detailed maps are available from bookshops, news agencies, kiosks and railway station booking offices. Local village maps can usually be obtained from community offices.

- A safety road map of Switzerland is available from the Red Cross for SFr.15.80 (✉ christine.beyeler@redcross.ch).

Unfortunately Switzerland doesn't have any large-scale maps for rural areas containing a comprehensive street index.

CAR RENTAL

Major international car rental companies (e.g. Avis, Budget, Europcar and Hertz) are represented in most cities in Switzerland and at international airports (offices are open from around 6.30am until 11pm). Cars can also be rented from local garages and car rental offices in most towns. Look under car rentals (*Autovermietungen/Mietwagen, location de voitures*) in the telephone directory or on the Internet (e.g. 💻 www.avis.ch, www.budget.ch, www.europcar.ch or www.hertz.ch). Rental cars in Switzerland have a special registration plate with a 'V' (for *vermietet* or rented) after the number.

Car rental is generally **very** expensive in Switzerland and around double the cost in many other European countries and up to three times the rate in the US. Rental costs vary considerably between rental companies, particularly over longer periods (weekly and monthly rates are lower). Renting a car from an airport is the most expensive, as are one-way rentals. Older cars can be rented from many garages at lower rates than those charged by the multinational companies. In winter, rental cars are fitted with winter tyres and usually supplied with snow chains and ski racks at no extra charge. Rental cars can be ordered with a portable telephone, a luggage rack and child's seats (for an extra charge).

A new service introduced by the SBB in 1998 is Mobility Car Sharing, where you pay an annual subscription of SFr. 250 or SFr.150 when combined with a half-fare travel card, a *Streckenabonnement* of the Swiss federal railway, a *Generalabonnement*, or a Migros membership card. You can reserve a car from some 980 railway stations and are charged a low rate based on the time used and the kilometres travelled. For more information contact Mobility Car Sharing, Schweiz, Gütschstrasse 2, CH-6000 Lucerne 7 (☎ 041 248 22 22, 💻 www. mobility.ch). Mobility members also receive a 20 to 30 per cent discount on Hertz car rentals in Switzerland and a 10 per cent discount in Europe.

In addition to standard saloon cars, you can also rent a 4-wheel-drive car, station wagon, minibus, luxury car, armoured limousine or a convertible, often with a choice of manual or automatic gearbox. Minibuses accessible to wheelchairs can also be rented, e.g. from Hertz. In some cities, e.g. Geneva, electric cars with a limited range can be rented from Avis, Hertz and Sixt-Alsa. Vans and pick-ups are available from the major rental companies by the hour, half-day or day, or from smaller local companies (which are cheaper than the major companies). When you have your car serviced or repaired, most garages will rent you a car for a nominal sum or even lend you one free of charge (see **Garages** on page 230).

To rent a car in Switzerland you require a valid Swiss, European or international driving licence, which must have been held for a minimum of one year. The minimum age of a driver must usually be 20 or 21 and can be as high as 25 for some categories of cars. It's usually necessary to have a credit card to rent a car in Switzerland. **Don't be late returning a car as it can be expensive.**

One way to reduce the cost of car rental in Switzerland is to rent a car through the US office of an international car rental company and pay by credit card. This is a legitimate practice and can save you up to 50 per cent on local rates. The US freephone (800) numbers of rental companies, such as Alamo, Avis, Budget and Hertz can be obtained from international directory enquiries and must be prefixed by the international access number.

MOTORING ORGANISATIONS

There are three Swiss motoring organisations:

- **The Automobile Club of Switzerland** (*Automobil Club der Schweiz (ACS), Automobile Club Suisse*);
- **The Touring Club of Switzerland** (*Touring Club der Schweiz (TCS), Touring Club de Suisse*);
- **The Transport Club of Switzerland** (*Verkehrs-Club der Schweiz (VCS), Association Suisse des Transports*).

There are few essential differences between the services provided by the two largest Swiss motoring organisations, the ACS and TCS, although charges vary. The services provided by the VCS are more limited. The annual membership fee is around SFr. 75 for one vehicle (VCS around SFr. 50) plus a registration fee (e.g. SFr. 20). There are reduced fees for spouses and juniors, and company membership is also possible.

The ACS and the TCS (and, to a lesser extent, the VCS) provide a wide range of services, which may include official control and pre-control serviceability tests; estimation of repair costs; verification of repairs and bills; guarantee claims; holiday luggage and travel insurance; car, motorcycle and cycle insurance; travel bureau and ticket office services; hotel reductions; valuations of used cars; legal and technical advice; advice on buying cars; running cost estimates (per km); tyres and car accessories; customs' documents; information about road conditions; tourist information; road maps and tourist guides; free national and canton newspapers; international driving licences; and translations of Swiss driving licences.

Members of Swiss motoring organisations who break down anywhere in Switzerland can call service telephone number 140 (24-hour service) for free help (non-members can also obtain assistance, but it can be expensive). Emergency SOS roadside telephones (painted orange) are provided throughout Switzerland on motorways, mountain passes and in tunnels. Black arrows on white posts at the side of motorways show the direction of the nearest telephone (situated every 1.6km/1mi). Keep your membership card in your car and quote your number when calling for help. In Switzerland, membership includes the breakdown patrol service, towing to a garage, or transportation of your car to your home garage. In addition, when necessary, the cost of a taxi to the nearest bus or rail station, a taxi home or a hotel room will be paid. Swiss motoring organisations have reciprocal arrangements with motoring organisations in most European countries.

All Swiss motoring organisations provide a comprehensive international travel insurance policy, called a 'protection letter' (*Schutzbrief, livret*), which covers most travel accident possibilities. If you have a car accident or a breakdown abroad the protection letter insurance will pay for hotel and medical costs, car rental and essential repairs, or shipment of your car back to Switzerland. This insurance is valid irrespective of the mode of transport used and can be taken out with the TCS for Europe (including Russia) and the Mediterranean countries or the whole world. The VCS insurance covers only Europe and the Mediterranean countries, while ACS offer world-wide cover only. Insurance costs from around SFr. 50 to 160 a year, depending on the motoring organisation and whether you have European or world-wide cover.

Letters of credit cover car rental (vouchers for Avis or Hertz), repairs, emergency medical attention, legal aid, technical survey and police fines (resulting from an accident). The letters of credit and your identity card (*Ausweiskarte, carte d'authentification*), which must be signed, should be kept in a safe place. The TCS protection letter also covers holiday or travel cancellation fees, or fees incurred by curtailment of a holiday when caused by an emergency. The insurance provided by the protection letter is much cheaper than most holiday travel insurance, **but you should ensure that it includes all your travel insurance requirements.**

Legal expenses insurance (*Rechtsschutz, assurance de la protection*, covering legal costs in the event of an accident, is available from Swiss motoring organisations but is usually cheaper from Swiss motor insurance companies. The ACS or TCS can also help you when you're locked out of your car (better still to have spare keys or a friend who's a car thief).

Swiss motoring organisations have offices in all major cities and large towns and the head offices of the these organisations are as follows:

- **The Automobile Club of Switzerland (ACS)**, Wasserwerkgasse 39, Postfach, CH-3000 Berne 13 (☎ 031 328 31 11, ⌨ www.acs.ch);

- **The Touring Club of Switzerland (TCS)**, ch. de Blandonnet 4, Case postale 820, CH-1214 Vernier (☎ 022 417 27 27, ⌨ www.tcs.ch);

- **The Transport Club of Switzerland (VCS)**, Lagerstr. 18, CH-3360 Herzogenbuchsee (☎ 062 956 56 56, ⌨ www.vcs-ate.ch);

PARKING

Parking in Swiss towns can be a problem, particularly on-street parking. In most towns there are many public and multi-storey car parks, indicated by the sign of a white 'P' on a blue background. In cities there are also hundreds of parking meters, but they usually all seem to be constantly occupied, particularly on Saturdays. In some cities, e.g. Berne, there are signs that direct you to a car park with free places. Parking in towns costs SFr. 2 to 3 per hour. Parking in a centrally located city car park costs at least SFr. 2 an hour and 24 hours can cost SFr. 25 or more. Geneva introduced an obligatory parking sticker for the central area in an effort to reduce traffic pollution. Cheaper parking is often available not far from city centres and some city shopping centres allow a period of free parking, e.g. three hours. You may prefer to drive to a convenient railway station or a park and ride (P+R) area, where bus or train connections are available to city centres. A 'P+R' parking ticket may also include the cost of the bus or tram journey to and from the local town centre. P+R parking at railway stations costs from SFr. 2 to 10 per day (average SFr. 4) and monthly rates are available for commuters (typically a 50 per cent reduction).

If you park in a multi-storey car park, make a note of the level and space number where you park as it can take a long time to find your car if you have no idea where to start looking! Tear-off slips showing the parking level (*Geschoss/Stockwerk, etage*) are sometimes provided at lifts in multi-storey car parks. On entering most car parks you take a ticket from an automatic dispenser. You must pay **before** collecting your car, either at a cash desk (*Kasse/Caisse*) or via a machine, which may accept both coins and notes. Some of them also accept credit cards. **You cannot pay at the exit.** After paying you usually have around 15 minutes to find the exit, where you insert your ticket in the slot of the exit machine (in the direction shown by the arrow on the ticket). In some ski resorts, parking in a multi-storey car park is free for skiers or anyone using the ski lifts. You must stamp your car park ticket in a machine, usually at the station above the car park level, in order to exit from the car park without paying. **Headlights should be used in all underground and badly lit garages.**

Swiss companies don't usually provide employees with free parking facilities in large cities and towns. Outside main towns, free parking is usually available at or near offices or factories. Disabled motorists are provided with free or reserved parking spaces in most towns, shopping centres and at airports, but must display an official disabled motorist badge inside their windscreen (some city car parks also have spaces reserved for women near the exit). Regular drivers for the disabled can also obtain special parking permits in some cities. Apart from off-street parking, e.g. multi-storey car parks, the following kinds of on-street parking are provided in most towns:

- **Parking meters**, where the maximum permitted parking period varies from 15 minutes to ten hours. Meter-feeding is illegal and you must vacate the parking space when the meter time expires. Meters usually accept a combination of 50 cent and one franc coins. The costs varies, e.g. in Zurich it's SFr. 1 per hour in the city centre and SFr. 0.50 outside. Most meters are in use from 7am to 7pm, Monday to Friday and from 7am to 4pm on Saturdays (check the meter to be sure), and some are free during lunch periods, e.g. noon to 2pm. Meters at railway stations may be in use 24 hours a day.

- **White zones**, indicated by white road markings and a sign, permit free unlimited parking.

- **Blue zones** (*Blaue Zone, zone bleue*), indicated by blue road markings, require a parking disc (*Parkscheibe, disque de stationnement*) to be displayed behind your car windscreen. Parking discs are available free from Swiss motoring organisations, police stations, banks, hotels, insurance offices, kiosks and tourist offices. Motor accessory shops and garages also sell them for a few francs. A new EU-compatible parking disk was introduced in January 2003. The parking disk has to be set to the next half or full hour and then allows one hour of parking from that time. For example, if you arrive at 9.50am you set your parking disk on 10am and can leave the car in the parking space until 11am. If you arrive at 10.05 am you set the car to 10.30 am and are allowed to use the parking space until 11.30am. Free parking is also permitted from 6pm until 9am the next day. In some towns, it's possible to purchase a permanent pass from your local traffic office or some police stations, valid for extended parking in a blue zone. However, it's normally valid only in your local postcode area.

- **Pay and display** parking areas, where you must buy a parking ticket (showing the parking expiry time) from a ticket machine and display it behind your car windscreen. These areas include both on and off-street parking areas and may include park and ride (P+R) car parks, e.g. at railway stations. There may be a maximum parking period of around two hours in town centres.

The attitude towards illegal parking is much stricter in Switzerland than in most other European countries, although the Swiss still seem to park anywhere in the cities. You're forbidden to park on footpaths (even with one or two wheels) anywhere in Switzerland, unless signposted and marked otherwise (in some towns parking spaces include part of the footpath, shown by a line).

You can be fined for parking illegally in a private parking area. Parking illegally in reserved car parking spaces can result in a heavy fine, e.g. SFr. 100 (private parking spaces may be reserved by local residents and aren't used during business hours only). Private parking spaces are sacred in Switzerland and **very** expensive. For minor parking offences in some car parks, e.g. exceeding the permitted parking time by up to half an hour, you may be fined

SFr. 10, which must be inserted in the envelope provided and deposited in a special box at the exit. Parking fines were increased considerably in 1996, e.g. SFr. 40 for exceeding the allowed/paid time by up to two hours, SFr. 60 from two to four hours and SFr. 100 for four to ten hours. In some towns you can be fined for parking facing the wrong way, i.e. you must be able to pull out directly into the flow of traffic on the same side of the road as you're parked. If you receive a parking ticket, it's usually thoughtfully accompanied by a giro payment form (*Einzahlungsschein, bulletin de versement*) and is payable within ten days. You will be sent a reminder letter if you don't pay a fine on time and it may be increased as a consequence.

Be careful where you park your car in the mountains, particularly during spring when the snow is melting and the weather is wet and/or stormy. It isn't unknown for falling rocks (even small ones) to make large dents in cars.

PEDESTRIAN ROAD RULES

The following road rules apply to pedestrians in Switzerland:

- Motorists **must** stop for a pedestrian waiting at a pedestrian crossing if the pedestrian shows by any action his intention to cross the road. However, you should still take extra care when using pedestrian crossings in Switzerland as Swiss motorists aren't fond of stopping. If you come from a country where motorists routinely approach pedestrian crossings with caution and stop when pedestrians are waiting, **take extra care** (20 per cent of Swiss road fatalities are pedestrians).

- Pedestrians are forbidden to cross a road within 50 metres of a pedestrian crossing, bridge or subway (pedestrian underpass).

- Teach your children the green cross code: look **left**, look **right**, look **left** again, before crossing the road (remember that traffic drives on the **RIGHT** hand side of the road). In school, children are taught to stop, look, listen and walk.

- Pedestrians must wait for a green light before crossing the road at a pedestrian crossing with pedestrian lights, regardless of whether there's any traffic. You can be fined for jay walking, i.e. crossing the road where it's prohibited or against a red pedestrian light.

- Pedestrians must use footpaths where they are provided or may use a bicycle path when there's no footpath. Where there's no footpath or bicycle path, you must walk on the left side of the road facing the oncoming traffic.

MOTORING ABROAD

When motoring abroad **NEVER** assume that the rules, regulations and driving habits are the same as in Switzerland. Always take your Swiss (or foreign) driving licence, car registration and insurance papers (e.g. green card), and bear in mind such things as breakdown insurance, essential spares, and security for your car and belongings. Check that your car complies with local laws and that you have the necessary equipment, such as a warning triangle(s), first-aid kit and fire extinguisher. If in doubt, check the latest laws and regulations with a Swiss motoring organisation.

The most dangerous European countries for motorists vary depending on which newspapers or magazines you read and whose statistics they use. However, it's undeniable that the likelihood of having an accident is much higher in some countries. Driving in some European cities is totally chaotic, a bit like the dodgems without the fun, and nerve-wracking at the best of times. It's no way to spend a relaxing holiday. If in doubt about your ability to cope with the stress or the risks involved, you'd be wiser to fly or take a train.

LEARNING TO DRIVE

The following points are applicable to learner drivers in Switzerland:

- You must be at least 18 years old.
- You must have attended a first-aid-course and passed a written road rules test which can be taken in English and other foreign languages.. There are 50 questions in each of the ten possible examinations (one is randomly chosen for you). A booklet containing the 850 possible questions of the basic theory examination (in German, French and Italian) is available from your canton's motor registration office. Once you've passed the test you can apply for a provisional driving licence.
- You must attend eight hours of compulsory traffic theory (costing for example round SFr. 240 at Migros Club School). This cannot be done before the road rules test has been passed.
- You must display an 'L' plate (white L on a blue background) at the rear of your car.
- You aren't permitted on busy roads, including motorways, until you're proficient enough.
- A fee of around SFr. 250 is payable (depending on your canton), which includes the cost of the provisional driving licence, the test fee (written and practical), and a book of the rules of the road.

- You must always be accompanied by a qualified driver who has held a full driving licence for at least three years.

- It isn't compulsory to take driving lessons with a driving school (*Fahrschule, auto-école*) before obtaining your licence. Nevertheless it's advisable as the instructors know the standard demanded by examiners. Instruction is available in most languages. Reckon on around 20 to 30 hours of instruction costing from around SFr. 75 an hour (plus a one-off insurance fee of about SFr. 60).

- You must complete a 10-hour first-aid course (*Nothelferkurs, cours de premier secours*) at a federally approved institute, e.g. the Migros Club School (see **Day & Evening Classes** on page 316) or a motoring organisation.

In some cantons, the practical driving test can be taken only three times. After the third failure you must see a psychologist who will decide if you're psychologically fit to drive (many 'qualified' drivers would immediately be confined to a padded cell if they had to take this test!). On the recommendation of the psychologist you may take the test a fourth **and final time**. In other cantons, (e.g. Zurich), after the 3rd failure of the practical exam, you're put into a special, smaller class where you can receive the personal attention required to pass the exam. Swiss motoring organisations run 'refresher' courses for senior citizens (aged 55 plus). If you're over 70 years old you need confirmation from your GP every year that you're still fit to drive.

USEFUL TELEPHONE NUMBERS

Number	Service
117	Police (emergencies only)
118	Fire (emergencies only)
144	Ambulance (emergencies only)
1414	Rega Helicopter Rescue
140	Vehicle Breakdown
163	Road Reports (recorded information)

The above telephone numbers can be dialled from anywhere within Switzerland and are manned or provide recorded information (in the local language: French, German or Italian) 24-hours a day.

12.

HEALTH

Switzerland spends around 10 per cent of its GDP on health, some SFr. 40,000 million a year, which is one of the highest percentages in the OECD. Although Swiss health insurance is expensive (only North Americans and Swedes spend more on health care) and becoming more so every year, value for money and the quality of health services are among the best in the world. Switzerland has a wealth of modern hospitals, excellent doctors (the highest ration of doctors to patients in the world) and highly-trained nurses, employing the latest equipment and medical techniques. If you must get sick you could hardly choose a better place, provided of course that you're insured or can afford to pay the bill! There are generally no waiting lists for operations or hospital beds and the standard of treatment is second to none. Two yardsticks used to measure the quality of health care are the infant mortality rate and life expectancy. Switzerland has the lowest infant mortality rate in the world (around five deaths in the first year for every one thousand live births) and its life expectancy of 83 for women and 77 for men is exceeded only by Japan.

The Swiss are among the healthiest people in the world, although according to some reports, the famous Swiss air isn't always as fresh as the guide books would have you believe. Despite strenuous efforts to reduce pollution, impure air and high ozone levels in summer in the major Swiss cities is causing health problems (mainly respiratory ailments and allergies), particularly among children. However, the Swiss are excessive when it comes to health matters and compared with what passes for fresh air in most countries, their city air is pure oxygen. Some of the pollution may be caused by smokers, as Switzerland rates highly in the world smoking league (per head of population) and has a particularly high proportion of young women smokers. The main causes of death in Switzerland are heart disease (around 45 per cent) and cancer (some 25 per cent).

The Swiss are prominent in the lucrative immortality business (body, mind and soul transplants), including plastic surgery, rejuvenation and regeneration clinics, spa treatment centres and therapies by the dozen. Cellular rejuvenation (a snip at around US$10,000) patients are injected with live sheep cells – Switzerland abounds with geriatrics prancing around like spring lambs. Complementary medicine is also popular in Switzerland (particularly homeopathy) and is usually paid for by Swiss health insurance. Hay fever sufferers can obtain the daily pollen count (*Pollenbericht, pollen bulletin*) between March and July from Swiss television teletext and the daily newspapers. You can safely drink the water in Switzerland, but the wine and beer taste much better.

EMERGENCIES

The action to take in a medical 'emergency' (*Notfall, urgence*) depends on the degree of urgency. The emergency medical services in Switzerland are among the best in the world. Keep a record of the telephone numbers of your doctor and local emergency hospital and other emergency telephone numbers (see page

133) near your telephone. Emergency first-aid information is available at the back of all telephone directories in French, German and Italian. If you're unsure who to call, dial the police on 117, who will either tell you who to contact or will contact the appropriate service for you. The action to take in an emergency may include one of the following:

● Call 144 for an ambulance. Most ambulances are equipped with cardiac equipment and special cardiomobiles are provided for emergency cases. See also the Swiss air rescue service (REGA) on page 134.

● Call your family or personal doctor. Outside surgery hours a telephone answering machine will give you the telephone number of the doctor on call. If you're physically capable, you can go to the emergency treatment centre (*Notfalldienst, service d'urgence*) of a hospital or an emergency clinic (*Pikett-Dienst, permanence*) for minor casualties in French-speaking Switzerland. You may need to show proof of your health insurance. Emergency cases involving non-Swiss residents without insurance and no means to pay may be turned away, although this is unlikely and won't happen in a life or death situation.

In major cities a telephone number is provided where a doctor is available to advise you on medical and psychiatric emergencies. Call the telephone operator on 111 and ask for the emergency medical Service (*Ärztlicher Notfalldienst/Zentrale Örtliche Notfalldienst, médecin de service/médecin de jour*). The operator keeps a list of doctors, dentists, pharmacies and veterinarians who are on call 24-hours a day. Doctors and dentists are categorised by speciality, location and the languages spoken.

If you have an existing medical problem that cannot easily be seen or recognised, e.g. a heart condition, diabetes, a severe allergy (e.g. penicillin), epilepsy or a rare blood group, you may be interested in Medic-Alert. Medic-Alert members wear an internationally recognised identification bracelet or necklace emblem. On the back of the emblem is engraved your medical problem, membership number and a telephone number. When you're unable to speak for yourself, doctors, police or anyone providing aid can obtain immediate vital medical information from anywhere in the world by telephoning a 24-hour emergency number. Medic-Alert is a non-profit registered charity. Members pay for the cost of the emblem and a small annual fee. For more information contact the Medic-Alert Foundation, 1 Bridge Wharf, 156 Caledonian Road, London N1 9UU, UK (☎ 020-7833 3034, 🖥 www.medicalert.co.uk).

ACCIDENTS

If you have an accident resulting in an injury, either to yourself or a third party, inform the following, as necessary:

- Your family or any doctor (if treatment is necessary);
- The police (may be compulsory within 24 hours);
- Your accident insurance company (who will send you a form to complete);
- Your employer. If you have an accident at work, report it to your manager or boss as soon as possible. If you have an accident outside work, you need to inform your employer if you work more than eight hours a week as you will have accident insurance through your employer.

An accident report form must be completed for all accidents where medical treatment is necessary and which result in a claim on your accident insurance. As a general rule, Swiss accident or health insurance policies pay for medical treatment only when the patient remains in Switzerland. Journeys abroad while undergoing a course of treatment as the result of an accident may require the consent of your insurance company. The length of time during which you remain on full pay after an accident, usually depends on your length of service (see **Salary Insurance** on page 264).

For information on how to prevent and avoid accidents (road, sport, household, garden and leisure), contact the Swiss Bureau for the Prevention of Accidents (*Schweiz. Beratungsstelle für Unfallverhütung, Bureau suisse de prévention des accidents*), Laupenstr. 11, Postfach 8236, CH-3001 Berne (☎ 031 390 22 22, 💻 www.bfu.ch). The bureau publishes numerous free leaflets and a magazine, available on subscription. See also the Swiss air rescue service (REGA) on page 134.

DOCTORS

There are excellent doctors (*Arzt, médecin*) everywhere in Switzerland, many of whom speak reasonable or good English. Many embassies in Switzerland keep a list of English-speaking doctors in their area or doctors who speak their national language, and your employer or colleagues may also be able to recommend someone. Doctors are listed in telephone directories under *Aerzte, médecin* and their speciality. General practitioners (GPs) or family doctors are listed under *Allgemeine Medizin or médecin général* (alternatively you can try the Internet at 💻 www.doktor.ch). A zero with a diagonal line through it alongside a telephone number signifies a 24-hour answering service. Most doctors list both their surgery and home telephone numbers. Many major cities operate an emergency medical service (*Ärztlicher Notfalldienst, médecin de service*) where a list of doctors is kept, categorised by speciality, location and languages spoken.

If you're working or studying in Switzerland it's mandatory to have health insurance (see page 266), which may influence your choice of doctor. You may usually go to any doctor anywhere, although each canton has different rules and procedures. An appointment must usually be made before visiting a doctor (except in 'emergencies'). Most surgeries are closed on one day or afternoon a week and many doctors have Saturday morning surgeries. Be prepared to wait anything up to an hour past your appointment time (the only time your doctor will be punctual is when you're late!). Doctors in Switzerland make house calls only in dire emergencies.

There are specialists for many fields of medicine in Switzerland, which in many other countries are treated or dealt with by a general practitioner (GP). These include specialists for children's illnesses, internal disorders and maternity related problems. Your doctor is able to proffer advice or provide information on all aspects of health or medical after-care, including blood donations, home medical equipment and special counselling. Many doctors' surgeries in Switzerland are equipped to do simple tests (e.g. blood and urine), take X-rays and carry out most out-patient treatment performed in a clinic or small hospital. This is particularly true in villages and remote areas, where the nearest clinic or hospital may be some distance away.

It isn't always necessary to be referred to a specialist by your family doctor and you're usually free to make an appointment directly with, for example an eye specialist, gynaecologist or orthopaedic surgeon. If in doubt, ask your health insurance company for advice. There may be a long waiting list for an appointment with a specialist if you aren't an urgent case and your GP may be able to get you an earlier appointment. If you go to your doctor for treatment of an injury as the result of an accident, e.g. skiing, you must inform your accident insurance company within a few days. If you work over eight hours a week, treatment is free, as you're covered by your compulsory accident insurance (see page 263).

When you receive a bill from your doctor, you should pay it within the period specified (usually 30 days) and send it to your health fund or insurance company. Your health fund (see **Health Insurance** on page 266) usually reimburses up to 90 per cent of the cost. If you send your health fund your bank account details (bank name, branch and account number) or post office account number, they will pay refunds directly into your account and advise you when payment has been made. You should scrutinise all bills carefully, as it isn't unknown for doctors to overcharge.

Keep all receipts for health treatment. If your family's total health bills (including dental bills) that **aren't** covered by health insurance amount to 5 per cent or more of your annual income, then you're able to offset the cost against your income tax bill.

DRUGS & MEDICINES

Drugs and medicines prescribed by a doctor are obtained from a pharmacy (*Apotheke, pharmacie*) denoted by the sign of a green cross on a white background. At least one 'duty' pharmacy is open outside normal opening hours in all areas (a list is published in local newspapers and posted on pharmacy doors) for the emergency dispensing of drugs and medicines. In most cities, several pharmacies are open until late evening (e.g. 10pm) and some provide a 24-hour service on certain days or even seven days a week. Ask the telephone operator (111) for the address. **A surcharge (e.g. SFr. 2) is made on medicines purchased after normal closing hours and before 10pm, and a surcharge of SFr. 10 between 10pm and 8am.**

If there isn't a pharmacy in the village where your doctor practises, he'll usually supply you with medicines or drugs from his own supplies. If he doesn't have them in stock he'll write a prescription. Some medicines aren't recognised by a health fund and you must pay the full cost for them. Usually your doctor will tell you when this is the case and may offer to prescribe an alternative. Herbal and homeopathic medicines are popular in Switzerland. The Swiss take a lot of drugs (including spending more on pain-killers than any other country in Europe) and have the second largest per capita consumption in Europe after the Germans. It also has the highest prices in Europe for prescribed medicines, some 40 per cent higher than the EU average. As with various other items, many drugs and medicines are sold much cheaper (e.g. less than 50 per cent of the Swiss price) in Switzerland's neighbouring countries, particularly France and Italy.

Non-prescription medicines or drugs can be purchased from a pharmacy or a drug store (*Drogerie, droguerie*) and are expensive. A drug store stocks non-prescription medicines, cosmetics, toiletries and cleaning supplies. They also sell a few unexpected items, such as alcohol – official recognition of its medicinal qualities perhaps (but **only** when taken in moderation!). A health food shop (*Reformhaus, magasin de produits diététiques*) sells health foods, diet foods and eternal-life-virility-youth pills and elixirs, for which the Swiss are famous. Medicines or drugs are prescribed in the following three ways:

- Once only when the prescription is filled;
- One repeat dose without the need for a second prescription;
- Repeat doses as often as necessary within a three-month period.

The procedure for filling prescriptions when you're a member of a health fund (*Krankenkasse, casse maladie*) varies, but is usually as detailed below.

Most health insurance companies issue a credit card size insurance card that you show at the pharmacy together with the prescription from the doctor. The pharmacy will take your insurance number and the company details and invoice the health insurance directly. The health insurance company will send you an invoice for the annual excess and/or the 10 per cent you have to pay yourself. Pharmacies are allowed to charge a special fee for giving advice (irrespective if they really give any advice or simply hand you the medication) and another fee for having your details on their computer. These fees were introduced to compensate the pharmacies for a reduction of margins on medication in 2001 and are covered by the health insurance.

Some health companies – usually the ones with the cheapest premiums – do not automatically pay the pharmacies but require you to pay for the medication and to then send the invoice to the health insurance company for a refund.

HOSPITALS & CLINICS

Most Swiss towns have a hospital (*Krankenhaus/Spital, hôpital*) or clinic signposted by the international hospital sign of a white 'H' on a blue background. Hospitals are listed in telephone directories under *Spitäler, hôpitaux*. Depending on the canton and area of Switzerland, hospitals may be designated as cantonal, zonal, regional, specialised or a private clinic-hospital. A general hospital (*Kantonsspital, hôpital cantonal*) is the largest and best equipped, with the most experienced staff. Clinics are usually private and treatment there isn't generally covered by a health fund or medical insurance, unless specifically stated in your policy. In French-speaking Switzerland there are emergency clinics (*Piquet-Dienst, permanence*) providing 24-hour treatment for minor accidents and medical emergencies (there are also 24-hour emergency dental clinics).

Except for emergency treatment, you may be admitted or referred to a hospital or clinic for treatment only after consultation with a doctor. Normally you're admitted to a hospital in your own canton (or zone in a city), unless specialist surgery or treatment is necessary that's unavailable there. In an emergency outside your canton of residence, you will obviously be treated in the nearest suitable hospital. Children are usually treated in a special children's general ward, well stocked with games, toys, books and other children. Children who require long-term hospitalisation may, depending on their health, be given school lessons in hospital.

Your choice of hospital and doctor depend on your level of health insurance cover (see page 266) and the particular medical problem. The type of hospital accommodation also depends on your level of insurance. Patients with standard cover are accommodated in a general ward (two to four beds), half private in a two-bed ward and private in a private room. Many doctors treat patients only at certain hospitals and you may have to choose between having your usual doctor or specialist attend you, or treatment in a particular hospital. Patients in general wards, i.e. without private or half-private insurance, are usually unable to choose their doctor. This may be important as not all doctors speak good English. Nurses are also unlikely to speak English, particularly in French and Italian-speaking areas.

If you're a non-resident and aren't a member of a health fund or don't have Swiss medical insurance, hospitals usually require a deposit on your admittance (they aren't taking any chances on your survival!). The deposit may range from SFr. 2,000 to 10,000 and will depend on whether you're resident in the canton where the hospital is located, elsewhere in Switzerland or abroad. The actual cost of treatment is calculated later and you will receive a rebate or a bill for the difference (usually they overestimate the cost). In some private clinics, foreign patients must make deposits of up to SFr. 50,000 on admission!

Hospital visiting times are shown in telephone directories. Visiting hours vary depending on whether you're in a private, half private or general ward (no prize for guessing which patients have the longest visiting hours). In private clinics there may be no restrictions on visiting.

A publication entitled *Private Clinics in Switzerland* (there are over 100) and a brochure giving particulars of convalescence homes and hotels are available from Switzerland Tourism (see page 305). Information is also available from the Association of Swiss Private Clinics (*Vereinigung der Privatkliniken, Association Suisse des cliniques privées*), Moosstr. 2, Postfach 29, CH-3073 Gümligen-Berne (☎ 031 952 61 33 ▣ www.privatkliniken.ch)

CHILDBIRTH

Childbirth in Switzerland usually takes place in a hospital, where a stay of three to five days is usual. The husband is usually encouraged to attend the birth, unless difficulties are expected or he looks like he is about to faint or worse. You can also have a baby at home. Ask your family doctor or obstetrician for information and advice.

Maternity costs (general ward) are fully covered by the basic Swiss health insurance. Most Swiss hospitals are like hotels, where you can choose between a single or double room, with or without a bath or toilet (there's sometimes a long wait to use a shared toilet) and meals are served *a la carte* with wine (if permitted). Your insurance cover may be the deciding factor, unless of course someone else is footing the bill. Some private clinics are covered by health fund insurance (private hospital cover) and have special rates for childbirth, but may not cover a birth by caesarean. Ask for a list of charges in advance. You may choose a gynaecologist in advance (if you don't, one will be assigned at the hospital) and you can usually request an English-speaking midwife (see also **Hospitals & Clinics** above).

When you give birth in a Swiss hospital, you must provide a name or names for both sexes in advance, **from an approved list of names**. The approved list of names may not apply to foreigners, although you may need to show that the name you choose is normal in your country (although how do you do that is another question). Foreigners giving birth in a Swiss hospital must bring the following papers with them on admittance:

- Passport;
- Swiss residence permit;
- *Marriage licence or divorce papers;
- *Birth certificates of both parents.

* These may not be necessary, but check in advance.

Don't forget to notify your health insurance company of your new arrival, as babies must be insured within three months of their birth (it can be done in advance from the expected month of birth). If you give birth prematurely, don't forget to inform your health insurance company. Notify your employer of the birth and check that the child allowance (see page 55) is paid with your salary.

Most communities provide a free post-natal nursing service (*Säuglings schwester, nurse*). The nurse will visit you at home (usually once only) after you've given birth. Thereafter you may take your child to the nurse's clinic for regular check-ups during the following year. She is an excellent source of advice on any baby health questions, but may not speak English. The nurse will provide a certificate if you breast-feed your child, for which many communities pay an allowance. Switzerland has a comprehensive vaccination programme for babies and children of all ages.

Your local community may present you with a toy for your child and around ten cantons pay a birth allowance, e.g. SFr. 500 to 1,200. You will also be inundated with advertisements for everything from baby food and toys, to banks offering to make a donation of SFr. 20 to 50 if you open a savings account for your child. Baby facilities are provided in some public toilets and by most department stores in cities.

Useful newsletters for new mothers include *Mothering Matters*, available from Susan Straubinger (In der Würz 1, 8800 Thalwil, ☎ 01 722 36 55) and *The New Stork Times*, available on subscription from Andrea Bader-Rusch (Wässerwies 11, 8712 Stäfa, ☎ 01 926 57 48, 🖳 www.thestork.ch).

DENTISTS

There are excellent dentists (*Zahnarzt, dentiste*) everywhere in Switzerland, many of whom speak reasonable or good English. Many embassies keep a list of English-speaking dentists in their area (or dentists who speak their national language) and your employer or colleagues may also be able to recommend someone. Dentists are listed in telephone directories under *Zahnärzte, dentiste*. A zero with a diagonal line through it alongside a telephone number indicates a 24-hour answering service. Some dentists have Saturday morning surgeries. Most major cities have a special dental emergency telephone number, where a list of dentists is kept, categorised by speciality, location and the languages spoken. In some areas, e.g. Geneva, there are 24-hour emergency dental clinics. Call the telephone operator on 111 for information.

Many family dentists in Switzerland are qualified to perform special treatment, e.g. periodontal work, carried out by a specialist in many countries. Dental treatment is expensive, so it pays you to keep your mouth shut during dental visits. For example, over SFr. 5,000 to straighten a child's teeth isn't unusual. Fees are calculated according to a points system and you're entitled to an itemised bill. Dental treatment is cheaper in all of Switzerland's neighbouring countries and may be even lower in your home country – even the US, home of the million dollar smile, is cheaper! This option, although less convenient, may be worth considering if you're faced with expensive treatment (see also **Dental Insurance** on page 273). You should, in any case, obtain a detailed written estimate before committing yourself to an expensive course of treatment.

Switzerland's annual consumption of around 11kg of chocolate per head annually is the world's highest and ensures that dentists (and Swiss chocolate manufacturers) remain financially healthy.

OPTICIANS

The optician or optometrist (*Optiker, opticien*) business is competitive in Switzerland. Prices for spectacles and contact lenses aren't fixed, as they are for many other professional services, so it's wise to compare costs before committing yourself to a large bill. The prices charged for most services, e.g. spectacles, lenses, and hard and soft contact lenses, vary considerably and are usually more expensive than in most other European countries. For example, soft contact lenses cost less than half the average Swiss price in the UK and Germany. Disposable and extended-wear soft contact lenses are also widely available, although medical experts warn that they should be treated with caution as they increase the risk of potentially blinding eye infections. **Obtain advice from your family doctor or an ophthalmologist before buying them.**

You may go to an oculist or eye specialist (*Augenarzt, occuliste*) for an eye test. An oculist can usually make a more thorough test of your eyesight than an optician and is able to test for certain diseases that can be diagnosed from eye abnormalities, for example diabetes and certain types of cancer. The costs are covered by your medical insurance.

COUNSELLING & SOCIAL SERVICES

All cantons in Switzerland provide counselling (*Beratung, conseil*) and assistance for certain health and social problems. These include drug rehabilitation; alcoholism (Alcoholics Anonymous); gambling; attempted suicide and psychiatric problems; youth problems; battered children and women; marriage counselling; and rape. Many cantons also have a special telephone number for children, where they can obtain confidential help, e.g. in cases of physical or sexual abuse. Counsellors provide advice and help for sufferers of various diseases (e.g. multiple sclerosis and muscular dystrophy) and the disabled (e.g. the blind and deaf). They also help very sick and terminally ill patients (e.g. AIDS and cancer) and their families to come to terms with their situation. The Samaritans (*Die dargebotene Hand, la main tendue*) also provide a free telephone (143) counselling service in times of personal crisis (see page 134).

In times of need there's **always** someone to turn to and all services are provided in the utmost confidentiality. In major towns, counselling is usually available for foreigners in their own language. If you need help desperately, someone speaking your language will be found. Many cantons publish a handbook of counselling centres. Contact your canton's health service (*Kantonärztlicher Dienst des Gesundheitsdepartment, service médical cantonal*) or ask your family doctor for advice. You can also the Internet (e.g. 🖥 www. infoset.ch) to find resources in German and French regarding addiction therapy in Switzerland.

In a move to combat AIDS, local authorities in some Swiss cities provide free needles and a 'fixing' room for addicts use with a nurse on hand. Some cantons treat drug addiction as a social rather than a criminal problem and provide medical support; social workers; methadone treatment; and free or inexpensive food and drink, syringes and accommodation. In an attempt to combat one of the highest per capita rates of drug addiction in Europe, free drugs are provided for registered addicts in some cities (e.g. Basle and Zurich) in a controlled programme to help them kick the habit.

BIRTHS & DEATHS

Births and deaths in Switzerland must be reported to your local registrar office (*Zivilstandamt, bureau de l'état civil*). In the case of a birth in Switzerland, registration is carried out by the hospital where the child is born. However, if you have a child at home or in a different community from where you live, you must complete the registration yourself within three days. Ask your registrar office for information. A Swiss birth certificate (*Geburtsschein, acte de naissance*) is issued automatically. If a child is born en route to the hospital, there will be an exciting legal wrangle to decide its community of birth.

In the event of the death of a resident of Switzerland, all interested parties must be notified (see **Chapter 20**). A doctor will provide a certificate specifying the cause of death for insurance companies and other interested parties. You should make around ten copies as they're also required by banks, insurance companies and various other institutions. A death certificate may be required before probate can be granted for a will. A body can be buried or cremated in Switzerland or the body or ashes can be sent to another country. In some cantons (e.g. Geneva) burial is free in your local commune. **Burial land in Switzerland is recycled after 25 years, when graves are excavated and the land reused for further burials.** For more information contact your local community office.

Births and deaths should be reported to your local consulate or embassy, for example to obtain a national birth certificate, passport and social security number for a child.

SEXUALLY-TRANSMITTED DISEASES

Switzerland has one of the highest per capita levels of AIDS cases in Europe. AIDS is the most frequent cause of death among those aged 25 to 34 followed by suicide. As part of the Swiss campaign against AIDS, many supermarkets and department stores (e.g. Migros, Coop) stock condoms (*Präservatives, préservatif*) in the cosmetic sections. (Although they're called 'preservatives' in German, don't expect to find them in the food section in different flavours.) Condom dispensing machines have also been installed in some schools and in many public toilets. As the Swiss campaign advertisement says, 'For AIDS protection, use condoms' (*Vor AIDS schützen, Präservative benützen, pour la lutte anti-SIDA utiliser des préservatives*).

All cases of AIDS and HIV positive blood tests in Switzerland must be reported to the federal authorities (patients' names remain anonymous). The spread of AIDS is accelerated by the sharing of needles among drug addicts, among whom AIDS is common (many of Switzerland's estimated 25 to 30,000 hard drug addicts are believed to be infected with the HIV virus).

HOME-NURSING SERVICE

Most communities operate a home nursing service for house-bound invalids, the cost (e.g. SFr. 20 per hour) of which depends on the patient's or family's income. You can join a housekeeping and nursing service association (*Haus- und Krankenpflegeverein, sociéte des aides familiales et des soins à domicile*) like the Spitex, Belpstrasse 24, Postfach 329, 3000 Bern 14 (☎ 031 381 33 81, 🖳 www.spitex.ch) This reduces the cost of home nursing and household help. Free services such as blood pressure checks may be provided for members. Many communities provide families with a cleaning and general household service (including cooking) when the mother is ill. The service is cheaper if you're a member of a housekeeping and nursing service association. An optional premium is also payable with most health insurance companies to cover the cost of home help when a mother is ill for more than a few days. The cost of a stand-in mother/housekeeper is tax deductible. For information contact your community.

Pro Senectute provides help for the elderly, including social and community work and homecare, e.g. homehelps, cleaning services, mobile mending and laundry service, meals-on-wheels, pedicure, transport and home visits. The charge for services varies depending on the canton and is usually the actual cost incurred (those on low incomes may be partly or fully reimbursed). Foreigners are treated the same as Swiss, except that they must have five years continuous residence in Switzerland to qualify for financial support. For information contact Sozialberatung Pro Senectute, Lavaterstr. 60, Postfach, CH-8027 Zurich (☎ 01 283 89 89, 🖳 www.pro-senectute.ch). The Red Cross and local nursing societies provide nursing services and the rental of apparatus for the sick and disabled.

SPAS

There are 19 spas or thermal baths (*Bad/Kurort, station thermale*) in Switzerland, which although called a *Bad* in German are good for you and provide therapeutic and medicinal benefits. Spa treatment is recommended for a number of illnesses, including the alleviation of arthritic and rheumatic pains. The cost of treatment may be paid by your health fund when prescribed by a doctor. Most spas can be visited on a daily basis for a single entry fee. The usual maximum immersion time is 20 to 30 minutes, followed by a rest period (reclining chairs are provided) of about the same duration. Day tickets usually have a time limit of around two hours.

A *Swiss Spa Guide* is published by the Swiss Spa Association, listing the facilities and accommodation provided at major Swiss spas, and containing general information in English, French and German. It's available free from Schweizer Heilbäder, Avenue des Bains 22, 1400 Yverdon-les-Bains (☎ 024 420 15 21, 💻 www.heilbad.org). Switzerland Tourism also publishes a brochure about Swiss spas in French and German entitled *Wellness vacation*.

13.

INSURANCE

Switzerland isn't exactly a nation of gamblers, a fact reflected by the amount the Swiss spend on insurance (*Versicherung*, *assurance*), which at around 20 per cent of the average family budget is the highest in the world. Each household spends an average of around SFr. 40 a day on insurance (excluding car insurance). The Swiss don't care to take any chances, particularly when they can insure against them – they spend some SFr. 20 billion a year on life insurance premiums alone! The Swiss government and Swiss law provides for various obligatory federal and employer insurance schemes. These include federal pension and disability insurance, company pension funds, health insurance, accident insurance, unemployment insurance and salary insurance. The Swiss government spends a quarter of its budget on social security and other insurance schemes. Other insurance may also be obligatory depending on your age, canton of residence or employer, for example house contents insurance and private liability insurance.

It's important to ensure that your family has full health insurance during the period between leaving your last country of residence and when you obtain new health insurance in Switzerland. This is particularly applicable if you're covered by a company health insurance policy, terminating on the day you leave your present employment. One way to do this is to take out a travel or holiday insurance policy, although this could be inadequate, particularly if a serious illness for which you aren't covered is diagnosed in the interim period. If possible, it's better to extend your present health insurance policy. If you come to live in Switzerland, health insurance starts on the day you enter the country, even if you choose your insurance company a few weeks later. Of course this also means that your premiums start from your first day in the country.

In all matters regarding insurance you're responsible for ensuring that you and your family are legally insured in Switzerland. If you wish to make a claim against your insurance or a third party is claiming against you, you'd be wise to report the matter to the police within 24 hours, which may in some cases be a legal requirement, e.g. if you set fire to a rented apartment. Obtain legal advice for anything other than a minor claim. Swiss law may be different from that in your home country or your previous country of residence and may also vary from canton to canton. As an additional warning that disaster can strike at any time, some insurance companies provide policyholders with an emergency telephone number for use at nights and weekends. It's wise to follow the example of the Swiss and make sure you're covered against most disasters. Regrettably you cannot insure yourself against being uninsured or sue your insurance agent for giving you bad advice!

INSURANCE COMPANIES

Insurance is one of Switzerland's major businesses and there are numerous insurance companies from which to choose, many providing a range of insurance services, while others specialise in certain fields only. The major insurance companies have offices or agents throughout Switzerland, including most small towns. Telephone insurance companies (such as Züritel) have been introduced in recent years and usually offer lower premiums than traditional agents. All Swiss insurance companies provide a free analysis of your family's insurance needs and your Swiss bank may also provide independent advice (although they usually have a deal with one insurance company). Obtain a few quotations before signing a contract and ask the advice of your colleagues and friends (but don't believe everything they tell you!).

In most cities you can find English-speaking Independent Financial Advisers or Insurance Brokers who can help you obtain appropriate cover and find the best companies. Before choosing an advisor, ask whether he has experience dealing with expatriates, as your needs might be considerably different from those of a Swiss family who never leave the country. A good financial adviser or broker can also help you if you have any insurance claims.

INSURANCE CONTRACTS

Read all insurance contracts before signing them. If you cannot obtain an English translation and you don't understand everything, ask a friend or colleague to translate it or take legal advice. Most insurance companies have English-speaking representatives and some provide information and a translation of policies in English, e.g. Winterthur.

Most insurance policies run for a calendar year from 1st January to 31st December. If you take out, change or cancel a policy during the year, you will be billed or reimbursed the balance to the end of the year. All insurance policy premiums should be paid punctually, as late payment may affect your benefits or a claim (although, if this is so, it should be noted in your policy). Whilst most policies have what looks like a fixed term, for example 3 years, they still renew themselves automatically by another year if you don't give notice 3 months before the end of the term.

SOCIAL SECURITY SYSTEM

Switzerland has a three part social security system for all employees, called the 'three pillar' system (3-Säulen-Konzept, système des 3 piliers). It consists of:

1. Compulsory federal old age and survivors insurance (AHV/OASI) and disability insurance (IV/DI), which is the Swiss federal social security pension scheme.
2. Compulsory private company pension funds for employees.
3. Voluntary tax-deductible private pension savings and life insurance.

The aim of the federal social security system is to guarantee employees at least a subsistence income on retirement or in case of disability. To receive a full pension you must contribute for the maximum number of years.

OBLIGATORY INSURANCE

The following insurance premiums are obligatory for all employees in Switzerland and are automatically deducted from your gross monthly salary by your employer:

- **Old Age & Survivors Insurance** (*Eidgenössische Alters- und Hinterlassenversicherung/AHV, Assurance-Vieillesse et Survivants fédérale/AVS*) and **Disability Insurance** (*Invalidenversicherung/IV, Assurance Invalidité/AI*). The contribution for all employees is 5.05 per cent of their gross monthly salary.

- **Company Pension Fund** (*Berufliche Vorsorge/BVG, Prévoyance Professionelle/LPP*). Contributions vary from around 5.5 to 11 per cent of your gross monthly salary, depending on your age and your employer's pension fund.

- **Accident Insurance** (*Unfallversicherung, assurance accidents*). Occupational accident insurance is non-contributory. Private accident insurance contributions vary depending on your employer from non-contributory to around 2 per cent of your gross monthly salary.

- **Salary Insurance** (*Salärversicherung/Lohnversicherung, assurance salaire*). Contributions vary from non-contributory to around 2 per cent of your gross monthly salary.

- **Unemployment Insurance** (*Arbeitslosenversicherung, assurance chômage*). The contribution for all employees is 1.25 per cent of your gross monthly salary up to SFr. 8,900 per month and 0.5 per cent on the amount above this.

- **Health Insurance** (*Krankenversicherung, assurance maladie*). Health insurance has been compulsory for everyone (except foreign diplomats) living in Switzerland since 1st January 1996 (see page 266).

- **Third Party Insurance** (*Haftpflichtversicherung, assurance responsibilité civile*). Third party insurance is obligatory for motor vehicles (see page 212), motorcycles, bicycles and some sports.

The following insurance isn't obligatory, but is recommended:

- **House Contents Insurance** (*Hausratsversicherung, assurance des effets mobiliers*). House contents insurance is obligatory in most cantons.

- **Private Liability Insurance** (*Privat-Haftpflichtversicherung, assurance responsibilité civile*).

OLD AGE & SURVIVORS INSURANCE

The federal Old Age and Survivors Insurance (OASI) and Disability Insurance (DI) is the Swiss federal social security pension scheme (*Staatliche Vorsorge, prévoyance sociale*). It's the first part of the three-part Swiss social security system and is referred to as pillar one. OASI and DI include the following:

- A retirement pension for a single person or a couple;
- A supplementary pension for a younger wife;
- A child's pension for the child of the beneficiary of a retirement pension;
- A widow's pension or gratuity (a widower cannot claim a pension!);
- An orphan's single (one parent deceased) or double (both parents deceased) pension;
- Long-term treatment and all associated costs for the disabled;
- An invalidity pension for a disabled person;
- A disability allowance for those requiring full-time personal supervision (to qualify for a disability pension, contributions must have been paid for one year);
- Appliances for a disabled person.

All employees in Switzerland pay OASI/DI from 1st January of the year following their 17th birthday. Non-employed people pay OASI/DI from 1st January of the year following their 20th birthday until the official age of retirement. This includes all non-employed 'leisured foreigners' (retirees or the 'idle rich'), who are assessed on their assets, i.e. capital, investment income or pension, and income from annuities. Contributions continue until the official retirement age of 65 for men and between 62 and 64 for women (depending on your date of birth – see below), for both the employed and unemployed, or until the age of retirement if later. If you retire before the official retirement age, you must continue to pay OASI contributions until the official retirement age. If you continue to earn above a certain sum after the official age of retirement, you must also continue to pay OASI, although this won't increase your pension above the maximum amount when you finally retire.

If your spouse works and you don't, you're automatically included in his/her contributions. Contributions and years are also allocated to your pension for the time spent looking after children aged under 16.

The retirement age for women is being increased from 62 to 64, in order to reduce pressure on the state pension fund. As in most western countries, Switzerland has too few employed people to pay the pensions of the increasing number of retirees. The over 65 population is expected to double in the next 50 years to around 40 per cent of the population, which, if unchecked, will cause social costs to explode from today's 7 per cent of GDP to 33 per cent! Pensions are adjusted, usually every two years, according to the wage and price index. Complementary benefits are payable to foreigners with low incomes who have lived continuously in Switzerland for at least 15 years.

If you defer receipt of your pension for one to five years, the following increases are paid:

No. Of Years	Increase (%)
1	5.2
2	10.8
3	17.1
4	24.0
5	31.5

When your salary includes income 'in kind', for example board and lodging or a car, the value is added to your salary and OASI/DI is payable on the total sum.

Employees pay OASI/DI of 5.05 per cent of their monthly gross income and employers pay the same amount. The total of 10.1 per cent includes 8.4 per cent for AHV/OASI, 1.4 per cent for IV/DI and 0.3 per cent for APG/EO (salary compensation insurance for the loss of earnings incurred during military service or women's military corps, Red Cross and civil defence service). If you're self-employed, your contributions depend on your income and are between 5.1 per cent and 9.5 per cent (AHV/OASI 7.8 per cent, IV/DI 1.4 per cent and APG/EO 0.3 per cent) if you earn over SFr. 50,700 a year. The minimum contribution is SFr. 425.

Everyone who pays OASI/DI receives an insurance certificate (*Versicherungsausweis AHV-IV, certificat d'assurance AVS-AI*). The certificate contains your personal insurance number and the number of the OASI/DI compensation office (*Ausgleichskasse, caisse de compensation*) that has opened an account in your name (addresses are listed on the last two pages in telephone directories). Make a note of this number and keep both it and the certificate in a safe place. If you change jobs, you must give your insurance certificate to your new employer so that he can register you with the local OASI/DI compensation office.

The pension you receive on retirement depends on your average annual contributions and the number of years you've contributed. The minimum annual full pension on 1st January 2003 was SFr. 12,660 (SFr. 1,055 a month) for a single person and SFr. 18,990 (SFr. 1,582 a month) for a couple. The maximum full pension in the autumn of 2003 was SFr. 25,320 a year (SFr. 2,110 a month) for a single person and SFr. 37,980 a year (SFr. 3,165 a month) for a married couple (a married couple's pension is divided into two equal portions and paid separately to each individual). A full pension is paid only when you've contributed for at least 44 years.

Foreigners qualify for a reduced pension after contributions have been paid for one year. Switzerland has bilateral agreements with over 20 countries including all western European countries, Canada, Australia and the US. Foreigners who are citizens of countries with which Switzerland has a bilateral insurance agreement receive a Swiss pension irrespective of where they live. Citizens of countries without a bilateral agreement only receive a Swiss pension when they're living in Switzerland. Contributions to OASI/DI aren't transferable to foreign national insurance schemes and aren't refundable if your country of domicile has a bilateral agreement with Switzerland. If a bilateral agreement isn't applicable and you aren't entitled to a pension under Swiss law, your OASI/DI contributions will be refunded when you leave Switzerland.

If you live in Switzerland for a short period only, you may be exempt from paying OASI/DI, particularly if your country of origin has a bilateral agreement with Switzerland regarding pension contributions. To qualify you must usually be transferred to Switzerland by your employer for a temporary period only (maximum 24 months) and must remain covered by your home country's social security system. Non-working spouses and employees of international organisations (e.g. The United Nations) and diplomatic missions are exempt from paying OASI/DI.

For further information contact the Federal Office for Social Insurance (*Bundesamt für Sozialversicherungen, Office Fédéral des Assurances Sociales*), Effingerstr. 33, CH-3003 Berne (☎ 031 322 90 11, ⌨ www.ahv.admin.ch) or the Central Compensation Office (*Zentrale Ausgleichsstelle, Centrale de compensation*), av. Edmond-Vaucher 18, CH-1211 Geneva 28 (☎ 022 795 91 11).

COMPANY PENSION FUND

A company pension fund (*Berufliche Vorsorge/BVG, Prévoyance Professionelle/LPP*) is a compulsory (since 1st January 1985) contributory pension scheme for employees. It's the second part of the Swiss social security system, called pillar two. All employees earning over SFr. 25,320 a year and over 17 years of age must be members of a company pension fund, which may be run by the company, a professional association or an insurance company. The maximum insured salary on 1st January 2003 was SFr. 75,960. From this amount the minimum insured salary of SFr. 25,320 (insured by OASI/DI) is deducted. The remainder, SFr. 50,640 is the insured annual earnings or co-ordinated earnings.

From the 1st January after your 17th birthday until the age of 24, contributions are lower as only accident, death and disability are covered. From 1st January of the year following your 24th birthday, your contributions are increased to include retirement benefits. Total contributions to a company pension fund vary from around 7 to 18 per cent, depending on your salary, age, sex and your employer's particular pension fund, and are approximately as shown below:

Age		Contribution (%)
Men	**Women**	
25-34	25 – 31	7
35-44	32 – 41	10
45-54	42 – 51	15
55-65	52 – 62	18

Contributions are increased by between 3 to 4 per cent for additional premiums for risk insurance, special measures and a security fund. Of the total pension fund premium of 11 to 22 per cent, your employer pays at least 50 per cent, meaning that the amount you pay varies from around 5.5 to 11 per cent of your gross salary. The benefits paid on retirement depend upon your accrued fund assets. The fund provides retirement, survivors and disability pensions. A widow's pension is 60 per cent of the disability or retirement pension, and an orphan's and children's pension 20 per cent.

If you join a company after the age of 24, you often have the option of paying a lump sum into the pension fund or of paying higher monthly contributions in order to qualify for a larger pension. The OASI/DI and company pension fund bring your pension to around 60 per cent of your final salary, provided you've paid contributions for the maximum number of years without interruption. If you change your employer, the accrued amount you've paid (plus interest) will be credited to your new employer's pension scheme. Under new rules introduced in 1995, employees who change employers also receive the employer's contributions plus accrued interest.

In a move designed to encourage home ownership, employees may withdraw money from their company pension fund to buy a home in Switzerland, pay off an existing mortgage, or pay for renovations or alterations. The money must be used for their primary residence. Until the age of 50 the total accrued sum can be withdrawn, after which you can withdraw the total sum that was accrued when you reached the age of 50 or half the total sum currently accrued, whichever is the highest. You can repay money to your pension fund at any time in order to restore your pension. If you sell your primary residence and don't buy another, you must pay back any money withdrawn. A cash payment of the accrued capital is possible only with the following:

- When you leave Switzerland for good;
- When you become self-employed (your local OASI/DI office must provide proof so that your pension fund recognises you as self-employed);
- When the total sum accrued is less than one year's pension payments.

Pensions are indexed to the cost of living. Your company pension fund rules are detailed in your employment conditions or in a separate document and you will receive regular pension fund statements from your employer or fund. Self-employed people aren't required to belong to a company pension fund and can choose to pay higher tax-deductible private pension contributions to compensate for the lack of a company pension (see **Private Pension** on page 272).

For more information contact the BVG Foundation Institution (*Stiftung Auffangeinrichtung BVG, Fondation institution supplétive LPP*), Postfach 4338, CH-8022 Zurich (☎ 01 206 44 36).

ACCIDENT INSURANCE

There are two categories of mandatory accident insurance (*Unfallversicherung, assurance accidents*) for employees in Switzerland, as follows:

- **Occupational Accident Insurance** (*Betriebsunfallversicherung, assurance accidents professionels*). Occupational accident insurance is compulsory and is paid by your employer. It covers accidents or illness at work and accidents that occur when travelling to and from work, or when travelling on company business. One of the best known accident insurance companies is SUVA or CNA (*Schweizerische Unfallversicherungs-anstalt/SUVA, Caisse nationale suisse d'insurance en cas d'accidents/CNA*).

- **Non-Occupational Accident Insurance** (*Nichtbetriebsunfallversicherung, assurance accidents non-professionels*). Non-occupational accident insurance is compulsory for all employees who work over 8 hours per week. An employer may pay the whole cost of non-occupational accident insurance or pass the cost onto employees. Where applicable, the portion payable by the employee varies up to a maximum of around 2 per cent of his gross monthly salary, up to a salary limit of SFr. 106,800 per year (SFr. 8,900 a month). You may be covered by your employer for a higher salary by additional complementary accident insurance. Where applicable, your contribution is deducted from your salary at source.

Accident insurance allows for total disability pensions of 80 per cent of your annual salary, and in the event of death, a survivors pension of up to 70 per cent of your annual salary. If you engage in dangerous or high-risk pursuits, you should check whether your accident insurance has any exclusion clauses. Skiing and most sports accidents are, however, fully covered by your non-occupational accident insurance. If you work less than 8 hours a week, you will usually only have occupational accident insurance (but you will be covered for other accidents by your health insurance), although non-occupational accident insurance is compulsory for part-time employees who pay OASI/DI.

When medical treatment is necessary abroad as the result of an accident, you will be refunded a maximum of double the costs that would have been incurred in Switzerland (medical treatment in some countries is actually **more expensive** than in Switzerland). You must usually make a claim on your accident insurance within three months of an accident. If you fail to meet this deadline, you must either pay the bill yourself or make a claim on your health insurance. The self-employed and anyone else who isn't covered by an employer are covered for accidents by their health insurance.

Accident insurance paid by employers only includes employees and not family members. Ensure that your family is covered by private accident insurance, which can be combined with a health fund insurance, otherwise you must pay the full cost of any treatment yourself.

SALARY INSURANCE

Many companies provide salary (or salary continuation) insurance (*Salärausfall-versicherung/Salärlosenversicherung, assurance salaire*), which provides sick pay (*Taggeld, indemnité journalier*) in the event of illness or an accident, although it may cover you for a limited period only (usually 720 days). These schemes may be non-contributory, although employees usually pay a part of the premium, e.g. 50 per cent of contributions. The maximum salary covered may be as high as SFr. 243,000 a year.

Salary insurance also applies to part-time employees who have been employed for three months or longer. If the company has no insurance, the period for which you're entitled to sick pay depends on your length of service and may be calculated as a percentage of your hourly rate. The minimum period is usually three weeks in your first year of service.

Your salary is usually paid in full during the first month of an illness or accident. After the first month, your salary is paid in full or 90 per cent up to a maximum of two years (may be 80 per cent for single employees and 85 per cent for married employees with no children). Your employer may pay the whole salary insurance premium or pass part or the whole cost onto you. Where applicable, the percentage payable by the employee varies up to a maximum of around 2 per cent of his gross monthly salary.

UNEMPLOYMENT INSURANCE

Unemployment insurance (*Arbeitslosenversicherung/ALV, assurance chômage*) is compulsory for all employees. Your contribution, deducted at source from your gross monthly salary, is 1.25 per cent up to a maximum salary of SFr. 106,800 a year (SFr. 8,900 a month). Unemployment insurance is often included with OASI/DI on your salary statement (total 6.55 per cent). On the portion of salaries of between SFr. 106,800 and SFr. 267,000 the employee's ALV contribution is 0.5 per cent. The chances of being unemployed in Switzerland have increased considerably in the last few decades, during which unemployment rose from below 1 per cent in the 1980s to reach around 6 per cent in 1993. Since then it has fallen again and in 2002 was around 2.9 per cent. To fund the increase in unemployment benefits (and reduce the fund deficit) both employees' and employers' contributions were raised to 1.5 per cent (total 3 per cent) in 1994 but – in spite of rising unemployment – have been cut back to 1.25 per cent (total 2.5 per cent).

Unemployment benefits are paid when you're unemployed, on short time or when an employer is unable to pay your wages, e.g. he has gone bankrupt. Part-time employees are also entitled to unemployment benefits when wholly or partly unemployed. Unemployment benefits also provide for retraining, further education and schemes for the unemployed. To qualify for unemployment benefits when fully unemployed, you must have worked and contributed in Switzerland for at least twelve months during the previous two years. You must register within a few days of losing your job or of your employer being unable to pay you.

The amount of benefits paid depend on your previous salary and marital status, and may also depend on whether you were made redundant or were fired or resigned voluntarily (not advisable if you wish to receive unemployment benefits!). Unemployed people with a family and the disabled receive a higher percentage of their previous salary (up to a maximum salary of SFr. 106,800 a year or SFr. 8,900 a month) than single people who aren't disabled. Lower benefits are paid if you resigned your job, unless you can prove that your working conditions were intolerable (which is extremely difficult). Additional payments are made to cover children's allowances and educational costs, as prescribed by Swiss law. The length of time you receive unemployment benefits depends on your length of employment.

When you're unemployed you must report monthly to your local unemployment. The payment of benefits depend on you actively seeking employment, although you may restrict your job hunting to the area where you live and the field or profession in which you're qualified to work. During a period of unemployment, it's your responsibility to find new employment with the help of the labour exchange and your community. You should apply in writing for around ten suitable jobs each month and the authorities may ask to see your letters and any replies.

You're obliged to accept any reasonable job offered you by the employment office, however, if you're a brain surgeon you won't be offered a job as a waiter or waitress! If you're offered a job with a lower salary than the amount you receive in unemployment benefits, you must accept it, although you're compensated by the unemployment office for one year. This ensures that you don't receive less income by working than you would by remaining unemployed.

Benefits are paid only while you live in Switzerland. If you leave Switzerland before the benefit period has ended, no further monthly payments or lump sum payment will be made. If your residence permit expires before the benefit period has elapsed, it will be extended on application. If you're unemployed and no longer entitled to unemployment benefits, your residence permit may be cancelled. Benefits for non-payment of your salary by an employer, e.g. when he has gone bankrupt, will be paid even if you've already left Switzerland.

Additional information can be obtained at your local labour exchange (*Arbeitsamt, office du travail*). Employees of foreign embassies, missions and international organisations who don't pay OASI/DI or unemployment insurance, aren't eligible for unemployment benefits.

When your entitlement to federal unemployment benefits has expired, you're dependent on supplemental canton programmes, which vary depending on the canton. Under federal law, those earning below a maximum amount per year are eligible for public welfare (such as rent assistance) and cantons and communities also provide financial assistance to families whose income falls below a minimum figure, e.g. around SFr. 18,000 a year in Zurich.

Employers in Switzerland aren't required to make redundancy payments. Irrespective of how long you've been employed, you're entitled only to the notice period stated in your employment contract or conditions, or payment in lieu of notice. Executive positions may, however, provide for a cash payment (a 'golden handshake') if you're sacked or made redundant.

HEALTH INSURANCE

From 1st January 1996, basic health insurance (*Krankenversicherung, assurance maladie*) has been compulsory for everyone living in Switzerland for three months or more with the exception of foreign diplomats and employees of international organisations. Foreigners must obtain health insurance within three months of their arrival in Switzerland and babies must be insured within three months of their birth. Some large companies have their own health insurance schemes offering advantageous conditions and reduced premiums for employees and their families. If you're a member of a health insurance scheme sponsored by your employer or a professional association, your premium may be deducted at source from your salary. Private health insurance premiums may be paid annually, quarterly or monthly, by giro payment or by standing order from a bank or post office account. Your employer may pay a part or the total cost of your health insurance, although this isn't usual.

Health insurance in Switzerland can be taken out with a health fund (*Kranken-kasse, caisse maladie*) or a private health insurance company (*Krankenversicherung, assurance maladie*). Health funds, of which there are over 100 in Switzerland, are of the mutual benefit or friendly society type and mostly non-profit organisations. They try to exert some control over doctor's and hospital fees, and are the cheapest form of health insurance in Switzerland. Premiums, which prior to 1996 were subsidised by the state or cantons, have increased by an average of over 50 per cent in some cantons in recent years, although rises have now slowed and they were 'only' expected to rise by an average of 10 per cent from 2003 to 2004. It's important to shop around as costs vary considerably between the cheapest and most expensive insurance companies in different cantons (you can do this on the Internet at 🖥 www. comparis.ch). The premiums of those with low incomes are subsidised by the cantons – in most cantons only by application.

All companies must offer identical basic cover as prescribed by law, which includes treatment by doctors, chiropractors, mid-wives and certain other practitioners (e.g. nurses and physiotherapists) when treatment is approved by a doctor; medication and laboratory tests; dental treatment necessary as the result of an accident or illness; hospitalisation in a general ward; and emergency treatment abroad. Pre-existing conditions cannot be excluded from the basic cover (including pregnancy). Hospital treatment in a general ward is usually restricted to hospitals in your canton of residence, although you can choose to pay extra to be hospitalised in a public hospital outside your canton of residence and for a half-private (two-bed) room or a private room. A health fund will pay for treatment in a private clinic only when similar treatment isn't available locally in a general hospital. A private health insurance scheme usually includes half-private or private hospital cover as standard and may include medical services and medicines that aren't covered by a health fund.

Standard cover (hospital general ward) from a health fund usually costs between SFr. 200 and 400 a month for an adult, depending on the insurer and where you live. Premiums have been increasing in leaps and bounds in recent years, particularly private and half-private hospital cover (which can double your premium), although steps have been taken to curb increases. Premiums for private and half-private cover can be reduced by payment of an excess or deductible (selbstbehalt, franchise). The minimum compulsory excess is SFr. 300 a year for adults (zero for children), although you can choose to pay from SFr. 400 to SFr. 1,500 (which reduces premiums). Patients must pay 10 per cent of all non-hospital costs (treatment, drugs, etc.) above the excess. Standard cover is valid world-wide and pays a maximum of twice what the same treatment would cost in Switzerland, which could be a problem in the US where it's advisable to take out supplemental cover or travel health insurance. However, under the bilateral treaties between Switzerland and the EU, Swiss and EU citizens travelling to an EU country will only receive the cover that is compulsory in that country (which may be different to Switzerland and where additional excesses may have to be paid). It's therefore advisable to have additional travel insurance that can be obtained from many Swiss insurers for an annual premium of approximately SFr. 160 for a family. Swiss and EU citizens should carry a form E-111 (obtainable from your Swiss insurance company) when travelling to an EU country in order for the medical costs to be charged to the Swiss insurance system directly. Without the form you might be required to pay any doctor's or hospital fee yourself and then have them refunded by the Swiss insurance company – usually a time-consuming process!

If you will be working in Switzerland for less than three months (e.g. on a contract basis) and won't be covered by Swiss compulsory health insurance, you will need an international health insurance policy. These usually offer members a choice of benefits covering average health costs or a super scale for countries with high medical costs, which includes Switzerland. Besides the usual doctor's and hospital fees, claims can generally be made for body scans, convalescence, home nursing, outpatient treatment, health checks and surgical appliances. With an international health insurance policy, you may be able to renew your cover annually, irrespective of your age, which could be important. If you have a foreign health policy, ask your insurance company what it will cost for cover in Switzerland.

Checklist

When comparing the level of cover provided by different health insurance schemes, the following points should be considered:

- Does the scheme have a wide range of premium levels and are discounts or special premium rates available for families?
- Is private, half-private and general hospital cover available? What are the costs? Is there a limit on the time you can spend in hospital? Are private and half-private rooms available in local hospitals?
- Is optional dental cover provided? What exactly does it include? Can it be extended to include extra treatment? Dental insurance usually contains numerous limitations and doesn't cover cosmetic dental treatment.
- Are accidents covered. e.g. sports injuries and dental treatment? Employees in Switzerland are automatically covered by their employer's obligatory accident insurance. Car accidents are usually covered by Swiss motor insurance. Those with separate accident insurance (UVG) can reduce their premiums by up to 10 per cent by omitting accident insurance. As a general rule, health insurance includes cover for accidents.
- What are the restrictions regarding hospitalisation in a canton other than your canton of residence?
- What emergency ambulance or other transportation fees are covered?
- What is the qualification period for special benefits or services?
- What level of cover is provided for Europe and/or the rest of the world? What are the limitations?
- Are all medicines covered for up to 90 per cent of their cost or are there restrictions?
- Are convalescent homes or spa treatments covered when prescribed by a doctor?
- What are the restrictions on complementary medicine, e.g. chiropractic, osteopathy, naturopathy, massage and acupuncture? Are they covered? Must a doctor make a referral? Complementary medicine is popular in Switzerland and is often paid (or partly paid) by Swiss health insurance companies.
- Are possible extra costs likely, and if so, what for?

- Are spectacles or contact lenses covered, and if so, how much can be claimed and how frequently? Some Swiss health funds allow you to claim for a new pair of spectacles every two or three years.
- Is the provision and repair of artificial limbs and other essential health aids covered?

General Information

The following general points apply to most health insurance policies in Switzerland:

- You must enrol your spouse and children as members, as they aren't automatically covered by your membership.
- It's important to consider the extra levels of insurance and benefits available from health funds and insurance companies. For example, you can usually choose to pay extra for private or half-private hospital treatment and extra dental cover. When hospitalised, private and half-private patients can usually choose to be attended by the doctor of their choice.
- Private medical and extra dental cover (and other optional benefits) may become effective only after a qualifying period of around three months. This period may be waived if you can prove membership of another insurance scheme (Swiss or foreign) with the same or a higher level of cover.
- Usually your doctor will send you a bill for each separate illness within a three-month period. If you're forced to visit different doctors (for example your doctor is sick or doing military service) for the same illness, the separate bills should be sent to your health fund together. If you change doctors of your own accord during a course of treatment you must pay twice.
- If you wish to see a complementary medical practitioner, you must usually be referred by your doctor (unless you go as a private patient and pay the bill yourself). Your health fund **may** pay all or part of the cost of acupuncture treatment, an osteopath or chiropractor, massage (**not** the sort provided in 'massage' parlours), spa treatment, chiropodist or witch doctor. From June 1999, standard cover has also included Chinese medicine, homeopathy, anthroposophic medicine and neural therapy. Check with your health fund what percentage of the bill (if any) they will pay, before committing yourself to a course of treatment and a large bill.
- Specialists in Switzerland are usually free to charge what they like and their fees are significantly higher than family doctors. Hospitals and doctors generally have different charge rates, as follows (lowest rate first):
  - Patients who have health insurance cover within the canton;

- Patients who have health insurance cover in another canton;
- Private patients who don't belong to a Swiss health fund or Swiss health insurance scheme.

● All bills, particularly those received for treatment outside Switzerland, must include precise details of treatment and prescriptions received. **Terms such as 'Consultation' or 'Dental Treatment' are insufficient.** It's helpful if bills are written in a language intelligible to your health fund, for example English, French, German or Italian.

● There are no restrictions on changing insurance companies, although the cancellation period for basic insurance is three months and policies can be terminated only on the 30th June and the 31st December (in writing by registered post). However, a policy with a higher deductible than the legal minimum can only be cancelled annually on 31st December, although if premiums are increased policies can be terminated with one month's notice. If you're planning to change your health insurance company, ensure that no important benefits are lost. If you change your health insurance company, it's advisable to inform your old company if you have any outstanding bills for which they're liable.

● If you're leaving Switzerland, you must cancel your insurance in writing and give at least one month's notice. **When leaving Switzerland, you should ensure that you have continuous medical insurance.** Note, however that if you're elderly or have a poor health record, you may find it difficult or impossible to obtain health insurance in some countries at an affordable price.

HOME CONTENTS INSURANCE

In most cantons it's mandatory to take out house contents insurance (*Hausratsversicherung/Haushaltversicherung, assurance des effets mobiliers*) covering your personal property against natural hazards such as fire, floods, gas explosions and theft. House contents insurance is inexpensive at around SFr. 200 a year for cover totalling some SFr. 50,000, or about SFr. 4 for each SFr. 1,000 of cover. Most house contents insurance policies cover the cost of replacing items at their new cost (new for old) and **not** their second-hand value (except bicycles, skis and snowboards, although you can include 'new for old' cover for these items for a small fee). House contents insurance doesn't include accidental damage caused by you or members of your family to your own belongings. It may also exclude accidental damage to fixtures or fittings (e.g. baths, wash basins, electrical fittings and apparatus), which can be covered by a private liability insurance policy (see below). A supplement may be payable to cover special window glass in modern homes, which is expensive to replace.

Take care that you don't under-insure your house contents and that you periodically reassess their value and adjust your insurance premium accordingly. You can arrange to have your insurance cover automatically increased annually by a fixed percentage or amount by your insurance company. If you make a claim and the assessor discovers that you're under-insured, the amount due will be reduced by the percentage by which you're under-insured. For example, if you're insured for SFr. 50,000 and you're found to be under-insured by 20 per cent, your claim totalling SFr. 5,000 will be reduced by 20 per cent to SFr. 4,000. Keep a list of all major possessions and receipts.

Insurance companies will provide you with a free estimate based on the number of rooms in your home, the number of occupants and whether you have expensive possessions or worthless stuff (like poor struggling authors!). Don't forget to mention any particularly valuable items, e.g. the family jewels or antique collection. House contents insurance can be combined with private liability insurance (see below).

If you own a property in Switzerland, you must insure it against fire with the local Cantonal Insurance Office (offices also provide insurance against water damage, although this isn't obligatory).

PRIVATE LIABILITY INSURANCE

It's customary in Switzerland to have private liability insurance (*Privat-Haftpflichtversicherung, assurance responsabilité civile*). To take an everyday example, if your soap slips out of your hand while you're taking a shower, jumps out of the window and your neighbour slips on it and breaks his neck, he (or his widow) will sue you for millions of francs. With private liability insurance you can shower in blissful security (but watch that soap!). If you set fire to your rented apartment, your landlord will claim against your private liability insurance (if you don't have insurance, they will lock you up and throw away the key). The cost is around SFr. 100 a year for cover of SFr. 5 million (which is the recommended cover). For some claims you may be required to pay the first SFr. 100 to 200.

Private liability insurance covers all members of a family and includes damage done or caused by your children and pets (for example if you dog or child bites someone). Where damage is due to severe negligence, benefits may be reduced. Private liability insurance can be combined with house contents insurance (see above). Check whether it covers you against accidental damage to your apartment's fixtures and fittings. Some sport accidents aren't covered by private liability insurance, for example if you accidentally strike your opponent with your squash racket, he cannot claim against your private liability insurance to have his teeth fixed (but can claim against his accident insurance). **If you cause an accident through your negligence, e.g. while skiing, you can be sued for heavy damages.** Another excellent reason to have private liability insurance.

OPTIONAL INSURANCE

The most common types of optional insurance available in Switzerland are the following:

- Private pension;
- Dental insurance;
- Travel insurance;
- Personal effects insurance;
- Motor breakdown insurance;
- Comprehensive motor insurance;
- Life & annuity insurance.

The above insurance is described below or a reference is made to the chapter where it's described in detail.

Private Pension

The federal (see page 259) and company pension schemes (see page 261), are often equal to a maximum of 60 per cent of earnings (for those who have worked in Switzerland their whole working life!). To supplement these pensions and bring your pension closer to your final salary, you can contribute to a private pension fund (*Alterssparheft, caisse privée prévoyance-vieillesse*) and receive tax relief on your contributions (up to a limited amount). This is the third part of the Swiss social security system, called pillar three (*Selbstvorsorge, épargne personelle*). If you're a member of a company pension fund, you may pay up to 8 per cent of the maximum average pensionable AHV/AVS salary, which was SFr. 5,933 a year on 1st January 2002, tax-free into a private pension fund or a special bank account. If you **aren't** a member of a company pension fund, you may save up to 20 per cent of your annual income tax-free (but not more than 40 per cent of the maximum average pensionable AHV/AVS salary), up to a maximum of SFr. 29,664.

You can receive the benefits of a private pension scheme up to five years before the Swiss retirement age of 65 (men) or 62-64 (women), although you must pay a reduced rate of tax on a portion of the amount. Repayment can also be made in the following circumstances:

- If you become an invalid;
- If you leave Switzerland permanently;
- If you become self-employed (after being an employee);
- If you join another pension scheme.

The interest paid by banks on private pension savings in Switzerland is around 2 to 2.5 per cent. There are no bank charges or bank taxes. You might find it worthwhile to compare the interest received from a private pension fund in Switzerland with that paid in other countries. However, you should take care which currency you choose, as your savings could be considerably reduced if the currency is devalued (and you may have to pay tax on the interest).

Dental Insurance

Basic dental insurance (*Zahnarztversicherung, assurance dentaire*) can be taken out as a supplement to Swiss health insurance. Health funds and health insurance companies offer dental cover or extra dental cover for an additional premium, although there are many limitations and cosmetic treatment is excluded. It's unusual to have full dental insurance in Switzerland as the cost is prohibitive. A dental inspection is usually required before you're accepted as a reasonable risk. Dental treatment can be **very** expensive in Switzerland (you don't always receive gold fillings, but you usually pay your bills in gold!) and you should obtain an estimate before committing yourself to a large bill.

In primary and possibly secondary school, children receive a free annual dental inspection from a school appointed dentist. An estimate is provided for any dental treatment required and communities may pay a percentage of bills for low income families. Your health insurance company may also pay a percentage, if your child is insured for dental treatment. If you or your children require expensive cosmetic dental treatment, e.g. crowns, bridges, braces and false teeth, it's usually cheaper to have the treatment outside Switzerland, as dental costs are lower in all of Switzerland's neighbouring countries. Alternatively, ask your dentist if he can reduce the cost by reducing the work involved. This may be possible as Swiss dentists usually strive for absolute perfection, e.g. when straightening a child's teeth. It could be a lot cheaper to settle for less. The amount payable by your health insurance for a particular item of treatment is fixed and depends on your level of dental insurance. A list of the amounts refunded are available from health insurance companies.

There are usually no restrictions on where (either in Switzerland or abroad) you obtain dental treatment, although you must provide your health insurance company with a detailed itemised bill. You can use a health insurance form to pay your dental bill (see page 266), although most people pay their dental bills directly (after pawning the family jewels and taking out a second mortgage) and then send the bill to their health insurance company for a refund.

Travel Insurance

Travel insurance (*Reiseversicherung, assurance voyage*) is available from insurance companies, travel agents, airports and railway stations in Switzerland. Worthy of special mention is the protection letter (*Schutzbrief, livret*), a comprehensive travel insurance policy, available from Swiss motoring organisations (see page 232). It includes most travel and holiday emergencies and is valid irrespective of the mode of transport used. Short-term holiday insurance is also provided by the ACS and TCS and the Swiss railways (SBB).

Carefully check the level of travel insurance required. For example, you may require insurance for loss of deposit or holiday cancellation, personal effects and baggage, health and accidents, personal money and private liability. **Travel insurance usually excludes high-risk sports such as skiing and jet-skiing, unless specifically covered.** You must never admit liability and never pay out a cent without written permission from your insurers.

If you belong to a Swiss health fund or health insurance scheme, you're usually covered for health insurance world-wide for up to twice the cost of treatment in Switzerland.

Personal Effects Insurance

You can take out personal effects insurance (*Mobiliarversicherung, assurance mobilière*) to cover your belongings world-wide when travelling or when you're away from your normal home (this can also be included in your house contents insurance). The cost is around SFr. 80 a year for cover of SFr. 2,000. Some companies may require you to pay the first 10 per cent or SFr. 200 of a claim.

Motor Breakdown Insurance

Motor breakdown insurance (*Autopanneversicherung, assurance dépannage*) for Switzerland and foreign countries is available from Swiss motoring organisations (see page 232), which also provide insurance for motorcycles, mopeds and bicycles.

Comprehensive Motor Insurance

Full comprehensive (*Vollkasko, casco intégral*) or partial comprehensive (*Teilkasko, casco partiel*) motor insurance may be taken out with any motor insurance company in Switzerland (see page 212). Third part motor insurance is obligatory.

Life & Annuity Insurance

Some Swiss companies provide free life insurance (*Lebensversicherung, assurance vie*) as an employment benefit, although it may be accident life insurance only. You can take out a life insurance or endowment policy with numerous Swiss and foreign insurance companies. Swiss policies are usually for life **insurance** and not, as for example in the UK, for **assurance**. Assurance is a policy which covers an eventuality which is certain to occur, for example, like it or not you must die one day (unless the Swiss invent an immortality drug). Thus a life assurance policy is valid until you die. An **insurance** policy covers a risk that **may** happen but isn't a certainty, for example accident insurance (unless you're **very** accident prone).

In Switzerland a life insurance policy is generally valid until you're 70 years old, depending on the company. If you die before you're 70 they pay up, but if you live longer than 70 years they pay nothing. Health insurance companies work closely with the medical profession to ensure that you don't die before you're 70! The reason insurance companies sponsor fitness courses is to keep people fit and healthy so they live to a ripe old age (it works remarkably well in Switzerland). A life insurance policy is useful as security for a bank loan and can be limited to cover the period of the loan (some lenders insist upon it).

14.

FINANCE

Switzerland is (per capita) the wealthiest country in the world, with one of the world's highest Gross Domestic Products (GDPs) per head (around US$31,005) and some 100,000 millionaires (the Swiss are the richest people in Europe in terms of average personal wealth). Swiss banks and financial institutions are renowned for their efficiency and security, and Zurich is one of the world's major financial centres and Switzerland is the world capital of private banking. The Banking Commission has estimated that Swiss banks have some SFr. 2,500 billion under management, at least half of which is deposited by overseas clients. However Switzerland's prosperity has been damaged by an over-valued Swiss franc (the world's strongest currency) in the last decade, although it's value has fallen slightly in recent years.

Financially, Switzerland is the safest country in the world and it has traditionally been a favourite bolt-hole for 'hot' money. The world-famous (infamous) secrecy surrounding Swiss numbered bank accounts extends to all customer accounts, and heavy fines and even imprisonment can result for employees who breach this confidentiality. The Swiss have, however, succumbed to international pressure in recent years and introduced tougher rules to combat money laundering. This hasn't stopped some critics labelling Swiss banks 'launderettes' and Russian and other 'Mafia' money is allegedly still flooding into the country. Switzerland's reputation has also been tarnished in recent years by the furore over Nazi gold and dormant Jewish funds dating back to the second world war, as a result of which Swiss banks agreed to pay holocaust survivors US$1.5 billion.

Competition for your money is fierce and financial services are provided by numerous Swiss and foreign banks, investment brokers, post offices and even railway station booking offices. One of the surprising things about the Swiss is that they don't usually pay bills with cheques or credit cards and use cash more than anywhere else in the western world. Over 90 per cent of all retail purchases are paid for with **real** money, compared with less than 70 per cent in the UK and the US.

When you arrive in Switzerland to take up residence or employment, ensure that you have sufficient cash, traveller's cheques, credit cards, luncheon vouchers, gold and diamonds, to last at least until your first pay day, which may be up to two months after your arrival. During this period you may also find an international credit card useful.

See also **Chapter 13** for information regarding company and private pension schemes, and life and annuity insurance.

SWISS CURRENCY

As you may already be aware, the Swiss unit of currency is the Swiss franc (*Frank, franc*), the most stable currency in the world. The Swiss franc has been allowed to float on the foreign exchange markets since 1973, since when it has increased in value against the US$ and £sterling by over 250 per cent (which naturally has **nothing** whatsoever to do with why foreigners are so eager to work in Switzerland!). In fact the Swiss franc appreciated so much in the early 1990s that it made life difficult for Switzerland's exporters and the tourist industry. In September 2003, one Swiss franc was equal to around GB£0.45, □0.65 and US$0.75.

The Swiss franc is divided into 100 cents (*Rappen, centime*) and Swiss coins are minted in 5, 10 and 20 cents and half, 1, 2 and 5 francs. Banknotes are printed in denominations of 10, 20, 50, 100, 200, 500 and 1,000 francs. **Beware of counterfeit banknotes, some of which are made with sophisticated colour laser copiers.** New high-tech banknotes with a wide range of security features are being gradually introduced and are allegedly 'virtually impossible' to counterfeit. The new notes contain five visible safety features plus a second level detectable by special equipment and a third level known only to the central bank. The franc is usually written as SFr. When writing figures in Switzerland, a quotation mark (') is used to separate units of millions, thousands and hundreds, and a comma (,) to denote cents, e.g. 1'500'485,34 is one million, five hundred thousand, four hundred and eighty five francs and 34 cents – a nice healthy bank balance! Values below one franc are written with zero francs, e.g. 0,75 is seventy five cents (**note that in this book they're written as SFr. 0.75**).

FOREIGN CURRENCY

Buying foreign currency with Swiss francs is invariably a pleasant experience. The major Swiss banks change practically all foreign banknotes without batting an eyelid and even most coins, although at a lower exchange rate than banknotes. Banks give a higher exchange rate for traveller's cheques than for banknotes. Foreign currency can also be purchased from special foreign currency dispensing machines at selected branches of major Swiss banks, e.g. in shopping centres and at airports. The most popular foreign currencies can also be changed to Swiss francs via machines at airports and major railway stations. The big banks (UBS and CS) charge a fee of SFr. 5 for cash currency exchanges unless you have a bank account with them. The Coop Bank and Migros Bank and many cantonal banks don't charge such fees and often have better exchange rates.

Switzerland has no currency restrictions. You may bring in or take out as much money as you wish, in any currency. Many Swiss hotels and shops accept and change foreign currency, but usually at a less favourable exchange rate than banks. The Swiss franc exchange rate (*Wechselkurs, cours de change*) against most European and major international currencies is listed in banks and daily newspapers. Most Swiss banks sell palladium, platinum, gold and silver (bars and coins), which are a popular investment – particularly when the world's stock markets are in a panic. Swiss gold coins are a favourite gift from Swiss godparents to their godchildren (in fact most people are happy to receive them).

Many railway stations provide a money changing service, which is particularly handy for 'spur of the moment' motoring trips abroad. Major SBB stations have change bureaux (with extended opening hours) where you can buy or sell foreign currencies at favourable rates, buy and cash traveller's cheques, and obtain a cash advance on credit cards. In over 300 smaller stations, you can buy currency and traveller's cheques in the most popular foreign currencies. Railway station change offices are open during normal railway booking office hours from around 6am until 7.30pm, including weekends, and are open even later at major stations. The SBB and the Swiss Post are also representatives of Western Union in Switzerland and cash can be sent or received by telegraphic transfer in as little as ten minutes, although the cost is high. **When sending money abroad, you may get a better exchange rate from a post office than a bank.**

BANKS

If there's one place in Switzerland where you can be sure of a warm welcome, it's a Swiss bank (unless you plan to rob it!). It will probably come as no surprise to hear that there are **lots** of banks in Switzerland (around 600), although many have closed in recent years or have been swallowed up by the major banks. The three major Swiss banks became two in 1998, when the Union Bank of Switzerland (*Schweizerische Bankgesellschaft, Union de Banques Suisses*) merged with the Swiss Bank Corporation (*Schweizerische Bankverein, Société de Banque Suisse*). The merged bank has been named UBS and is the world's second largest bank after HSBC with some has 40 per cent of the Swiss market. A further 20 per cent of the home market is taken by the only other Swiss national bank, Crédit Suisse (*Schweizerische Kreditanstalt, Crédit Suisse*). However, big doesn't mean better to many Swiss and up to a quarter of the merged banks' domestic customers have deserted to the smaller canton banks which offer a more personal service and in most cantons provide a guarantee for deposits.

Switzerland is one of the most over-banked countries in the world and in addition to the two major banks, which have branches in most towns, there are many smaller regional, canton (around 25), loan and savings banks, plus private (mainly portfolio management) and foreign banks (around 150). If you do a lot of travelling abroad, you may find that the comprehensive range of services offered by the major Swiss banks is more suited to your needs. The major banks are also more likely to have staff who speak English and other foreign languages, and they can provide statements and other documentation in English and other non-Swiss languages.

In a small country town or village, there's usually a branch of one of the local banks (e.g. *Raiffeisenbank, Caisse Raiffeisen*) and a post office, but not a branch of a major bank. Local banks usually provide a more personal service and may offer cheaper loans and mortgages than the major banks. Recent years have seen the introduction of 24-hour telephone and Internet banking by the major Swiss banks, although Internet banking hasn't taken off in Switzerland like it has in some other countries.

Opening Hours

Normal bank opening hours are from between 8 or 8.30am to 4.30 or 4.45pm Monday to Friday, with no closure over the lunch period in cities and large towns. Most banks are open late on one day a week, e.g. until 5.30 or 6.30pm, depending on the bank and its location. In cities, a few banks have extended opening hours during the week and are open on Saturdays from around 9am to 4pm. In large shopping centres (*Einkaufszentrum, centre commercial*) most banks are open until 5pm on Saturdays and major banks are also open on Saturdays in many tourist areas. There are no general opening hours for country or village banks, which may be closed on Monday mornings and Wednesday afternoons and open on Saturday mornings. They usually close for lunch, which may extend from 11.45am until 2pm, but often remain open until 5.30pm, Monday to Friday. Banks at Swiss airports and major SBB stations are open from around 6.30 or 7am until 6.30pm (10.30pm at airports).

In major cities there are automatic 'electronic' 24-hour banking centres, where you can purchase foreign currencies, change foreign currency into Swiss francs, buy traveller's cheques and gold, change Swiss banknotes and coins, and rent safety deposit boxes. You can also obtain 24-hour telephone customer advice, and stock market and general banking information via computer terminals. These services are provided in addition to the usual automatic banking facilities, such as cash withdrawals, deposits and checking account balances.

Opening An Account

One of your first acts in Switzerland should be to open a bank account. Simply go to the bank of your choice and tell them you're living or working in Switzerland and wish to open a salary (*Salärkonto/Lohnkonto, compte salaire*) or personal account. After opening an account, don't forget to give the details to your employer (the bottom line is **always** getting paid). Some companies have a preferential arrangement with a particular bank, which may result in lower bank charges for employees. Your salary is normally paid by your employer directly into your bank or post office account. Your monthly salary statement will be sent to your home address or given to you at work. On arrival in Switzerland you may need to wait up to two months for your first pay cheque. This is unusual but check with your employers. If necessary they may give you an advance on your salary.

Bank statements are usually issued monthly (optionally daily, weekly or quarterly), interest is paid on deposits and an overdraft facility is available. **Note**

that if you ask your bank to retain your post for collection, fees can be astronomical. You won't receive a cheque book with a salary account, but an account card containing your encoded account information. Current accounts in Swiss francs and foreign currencies are available to all residents. Lower interest is paid on current accounts than on a salary account and a cheque book is only issued on request. Bank statements are issued quarterly and cheques aren't usually returned. A charge isn't made per cheque, but bank charges are levied annually, plus postal and other charges.

All banks offer many kinds of accounts in addition to salary and current accounts, including a range of savings accounts providing higher interest rates than a personal, salary or current account. Ask at your bank.

There are considerable differences in the fees banks charge, with UBS and Crédit Suisse more expensive for accounts with relatively small balances (if the balance averages over SFr. 10,000 in an account, fees are reduced). The smaller banks (cantonal banks, Migros and Coop bank) usually have lower fees. Migros bank (⌨ www.migrosbank.ch), owned by Switzerland's biggest supermarket chain (which also owns Globus and OfficeWorld), usually pays an interest rate that's 0.25 to 0.5 per cent higher than most other banks.

General Information

The following points are applicable to most Swiss banks:

- All bills can be paid through your bank. Simply send the payment forms to your bank with a completed payment advice form, provided free by your bank on request, or drop them in your bank's post box using the free envelopes provided. Your bank will make a payment order (*Zahlungsauftrag, ordre de paiement*). This method of payment is free and has the advantage that your payments (or the total payment) are recorded on your monthly bank statement. Alternatively you can pay your bills at a post office (see page 121).

- Buying stocks and bonds in Switzerland is normally done through a bank and not through a stockbroker. Most banks post the latest Swiss share prices in all branches and some have enquiry systems where information can be displayed on a computer screen.

- You can open a foreign currency account with any Swiss bank, although no interest is paid. If you receive a transfer from abroad, make sure that it's deposited in the correct account.

- With a salary account you will receive a monthly or quarterly statement (optionally daily or weekly), confirmation of payment of standing orders and cheques (debit advice), and a credit advice for payments made into your account other than your salary. All correspondence from the major Swiss banks can be requested in English and certain other non-Swiss official languages, in addition to French, German and Italian. **Note that banks charge postage of SFr. 0.70 or 0.90 for each transaction posted to you, depending on whether you choose 'A' or 'B' class post.**

- Many banks offer extra interest to students or youths aged, for example, from 16 to 20. This costs the banks very little as most students are broke, but all banks know that you need to 'get 'em while they're young', as few people change banks (which is why some banks offer to open a savings account for your new baby with a free deposit of SFr. 25 or 50).

- Any account holder can create a joint account by giving his spouse (or anyone else) signatory authority. A joint account can be for two or more people. You can specify whether cheques and withdrawal slips need to be signed by any 'partner' or require all partners' signatures.

- At the end of the year (or more frequently, depending on your bank) you will receive a statement listing all bank charges, interest paid or earned and the taxes, e.g. Federal Withholding Tax (see page 294), deducted during the previous year. Keep this in a safe place as when you complete your income tax return (see page 288) you can reclaim the withholding tax and any interest paid is also tax deductible.

- If you have insufficient funds in your account, your bank may not pay your standing order payments (*Dauerauftrag, ordre permanent*) **and may not inform you of this**. Standing orders are paid automatically, providing there's sufficient funds in the account to cover them. Check your monthly payment advices, sent as confirmation of payment of all standing orders, and your monthly bank statement. Standing orders cost around SFr. 15 a year from a salary account.

- If an American citizen wishes to hold US securities in a Swiss custodian account, he must sign a form stating that the Swiss bank is either allowed to inform the IRS about the account or that on the sale of the securities a withholding tax of 31 per cent of the profits or capital gains will be levied. All other citizens must sign a statement to the effect that they aren't American and have no tax liabilities in the US.

  All major Swiss banks produce numerous free brochures and booklets (many that are published in English) describing their services and containing interesting and useful information. The major banks also publish newsletters in English and other foreign languages, which are sent free to customers.

- Internet banking is available with most Swiss banks, usually free of charge. In 2003 UBS was the first (and so far only) bank to introduce additional charges for payments over the Internet (SFr. 0.30 for payments to a Swiss bank account, SFr. 5 for payments to accounts outside Switzerland).

Account Cards

Most banks issue account cards (*Bankkarte, carte bancaire*) which can be used at any branch to withdraw cash and carry out other transactions over the counter, and to withdraw up to SFr. 5,000 per day from cash dispensing machines (ATMs). When using your account card over the counter, identification must be provided, for example your Swiss residence permit, passport or driving licence. Account cards can also be used to make deposits (*Anzahlung, acompte*) or payments via machines (envelopes are provided), check account balances, order forms, and print a mini-statement and balance. Foreign currency can also be obtained via special foreign currency machines. Account cards are issued free to salary, personal and current account holders.

LOANS & OVERDRAFTS

Interest rates for people wishing to borrow are low in Switzerland, but then so is the interest paid on deposits. Some banks won't give foreigners with a B permit an unsecured loan (*Darlehen, emprunt/prêt*) during their first year in Switzerland. You will generally be unable to obtain a loan or overdraft (*Kontoüberziehung, dépassement de crédit*) until you've been in Switzerland at least three months.

The net interest margin charged by most Swiss banks is among the lowest in the world, although you should still shop around for the best deal (Migros bank's rates are among the lowest). Interest rates vary considerably depending on the bank, the loan amount and the period of the loan. Don't neglect the smaller banks as it isn't always necessary to have an account with a bank in order to obtain a loan. Ask your friends and colleagues for their advice. Some insurance companies also provide loans. If you have collateral, e.g. Swiss property or insurance, or can get someone to stand as a guarantor for a loan, you may be eligible for a loan at the (lower) mortgage interest rate. Some banks may require you to take out a life insurance policy for the duration of the loan.

It's usually easier to obtain an overdraft than a loan, particularly during your first year in Switzerland, although credit may be a limited, e.g. to SFr. 10,000. The overdraft interest rate is usually a few percentage points higher than the mortgage rate, but is much lower than the rate for a standard loan. Some banks allow salary or personal account holders to overdraw one month's net salary without making special arrangements, for which the current overdraft rate applies. Check with your bank. Overdrafts are insured free by some banks against customers being unable to repay them. If you have a hire purchase (credit) agreement, e.g. for a car, a bank won't usually give you a loan or overdraft, but they may offer to pay off the outstanding debt with a loan.

Borrowing from private loan companies, as advertised in some newspapers and magazines, is expensive (very high interest rates). **Use them only as a last**

resort when all other means have been exhausted. Even then, as a foreigner, you may need to find a homeowner or Swiss citizen to act as a guarantor (in which case you'd be better advised to borrow from a bank). In general, the more desperate your financial situation, the more suspicious you should be of anyone willing to lend you money (unless it's your mum!).

CREDIT CARDS

Most large Swiss businesses accept major international credit cards, although they don't always advertise this fact. Credit cards aren't so readily accepted by small businesses, for whom the commission charge can be prohibitive. The Swiss generally mistrust plastic money and prefer payment in cash, gold or diamonds. You can apply for certain credit cards through your bank. A Eurocard is the most commonly used credit card in Switzerland and the following conditions apply:

- The Eurocard costs from SFr. 50 a year (SFr. 150 for a Eurocard Gold) from banks, motoring organisations (e.g. the TCS), the post office and the SBB;
- It has a maximum spending limit of up to SFr. 10,000;
- It can be used to obtain up to SFr. 1,000 in cash per day in Switzerland or up to SFr. 10,000 a month from over 200,000 cash dispensing machines world-wide (there's a 2.5 per cent fee for cash withdrawals and a minimum charge of SFr. 10 outside Switzerland);
- It can be used to buy petrol from petrol stations with credit card pumps;
- The card provides free travel accident insurance up to SFr. 200,000 (SFr. 500,000 with a gold card) when travel costs are paid with the card;
- It is also a Mastercard, the most widely accepted credit card in North America;
- The allows you to pay the monthly bill by direct debit from a bank account (which is naturally preferred by card companies);
- It doesn't hold the card holder responsible for a lost or stolen card, provided it's reported immediately (☎ UBS card centre 01/828 31 34, CS card centre 0848/800 860, VISECA card services 044 200 83 83), when liability is limited to SFr. 100.

In comparison with Eurocard, the annual charge for a Visa/Classic card is SFr. 50 or 100, and Diners Club and American Express around SFr. 150. Gold cards are available with a higher spending limit and other benefits. There's a higher annual fee for a gold card plus an 'entrance' fee, although the annual fee may be reduced by 50 per cent if you spend SFr. 7,500 during a year and may be waived altogether if you spend SFr. 15,000 a year. Special edition cards are issued with

colourful designs by Swiss artists, for which there's an extra fee. Visa cards, Eurocards and the Migros bank M-Card can be combined with a half-fare travel card (see page 181).

Some credit cards provide free travel and accidental death insurance, when travel costs are paid with the card. Before obtaining a card, compare the costs and benefits provided, particularly the interest rates charged. Major department stores issue their own account cards, e.g. Globus, Jelmoli and Manor. Some store cards allow credit, whereby the account balance may be repaid over a period of time, although interest rates are usually high.

Many foreigners can obtain an international credit card in a country other than Switzerland and be billed in the currency of that country (or can retain existing 'foreign' credit cards). You may, however, find it more convenient and cheaper to be billed in Swiss francs rather than a foreign currency (e.g. US$ or sterling), where you must wait for the bill from outside Switzerland and payments vary due to exchange rate fluctuations.

If you happen to lose a bank or credit card, report it immediately to the issuing office, when your liability is usually limited to SFr. 100. Even if you don't like credit cards and shun any form of credit, they do have their uses such as no deposits on rental cars, no prepaying hotel bills, safety and security, and above all, convenience.

VALUE ADDED TAX

After rejecting the imposition of value added tax (*Mehrwertsteuer/MWSt, taxe sur la valeur ajoutée/TVA*) in referendums on three previous occasions, it was finally approved by voters on Nov 28th 1993. Value added tax (VAT) was introduced on 1st January 1995 and replaced the old purchase tax (WUST, ICHA). The low standard rate of just 7.6 per cent (increased from 6.5 per cent on 1st January 1999) compares favourably with the average of over 15 per cent in EU countries.

Certain products and services are exempt from VAT including postal services, health care, social security, sport, culture, insurance, the granting of free credits, factoring, current-account transactions and the export of goods. VAT applies to other goods and services at the following rates:

Rate (%)	Applicability
Reduced (2.4)	Food and drinks (excluding alcoholic drinks and cooked meals); meat; cereals; plants, seeds and flowers; some basic farming supplies; piped water; medicines and drugs; books, newspapers, magazines and other printed materials; and non-commercial services of radio and TV companies;
Hotel Rate (3.6)	Overnight stays in hotels and other accommodation;
Standard Rate (7.6)	All goods and services that aren't listed above.

Most prices in Switzerland are quoted inclusive of VAT, although some prices are occasionally quoted exclusive of VAT. Individuals are liable for VAT if their annual local and foreign taxable and tax-exempt turnover exceeds SFr. 75,000.

INCOME TAX

The rate of income tax (*Einkommenssteuer*, *impôt sur le revenu*) levied in Switzerland varies between around 15 and 35 per cent, which is good news for many foreigners, particularly those from most European countries and especially single people, although rates are rising faster than in most other industrialised countries. Income tax is levied by the federal government (direct federal tax) and by cantons and communities, and each of the 26 Swiss cantons is autonomous as far as taxes are concerned, which makes it impossible to provide comprehensive figures here, although some examples are given below. If you want to check the tax rates in a particular area, contact a local tax adviser (*Steuerberater*, *fiduciaire*), who will usually be able to provide you with a comparison between rates in different cantons and communities.

Income tax consists of the following taxes:

- **Federal Tax** (*Direkte Bundessteuer*, *impôt fédéral direct*) is levied at between 1 and 5 per cent according to your income and comprises around 20 per cent of your total tax bill. It's assessed differently from canton and community tax and entered on a separate tax form, sent with your community and canton tax forms. The deductions allowed against federal tax, based on your net annual salary, aren't the same as for canton and community tax.

- **Canton and Community Taxes** (*Staatssteuer/Kantonssteuer*, *impôt cantonale* and *Gemeindesteuer*, *impôt commune*) comprise by far the major part of your total tax bill. Generally, the richer the community, the lower its tax rate.

- **Fire Service Tax** (*Feuerwehrsteuer*, *taxe d'exemption au service de feu*) is paid by all community residents who aren't active members of the local fire service. It may be calculated as a percentage of your basic tax value or may be a fixed sum (e.g. SFr. 100 a year), depending on your canton.

- **Church Tax** (*Kirchensteuer*, *impôt du culte*) is calculated as a percentage of your basic tax value and is payable by all who pay direct tax, but can be reclaimed by those who aren't registered as members of an official Swiss religion (see page 80). The amount payable varies from community to community depending on your canton and church, and may be up to 20 per cent of your basic tax value.

Tax rates are progressive – the more you earn the more tax you pay – and vary according to whether you're married and how many children you have as well as where you live. Married couples and their minor children are assessed jointly.

A divorced or legally separated person is assessed separately. Unmarried couples often delay getting married in Switzerland because their joint income would put them in a higher tax bracket.

In 2003, income tax on selected incomes for a married man without children in the capital cities of the cantons that are most popular with English-speakers (which happen to include those with the highest and the lowest tax rates in Switzerland) were as shown below:

Community (Canton)	Annual Income (SFr.)		
	50,000	100,000	200,000
Basle (BS)	3,960	16,410	51,140
Berne (BE)	3,948	15,510	48,720
Fribourg (FR)	3,760	14,720	47,840
Geneva (GE)	2,510,	15,100	49,580
Lausanne (VD)	3,655	14,810	46,660
Lugano (TI)	2,810	13,780	48,580
Moutier (JU)	4,245	16,320	50140
Zug (ZG)	1,800	7,900	29,440
Zurich (ZH)	2,790	11,160	40,260

Foreigners usually pay direct (withholding) income tax (*Quellensteuer, impôt à la source*), which is deducted from salaries at source by employers and generally settles their income tax liability (direct income tax only applies to foreigners). This may result in foreigners paying a higher tax rate than the Swiss. If you pay source tax you should be aware of anything which entitles you to a refund such as mortgage interest. You should write to your canton's tax authorities requesting a reduction of your tax liability if you have interest expenses such as credit cards, car loans, mortgages or child support payments, whether in Switzerland or another country (a letter documenting the expenses and requesting a refund will suffice). Most cantons require the letter to be received by 31st March of the year following the tax year for which you are claiming.

Some cantons don't require foreigners to pay direct income tax when they earn above a certain amount (e.g. SFr. 120,000 per year), or when their cantons of residence and employment are different, although foreigners without a C permit must pay direct income tax in most cantons irrespective of their income level. You're always subject to tax in your canton of residence and not your canton of employment (which is a constant source of conflict between Geneva and Vaud – thousands of residents of Vaud work in Geneva, but pay no taxes there), if different. Foreigners paying direct income tax aren't generally required to file a tax return, although it's usually necessary if your gross earnings exceed SFr. 120,000 a year and/or you have considerable assets (such as property and investments), either in Switzerland or abroad.

When a foreigner obtains a C permit after five or ten years (see page 70), he automatically ceases to pay direct income tax and must complete an income tax return every one or two years and pay tax annually. **If you work in Switzerland and live in another country (e.g. Austria, France, Germany or Italy), you must usually pay income and other taxes in the country where you're resident.**

Unemployed 'leisured foreigners' (retirees or the 'idle rich') can choose to be taxed on a special basis (*Pauschalbesteuerung, forfait fiscal*) in many cantons, where assessment is based on a lump-sum figure according to a person's 'lifestyle'. In the cantons of Geneva and Vaud the assessment is based on five times the annual (theoretical) rental of accommodation (including a garage) or around 3 to 7 per cent of the property value. No wealth tax is payable on this figure. A minimum taxable income of SFr. 300,000 may be required to qualify under the special tax basis, which may not be advantageous to those whose only income is a pension or annuity. To qualify you must usually have a net wealth of at least SFr. 2 million. Under this scheme, you pay a fixed lump sum in income tax that's agreed with your local canton tax authorities and isn't related to your actual income. To qualify you should spend a minimum of 180 days a year in Switzerland.

In addition to Swiss taxes, you may also be liable for taxes in your home country. Citizens of most countries are exempt from paying taxes in their home country when they spend a minimum amount of time abroad, e.g. one year, although US nationals remain subject to US income tax while living abroad. It's usually your responsibility to familiarise yourself with the tax laws in your home country or country of domicile. If you're in doubt about your tax liability in your home country, contact your nearest embassy or consulate in Switzerland. US citizens can obtain a copy of the *Tax Guide for Americans Abroad* from American Consulates.

Tax Deductions

The following list is a rough guide to the deductions you can make from your gross salary when calculating your taxable income. Deductions are different, however, for federal and canton/community taxes.

- Obligatory insurance contributions such as federal old age and survivors insurance, disability insurance, company pension fund, accident insurance, health insurance and unemployment insurance. Most obligatory insurance contributions (see page 258) are deducted from your gross salary by your employer;

- Premiums for life insurance, endowment, annuity, private pension, accident, sickness, invalid and unemployment insurance, up to a maximum amount;

- Business expenses, e.g. car expenses (including travel to and from your place of work), entertainment (if not paid or reimbursed by your employer), outside or subsidised meals (not free meals), employment-related education and books;

- Standard allowances are permitted on many items, without proof of expenditure. Personal allowances vary depending on individual circumstances, e.g. single or married, divorced or widowed, and the number of children or dependants. Allowances vary from canton to canton.

- Interest charges on mortgages, loans and overdrafts;

- Medical expenses for your family that aren't reimbursed by an insurance policy and which total 5 per cent or more of your annual income (in some cantons: all medical expenses);

- Study costs, if not reimbursed by your employer;

- Donations to recognised charities up to a maximum amount;

Tax Calculation

Your income tax assessment is based on a 'basic tax value' (*Ordentliche Steuer/Einfache Steuer*, *impôt de base*), calculated from your taxable income after all deductions have been made. The basic tax value is derived from tables produced by each canton and is different for single and married people. A simple example of a tax calculation for federal and canton/community taxes is shown below:

Federal Tax	
	SFr.
Net annual salary	100,000
Deductions	(18,000)
Taxable income	82,000
Federal tax due	4,000
Canton/Community Taxes	
	SFr.
Net annual salary	100,000
Deductions	(12,000)

Taxable income	88,000
Basic tax value	6,000
Canton tax (120% of basic tax value)	7,200
Community tax rate (120% of basic tax value)	7,200
Parish church tax (20% of basic tax value)	1,200
Community fire tax	100
Total Canton/Community Tax	15,700
Grand Total Tax Bill	19,700

* Calculated from tables provided by your community tax office.

Annual Tax Bill

Income tax for Swiss and foreigners with a C permit, or others who aren't eligible to pay direct income tax, is payable annually. Tax is calculated on your net assets. Nearly all cantons have now switched to a system whereby tax is based on the income of the preceding year and an assessment is made annually. If you have no previous income record in Switzerland, you will receive a provisional assessment until a full tax period has passed. The difference between what you've paid and your final tax bill will either be payable or refunded. Your tax bill (*Steuerrechnung, prélèvement fiscale*) usually comes in two or three parts. The Swiss don't call it a tax **demand**, but an 'invitation to pay' – if you decline the invitation, they lock you up! There will be a tax bill for the cantonal tax and one for the community tax (these two together make around 80 per cent of your tax liability). The remaining 20 per cent is federal tax, which is calculated separately.

Canton & Community Tax

You usually receive your canton and community tax bills for the current year a few weeks after filing your tax return. **Note that the dates the tax is due can be different for federal, cantonal and community tax.** In some cantons, cantonal tax is due even before the end of the year you file a tax return for, and it's up to you to guess the amount in order to pay it on time. When you pay late interest of approximately 5 per cent is charged. If you pay a bill early, the tax office pays you interest, which is usually higher than if you had left the money in a savings account (and the interest isn't taxable). Payment slips for advance payments are available at tax offices. If you prefer to pay your tax bill monthly or quarterly, inform your tax office and they will send you the appropriate payment advices. If you receive a late assessment and bill for tax, you may be given an extra month or two to pay it. In this case your tax bill may consist of various parts, payable at different times.

Federal Tax

The second part of your tax bill is for direct federal tax (*direkte Bundessteuer, impôt fédéral direct*) and represents approximately 20 per cent of your total tax bill. Bills are payable by 1st March annually. If you don't pay your bill by the due date, you can be charged interest on any outstanding sum. In practice it may be possible to pay your tax bill, or part of it, a month or two late without paying interest (but don't count on it). If you aren't going to be able to pay your tax bill on time, it's advisable to inform your community tax office (so they won't think that you've absconded).

Income Tax Return

If you don't pay direct income tax, you must complete an income tax return annually. The forms are sent to you by your community tax office, usually in January, and must usually be completed and returned by the 31st March. If necessary, ask for a delay in completing the return, which should be a formality as it takes months to process them all. It's advisable to contact a tax accountant (*Steuerberater, conseiller financier/fiduciaire*), your local tax office (*Steueramt, bureau des impôts*) or your bank for help in completing your tax return. Apart from language problems and the tax knowledge necessary, a pile of forms must be completed. For most people it simply isn't worth the effort doing it themselves, particularly as a tax accountant may charge 'only' a few hundred francs to complete a simple tax return. If you need information regarding your tax return or any correspondence from your local tax office, it's better to go in person rather than telephone. Take someone with you if you don't speak the local language. The tax authorities want to know about all your sources of income, including the following:

- Salary, commission or any other form of employment income, including allowances in cash or kind;
- Professional or business income (net of expenses);
- Pensions and annuities;
- Income from real estate, including the estimated rental value of personal occupancy (net of estimated maintenance costs);

- Dividends and interest from investments in Swiss or foreign securities, receivables or deposits, royalties, licence and similar fees;
- Interest you've paid on debts, loans or mortgages and on late tax payments (these can all be claimed).

Taxable income usually includes your total income from all sources and all net assets **world-wide**, excluding property. If part of your income is taxed abroad in a country with a double taxation treaty with Switzerland, you won't be required to pay Swiss tax on that amount. However, your Swiss tax rate (basic tax value) may be assessed on your total world-wide income, including the portion on which you've already paid tax. Despite the name, the double taxation treaty is designed to **prevent** you paying double taxes and not to ensure that you pay twice. Income derived from real estate outside Switzerland is exempt from Swiss tax, but may be taxed abroad. For information, write to the Swiss Federal Tax Office, Section for International Fiscal Law and Double Taxation Matters, Bundesgasse 32, CH-3003 Berne (🖳 www.estv.admin.ch).

If you pay direct income tax, you can request a tax review (by completing an income tax return) if you think you've paid too much tax. **Note, however, that there's the possibility that instead of giving you a rebate, the tax authorities may 'invite' you to pay additional tax.** Anyone can lodge an appeal against their tax assessment. In some cantons, foreigners with a B permit paying direct income tax and earning above a certain amount, e.g. SFr. 120,000 a year, must complete a tax return. If your tax status changes in the first year after completing a tax return, e.g. due to the birth of a child, marriage, a dependent relative or a large change in income, you can ask to have an intermediate assessment instead of waiting until the end of the tax period. If your spouse starts working, an intermediate assessment is obligatory.

All Swiss taxes must be paid when changing cantons or before leaving Switzerland. Tax for a period of less than one year is assessed on a pro rata basis.

FEDERAL WITHHOLDING TAX

A federal withholding tax (*Verechnungssteuer, impôt anticipé*) of 35 per cent is deducted directly from investment income, which includes all interest on bank balances in Switzerland. This tax is intended for businesses and although it's automatically deducted by all banks from the interest on deposits, it's reclaimable by individuals paying Swiss income tax, provided they declare their assets. You may, however, be liable for wealth tax on your assets (see below). If you pay direct income tax (*Quellensteuer, impôt à la source*), federal withholding tax can be reclaimed for the preceding three years via a form available from your community office. If you pay tax annually, a claim should be made on your income tax return. You can choose to have federal withholding tax repaid in cash, directly into a bank or post office account, or deducted from your next tax bill, when you will be paid interest on the amount due.

WEALTH TAX

A wealth tax (*Vermögenssteuer*, *impôt sur la fortune*) is levied by all cantons on net wealth. The rate is progressive and varies depending on the canton and community where you live, and is usually between 0.25 and 1 per cent. Where applicable, wealth tax is paid along with your canton and community taxes. Some cantons also impose a special real estate tax (this is instead of or in addition to wealth tax) which can range from 0.03 and 0.3 per cent of the gross value.

CAPITAL GAINS TAX

Capital gains tax is levied on property (real estate) but not on other assets and depends on the amount of profit made and the length of ownership. As with income tax, rates vary from canton to canton. Capital gains are usually taxed separately and not with general income.

INHERITANCE & GIFT TAX

There are no federal estate, inheritance or gift taxes in Switzerland, but these taxes are levied on residents by most cantons. Rates vary considerably with the canton and according to the relationship of the beneficiary to the deceased or donor, as shown in the tables below (selected communities only; note that there's no inheritance or gift tax in Schwyz).

Spouses

City (Canton)	Value of Estate (SFr.)	
	100,000	500,000
Basel (BS)	-	-
Berne (BS)	-	-
Fribourg (FR)	3,000	15,000
Geneva (GE)	3,050	21,550
Lausanne (VD)	984	14,295
Lugano (TO)	0	0
Moutier (JU)	1,125	9,500
Zug (ZG)	0	0
Zurich (ZH)	0	0

Descendants

City (Canton)	Value of Estate (SFr.) 100,000	500,000
Basel (BS)	-	-
Berne (BS)	1,000	7,125
Fribourg (FR)	-	-
Geneva (GE)	3,050	21,550
Lausanne (VD)	984	14,295
Lugano (TO)	2,750	29,000
Moutier (JU)	1,152	9,500
Zug (ZG)	-	-
Zurich (ZH)	-	19,600

Unrelated Beneficiaries

City (Canton)	Value of Estate (SFr.) 100,000	500,000
Basel (BS)	26,460	174,798
Berne (BS)	22,100	172,100
Fribourg (FR)	30,000	150,000
Geneva (GE)	49,896	268,296
Lausanne (VD)	24,354	125,000
Lugano (TO)	28,050	211,425
Moutier (JU)	27,500	187,500
Zug (ZG)	10,800	70,900
Zurich (ZH)	19,200	153,600

Generally, German-speaking cantons don't levy inheritance tax for spouses and descendants, whereas French-speaking cantons do. The duty levied upon the estate of a foreigner who's domiciled in Switzerland but has never been employed there is reduced in some cantons, e.g. by 50 per cent in Vaud.

WILLS

It's an unfortunate fact of life that you're unable to take all those lovely Swiss francs with you when you make your final departure (unless you're Swiss, in which case you will have access to heavenly 'bancomats'!). All adults should make a will (*Testament*) irrespective of how large or small their assets.

If you don't want your estate to be subject to Swiss law, you're usually eligible to state in your will that it's to be interpreted under the law of another country. This will depend on your and your spouse's nationality and your ties with that country. A foreigner who also holds Swiss nationality **must** make his will under Swiss law if he is resident in Switzerland. If your estate comes under Swiss law, your dependants may be subject to the weird and wonderful Swiss inheritance laws. **Swiss law is restrictive regarding the distribution of property and the identity of heirs, and the estate is divided according to the number of children, who may receive the lion's share of the spoils.** You might not be too concerned about this (wherever you end up), but your dependants might well be!

In order to avoid being subject to Swiss death duty (see above) and inheritance laws, you must establish your domicile in another country. Foreigners living in Switzerland with a C permit are usually considered under Swiss federal and private international law to be domiciled in Switzerland.

In general, all valid wills made in accordance with the law of the place of execution are recognised in Switzerland, both under the Hague convention, to which Switzerland is a signatory, and under the Swiss Private International Law Act 1987. It's possible to make two wills, one relating to Swiss property and another for foreign property (which is always advisable).

If you don't specify in your will that the law of another country applies to your estate, then Swiss law applies. If you live in Switzerland and wish your will to be interpreted under Swiss law, you can state this and that you've abandoned your previous domicile in your will. Your will must also be legal and valid in Switzerland.

Making a will in Switzerland is simple: it must be hand-written, state your full name, and be dated and signed. No witnesses are required. However, to ensure that the contents of your will comply with Swiss law, it's advisable to obtain legal advice.

Keep a copy of your will(s) in a safe place and another copy with your solicitor or the executor of your estate. Don't leave your will in a safe deposit box, which in the event of your death will be sealed for a period under Swiss law. You should keep information regarding bank accounts and insurance policies with your will(s) – but don't forget to tell someone where they are.

If you die while working in Switzerland, your salary will usually be paid for an extra month or two if you have more than five years' service (maybe the Swiss really do have bancomats in heaven!).

COST OF LIVING

No doubt you'd like to know how far your Swiss francs are likely to stretch and how much money (if any) you will have left after paying all your bills. First the good news. As you're probably aware, Switzerland has one of the world's highest standards of living, its per capita income and purchasing power is among the highest in the world, and executive salaries are the highest in Europe. On the other hand, some 300,000 people receive social assistance and it's estimated that up to double this number live on or below the official Swiss poverty line, defined as an income of around SFr. 1,700 a month. Switzerland generally has a very low inflation rate and although it reached 5.4 per cent in 1990 (which for Switzerland is hyper-inflation), it was just 0.6 per cent in late 2002.

The bad news is that Switzerland has one of the highest costs of living in Europe and Swiss cities, particularly Zurich and Geneva, are among the most expensive in the world. The prices of some goods are unnecessarily high for no apparent reason, other than Switzerland's cartels and anti-competitive practices. The average price of many goods and services in Switzerland are up to 40 per cent higher than in EU countries and up to 60 per cent higher than in the US. However, prices of many goods and services (e.g. most retail goods; government-fixed prices such as hospital, postal and railway charges; insurance premiums; and credit costs) are monitored and controlled by the office of Price Controller to prevent unjustifiable price increases. If you wish to make comparisons, the UBS bank publishes a free annual booklet in English entitled *Prices and Earnings Around the World*.

It's difficult to calculate an average cost of living in Switzerland, as it depends on your circumstances and lifestyle. Although the cost of living in Switzerland is high, costs are offset by much higher salaries and lower taxes than in many other countries. What is important to most people is how much money they can save or spend each month. Overall your food bill will almost certainly be higher, as Switzerland has **very** high food prices (only exceeded world-wide by Tokyo). The actual difference in your food bill will depend on what you eat and where you lived before coming to Switzerland. Due to the high subsidies paid to Swiss farmers, food in Switzerland is 25 to 50 per cent more expensive than in most EU countries and North America. Around SFr. 600 should feed two adults for a month in most areas, excluding fillet steak, caviar and alcohol (living in Switzerland provides an excellent incentive to cut down on all those expensive, rich foods).

Despite the high cost of food, the cost of living in Switzerland needn't be astronomical. If you shop wisely, compare prices and services before buying, and don't live too extravagantly, you may be pleasantly surprised at how little your can live on (provided you don't want to buy a house). In fact, with the notable exception of housing, many people find that the cost of living in Switzerland isn't as high as they expected. Shopping abroad (see page 362), particularly for expensive purchases and food, can help reduce your living costs considerably. When possible, many foreigners choose to live in a neighbouring country (where the cost of living is significantly lower) and commute to their jobs in Switzerland.

A list of the approximate **MINIMUM** monthly expenses for an average single person, couple or family of four is shown in the table below (the numbers indicated after some of the items refer to the notes below). When calculating your cost of living, remember to deduct the appropriate percentage for income tax (see page 288) and obligatory insurance deductions (see page 258) from your gross salary.

ITEM	MONTHLY COSTS (SFr.)		
	Single	**Couple**	**Couple & 2 Children**
Housing (1)	1,000	1,500	2,000
	(1 bed)	(2 bed)	(3 bed)
Food (2)	400	600	800
Utilities (3)	200	250	300
Leisure (4)	400	450	500
Car (5)	250	250	250
Travel	100	150	200
Insurance (6)	450	700	900
Clothing	100	200	300
TOTAL	**2,900**	**4,100**	**5,250**

Notes

1. Rent or mortgage payments for a modern or modernised apartment or house in an average small town or suburb, excluding major cities and other high cost areas. The properties envisaged are a studio or one bedroom apartment for a single person, a two-bedroom property for a couple, and a three-bedroom property for a couple with two children. **Note that in some cities, e.g. Geneva and Zurich, housing can cost double or treble these figures.**

2. Doesn't include luxuries or liquid food (alcohol).

3. Includes electricity, gas, water, telephone, cable or satellite TV, and heating and air-conditioning costs.

4. Includes all entertainment, dining out, sports and vacation expenses, plus newspapers and magazines.

5. Includes running costs for an average family car, plus third party insurance, annual taxes, petrol, servicing and repairs, but excludes depreciation or credit costs.

6. Includes standard Swiss health insurance (but not expensive international health insurance), household (building and contents), third party liability, travel, automobile breakdown and life insurance.

15.

LEISURE

The above paragraph was how Switzerland was cursorily dismissed in a travel book describing the world and its regions, published in 1928. Some 70 years later, not surprisingly, a few things have changed (there are fewer goats and trees). However, Switzerland still has immense wealth and catering for visitors has developed into a very profitable tourist industry. Tourism is Switzerland's third largest industry, employing some 300,000 people directly or indirectly and earning around SFr. 12 billion annually. One in every three people in mountain areas relies on tourism for a livelihood, although visitor numbers have been hit by the strength of the Swiss franc in recent years, during which earnings (some 6 per cent of GDP) have fallen.

Leisure activities and entertainment in Switzerland are of the high standard and diversity you'd expect from a country that celebrated 200 years of tourism in 1987 (and its 700th anniversary in 1991) and is credited with having invented tourism. It offers a huge variety of entertainment, sports (see **Chapter 16**) and pastimes and is blessed with a wealth of natural beauty hardly matched anywhere in the world in such a small area. The majority of tourists come to Switzerland to participate in outdoor sports, e.g. skiing and hiking, and not, for example, to savour the night life (which although lively enough for most people, may disappoint the international jet set). If you want to avoid road traffic and its ever-attendant pollution, visit one of Switzerland's delightful car-free Alpine resorts (Bettmeralp, Braunwald, Mürren, Riederalp, Rigi-Kaltbad, Saas-Fee, Stoss, Wengen and Zermatt).

Switzerland is a small country and no matter where you live you can regard the whole country as your playground. Due to excellent road and rail connections, a huge area is accessible for day excursions and anywhere within Switzerland (and many neighbouring countries) is within easy reach for a weekend trip. The maximum distance from east to west is only 348km (216mi) and from north to south it's just 220km (137mi).

Information regarding local events and entertainment is available from tourist offices and local newspapers. In most cities there are magazines or newspapers devoted to entertainment, e.g. *Panorama* and *Scoop* in French-speaking Switzerland. Free weekly or monthly programmes are published by tourist offices in all major cities and tourist centres. Many city newspapers publish free weekly magazines or supplements containing a detailed programme of local events and entertainment. Other useful sources of information are the monthly English-language magazines *Swiss News* (🖳 www.swissnews.ch) and *GT Magazine* (🖳 www.genevanews.com), plus *Revue Switzerland* (🖳 www.revue.ch), which is published only in French and German. The latest entertainment information can also be obtained from the Swiss television teletext service as well as the Internet (🖳 www.myswitzerland.com).

The main aim of this chapter, and indeed the purpose of the whole book, is to provide information that isn't found in standard guide books. General tourist information is available in many excellent Swiss guide books including the *Michelin Green Guide to Switzerland, Baedeker's Switzerland, Fodor's Switzerland* and *Lonely Planet Switzerland* (see **Appendix B** for a list).

TOURIST OFFICES

There are tourist offices in all Swiss cities and tourist areas, where English-speaking staff can provide you with a wealth of information and also find you a hotel room. They're open daily, including Saturdays and Sundays, in most major cities and tourist centres. Telephone the tourist office or consult a guide book to find the exact business hours. In major towns, reduced opening hours are in operation during winter, while in smaller towns and resorts tourist offices close for lunch and may open during the winter **or** summer season only. Services provided by tourist offices include local information; hotel reservations; local and city tours; excursions; congresses; car rental; guides and hostesses; and train and bus information. In some towns, a walking tour on cassette (with free map) can be rented for a small fee.

In an effort to enhance Switzerland's image, the Swiss National Tourist Office was renamed Switzerland Tourism (*Schweiz Tourismus*, *Suisse Tourisme*) in 1995 and given a new logo. Switzerland Tourism (ST) is a mine of information and in addition to promoting tourism its aim is to further understanding of Switzerland's special political, cultural and economic characteristics, in close co-operation with the 12 regional tourist promotion boards. ST has offices in many countries including Australia, Austria, Belgium, Brazil, Canada, China, Egypt, France, Germany, Hong Kong, India, Israel, Italy, Japan, the Netherlands, Spain, Sweden, Taiwan, the UAE, the UK and the US. It produces over 100 publications (one in over 30 languages) totalling around four million copies and distributes many more. **ST is continually revising, updating and replacing its publications, and therefore some of the brochures mentioned in this book may no longer be available – contact ST's toll-free call centre (☎ 0800 100 200 30) for information.**

Whatever you'd like to know, ST will either provide you with the information directly or will give you the name of someone who can help you. They answer telephone enquiries and will send information by post, including an annual booklet entitled *Events in Switzerland*, listing music, theatre and film, folklore, public festivals, sports events, exhibitions, fairs, markets and congresses. ST is Switzerland's ambassador of tourism and in contrast to the sometimes frosty reception from Swiss embassies, particularly when enquiring about employment in Switzerland, they're a paragon of co-operation and friendliness. The head office is Switzerland Tourism, P.O. Box 695, CH-8027 Zurich (☎ 01 288 11 11 or 0800 100 200 30, 🖳 www.myswitzerland.com).

HOTELS

All Swiss hotels are comfortable, clean and efficient. The standard of hotel accommodation and service is excellent; whether a luxury 5-star hotel or a humble pension, it's almost impossible to find a bad hotel in Switzerland (the Dolder Hotel in Zurich has been chosen as the world's best hotel by the US trade journal *Conde Nast Traveler*). Not surprisingly, Swiss hotels and hotel training schools provide the best training for hotel staff in the world. Swiss hotels are, however, **very** expensive (the Royal Suite in the Hotel President Wilson in Geneva costs over SFr. 20,000 a night!), particularly in major cities, and the most expensive in Europe (the average is over SFr. 200 per night!). Prices vary considerably depending on the standard, location, season (low, middle or high) and the amenities provided. The following table can be used as a **rough** guide:

Class	Star Rating	Price Range (SFr.)
Luxury	5	250 – 500+
First	4	100 – 250
Middle	3	75 – 150
Comfortable	2	50 – 100
Simple	1	40 – 80

The prices quoted above are **per person, per night**, sharing a double room with bath (prices are usually quoted per person and not per room in Switzerland). There's usually no charge for children up to six years old when sharing their parents' room and reductions for older children are usually provided, e.g. 50 per cent for those aged 6 to 12 and 30 per cent for those aged 13 to 16. Continental breakfast is often included in the cost and a British or American style cooked breakfast, sometimes buffet style (self-service), is available in many first class hotels (although it may be an extra). Many hotels with restaurants offer half-board (breakfast and dinner) or full-board (breakfast, lunch and dinner) on favourable terms. A hotel *Garni* provides bed and breakfast and beverages, but no meals.

Inexpensive accommodation, e.g. small one-star hotels and pensions, is usually difficult to find in the main cities. Outside major cities it isn't necessary to pay a fortune. A guide to around 200 'simple & cosy' hotels is available from E&G Swiss Budget Hotels, Route des Layeux, Case Postale 160, CH-1884 Villars (☎ toll-free 0848 80 55 08, 🖳 www.rooms.ch). E&G hotel accommodation varies from dormitory beds at SFr. 20 per night up to the most expensive rooms at around SFr. 80 per person, per night. A brochure (provided by E&G) listing inexpensive hotels, inns and pensions for an average of around SFr. 40 per night (including breakfast but without a bath or shower) is available from Switzerland Tourism (see also **Youth Hostels** on page 309). Many hotels in Switzerland have special rates for senior citizens and children. Most people should be able to find something to suit their budget and taste among over 6,000 hotels and boarding houses in Switzerland, offering a total of over 200,000 beds.

The *Swiss Hotel Guide* (*Schweizer Hotelführer*, *Guide Suisse des Hôtels*) is published annually by the Swiss Hotel Association (SHA), and is available free from them (see address below) and Switzerland Tourism (ST) offices. It contains the addresses, telephone/fax numbers, opening dates, room rates and amenities of over 2,500 hotels, guesthouses and pensions, including hotels with special facilities for the disabled. It also lists restaurants, spas and climatic resorts. The SHA also publish brochures for senior citizens, a list of hotels with special facilities for families and information about country inns. For more information contact the Swiss Hotel Association (*Schweizer Hotelier-Verein, Société Suisse des Hôteliers*), Monbijoustr. 130, Postfach, CH-3001 Berne (☎ 031 370 41 11, 🖳 www.swisshotels.ch).

An organisation catering particularly for families is Happy Family Swiss Hotels, Postfach, CH-8784 Braunwald (☎ 055 643 38 44, ✉ kinderhotels@ bluewin.ch). Special holiday deals are available throughout the year at most large hotels, e.g. skiing holidays, including half board and a ski pass. Holidays tailored specially for pensioners are organised by Pro Senectute Schweiz, Lavaterstr. 60, Postfach, CH-8027 Zurich (☎ 01 283 89 89, 🖳 www.pro-senectute.ch). Information about hotels with special facilities for the disabled is available from Procap, Reisen für Menschen mit Handicap, Froburgstr. 4, CH-4600 Olten SO (☎ 062 206 88 30). They also produce holiday catalogues for disabled people and city guides for the disabled for 26 Swiss towns and cities.

In most Swiss cities and resorts, the local tourist office will find you a hotel room for a charge of around SFr. 2. They may also provide brochures and information regarding youth accommodation, hotels catering specially for children, and hotels with swimming pools and sports facilities. Residential hotels and one-room hotel apartments are available for longer stays. Hotel apartments in cities aren't often let for less than six months, due to the difficulty of finding replacement tenants, particularly in winter. In mountain resorts, many hotels close for the summer months or close between the end of the summer season and the start of the winter season, e.g. October to November. If you want a room in a top class hotel during an international convention or fair, or in a city or popular resort (particularly during school holidays), you should book well in advance.

In addition to hotels, bed and breakfast (*Zimmer zu vermieten, chambre à louer*) accommodation is available throughout Switzerland, particularly in small towns and villages in tourist areas. Local tourist offices may keep a list of rooms to let in private homes. An excellent resource is provided by Cathy Renggli and her associates, who have a website listing bed and breakfast accommodation throughout Switzerland (☎ 027 456 20 06, 🖳 www.bnb.ch).

SELF-CATERING ACCOMMODATION

You can find self-catering accommodation, e.g. apartments and chalets, in all holiday areas in Switzerland. Chalets and apartments can be rented through agencies or direct from owners. An apartment is generally much cheaper than a hotel room, you have more privacy and freedom, and you're able to prepare your own meals. Standards, while generally high, vary considerably, and paying a high price doesn't always guarantee a good location or a well furnished or well appointed apartment (most look wonderful in brochures).

Most holiday apartments are, however, comfortable and all are spotlessly clean. Apartments are generally well-equipped with bed linen, towels, cooking utensils, crockery and cutlery, although there may be an extra charge for bed linen. Some basic food stuffs (e.g. salt and sugar) and such essentials as toilet paper and soap may be provided, but don't count on it. Most people take essential foods and supplies with them, and buy fresh food on arrival. Shops in holiday areas may be open for a period on Sundays, particularly in ski resorts during the winter season.

You're normally required to do your own daily cleaning as apartments aren't serviced unless part of a large private chalet or a hotel apartment complex, when chambermaids are provided. Don't overdo the cleaning as you usually have to pay for an apartment to be cleaned on your departure. Apartments are normally let on a weekly basis from Saturday to Saturday. You're required to move out by around noon on your last day, when a veritable army of cleaning ladies march in.

Apartments are best rented from the owners and not through agents. Write to the tourist office of the town or village where you wish to stay and book well in advance for public and school holiday periods, e.g. three to six months in winter. Tourist offices usually send a list of apartments with prices and a map showing their location. The location is of particular importance if you're going to be skiing, as you will want to know how far the apartment is from the nearest ski lift; generally the nearer apartments are to ski lifts, the more expensive they will be. Other aspects that influence the rental cost are the size, amenities, general quality and the season. Budget for around SFr. 150 to 250 per person, per week, for a four-bed apartment in high season, and up to 50 per cent less during the low season.

If you obtain a list of apartments from the tourist office, you must contact the owner or agent directly to find out the availability and further details, and to make a booking. You may need to pay a deposit or the full cost in advance. Check whether there are any extras for cleaning or breakages (sometimes included in the rent). In most ski resorts, landlords collect a small visitor's tax (*Kurtaxe, taxe de séjour*), which may amount to a few francs per adult, per day.

In summer you can usually find an apartment on the spot without any trouble, particularly in resorts that cater mainly for winter sports fans. Chalets and apartments can also be rented from many agents in Switzerland including the Automobile Club of Switzerland (ACS), Wasserwerkgasse 39, CH-3000 Berne 13 (☎ 031 328 31 11), Interhome (Schweiz) AG, Buckhauserstr. 26, CH-8048 Zurich (☎ 043 211 77 77, 🖳 www.interhome.ch) and Utoring AG, which has recently been acquired by Interhome (☎ 01 497 27 27, 🖳 www. utoring.ch). Self-catering accommodation can also be found via the Internet (e.g. 🖳 www. vacanca.com and www.holiday-home.ch). One way to enjoy a relatively inexpensive self-catering holiday in Switzerland is to exchange your home abroad with someone who lives in Switzerland. For information send two international reply coupons to International Home Exchange, Fair Tours, Postfach 615, CH-9001 St. Gallen (🖳 www.gn.apc.org/fairtours, ✉ fairtours@gn.apc.org).

CARAVANNING & CAMPING

Switzerland has around 450 camping and caravan (trailer) sites, graded from one to five stars according to their amenities, location and other factors. Many are open all year round. The cost varies and averages around SFr. 15 per night for a family of four. Campers must have an international camping carnet, available from Swiss camping associations (see below). Permission is required to park or camp on private property or anywhere outside official camping sites. Caravans can be rented in most areas of Switzerland.

For detailed information about campsites, contact the Swiss Camping and Caravanning Federation (Verband Schweizer Campings Fédération Suisse de Camping et de Caravanning Bahnhofstrasse 2, Postfach, 3322 Schönbühl, (☎ 031 852 06 26, 🖳 www.camping.ch, 🖳 www.camping-switzerland.ch). They publish handbooks, which are available from bookshops in Switzerland, listing all Swiss campsites and their facilities. The Touring Club of Switzerland (TCS) publish the *TCS Camping Guide*, available from TCS offices and bookshops. In addition to listing campsites in Switzerland, it also lists sites in France, Italy and Spain, including a section on naturist camp sites for those wishing to save on laundry costs. A list of campsites is also available from Switzerland Tourism (ST) offices.

YOUTH HOSTELS

If you're travelling on a tight budget, one way to stretch your precious financial resources is to stay in youth hostels, of which there are around 60 in Switzerland. Youth hostel accommodation is open to all, although members under seven years of age must be accompanied by an adult. All youth hostels provide separate dormitories for men and women and hot showers, and some provide cooking facilities, a laundry and an inexpensive restaurant. The cost of accommodation at most youth hostels ranges from around SFr. 12 to over SFr. 40 per night (average SFr. 20 to 30) and includes a cotton sleeping bag or bed linen.

You don't need to be a member of the Swiss Youth Hostels (SYH) to stay in one, although membership provides reduced prices and an international membership card. Membership costs SFr. 22 for those aged under 18 and SFr. 33 for those over 18. Family membership is also available for SFr. 44 (parents and children aged up to 18) and group leaders' membership for groups of ten or more (SFr. 55). To avoid disappointment you're advised to book at least five days in advance. In February, July, August and holiday periods, pre-booking is usually essential. Youth hostels require guests to remain quiet until 7am and don't allow alcohol on the premises. Smoking is restricted to designated rooms only.

For more information contact Swiss Youth Hostels/SYH (Schweizer Jugendherbergen, Auberges de Jeunesse Suisses), Schaffhauserstr. 14, Postfach, CH-8042 Zurich (☎ 01 360 14 14, 🖳 www.youthhostels.ch ✉ marketing@ youthhostel.ch). The SYH publish a free 'Know How' map showing hostel locations and listing their facilities and a free booklet entitled *Downtown*

Switzerland. Youth hostel information is also available from Switzerland Tourism (ST) who publish a free *Swiss Youth Hostel Guide.* The SYH travel service, Jugi Tours (☎ 031 380 68 68, 🖳 www.jugitours.ch), organises trekking, adventure, culture and education tours, as well as flights for youth hostellers. The former Swiss Student Travel Service (*Voyages SSR-Reisen*), recently taken over by STA Travel (Ankerstr. 112, Postfach, CH-8026 Zurich (☎ 01 297 11 11, 🖳 www.statravel.ch), provides information for travellers aged from 16 to 35 and has offices in all major Swiss cities and towns.

MUSEUMS & ART GALLERIES

Switzerland has over 700 museums, art galleries, gardens and zoos (Basle and Zurich zoos are world-famous and offer family and individual annual season tickets for regular visitors). Art treasures are housed in two National Museums in Zurich and at the Château de Prangins (near Nyon, Vaud), and in historical museums in Basle, Berne, Geneva and Zurich. Most museums are closed on Mondays and on public holidays, which is unfortunately standard practice on the European continent. Admission is usually free on Sundays (one Sunday a month in Geneva). Many museums close during lunch periods and opening times vary greatly, so check in advance. Some exhibitions make reductions for foreigners on production of a passport and reduced-price local transport tickets are often available for visitors to trade exhibitions.

Lists of museums, zoological gardens and botanical gardens are available from ST offices or the Internet (🖳 www.museums.ch). Museum lovers may also be interested in the *Swiss Museum Guide,* available from Swiss bookshops. All tourist information offices provide information about local attractions. A monthly (SFr. 30) or annual (SFr. 90) Swiss Museums Passport is available from tourist information offices and valid at over 300 museums throughout Switzerland. The *Michelin Green Guide to Switzerland* includes a list of the major museums, sights, tourist attractions and summer cable-cars and chair-lifts, including costs and opening times. News about exhibitions and fairs can be obtained from the telephone service number 1600.

CINEMAS

Around 450 cinemas (*Kino, cinéma*) throughout Switzerland show English-language films in the original language with German and French subtitles. Cinema listings in German-language newspapers show the original soundtrack language (first upper-case letter) and the subtitle languages (lower-case letters). For example, E/d/f denotes a film with English as the original language with German (*Deutsch*) and French (*Français*) subtitles, F/d denotes French language with German subtitles. In French-speaking areas, 'v.o.' denotes *version originale* (original language version). Programmes are shown on street posters in major cities.

Age restrictions vary from 6 years for Walt Disney type films to 9, 12 and 16 years for other films. In some cantons, cinemas must advertise the suitable age limit, but don't always enforce it when children are accompanied by an adult (children usually comfort their parents during the 'scary' bits). Otherwise, for children accompanied by adults, the age restriction is two years below the suitable age limit, e.g. if the general unaccompanied age limit is 12, then a child accompanied by an adult must be aged at least ten to see the movie. It isn't unusual for children (or adults) who look younger than their years to be asked for proof of their age, e.g. a school identity card.

Most cinemas accept telephone reservations and provide season tickets for movie fans. You can also purchase so called 'Movie Cards' or other membership-type cards for most cinemas. These allow holders to purchase subsidised tickets, advance booking via the Internet and other benefits. Ask at your favourite theatre for information. Film festivals are held in the major cities, when cinemas show films non-stop (24-hours a day) for a number of days and offer reduced admission prices. There are private film clubs in the main cities showing old classics.

THEATRE, OPERA & BALLET

Switzerland has many excellent theatres (around 150) and thriving opera houses, including many small theatres and troupes, with performances in French, German, Italian and other languages. In major cities, amateur English-language theatre companies periodically stage plays, and incidentally, are always on the lookout for new talent (see **Appendix A**). English and American repertory companies occasionally tour Switzerland (programmes are available from tourist information offices). Tickets for ballet and opera are in heavy demand, so apply well in advance (tickets can be purchased by subscription).

An annual calendar of music, theatre and dance events is available free from ST offices. A Swiss cultural magazine *Konzert & Theater* is available on subscription from Konzert & Theater, Museumstr. 1, Postfach 463, CH-9004 St. Gallen ☎ 071 242 05 05) Switzerland has an amazing number of travelling circuses (over 25), including the world-famous Circus Knie (the Swiss National Circus), which tours from March to November (⌨ www.knie.ch).

CONCERTS

Classical concerts, music festivals and solo concerts by international musicians and performers, are held regularly throughout Switzerland. Many Swiss international music festivals, from orchestral, choral and opera to jazz and rock, are world renowned. Season tickets are usually available for a whole season of classical performances or a selection of performances may be chosen from a prepared list. Although they aren't world-renowned, Basle, Geneva and Zurich all have excellent orchestras. Free organ and choral concerts are performed in churches throughout the year and free outdoor concerts are staged in summer. Look for announcements in your local newspapers or ask at your local tourist office.

The easiest place to purchase tickets for concerts and other events is from TicketCorner (☎ 0848 80 08 00, 💻 www.ticketcorner.ch). Tickets are also available at some department stores, music shops, and bookshops, most notably Manor department stores. **Ticket prices in Switzerland are generally high and can be astronomical for 'superstars'.**

For the musically talented there are musical (classical and brass bands) and choral societies in most towns and villages, and national orchestras for the really gifted (around 30 large professional orchestras). Those who cannot sing or play a musical instrument can join a yodelling group! A list of all major concerts and music festivals in Switzerland is provided in the Switzerland Tourism (ST) brochure, *Events in Switzerland*.

SOCIAL CLUBS

There are many social clubs and organisations in Switzerland, catering for both foreigners and Swiss. These include Ambassador clubs, American Women's and Men's Clubs, Anglo-Swiss clubs, Business Clubs, International Men's and Women's clubs, Kiwani Clubs, Lion and Lioness Clubs, and Rotary Clubs. Expatriates from many countries have their own clubs in major cities (ask at your local embassy or consulate in Switzerland). Many social clubs organise activities and pastimes such as chess, whist, art, music, sports activities and outings, and theatre and cinema visits.

If you wish to integrate into your local community or Swiss society in general, one of the best ways is to join a Swiss club. Most communities publish a calendar of local sports and social events. A list of social clubs and organisations for English-speaking foreigners is contained in **Appendix A**.

DISCOTHEQUES & NIGHT-CLUBS

There are discotheques and night-clubs in all major Swiss towns and cities. Discotheques and night-clubs in Switzerland are generally expensive. The entrance fee for discos, irrespective of whether they have a drinks licence, is usually between SFr. 10 and 30 (it sometimes includes a 'free' drink). When available, drinks are **very** expensive.

Although most Swiss aren't night owls, there are jazz and night clubs, bars, cabarets and discotheques open until between 2am and 6am in the major cities. Many clubs are private and don't admit casual visitors unless accompanied by members. At weekends in the major cities, it isn't uncommon to have 'after-hour parties' lasting until noon the following day. The Swiss are also known for rave-type parties that are held throughout the year, with house/techno and other youth-orientated music. Keep your eyes open for posters in cities.

CASINOS

Until recently, you could only play *Boule*, a sort of simplified roulette, in the 14 'B license' Swiss casinos in Bad Ragaz, Crans, Courrendlin, Davos, Granges-Paccot, Interlaken, Mendrisio, Meyrin by Geneva, Muralto, Pfäffikon, Schaffhausen, St. Moritz, and Zermatt. However, in a historic vote on the 7th March 1993, the Swiss voted to remove the long-standing ban on 'real' casinos to aid the declining tourist industry and bolster government coffers. After much debate, seven 'A licenses' (GrandCasino) were allocated at the end of October 2001 to Basle EuroAirport, Baden, Montreux, Berne, St. Gallen, Lugano and Lucerne.

'A license' casinos can offer unlimited betting with no maximum jackpot, while gamblers at 'B license' casinos are allowed to bet a maximum of SFr. 5 only, with a maximum jackpot of just SFr. 5,000 (not exactly big time for a millionaire). The new GrandCasinos (along with the smaller, B license ones) are expected to take in SFr. 900 million a year, with SFr. 400 million going to social security and a further SFr. 70 million to the cantons.

Before the introduction of the GrandCasinos, all the big Swiss gambling money flowed over the border into the strategically placed casinos surrounding Switzerland, which reap 25 times the revenues of the Swiss 'B License' casinos. There include casinos at Aix-les-Bains, Evian and Divonne (France), Campione D'Italia (Italy), Bregenz (Austria) Konstanz and Lindau (Germany).

BARS & CAFES

Bars and cafés abound throughout Switzerland, which, like most continental countries, has sensible licensing laws. Most bars and local restaurants (i.e. bars providing food) are open from morning to midnight, including Sundays. Hot food, snacks and excellent coffee are usually available. There are also many English and Irish-style pubs where you can buy British, Irish and other foreign beers. Local Swiss beers and wines are generally good and imported beverages are widely available (local **hell** beer won't kill you, it just means light beer). Spirits and cocktails are outrageously expensive, particularly in hotels. Good local mineral waters are available everywhere. Bear (beer?) in mind that some tea-rooms and cafés **don't sell alcohol**. In bars, a choice of non-alcoholic drinks should be available at prices below the cheapest alcoholic drink, although this isn't always the case (non-alcoholic wines and beers are also usually available).

In Swiss bars you don't pay for each drink as it's served, except in crowded tourist haunts or a pub with English bar service. You usually receive a total bill at the end of the evening (the system is designed to help you drive home, as the size of the bill has an immediate sobering effect). While on the subject of drinking and driving, the law is **very** strict in Switzerland and penalties are severe (see page 227). If you have more than a couple of small drinks you'd be well advised to hitch a ride with a sober friend or use public transport. The legal age for drinking beer and wine in public places in Switzerland is 16, and 18 for spirits and alcopops. Most cafés, bars and local restaurants provide free local newspapers and magazines, a common practice in continental Europe.

A popular card game named *Jass*, remotely similar to bridge and requiring a special deck of cards, can be played in most bars and local restaurants. Most local bars have a family or regulars' table (*Stammtisch, table des habitués*), reserved for regular customers. It's usually denoted by a huge ashtray and you may be asked to move if you sit there. Like restaurants, most bars and cafés close on one or two days a week (*Ruhetag, jour de repos*), usually posted on the door.

RESTAURANTS

There are around 27,500 restaurants in Switzerland, approximately one for every 250 inhabitants and one on top of every mountain (don't you find these statistics fascinating?). Restaurants in Switzerland invariably provide good food and service, although there's little original Swiss cooking on offer apart from fondue, raclette and rösti, and most serve international cuisine. Like most continental Europeans, the Swiss take their food seriously and the main meal of the day is usually eaten at midday (lunch time). Unlike in some countries, it isn't usually necessary to have a meal in a Swiss restaurant and you can order a snack or a drink only.

All restaurants are obliged by law to display their menu and prices outside. A good meal for two with a modest bottle of wine costs around SFr. 60 to 90 in an average restaurant (about the same price as in most northern European countries). Of course you can easily pay up to SFr. 200 a head if you want the best and the cost of wine can be astronomical. In many expensive restaurants, *nouvelle cuisine* is fashionable, consisting of tiny portions artfully arranged on large plates – if you're starving eat at a local bar. All restaurants offer a variety of house wines (*Offener Wein, vin ouvert*), which can be ordered by the deci-litre (but it's still expensive). Swiss restaurants and hotel bills include a service charge of 15 per cent, designed to cut out tipping (the price you see on the menu is the price you pay). Don't be concerned about not leaving a tip or leaving a few small coins only, as the waiter won't abuse you or spill soup over you on your return.

Most restaurants offer a daily menu (*Tagesmenu, menu de jour*) at lunch time, usually from noon to 2pm. It includes a choice of meals with soup or salad (and sometimes a dessert) and costs from around SFr. 14 Dinner in a local restaurant or bar is usually served from 7 to 10pm. Many restaurants offer half-portions for children or have a children's menu. Mövenpick restaurants are particularly good for children and offer a choice of menus, and McDonalds, the American chain of hamburger 'restaurants', have branches in most major cities and large towns (you can also hire restaurants for children's parties). Many department stores have good value for money restaurants. If you like a glass of wine or a beer with your meal, avoid alcohol free (*Alkoholfrei, sans alcool*) restaurants (e.g. Migros), tea-rooms and cafés.

Exotic foreign restaurants, which in Switzerland includes most foreign restaurants, aren't as common as in many other European countries and can be expensive. Most foreign cuisine is, however, available in the major cities. It's advisable to make a reservation for the more expensive or more popular restaurants, particularly during lunchtimes, on Friday and Saturday evenings, and at anytime for parties of four or more people.

In most bars and local restaurants you're given cash register receipts for each item ordered, which are totalled when you request your bill. Sliced bread is usually provided free with a meal, but bread rolls usually cost extra. If your waiter or waitress is going off duty, don't be surprised if you're asked to pay half-way through your meal. **Note that smoking is permitted in restaurants in Switzerland, which don't usually have a non-smoking area (somewhat surprisingly, dogs are also allowed into most restaurants).**

Most restaurants close on one or two days a week (*Ruhetag, jour de repos*), which is usually posted on the restaurant door. Many bars and restaurants have a private room that can be used (usually free) for a club meeting or social function, provided you buy coffee or other drinks. The continental game of skittles (*Kegelbahn, jeu de quilles*) can be played in many restaurants. Among the best Swiss restaurant guides are the *Michelin Schweiz* Red Guide and the *Gault-Millau Guide Schweiz*. You can also find Swiss restaurants on the Internet (🖳 www.restaurants.ch).

LIBRARIES

Most public libraries in cities and large towns have books in English, French, German and Italian. Opening times vary but are usually around 9am to 8pm from Monday to Friday and 9am to 4pm on Saturdays. Smaller libraries may open on only one or two days a week and opening hours may be reduced during the summer holiday period. Most large towns and cities have a central library (*Zentralbibliothek, bibliothèque centrale*) with a large selection of English-language books, and most universities also have libraries that are open to the public. Library membership is usually free or a nominal charge is made, for example SFr. 10 for ten years.

Private libraries are fairly common in major cities, some of which have a large collection of English-language books, magazines and newspapers. The American library in Geneva is the second largest English reading library on the continent, with around 17,000 titles. It's usually necessary to pay an annual membership fee to join a private library. American Women's Clubs (see **Appendix A**) run English-language libraries in most major Swiss cities, which are open to non-members for a small subscription fee.

FOREST HUTS

Most communities have their own forest hut (*Waldhütte, cabane*), which can be rented for social events (parties, drunken orgies, etc.). The fee is usually from SFr. 75 to 100 per day or night for a community resident or double this for a non-resident. The rent varies depending on the community and the amenities provided. In some huts, glasses, crockery and cutlery are provided besides electricity, running water and toilets, while others are more basic.

Forest huts are an excellent place to hold a party in summer or winter, when you can usually build a log fire. You can make as much noise as you like, as there are no neighbours to call the police at 10pm. It's also unnecessary to invite your neighbours and you don't need to worry about your guests spilling red wine on the carpet (there isn't one) or setting fire to the furniture (the community, on the other hand, won't be too happy if you burn down their hut!). You're required to clean the hut after your party or pay to have it cleaned. Book early, particularly for weekends and holiday periods.

If you're sick of cooking and don't fancy catering to an army of ravenous guests, party catering services are available, e.g. from Migros and Mövenpick, who can also provide staff. They provide both hot and cold buffet food and will deliver it to your party. A personal touch can be provided by a metre or two of bread with a personal message, courtesy of Migros and other bakers.

DAY & EVENING CLASSES

Adult day and evening classes are run by various organisations in all Swiss cities and large towns. The largest is the Migros Club School (*Klubschule Migros*, *école club Migros*, 🖳 www.klubschule.ch), funded by the Migros supermarket and department store chain. It has 12 regional co-operatives who operate over 50 centres in major cities and towns throughout Switzerland. Over 300 different subjects are taught, including foreign languages and local language courses for foreigners (about 40 per cent of total classes), handicrafts, hobbies and sports (also around 40 per cent), and further education, e.g. computer studies and typing (some 20 per cent). Migros schools publish regional programmes containing a list of all local clubs (available free from Migros clubs and stores).

Other companies and organisations providing day and evening classes include Coop Leisure Centres (*Coop-Freizeit-Center*, *centre de loisirs Coop*) and the People's High School (*Volkshochschule*, *université populaire*), both of which hold classes in general education, geography, culture and languages. American Women's Clubs and other expatriate organisations also organise day and evening classes in many subjects, and some organisations provide classes for children (e.g. English), particularly during school holidays.

Adult further education programmes are published in many areas (often delivered free to local residents) and include all courses organised by local training and education centres. Local newspapers also contain details of evening and day courses. Many communities publish an annual programme of events, including day and evening classes, and tourist offices may also be able to provide you with information. Many cantons publish a list of local adult education centres. Swiss universities organise non-residential courses and special language courses during their summer recess. See **Further Education** on page 169 and **Language Schools** on page 169.

16.

SPORTS

Sports facilities in Switzerland are excellent. Among the most popular sports are skiing and other winter sports, hiking, cycling, mountaineering, tennis, squash and swimming. Most water (sailing, windsurfing, water-skiing) and aerial sports (hang-gliding, ballooning, flying) also have many devotees. Participation in some sports is expensive, although costs can be reduced through the purchase of season tickets, annual membership or by joining a club. Switzerland Tourism (ST) can provide you with information about practically any sport and at the very least will provide you with a contact name and address. Various publications are available from tourist offices promoting special sports events and listing local sports venues.

The Swiss Olympic Association (*Schweiz. Olympischer Verband, Association Olympique Suisse*, Laubeggstr. 70, Postfach 202, CH-3000 Berne 32, ☎ 031 359 71 11, 🖳 www.swissolympic.ch) publishes a comprehensive annual year book, *Sport von A-Z*. Many cantons and cities publish comprehensive booklets listing local sports organisations, facilities and classes. Sports results are announced on the telephone service number 164 and on the Swiss television teletext service. Leaflets containing information about how to prevent and avoid sports accidents and injuries, e.g. cycling, hiking, skiing, soccer and water sports, are available from the Swiss Bureau for the Prevention of Accidents (see **Accidents** on page 243).

AERIAL SPORTS

The Alps are ideal for aerial sports (particularly gliding, hang-gliding, paragliding and hot-air ballooning), due to the updrafts and the low density of air traffic (apart from all the gliders, hang-gliders and balloons). Hang-gliding has become increasingly popular in Switzerland in recent years and there are over 20 hang-gliding schools. To obtain a glider pilot's licence you must make 40 flights in five different areas. For more information contact the Swiss Hang-Gliding Association (*Schweiz. Hängegleiter-Verband, Association Suisse de Vol Libre*), Seefeldstr. 224, CH-8008 Zurich (☎ 01 387 46 80, 🖳 www.shv-fsvl.ch).

Paragliding (*Gleitschirm, parapente*) entails jumping off steep mountain slopes (of which Switzerland has a few) with a parachute. There are over 20,000 registered 'pilots' in Switzerland and around 40 schools, and the sport even has its own magazine, *Gleitschirm*. Participants must have the proper equipment and complete an approved course of instruction lasting 20 hours, after which (if they survive) they receive a proficiency certificate and are permitted to go solo. For more information about paragliding contact the Swiss Hang-Gliding Association (address above). Ballooning has a small but dedicated band of followers. Participation is generally limited to the wealthy due to the high cost of balloons (lawyers and politicians receive a reduction for supplying their own hot air). A flight in a balloon is a marvellous experience, particularly over the Alps. There is, however, no guarantee of distance or duration, and trips are dependent on wind conditions and the skill of your pilot. A list of ballooning clubs is available from Switzerland Tourism (ST).

Light aircraft and gliders (sailplanes) can be rented with or without an instructor (providing you have a pilot's licence) from most small airfields in Switzerland. There are around 50 gliding clubs in Switzerland. Freefall parachuting (sky-diving) flights can be made from most private airfields in Switzerland; however, it's expensive and costs can run to over SFr. 7,000 for training and equipment. Information regarding free-fall parachuting, paragliding, gliding and flying is available from ST and the Aero-Club of Switzerland (*Aero Club der Schweiz, Aéro Club de Suisse*) Lidostr. 5, CH-6006 Lucerne (☎ 041 375 01 01, 💻 www.aeroclub.ch). A special weather report for aerial sports is provided on Swiss television teletext.

Before taking up the above sports, you're advised to make sure that you have adequate health, accident and life insurance and that your affairs are in order.

CYCLING

Cycling is popular in Switzerland, not only as a means of transport or a serious sport, but also as a relaxing pastime for the whole family. The weather from spring through to autumn is often fine for cycling, mainly dry and warm and generally not too hot – if only there weren't so many damn hills Switzerland would be ideal. There are over 6,000km (3,700mi) of marked bicycle paths are provided in country areas. These include the Cycling in Switzerland network which was officially opened in 1998, consisting of nine national cycle routes covering a total of over 3,300km (2,050mi) of cycle paths (maps are available from Switzerland Tourism and railway stations).

In Switzerland, as in most of Europe, cycling is a very popular sport and serious sports cyclists are to be seen everywhere. Cycle racing has a huge following and races are organised at every level. The *Tour de Suisse* is Switzerland's premier race, held in June over a 1,600km (1,000mi) route, and one of Europe's major events. For information contact the Swiss Cycling Federation (*Schweiz. Radfahrer-Bund, Fédération Cycliste Suisse*), Haus des Sportes, Laubeggstr. 70, Postfach 232, CH-3000 Berne 32 (☎ 031 359 72 33, 💻 www. cycling.ch). Information can also be obtained on the Internet (💻 www.ketten rad.ch or www.tourenguide.ch).

For the recreational cyclist, a standard bicycle (*Fahrrad, vélo/bicyclette*) can be purchased for SFr. 500 to 800 (cheaper bikes are also available); shop around for the best buy (a professional racing bicycle can cost thousands of francs). If you're feeling particularly energetic you can buy a 21-speed mountain bike and go cycling in the Alps (some resorts provide special mountain bike trails). Mountain bikes are currently all the rage and cost from around SFr. 900 for a good basic bike and many thousands for a top quality machine.

Apart from cycling to work, which many people do from spring to autumn, cycling is an excellent way to explore the countryside at your leisure and get some fresh air and exercise at the same time. Special cycling maps (*Velokarte, itinéraire pour cyclistes*) are produced by the Traffic Association of Switzerland (scale 1:50) and are available from bookshops everywhere. A *Bicycling in*

Switzerland booklet is available from Switzerland Tourism (ST), plus many regional cycling guides containing recommended one-day trips. Swiss motoring organisations also provide maps and books containing cycling tours (also have a look at 🖳 www.tourenguide.ch). **Note that mountain bikes are banned on many hiking paths due to the dangers and inconvenience to hikers, and cross-country 'off-piste' cycling is also prohibited in some areas to protect plant and wild life.** However, downhill cycling is an increasingly popular summer sport in ski resorts, where you can usually transport your bike on ski lifts.

Before a bicycle can be used on public roads it must be licensed (which includes third party insurance) at your local post office, bicycle shop or Migros store. The licence costs around SFr. 5 a year, depending on your canton of residence, and is valid until 31st May of the following year (the license includes third party insurance). When you licence a bicycle, you receive a self-adhesive vignette (*Kontrollschild, plaque d'immatriculation*) showing your canton initials, year and licence number, and a licence card, which must be signed and kept in a safe place. When you buy a bicycle in Switzerland you're given a small aluminium licence plate. This must be fastened vertically to your rear mudguard or rear frame, where it's easily visible, and your self-adhesive vignette affixed to it. In subsequent years you receive a new vignette and licence card when you buy your licence. Bicycle breakdown assistance and theft insurance is available from Swiss motoring organisations.

Important Notes

- All cyclists should be familiar with the road rules for cyclists contained in the *Handbook of Swiss Traffic Regulations*, available for around SFr. 5 from canton motor registration offices.

- Take **particular** care on busy roads and don't allow your children onto public roads until they're experienced riders. Children aren't permitted to cycle on a public road until they're aged seven and attending primary school; kindergarten doesn't count, even when a child is already seven. Bicycles aren't permitted on motorways.

- If you cycle in cities you should wear reflective clothing, protective head gear, a smog mask and a crucifix. It isn't necessary to wear expensive sports clothing when cycling, although a light crash helmet is advisable, particularly for children (and is much cheaper than brain surgery). Head injuries are the main cause of death in bicycle accidents, most of which don't involve accidents with vehicles, but are a result of colliding with fixed objects or falls. Always buy a quality helmet that has been subjected to rigorous testing and approved by a safety organisation.

- Children up to the age of seven can be carried on the back of an adult's bicycle in a specially designed chair. The rider must be aged over 16.

- Bicycles must be fitted with an anti-theft device blocking a wheel or the steering. A crude device is already fitted to bicycles purchased in Switzerland and you can buy a more secure steel cable or chain with a lock from bicycle accessory shops, e.g. Migros. **Note, however, that no devices are foolproof and some people take a wheel with them when leaving their bike unattended!** If your bicycle is stolen contact the local police.

- Where special cycle tracks or lanes are provided, they must be used. Unfortunately there aren't many off-road cycle lanes in cities and towns, and you often take your life into your hands when venturing onto main roads, particularly during rush hours.

- You aren't permitted to ride on footpaths unless signposted otherwise or two abreast on roads. Being pulled along by a moped (*Motorfahrrad/Mofa*, *vélomoteur*) is illegal and dangerous, and riding with your hands off the handlebars or feet off the pedals is also prohibited.

- If you import a bicycle, it must conform to Swiss safety standards. These include front and rear reflectors, front and rear lamps, pedal reflectors, bell, mudguards, front and rear brakes, and good tyres. Off-road bikes, e.g. some racing and mountain bikes, cannot be used on public roads (unless road legal), except when riding to and from race venues.

- Take drinks, first-aid kit, tool kit and a puncture repair outfit when on a long cycling trip.

- Take care not to get your wheels stuck in tram or railway lines.

Bicycle Rental & Transportation

Bicycles can be rented from over 150 Swiss railway stations and returned to any other participating station. Reservations should be made by 6pm the previous day or a week in advance for groups. You can choose from a country bike, mountain bike or children's bike, the fees for which are shown below:

- Half-day (until/after 12.30), returning to the station where you rented the bike: SFr. 23 (SFr. 18 for children under 16 or if you have a Swiss rail GA or a half-fare card).

- One day, returning to the station where you rented the bike: SFr. 30 (SFr. 25 for children under 16 or if you have a Swiss rail GA or a half-fare card).

- One day, returning to a different station from where you rented the bike: SFr. 36 (SFr. 31 for children under 16 or if you have a Swiss rail GA or a half-fare card).

With a family card (see page 183) children's bikes are free. A country bike can also be fitted with a free child's seat, but you need to book in advance. Bicycles can be left at any participating station for a fee of SFr. 7, which is waived if you rent a bike for more than one day. Further information is provided in a brochure available from railway stations, which also includes suggested routes. Bicycles can also be rented from cycle shops in many towns and mountain bikes are available in some mountain resorts for around SFr. 50 a day. At many stations you can hire suva-bike-helmets free.

You can transport your bicycle between any two stations for SFr. 15 per day, except for certain Eurocity and S-Bahn trains during peak periods. You must load and unload it yourself and have a valid ticket for the same destination (IC and fast trains excluded). Bicycles sent by train in Switzerland can be insured for SFr. 5 per SFr. 500 insured. Using the train allows you to cycle one way and return by train (or vice versa) or travel to an area by train, tour around by bicycle and return by train. Swiss railways (SBB) offer many special cycling tours and trips, and 'rail bicycle' brochures are available from railway stations. The SBB also publish a book entitled *40 Bicycle Tours* (with the train).

FISHING

Fishing facilities in Switzerland are superb. There are a huge variety of well-stocked waters totalling some 133,000hectares (330,000acres) of lakes and 32,000km (20,000mi) of running water; enough to keep even the keenest of anglers busy for a few weeks. Lakes and mountain streams are stocked annually with trout, grayling and pike. You must buy a fishing permit for rivers and some lakes. which are usually available for a day, week or month from the local tourist office or the area council office (*Bezirksamt, administration de district*). You can obtain an annual permit for your own canton and monthly permits for other cantons. Fishing licences for non-residents of a canton can be expensive, although there are some unrestricted waters that don't require a permit. Contact the local area council office or local tourist office for information.

Angling competitions are organised in many areas. The fishing season and rules and regulations regarding the permitted size of fish which can be taken vary from canton to canton, so check before planning a trip. For more information contact the Swiss Angling Association (*Schweiz. Fischerei Verband, Association Suisse des Pêcheurs*), Sekretariat Thomas Winzeler, Seilerstrasse 27, 3011 Berne ☎ 031 381 32 52 ⌨ www.sfv-fsp.ch)

GOLF

There are some 60 golf courses (9 and 18 holes) in Switzerland with many more planned, plus mini-golf courses. However, Switzerland has just one public golf course, the Executive Golf de Chessel between Aigle and the Lake of Geneva (there are also public driving ranges in some areas). Golf is an elitist and expensive sport in Switzerland and it's almost impossible to join a city club without excellent contacts and a low handicap (the waiting list for membership of some clubs is longer than the average expatriate's stay in Switzerland). The average joining fee for an 18-hole club is SFr. 20,000 to 25,000 and membership fees are an additional SFr. 2,500 a year. Members of foreign and other Swiss golf clubs can usually play at town clubs from Monday to Friday on production of a membership or handicap card. Green fees are from around SFr. 80 in urban areas and from SFr. 40 to over SFr. 100 in rural areas. Your best bet may be to play at a mountain resort course, where you can play golf in beautiful scenery (at around 1,500 metres) without being a member.

Many cities and resorts have indoor practice centres, where you can have a video analysis (demolition?) of your swing. Switzerland also has the world's largest indoor golf club (1,500m²/16,146ft²) at Zumikon, Zurich. Crazy golf (golf obstacle course) is played in many areas. It's taken seriously and competitions (even Swiss championships) are organised. For more information contact the Swiss Golf Association (*Schweiz. Golfverband, Association Suisse de Golf*), Place de la Croix-Blanche 19, Case postale, CH-1066 Epalinges (☎ 021 784 35 31, 💻 www. asg.ch). An excellent *Official Guide to Golf Courses in Switzerland* is available from Switzerland Tourism (ST). Many hotels offer special golf packages; for information, contact the Swiss Golf Hotels Group, Bahnhofstr. 8, Postfach, 7304 Maienfeld (☎ 081 300 44 22, 💻 www.swissgolfhotels.ch).

HIKING

Switzerland is a hiker's paradise with over 31,000km (over 19,000mi) of marked main routes, including ten national hiking routes each covering a distance of 200 to 400km (around 125 to 250mi), and some 400 secondary routes. The country boasts a grand total of over 50,000km (31,000mi) of hiking trails in some of the most beautiful scenery in the world. The Swiss are keen hikers and infants to pensioners can be seen everywhere in their hiking gear. Although the main hiking season is from around May to September, hiking in Switzerland isn't just a summer sport. Most winter sports resorts keep several hiking trails open for walkers throughout the winter – a total of some 4,600km (1,800mi). It's fun walking in the snow and the weather can be quite hot in the mountains in winter (you will also be hot after walking for a few kilometres).

Many local communities and walking clubs organise walks (*Volksmarsch, marche populaire*). There's a small fee (around SFr. 3) and a medal for any survivors (you will have earned it by the time you reach the top of the Matterhorn!). A complete programme of hikes organised by local walking clubs is available from the Federation of Swiss Hiking Trails (*Schweizer Wanderwege, Fédération Suisse de Tourisme Pédestre*), Im Hirshalm 49, CH-4125 Riehen (☎ 061 606 93 40, 💻 www.swisshiking.ch), who publish a bimonthly magazine (*Wander-Revue, Revue Sentiers*) for hikers, available in French and German editions. Membership of the Federation of Swiss Hiking Trails costs from around SFr. 10 to 30 a year, depending on your canton of residence. Guided hiking tours are organised in many resorts and the Swiss Alpine Club (SAC) organises excursions for experienced hikers (see page 330). Contact Switzerland Tourism and local tourist offices for information. Orienteering is also a popular sport in Switzerland.

Many mountain resorts have a special tourist information telephone number, where the latest information is recorded regarding local weather conditions, cable-cars and other mountain transport services, and the condition of hiking paths. Numbers are listed in telephone directories. The weather forecast is also available on service telephone number 162 and on Swiss television teletext. See also **Climate** on page 372.

An abundance of wild mountain flowers are in bloom in the Alps from around May to August, July usually being the best month. Many mountain areas have alpine gardens and guides to the local flora and fauna can be purchased from tourist offices. **Note that many plants are protected and you're forbidden to pick or uproot them (offenders can be fined).**

Signs

Hiking paths (*Wanderweg, chemin pédestre*) are indicated by yellow metal signs showing the altitude, destination and often the approximate time required to reach the destination. The times are based on a moderate walking speed of 4.2km (2.6mi) an hour on well-surfaced flat land, which is generous enough for anyone but a tortoise – provided of course you don't get lost. They sometimes show the distance to the destination. Mountain paths (*Bergweg, sentier de montagne*) are marked by yellow signs with a red and white tip or arrow point. Always stick to marked paths, particularly in difficult terrain. Where there are no signposts, routes are marked with yellow arrows or diamond-shaped signs on trees, rocks, posts and buildings (part of the challenge is trying to find the path). Signs may also be in canton colours. Some areas have special hiking paths for those confined to wheelchairs.

To commemorate Switzerland's 700th anniversary in 1991, the Swiss created the 'Swiss path' around lake Uri (part of the lake of Lucerne) at a cost of SFr. 12 million. Each canton was responsible for a stretch of the 35km (22mi) trail, which takes around 12 hours to negotiate (it's usually a two-day hike). A Swiss path train pass can be purchased from anywhere in Switzerland and a plan of the walk is available in English for around SFr. 5 and a more detailed book for around SFr. 30 (unavailable in English).

Books & Maps

You should plan a walk using a good map, for example Swiss ordnance survey maps (*Landeskarte der Schweiz, carte nationale de la suisse*). These excellent maps are produced in both 1:25 and 1:50 sizes and sold at stationers, railway stations, and shops in walking and climbing areas. Special hiking maps (*Wanderwegkarte, carte de chemins pédestres*) can also be purchased from most bookshops. A good general book on hiking is *Walking Switzerland - The Swiss Way* by Marcia & Philip

Lieberman (Cordee). It includes all the necessary advice required (unless you plan an assault on the north face of the Eiger) and includes a selection of walks. An excellent book of selected hikes of varying degrees of difficulty is the *Grosser Wander-Atlas der Schweiz* (Kümmerly + Frey). It contains summer, winter and town walks, cross-country skiing tracks, and excellent maps showing the gradients of walks (or how far you will fall if you don't take care). Another good book is the TCS *Grosse Freizeit und Ferienbuch* (Kümmerly + Frey), which not only includes hikes but also lists cycling tours, natural and cultural experiences, and paddle trips on rivers and lakes.

Free hiking brochures are produced by various organisations, including the post office, Swiss motoring organisations and some Swiss banks. Switzerland Tourism (ST) publish a series of hiking brochures, entitled *Switzerland Step by Step*, each containing 100 walks. They include town to town, mountain passes, and lake and panorama walks. Local hiking maps are available in all areas from shops and tourist and community offices. Plans showing local hiking paths are also displayed at many railway stations (although they're a bit difficult to fold up and put in your pocket). Many areas have a **hiking pass**, available from most railway stations and tourist offices, with suggested walking tours. See also **Appendix B** for a list of hiking books.

Emergencies

If someone is seriously injured, don't move him unless it's absolutely necessary to protect him from further injury. Keep him warm and seek help as soon as possible. The alpine SOS consists of a series of six signals evenly spaced over one minute (one every ten seconds) and then a repetition of six more after a minute's pause. The signals may consist of either six blasts on a whistle, six loud shouts, six flashes of a torch or six swings of an article of clothing (attached to a stick if possible) swung in a semi-circle from the ground. The reply to an emergency signal is three repeats of the visual or acoustic signal a minute, at one minute intervals.

Standing upright with both arms stretched above your head signals a request for a rescue helicopter. Holding one arm up with the other arm held down at your side indicates that a rescue helicopter isn't required. The Swiss REGA helicopter service (see page 134) is the ambulance of the Alps and all SAC huts have radio telephones that can be used to summon a helicopter. If you need to call REGA (☎ 1414) for a rescue helicopter, you should provide the following information:

- Your name, location of telephone and telephone number;
- What has happened where;
- Number of patients and their approximate injuries;
- Location – give exact details, e.g. map co-ordinates;

- Town, name and birth date of the injured person (it isn't essential to revive an unconscious patient and ask him, they just want to know where to send the bill!);
- Weather conditions and landing possibilities in the accident area;
- Any helicopter obstructions in the accident area, e.g. pylons, cables and power lines.

Some resorts, e.g. Sion and Zermatt, also provide a local helicopter rescue service. If you're going hiking with visitors to Switzerland, make sure that they have adequate accident insurance, including helicopter rescue. The cost of a rescue party or helicopter and medical treatment can be very expensive. If you work in Switzerland, you're covered for accidents by your compulsory employee non-occupational accident insurance.

General Information

The following notes may help you survive a stroll in the mountains:

- If you're going to take up hiking seriously, a good pair of walking shoes or boots is mandatory (available from most Swiss shoe and sports shops). Always wear proper walking shoes or boots where the terrain is rough. Unfortunately walking boots are usually uncomfortable or hurt your feet after a few hours (if they don't hurt, it isn't doing you any good). Wearing two pairs of socks can help prevent blisters. Break in a new pair of boots on some **gentle** hikes before setting out on a marathon hike around Switzerland.
- Don't over-exert yourself, particularly at high altitudes where the air is thinner. Mountain sickness usually occurs only above 4,000m/13,000ft, but can also happen at lower altitudes. A few words of warning for those who aren't particularly fit; take it easy and set a slow pace. It's easy to over-exert yourself and underestimate the duration or degree of difficulty of a hike. Start slowly and build up to those weekend marathons. If the most exercise you usually get is walking to the pub and crawling back, don't forget to take along a life-support machine (a crate of beer?). If you're unfit, use chair-lifts and cable-cars to get to high altitudes.
- **Don't attempt a major hike alone as it's too dangerous.** Notify someone about your route, destination and estimated time of return. Check the conditions along your route and the times of any public transport connections (set out early to avoid missing the last cable-car or bus). Take into account the time required for both ascents and descents. If you're unable to return by the time expected, let somebody know – if the rescue service is summoned in error, you may have to pay. If you realise that you're unable to reach your destination, for example due to tiredness or bad weather, turn

back in good time or take a shorter route. If you get caught in a heavy storm, descend as quickly as possible or seek protection, e.g. in an SAC hut.

- Check the weather forecast, usually obtainable from the local tourist office. Generally the higher the altitude, the more unpredictable the weather, even for Swiss meteorologists.

- Hiking, even in lowland areas, can be dangerous, so don't take any unnecessary risks. There are enough natural hazards including bad weather, rockfalls, avalanches, rough terrain, snow and ice, and wet grass, without adding to them.

- Don't walk on closed tracks at any time (they're signposted). This is particularly important in the spring when there may be the danger of avalanches or rockfalls. Tracks are sometimes closed due to forestry work or army exercises (falling trees and bullets can cause severe headaches). If you're in doubt about a particular route, ask in advance at the local tourist office. **Note that if the Swiss signpost anything as dangerous (*Gefahr/Lebensgefahr, danger*), you can bet it is!**

- Wear loose fitting clothes and not, for example, tight jeans, which can become uncomfortable when you get warmed up. Shorts (short trousers to Americans!) are excellent in hot weather. Lightweight cotton trousers are comfortable unless it's cold. You can wear your shorts underneath your trousers and remove your trousers when you've warmed up.

- Take a warm pullover, gloves (in winter) and a raincoat or large umbrella (an excellent plastic raincoat is sold at main post offices). Mountain weather can change suddenly and even in summer it's sometimes cold at high altitudes. A first-aid kit (for cuts and grazes), compass, identification, maps, small torch and a Swiss army knife may also come in handy. A pair of binoculars are handy for spotting wildlife (or hikers having fun in the bushes). Take a rucksack to carry all your survival rations. A 35 to 40-litre capacity rucksack is best for day trips or a 65-litre capacity for longer hikes.

- Take sun protection, for example a hat, sunglasses, and sun and barrier cream, as you will burn more easily at high altitude due to the thinner air. Use a total sunblock cream on your lips, nose and eyelids, and take a scarf or handkerchief to protect your neck from the sun. You may also need to protect yourself against ticks and mosquitos in some areas.

  Take a water bottle. This is much appreciated when you discover that the mountain restaurant that was just around the corner is still miles away because you took the wrong turn (there's a restaurant on top of every mountain in Switzerland).

- Beware of wild animals that appear ill or unnaturally friendly as they may have rabies (see **Pets** on page 380).

- If you're gathering mushrooms, always present them to your local official 'mushroom inspector', for checking, as some species are deadly poisonous (a number of people die each year in Switzerland from eating poisonous mushrooms or toadstools). **There's usually a limit to the amount of mushrooms which can be picked per person per day, e.g. 1 to 3kg (2.2 to 6.6lb).**

● Don't take young children on difficult hikes unless you enjoy carrying them. Impress upon children the importance of not wandering off on their own. If you lose anyone, particularly children, seek help as soon as possible and before nightfall. It's advisable to equip children with a loud whistle and some warm clothing, in case they get lost.

● Hikers are asked to observe the Swiss Nature Society's green rules:

  – Take care not to damage trees, flowers and bushes;

  – Leave animals in peace (dogs mustn't be allowed to disturb farm animals);

  – Be careful with fire and never start a fire in a forbidden area;

  – Watch where you walk and keep to the paths;

  – Don't litter the countryside;

  – Think of others;

  – Close all gates after use.

MOUNTAINEERING & CAVING

Those who find hiking a bit tame might like to try mountaineering, rock-climbing or caving (subterranean mountaineering), all of which are extremely popular in Switzerland. Switzerland has over 100 peaks of around 4,000m/13,000ft, which provide even the experts with plenty of challenges (usually consisting of trying to climb them all in one day!). If you're an inexperienced climber, you'd be well advised to join an alpine club before heading for the mountains. Contact the Swiss Alpine Club (*Schweizer Alpen-Club, Club Alpin Suisse/SAC*) Monbijoustr. 61, Postfach, CH-3000 Berne 23 (☎ 031 370 18 18, 🖥 www.sac-cas.ch) for information. The SAC maintain over 160 climber's mountain huts throughout Switzerland, listed in a book entitled simply, *Huts*.

Unless you're an experienced climber, you will need to hire a registered guide, particularly when climbing glaciers (don't, however, follow your guide too closely – if he falls down a crevice it isn't necessary to go with him). There are mountaineering schools (around 20 in total) in all the main climbing areas of Switzerland. Contact the Swiss Federation of Climbing Schools (*Schweiz. Verband der Bergsteigerschulen, Ecole Suisse d'Alpinisme*), Grand-Rue, CH-1874 Champery (☎ 024 479 16 15) for information. Guides are available at all mountaineering schools and in many smaller resorts. If you find a guide other than through a recognised school or club, ensure that he is qualified and registered. A good map is important. Swiss ordnance survey maps (*Landeskarte der Schweiz, carte nationale de la Suisse*) are the best. They're available in both 1:25 and 1:50 sizes from stationery stores, railway stations and shops in climbing areas.

Scores of climbers are killed each year in Switzerland, many of whom are inexperienced and reckless. Many more owe their survival to rescuers who risk their own lives to rescue them. Before taking up mountaineering, it's advisable to visit the alpine museum and graveyard in Zermatt (interesting even if you aren't planning to take up residence). Over 500 climbers have died attempting to climb (or descend) the Matterhorn. If this doesn't succeed in bringing you to your senses, all that remains is to wish you the best of luck.

It's extremely foolish – not to mention highly dangerous – to venture off into the mountains without an experienced guide, proper preparation, excellent physical condition, sufficient training, the appropriate equipment and accident insurance.

Mountain walking shouldn't be confused with hiking as it's generally done at much higher altitudes and in more difficult terrain. It can be dangerous for the inexperienced and should be approached with much the same degree of caution and preparation as mountaineering. A free brochure entitled *Safer Mountain Walking* (*Bergwandern Aber sicher!, la sécurité lors des radonnées en montagne*) containing advice about how to avoid accidents, fitness tips and safety rules, is available from Bundesamt für Unfallverhütung, Laupenstr. 11, Postfach 8236, CH-3001 Berne (☎ 031 390 22 22, 💻 www.bfu.ch). REGA, the Swiss helicopter rescue service (see page 134), has the job of rescuing climbers who get stuck on mountains and also provides safety guidelines for mountaineers. See also **Emergencies** on page 242.

RACQUET SPORTS

There are excellent facilities in Switzerland for most racquet sports, particularly tennis and squash. There are two main types of racquet clubs; sports centres open to anyone and private clubs. Sports centres require no membership or membership fees and anyone can book a court. Private clubs usually have high membership fees running into thousands of francs a year, although court fees are low or non-existent. Some private clubs are fairly exclusive and it's difficult to join unless you're introduced by a member and are wealthy.

Tennis is the most popular racquet sport in Switzerland and there's an abundance of covered and outdoor tennis centres. Courts are expensive in winter but are more reasonable in summer when outdoor courts come into play (tennis balls don't bounce too well on snow). Outdoor courts are in short supply in most areas and not surprisingly are difficult to book on sunny days. Tennis centres have coaches available for both private and group lessons. Many communities also have outdoor courts, often floodlit, for which fixed weekly bookings are taken for the whole summer season. Court costs are usually low at around SFr. 20 per hour.

Clubs catering exclusively for squash are rare, although most tennis centres have a number of squash courts, a total of over 600 in some 175 centres throughout Switzerland. The standard of squash isn't high due to the general lack of good coaching and top competition, although it's continually improving. Racquets and balls can be rented from most squash clubs for the American version of squash, called racquet ball, played in Switzerland on a squash court. Some tennis centres also provide badminton courts, which, due to their rarity, are fairly solidly booked on most weekday evenings (they're usually easier to book at weekends). Most badminton centres have clubs entitling members to play free of charge or on reserved courts at fixed times. Typical peak-hour evening court rental costs are:

Sport	Typical Costs Per Hour (SFr.)	
	Winter	Summer
Tennis	22 – 55	20 – 52
Badminton	18 – 30	16 – 27
Table Tennis	10 – 20 (45 mins)	10 – 20 (45 mins)
Squash	20 – 26 (45 mins)	20 – 26 (45 mins)

Court costs are usually cheaper before 5pm and at weekends. Costs can be further reduced by paying for a fixed number of periods (e.g. 5 or 10) or reserving a court for a fixed time each week throughout the season. Court costs are considerably higher than in many other countries, although they can be reduced substantially by joining a club. **Note that you must cancel a booked court 24 hours in advance, otherwise you must pay for it if it isn't re-booked.**

Most public swimming pools, many parks and school playgrounds have table tennis tables that you can use for free but you must take your own bats and balls.

Many clubs provide 'free' saunas and whirl-pools, and solariums are often available for a small extra cost. Racquet clubs sometimes have a resident masseur. Most public racquet clubs have a restaurant (possibly alcohol-free) or snack bar and some have swimming pools. A free list and map of local tennis and squash centres is available from many clubs. Some hotels have their own tennis and squash courts, and organise coaching holidays throughout the year. Information is available from racquet clubs, travel agents and resorts.

Most racquet centres run fee-paying clubs allowing members to play free of charge or at a reduced cost at certain times, and to participate in club competitions. League and knockout competitions are organised, both within clubs and nationally, through affiliation to Swiss sports federations. In order to play in inter-club competitions, competitors must be registered with the national federation for their sport. Fees include accident insurance. There's a full programme of local and national league competitions for all racquet sports.

Finally a few words for table tennis fans (which is **almost** a racquet sport). Table tennis is a sport that's rarely played socially in Switzerland. Normally you must be a member of a club, although you can play casually at hotels, swimming pools and youth clubs. Membership of a table tennis club is usually divided into 'active' (those representing the club in leagues and competitions) and 'passive' members (those playing socially only). Costs vary but it's an inexpensive sport with little equipment necessary. Typical annual club fees are from SFr. 50 to 100 for active membership.

To find the racquet clubs in your area, enquire at your local community or tourist office, or contact the Swiss national association.

RUNNING

Competitive running has a strong following in Switzerland, although jogging isn't very popular judging by the lack of joggers puffing their way up and down the hills. For serious competitive runners, a free annual booklet is produced by the Swiss Light Athletics Federation (*Schweiz. Leichtathletikverband, Fédération Suisse d'Athlétisme*), Industriering 43, Postfach 45, CH-3250 Lyss (☎ 032 387 38 00, 💻 www.swiss-athletics.ch). It contains a complete list of running events throughout Switzerland and is available from sports shops or from the above address.

For those who like to combine running and exercises there are around 500 planned courses (*Vita-Parcours*) throughout Switzerland, sponsored by the Zurich Life Insurance Company. Courses consist of a route of 3 to 4km, with an exercise stop every few hundred metres to keep you in good shape (or kill you if you're in poor shape). Contact the VITA life insurance company (💻 www.vitaparcours.ch) for a complete list of courses (or to insure your survival). Many communities organise local runs (*Volklauf, course populaire*) of around 10km (6mi), where all competitors receive a medal for finishing the course. Contact your local tourist office or community office for details of local races.

SKIING & SNOWBOARDING

A book about living in Switzerland would hardly be complete without a 'few' words (more or less) about skiing. Skiing is Switzerland's national sport and some 40 per cent of the population ski or snowboard regularly, including many foreigners, plus another two million visitors. Wherever you live you won't be far from the ski slopes, although in some areas the nearest facilities may be in a neighbouring country. Switzerland has around 200 ski resorts, most of which are located in attractive mountain villages. However, although Switzerland has largely resisted the temptation to construct purpose-built resorts in virgin areas, it has, like other countries, damaged its mountain environment by over development (the Alps are the world's most environmentally-threatened mountain range).

There are two main types of skiing in Switzerland: alpine or downhill (*Alpin*) and cross-country (*Langlauf/Ski Wandern, ski de fond/ski nordique*). Many downhill skiers look down on cross-country skiing (well they would, they're on top of a mountain!) as boring and lacking in excitement. This may be because it's too much like hard work to most of them, although it would be fair to say that if it's excitement and exhilaration (spelt F-E-A-R) that you're after, downhill skiing is hard to beat.

Whilst originally thought of as a sport for those who are too clumsy to master the art of skiing, snowboarding has picked up as a major winter sport in Switzerland since the mid 1990s. Whilst snowboarders can use the same pistes as skiers, many winter sport resorts have special snowboarding schools and half-pipes (barrel-run).

The skiing season in Switzerland lasts from December to April in most resorts and from November to May in resorts at around 2,000 to 3,000 metres, although it's possible to ski the whole year round on mountains with glaciers.

Alpine Skiing

First the bad news. Alpine or downhill skiing as well as snowboarding are expensive sports, particularly for families. The cost of equipping a family of four is around SFr. 2,500 for equipment and clothing (about SFr. 600 each). If you're a beginner, it's advisable to rent snowboarding or ski equipment (e.g. skis/board, poles, boots) or buy second-hand equipment until you're addicted, which, if it doesn't frighten you to death, can happen on your first day on the slopes. Many a would-be skier has invested a lot of money in new equipment, only to find he doesn't like skiing. Most sports shops have pre-season and end of season sales of ski equipment.

Ski-lift passes can cost over SFr. 50 a day for an adult in a top Swiss resort and skiing in some resorts, particularly at weekends (Sundays are worst), entails a lot of time-consuming and 'expensive' queuing. In many resorts you can buy a limited area ski-lift pass or a half-day pass, e.g. from noon, which is cheaper than buying a day pass for a whole area (you often need to be an Olympian to ski a large area in one day). You can buy a ski-lift pass in most resorts for almost any number of days or for the whole season. Generally, the longer the period covered by a pass, the cheaper the cost per day. In bad weather conditions, which is quite often, many runs are closed and there's usually no compensating reduction or refund in the price of ski-lift passes.

It's advisable to leave the top resorts to the experts and frequent some of the smaller, cheaper areas, at least until you make your first million francs or are sufficiently skilled and fit enough to take full advantage of the more difficult runs. That isn't to say that the bigger, more expensive resorts, don't provide good value for money. A top resort may offer up to ten times the number of lifts and prepared runs (*pistes*) than a small resort, while charging 'only' an extra 25 to 75 per cent for a ski-lift pass. A day's skiing for a family of four, including the cost of travel, ski-lift passes and food and drinks, costs around SFr. 200 in an average resort, but can be much higher.

In many areas, local coach companies organise day trips to ski resorts (usually on Sundays) and make stops in local towns to pick up skiers. They're reasonably priced and include a ski-lift pass. Swiss railways also offer special day-trip excursions which include a ski-lift pass. All large and many smaller resorts provide baby-sitting services or a ski nursery school, although most ski schools won't accept children below the age of three. Ask Switzerland Tourism for information or contact resort tourist offices directly (many are on the Internet).

Accommodation in ski resorts is more expensive during holiday periods (Christmas, New Year and Easter), when the pistes are **very** crowded. During public and school holiday periods, the crowds of schoolchildren may drive you crazy, both on and off-piste, particularly when queuing for ski-lifts (Swiss children aren't taught to queue and are born queue jumpers). Some resorts provide floodlit pistes in the evenings (information is available from ST), but make sure that you check what time the lights go out or you could find yourself skiing in the dark.

It's unlikely but not impossible to have your ski equipment stolen in Switzerland, although it's common in some of Switzerland's neighbouring countries. Take good care of your expensive equipment wherever you are, and when you must leave it unattended, mix your skis and poles with those of your friends (most people won't ski with odd skis and poles!). The price of new skis purchased in Switzerland often includes a year's insurance against theft or damage, or you can insure them separately for around SFr. 20 a year.

Learning To Ski Or Snowboard

If you're a newcomer to downhill skiing, it's worthwhile enrolling at a ski school for a week or two to learn the basics – and it's much safer than simply launching yourself off the nearest mountain, particularly for other skiers. Good skiing is all about style and technique, and the value of good coaching cannot be over-emphasised. Private and group lessons are available in all resorts, for toddlers to senior citizens. ST publish an *Index of Swiss Ski Schools* (see also 🖳 www.snow sports.ch). Many of the ski schools also provide snowboarding classes.

Don't let the 'experts' talk you into buying or hiring long skis. They usually have little or no idea what it's like to learn to ski (particularly as an adult), as most could ski before they could walk. **Putting a beginner on long skis is like putting a learner driver behind the wheel of a grand prix car.** If you're a complete beginner, you may like to try the French short ski (*Kurzski*, *ski-evolutif/ski moderne*) method of instruction using progressively longer skis. As a learning method for adults it's highly recommended by both former pupils and experts alike. As a beginner you want to be able to turn easily and you **don't** want to go fast. Short skis provide both of these advantages, plus better balance, and allow beginners to start learning parallel turns immediately. Adult beginners start on skis of around one metre in length and usually progress to 1.6 metre skis in a week, by which time most are making 'passable' parallel turns.

The main drawback is that the *ski-evolutif* method isn't taught in many resorts outside France (try Migros Club Schools in Switzerland – see **Day & Evening Classes** on page 316). A similar method is widely taught in North

America, where it's called the graduated length method (GLM). The traditionalists in Switzerland and Austria don't usually teach the *ski-evolutif* method, mainly because the locals learn to ski while 'in the womb'. There's also prejudice against *ski-evolutif* in Switzerland as it was invented by the French, who, as everyone knows, cannot ski (Killy was a rare exception).

Buy yourself a good skiing book. The Sunday Times book *We Learned to Ski* (Collins) is an excellent choice, not only for beginners but for any skier. It's expertly researched and written and cannot be too highly recommended. According to the experts, it's the best book ever written about learning to ski.

Preparation

As any boy scout will tell you, it's wise to do some preparation and take a few precautions before attacking the ski slopes:

Ski Exercises: It's advisable to perform some special ski exercises for a few weeks before taking to the pistes. This helps to increase your general flexibility and strength, and prepares your body for the unique demands of skiing. It also ensures that you don't ache quite so much after a day on the pistes. Special ski exercise classes are held in most cities and towns in Switzerland and shown on TV. Most ski books also contain recommended exercises. **Remember, grossly unfit skiers are a danger to everyone – not least themselves.**

Insurance: Check that your family and visitors are fully insured for ski accidents, including helicopter rescue (see page 134). If you live and work in Switzerland, you're covered for ski accidents by your compulsory employee, non-occupational, accident insurance, but this doesn't include family members.

Piste Plan: Always obtain a piste plan on arrival in a resort and check the connecting runs, so as not to get lost or take the wrong runs. In Switzerland runs are graded as follows: blue = easy, red = intermediate and black = difficult. In Austria and France there are green-graded runs for beginners. Unfortunately plans aren't always easy to read. There's sometimes a lot of walking between lifts and what appears on the plan to be the top of a lift, may turn out to be the bottom. Without a piste plan it's possible to end up by mistake on one of those dreaded 'north face of the Eiger' blackest-of-black runs. A piste plan also helps beginners avoid T-bars when skiing on their own, although they can be shared with another skier. Swiss resorts have mostly T-bars and few button (single tow) or chair-lifts.

Clothing: Besides proper ski clothes (jacket, trousers and gloves), long johns, thermal underwear, silk inner gloves, silk socks, scarves and woollen hats may be necessary. These may not sound too fashionable or glamorous, but are more welcome than the latest ski-wear fashions on freezing cold days – if you ski badly, you will look like an idiot no matter what you're wearing! A one-piece ski suit is best for beginners, as it keeps out the snow when you fall on your behind. Lightweight clothes and gloves can be worn on warmer days (gloves should always be worn to protect hands from injury). Après ski boots with non-slip rubber soles, e.g. moon boots, are essential and inexpensive.

Skin & Eye Protection: Your skin and eyes need protection from the sun and glare when skiing (snow blindness is rare, but not unknown). When skiing in bright sunlight, special ski sunglasses with side protection or mirror lenses are best. Buy the best you can afford. A loop connected to sunglasses and hung around your neck helps prevent their loss in a fall and is also handy to hang them from when you aren't wearing them. However, don't wear dark sunglasses or goggles that inhibit your vision in poor visibility, e.g. when it's snowing, as it makes it's difficult to see the bumps and dips. You can have a nasty accident if you hit an unseen bump (or a fellow skier) at speed.

It's easy to get sunburnt at high altitudes, even in winter. Use a total blockout cream for your lips, nose, ears and the rest of your face, even when it doesn't appear particularly bright. Apply often and liberally, particularly to lips (many a holiday is ruined by an outbreak of herpes) where it can be easily wiped off accidentally – hopefully by an attractive partner!

Safety

Safety is of paramount importance in any sport, but it's particularly important when skiing, where the possibility of injury is ever present (one in every ten participants suffers some sort of injury). In recent years, skiing-related deaths and serious injuries have increased considerably as slopes have become more crowded and skiers have looked further afield for more daring and dangerous thrills. Around 200 skiers die annually in Europe and a further 100,000 are injured. **Accident insurance is essential when skiing anywhere!**

Equipment: While it's unnecessary to wear the latest ski fashions, it's important to have suitable, secure and safe equipment – particularly bindings and boots. Although the latest high-tech bindings are a great help in avoiding injuries, the correct settings are vital. They should be set so that in the event of a fall, you part company with your skis before your leg (or part thereof) parts company with your body. Beginners' bindings must be set so that they release fairly easily, but not so easily that they open each time a turn is attempted. Have your skis and bindings serviced each season by a qualified ski mechanic (any ski shop can do this). If you're using rented or second-hand skis, double check that the bindings are set correctly and that they release freely in all directions. If you aren't entirely happy with rented equipment, never hesitate to request adjustments or an exchange. Young children should wear safety helmets at all times as soon as they're able to use normal pistes and lifts.

Ability & Injuries: Try to ski with people of the same standard as yourself or with an experienced skier who's willing to ski at your pace, and don't be in too much of a hurry to tackle those black runs. It isn't obligatory to ski from sunrise to sunset, although some fanatics may try to convince you otherwise. Stop skiing and rest when you feel tired. A sure sign is when you keep falling over for no apparent reason (unless you've had a large liquid lunch!). Most ski accidents happen when skiers are tired. If you injure yourself, particularly a knee, stop skiing and seek medical advice as soon as possible. If you attempt to ski with an injury or before an injury has had time to heal, you risk aggravating it and doing permanent damage. **It's better to ride down in the cable-car than on a stretcher!**

Weather: Unless you're an expert skier, it's best to avoid skiing in bad weather and in poor snow conditions. When snow cover is poor or runs are icy, the danger of injury increases dramatically, particularly for beginners and intermediates who often find it difficult or impossible to control their skis.

Avalanche Warnings: <u>NEVER</u> ignore avalanche warnings (*Lawinengefahr, danger d'avalanches*), denoted by black and yellow flags or signs and warning lights, or attempt to ski on closed (*gesperrt, barré*) pistes or anywhere there's a danger of avalanches (reports are issued at tourist offices). Avalanches on open pistes are extremely rare as the overloaded slopes overlooking pistes are blasted with explosives to remove excess snow. Don't ski or snowboard off-piste unless you're an experienced skier, and in an unfamiliar area you should hire an experienced local guide.

Each year 150 to 200 skiers and snowboarders are killed in avalanches in the Alps, usually when skiing off-piste (although in recent years there have been a number of disasters involving chalets situated directly below mountains). You can buy a small radio transmitter, e.g. an avalanche transceiver, that helps rescuers locate you if you're buried in an avalanche (some also have a flashing light system). They're expensive, although sensible off-piste skiers consider their lives are worth the cost (most guides insist upon them). You can also wear an ABS air balloon rucksack, which can be inflated like a car air-bag to protect you in the event of an avalanche (although experts are undecided about their effectiveness). Never ski off-piste on your own. Avalanche bulletins are given on the Swiss television teletext service and a special telephone service is also provided on service number 187 and the Internet (🖳 www.slf.ch) for ski tourers. Skiers who cause avalanches can be billed for the cost of rescue, damage to property and clean-up operations. Safety brochures for skiers are available from the Swiss Bureau for the Prevention of Accidents (see **Accidents** on page 243).

Restricted Areas: Only ski or snowboard where it's permitted. In some areas off-piste skiing is forbidden to protect plants and the wildlife habitat. Many animals are hibernating in winter and others need to preserve their precious reserves of fat to survive the winter. You won't help their chances of survival by frightening them. Trees are planted in many areas to help prevent avalanches and are easily destroyed by careless skiers. Some areas, which are signposted, are designated as preservation areas for wildlife, flora and fauna, and you can be fined for skiing there.

The Highway Code For Skiers & Snowboarders

As the ski slopes become more crowded, the possibility of colliding with a fellow skier has increased dramatically. Snowboarders have a reputation of being ruthless and leaving a trace of fallen skiers behind when speeding down the piste – using a different line than the skiers they have to be particularly careful. Happily, the result of most clashes is just a few bruises and dented pride, nevertheless the danger of serious injury is ever present. You cannot always protect yourself from the lunatic fringe. e.g. the crazy novice who skis way beyond his limits and the equally loony 'expert' who skis at reckless speeds with a total disregard for other skiers (Switzerland has a lot of these, particularly snowboarders and mono-skiers). Serious head injuries can often be prevented by wearing a helmet – many ski schools declare them compulsory for children. The following guidelines from the International Ski Federation's (FIS) Code of Conduct for skiers may help you avoid an accident:

- **Respect For Others** – A skier and snowboarder must behave in such a way that he neither endangers nor prejudices others.

- **Control Of Speed And Skiing** – A skier and snowboarder must adapt his speed and way of skiing to his own personal ability, and to the prevailing conditions of terrain and weather.

- **Control Of Direction** – A skier and snowboarder coming from above, whose dominant position allows him a choice of paths, must take a direction which assures the safety of the skier below.

- **Overtaking** – A skier and snowboarder should always leave a wide enough margin for the overtaken skier and snowboarder to make his turn. (As when motoring, the most dangerous skiing manoeuvre is overtaking.)

- **Crossing The Piste** – A skier and snowboarder entering or crossing a piste must look up and down to make sure that he can do so without danger to himself or to others. The same applies after stopping.

- **Stopping On The Piste** – Unless absolutely necessary, a skier and snowboarder must avoid making a stop on the piste, particularly in narrow passages or where visibility is restricted. If a skier and snowboarder falls, he must clear the piste as soon as possible.

- **Climbing** - A climbing skier must keep to the side of the piste and in bad visibility, keep off the piste altogether. The same goes for a skier or snowboarder descending on foot.

If you're hit by a reckless skier or snowboarder you can sue for damages or can equally be sued if you cause an accident. There's no foolproof way of avoiding accidents (apart from avoiding skiing altogether). Obey the FIS code and make sure that you're well insured for both accidents and private liability (see **Chapter 13**). If you're involved in an accident or collision you should do the following:

- Obtain the names and addresses (local and permanent) of all people involved and any witnesses.
- Report the accident to the local police within 24 hours. This is essential if you wish to make a claim against an insurance policy or a third party.

> - Make notes and diagrams of the accident scene while it's still fresh in your mind.
> - Notify your insurers as soon as possible and forward any documentation to them.

If you suspect any equipment was at fault, e.g. a ski binding, retain it (provided it wasn't rented) and note the precise type, size, adjustments and nature of the fault. If you work in Switzerland, your compulsory accident insurance covers you against ski accidents. However, it doesn't include cover for accidents caused by you, for which you need private liability insurance (see page 271) with an minimum insured sum of SFr. 2 million.

The Swiss Commission for the Prevention of Accidents on Ski-Runs and Cross-Country Trails (SKUS), Laupenstrasse 11,Postfach 8236, CH-3001 Berne (☎ 031 390 21 60)(💻 www.skus.ch) publish a booklet in English entitled *Guidlines for the Conduct of Skiers and Snowboarders.*

Snow & Weather Conditions

Information on alpine snow and weather conditions is provided on TV teletext on most stations during the skiing season. The DRS (Swiss German television service) provides the most comprehensive service. It lists resorts by area and gives snow depth (village and top station), the type of snow, piste conditions and whether the runs down to the village are open. It's updated twice a week on Mondays and Thursdays. The ARD/ZDF (German TV) service includes the major resorts in Austria, France, Germany, Italy and Switzerland. French teletext is unobtainable via a Swiss TV due to the different teletext system used in France. The Eurosport satellite TV station provides regular snow reports for major resorts, although not on teletext. Snow conditions are also available via the Internet (💻 www.skiinfo.ch).

It's important to check the snow conditions, as it's hardly worth skiing when there's little snow or snow conditions are bad, e.g. salt or slush. When snow cover is poor many runs are closed, particularly those down to the valley or bottom station, and you must endure a lot of queuing and walking between lifts. Many resorts have installed snow-making machinery on runs and are able to guarantee that a limited number of runs are open. However, when snow conditions are bad in most areas, the overcrowding is horrendous. Many ski resorts have a special ski information telephone number (*Schnee- und Pistenbericht, bulletin d'enneigement*) where the latest information is recorded including snow conditions, condition and number of runs open, local weather and the number of lifts in operation. Numbers are listed in telephone directories.

Before you set out or plan a day or weekend skiing trip, it's wise to check the weather forecast, as it isn't much fun skiing in a blizzard, rain, freezing cold or in bad visibility. Swiss weather forecasting is usually highly accurate and one of the best weather forecasts is provided by the Swiss television teletext service.

Ski Clubs

You may find that it's worthwhile joining a ski club affiliated to the Swiss-Ski, Haus des Skisports, Worbstr. 52, Postfach 478, CH-3074 Muri b. Berne (☎ 031 950 61 11, 💻 www.swiss-ski.ch). This usually entitles you to an Swiss-Ski booklet; skiing insurance; ski-lift vouchers; hotel and other discounts; membership of your local canton ski association; and a subscription to the Swiss-Ski magazine (in German), the official organ of Swiss-Ski.

All towns, most villages and many companies have their own ski clubs, and in some cities there are also international ski clubs for expatriates. Groups of ten or more skiers usually receive a reduction of around SFr. 5 per person off the cost of an individual day pass. A schedule of Swiss downhill skiing, cross-country and skating races (*Official Volkski-Kalendar, calendrier du ski populaire*) is published annually by the Swiss-Ski Federation (see page 341).

Summary

The above notes aren't intended to cause you to flee in panic at the sight of a snowflake or ski brochure. The pitfalls and dangers of downhill skiing have been highlighted with the sole aim of making your skiing safer and more enjoyable. In case you're still wondering what happened to the good news – here it is! Once you've overcome your initial fear and found your ski legs, skiing is one of the most enjoyable and addictive of all sports. On a beautiful spring day, with the sun and wind in your face and crisp powder snow under your skis, you may even imagine you've discovered heaven on earth.

If you're injured, don't despair, as you will have even more time for après ski activities, which is how the sport became so popular with many foreigners in the first place (skiing that is, not boozing). Some 'skiers' have taken the art of après ski to new heights and can make it last all day, although to retain your credibility it helps to have your leg in plaster (maybe you can rent a plaster cast from the local costume shop?).

Your chances of being injured, frozen or sunburnt are happily remote, **providing you take a few precautions**. Hals und Beinbruch (good luck)!

Cross-Country Skiing

Cross-country skiing (*Ski Langlauf/Ski Wandern, ski de fond/ski nordique*) doesn't have the glamorous jet-set image of alpine skiing, but nevertheless it's a popular sport in Switzerland. It appeals to both young and old, particularly those whose idea of fun is a million miles away from hurtling down a hill at 100kph (62mph), with a thousand metre drop on one side and a glacier on the other. Cross-country skiing can be enjoyed at any pace and over any distance, and therefore has great attraction for both those who aren't very fit and keen athletes. It can be exhilarating, particularly if you make the effort to learn the correct technique and persevere beyond the beginner's stage. It's also rates highly as a total body workout and is claimed by many to be one of the best of all forms of exercise.

Compared with alpine skiing, cross-country skiing has the advantages of cheaper equipment, lower costs, fewer broken bones **and** no queues. No expensive ski-lift passes are necessary, although skiers must buy a SFr. 90 annual Cross-Country Pass entitling them to use over 5,600km (3,500mi) of tracks throughout Switzerland (⌨ www.loipen-schweiz.ch). Alternately a local seasonal card can be purchased for around SFr. 35 or a day pass for SFr. 6 per day. Children (under 16) ski for free. Essential equipment costs as little as SFr. 300 to 400 for skis, bindings, poles, boots and gloves. No special clothing is necessary apart from gloves and boots, providing you have a warm pullover and tracksuit. You can, of course, buy more expensive equipment and special clothing.

Prepared cross-country trails, usually consisting of two sets of tracks (*Langlauf-Loipen*, *loipes/pistes de ski de fond*), are laid on specially prepared and sign-posted routes, where you ski in the direction of the arrows. There are cross-country ski trails in most winter ski resorts in Switzerland, Austria and Germany, although there are fewer in France and Italy (it isn't macho enough for Latins). You can enjoy cross-country skiing anywhere there's sufficient snow, although using prepared trails is easier than making your own, as is usually done in Scandinavia. The total number of kilometres of cross-country trails open in Swiss resorts is shown on the Swiss television teletext service. Many resorts have floodlit tracks for night skiing.

An annual booklet published by Swiss-Ski, *Ski Langlauf, Ski de fond*, is a must for all keen cross-country skiers. It contains information on all aspects of cross-country skiing (in English, French and German), a complete list of all Swiss cross-country skiing circuits, and race information. It's available from most sports shops or by post from Swiss-Ski (see address on page 341).

SKI VARIATIONS & OTHER WINTER SPORTS

When you get bored with all those 'easy' black pistes, you might like to try something different For information on the following winter sports, contact Switzerland Tourism (see page 305).

Bob-Sleighing

For the really brave or completely loony sensation-seeker (the famous Cresta run in St. Moritz is the world's fastest and most dangerous). Ladies aren't allowed to participate – unless they masquerade as men!

Curling

A bit like lawn bowls on ice, except that the 'balls' (called rocks) are flat with a handle on top. Curling rinks are generally located indoors, although some resorts have outdoor rinks. Demand for lessons has soared since Switzerland won the gold medal at the 1998 winter Olympics.

Dog Sledding & Horse Racing

Dog sledding and horse racing are popular in some resorts, although they generally aren't for novices.

Freestyle Skiing

Winter sport for circus acrobats and high-board divers. Involves doing a triple somersault on skis – among other things. For the brave and **very** accomplished skier. Spectacular but can be dangerous if you land on your head.

Heli-Skiing

No you aren't pulled along by a helicopter, but deposited by it in inaccessible places at around 4,000 metres (around 13,000 feet) from where you ski home (or get lost). For proficient off-piste skiers only. Heli-skiers in Switzerland must be accompanied by a licensed mountain guide.

Ice Hockey

A popular sport in Switzerland with both competitors (five leagues) and spectators. If only the Swiss could come up with a decent national team!

Ice Skating

Many towns and winter holiday resorts have outdoor ice rinks open from around October to April. There are also some 80 indoor rinks, many of which are open all year round. **Take extra care when skating on natural ponds and always observe warning signs. Rescue equipment (long poles) and alarms are usually prominently displayed.**

Luge

Single seat, feet-first toboggan used on a bob-sleigh run at break-neck speeds. Skeleton is a head-first (kamikaze position) version of the luge, hence the name.

Mono-Skiing

Equipment consists of one wide ski with two normal ski bindings side by side. Skiers use normal ski poles and wear ski boots. Usually requires good skiing ability, although it might appeal to those who have difficulty distinguishing between their left and right feet (see also **Snow surfing** below).

Off-Piste Skiing

Off-piste skiing in deep powder snow is what most advanced skiers dream about. It can be dangerous and aspirants should be able to handle black runs **with confidence**. See also **Avalanche Warnings** on page 338.

Ski-Bobbing

Similar to bicycling on snow and sometimes called snowbiking. Provides plenty of exhilarating, down-to-earth thrills. Ski-bobs can be rented in over 70 resorts, some of which have specially marked runs. However, some resorts ban them owing to the danger to skiers.

Ski Hang-Gliding & Paragliding

If jumping out of an aeroplane or off a mountain with a parachute or hang-glider (while wearing skis) is your idea of fun, these sports may appeal to you.

Ski-Joring

Skiers are pulled along by galloping horses at hair-raising speeds. An old 'sport' which is quite rare these days.

Ski Touring

Involves walking uphill and skiing downhill. Requires good off-piste skiing ability, excellent physical condition and special skis (skins) and equipment. Should never be attempted without a guide.

Snow Rafting

Participants sit in a rubber boat (or rubber tube), while it rockets down pistes at 100kph. It's best attempted on controlled and segregated slopes, where there are no trees or other obstacles (such as people). A dangerous 'sport' which is banned in many resorts.

Speed Skiing

Ski at up to 200kph/124mph (if you dare). For skiers who never got to lesson three – how to turn. Popular in France (enough said).

Tobogganing & Sledding

Many resorts have special runs reserved for tobogganing, while in others, runs may also be open to skiers. Great fun for children, both young and old (i.e. adults). Sometimes runs are floodlit during the evening. A brochure is available from Switzerland Tourism (ST) listing runs of up to 11km/7mph.

Some of the above sports are limited to a small number of resorts or are restricted to particular pistes or areas. If they don't provide enough challenges, you can always try skiing down the Matterhorn as a Japanese Kamikaze skier did in 1985 (he survived). Another Japanese (who else?) skied (he actually fell most of the way) down Mount Everest with a parachute, which was supposed to slow him down. He also lived to tell the tale and they even made a film of it – otherwise nobody would have believed it!

SWIMMING

There are heated indoor (*Hallenbad, piscine couverte*) and outdoor (*Freibad, piscine en plein air*) swimming pools in most Swiss towns, a total of around 1,000 when both public and hotel swimming pools are included (most hotel pools are open to non-residents for a small fee). Most towns and villages catering for winter sports and summer hiking have indoor swimming pools. The entrance fee is usually from around SFr. 5 and extras such as wave machines, saunas, solariums, table tennis, mini-golf and games areas may be provided. You can also swim at over 170 locations in Swiss lakes (*Strandbad, piscine naturelle*) from around June to September (the water temperature for the largest lakes is listed on Swiss television teletext). There are even a few areas set aside for nude sunbathing, although men and women are usually segregated and all are hidden from prying eyes (sexual thoughts are forbidden in Switzerland).

There are a number of large indoor swimming centres and water parks in Switzerland containing hot water pools, sulphur baths, thermal whirlpools, connecting indoor and outdoor pools, wave machines, huge water slides, solariums and saunas (some even have mixed saunas for those who like to indulge in **hot** sexual thoughts). Swimming centres have restaurants and are open daily from around 10am to 10pm. The entrance fee is high, e.g. SFr. 25 for just four hours, although they make a pleasant change from the local pool for a special day out. Spas throughout Switzerland (see page 252) have hot-spring pools where you may swim gently or relax in the water. Children aren't, however, always admitted. Most swimming pools and clubs organise swimming lessons (all levels from beginner to fish) and run life-saving courses.

WATER SPORTS

All water sports including sailing, windsurfing, water-skiing, rowing, canoeing and subaquatic sports are popular in Switzerland. This is hardly surprising as the country has over 1,600 natural lakes (totalling some 13,355,100km^2 or 330,000acres) and 32,000km (20,000mi) of rivers, perhaps including a few ponds and streams. Boats and equipment can be rented on most lakes and rescue services are provided, although they aren't usually free (they throw you back in if you cannot pay). Instruction is available for most water sports on major lakes and in holiday centres. There is unfortunately one small problem with sailing and windsurfing in Switzerland: a lack of wind, particularly in summer.

Rowing and canoeing is possible on most lakes and rivers. The Rotsee lake near Lucerne is the most famous Swiss rowing venue and one of the most beautiful courses in the world. Wetsuits are recommended for windsurfing, water-skiing and subaquatic sports, even during the summer. White-water rafting is an exciting and popular sport and is taught and practiced in many areas. Those who like something more adventurous might wish to try canyoning, which involves sliding down water channels (or ice channels) on your backside.

You must pass a written test before you can use a motorboat with a motor size of 6kW (7.5 PS) or a sailing boat with a sail area of over 15m^2 (161ft^2). Boats must usually have a mooring and cannot be stored at home except in a garage (unless you have a big, BIG bath). Sailing and windsurfing weather and the summer water temperature of the major lakes is provided on the Swiss television teletext service. Information regarding river rafting, kayaks and sailing schools is available from Switzerland Tourism (ST). **Be sure to observe all warning signs on lakes and rivers!**

OTHER SPORTS

The following are a selection of other popular sports in Switzerland:

Athletics

Most Swiss towns and villages have local athletics clubs and organise local competitions and sports days.

Ballet & Jazz Ballet

Hardly sports, but nonetheless excellent exercise. Dance, training and exercise classes are provided in many towns throughout Switzerland and are also organised by gymnasiums. Jazz ballet classes are also organised by Migros Club Schools (see **Day & Evening Classes** on page 316).

Billiards & Snooker

Many hotels, bars and sports clubs have billiard or snooker tables and there are a few billiards' clubs in the larger towns. English-style snooker isn't played in public clubs in Switzerland.

Bungee Jumping

If your idea of fun is jumping out of a cable car or a hot-air balloon with an elastic rope attached to your body to prevent you merging with the landscape, then bungee jumping may be just what you're looking for.

Darts

Not actually a sport but an excuse to get drunk (have you ever seen anyone playing darts in a milk bar?). Darts can be played at any of the Pickwick chain of pubs in Switzerland and other English-style pubs.

Gymnasiums & Health Clubs

There are gymnasiums and health clubs in most towns with tonnes of expensive bone-jarring, muscle-wrenching apparatus. Costs are around SFr. 100 a month or SFr. 1,000 a year, although they can be reduced by taking advantage of off-peak reductions. Many first class hotels have fitness rooms.

Gymnastics

An extremely popular sport in Switzerland and gymnastic clubs abound in all areas, even in small towns and villages.

Handball

Played indoors on a pitch similar to a five-a-side soccer pitch. Handball players pass the ball around by hand and attempt to throw it into a small goal..

Hockey

Called land hockey in Switzerland to avoid confusion with the more popular ice hockey.

Horse Riding

Popular but expensive. There are around 90 riding schools and equestrian centres in Switzerland. Hiring a horse from a farm is cheaper, but tuition isn't usually provided. Some resorts organise cross-country riding holidays.

Martial Arts

For those brought up on a diet of Bruce Lee, unarmed (?) combat such as Kung Fu, Judo and Karate are taught and practiced in most towns. There are over 300 judo clubs in Switzerland. Timid children are sometimes encouraged to learn judo to combat school bullies.

Roller Skating & Skate-Boarding

Rinks are provided in many towns and sometimes winter ice skating rinks are used for roller skating in summer.

Rugby

A surprisingly popular sport in Switzerland, where there are clubs in all the major cities (yet another 'habit' they picked up from the British – along with skiing).

Shooting

Shooting ranges abound in Switzerland and shooting is particularly popular on Sunday mornings to prevent you having a lye-in. Annual target shooting is compulsory for all Swiss men as part of their military service. Most towns and villages have a local shooting federation which organises local competitions. Crossbow shooting remains popular and modern William Tells are to be found in many crossbow clubs, although participants now use targets due to a dearth of brave little boys and big apples.

Football

Between mid-July and mid-June, the 10 first division clubs (formerly called *Nationalliga A*, from 2003 *Super League*) play each other home and away twice (36 rounds in total). The team finishing top is crowned the champions. At the end of the season the bottom team moves down to the second division (formerly called *Nationalliga B*, since 2003 *Challenge League*) and the team finishing ninth has to play against the team that has finished second in the Challenge League with the winner going to the Super League. The Challenge League consists of 16 teams. Most major Swiss cities and towns have either a first or second division football team. Many are professional and the standard of the best teams is similar to the English or German second or third divisions. Most towns and villages have amateur football clubs for all ages and standards.

Ten-Pin Bowling

Ten-pin bowling centres can be found in all major Swiss cities. Ten-pin bowling and skittles (*Kegelbahn, jeu de quilles*) can also be played in many hotels and restaurants.

Swiss Sports

The Swiss also have their own Alpine sports, which are usually incomprehensible to anyone but a Swiss mountain man. These include stone throwing (*Steinstossen* or *Steinwerfen*), traditional Swiss wrestling (*Schwingen*) and the strangest of all, *Hornussen*. In Hornussen a puck-like plastic object (the *Hornuss*) is placed at the tip of a curved rail planted in the soil. The striker hits the Hornuss with a whip-like cane around two metres in length, while the catchers (strategically placed in the field) attempt to bat it away with large wooden boards on poles before it hits the ground. Hornussen isn't expected to become an Olympic sport in the near future.

Miscellaneous

Many foreign sports and pastimes have a group of expatriate fanatics in Switzerland including cricket, American football, baseball, boccia, boules, croquet, polo and softball. For more information enquire at community and tourist offices, embassies and consulates, and social clubs (see **Appendix A**).

SPORT FOR THE DISABLED

Switzerland has an extensive sports programme for the disabled, organised by the Swiss Association for Handicapped Sport (*Plusport Behindertenspor Schweiz, Sport Handicap Suisse*), Chriesbaumstr. 6, CH-8604 Volketswil (☎ 01 908 45 00, 🖳 www.plusport.ch).

17.

SHOPPING

Shopping in Switzerland is among the best in the world, although you may sometimes wonder whether all Swiss are millionaires and just what they do with all those gold watches, diamond necklaces and fur coats. Actually millionaires make up only half the population of Switzerland – the rest are foreigners. Joking aside, it has been conservatively estimated that Switzerland has over 75,000 millionaires (including many foreigners) and the highest level of per capita accumulated wealth in the world. There are, however, a few shops that cater to the needs of poor foreigners and English is spoken in most major towns and tourist areas.

There's generally no bargaining in Switzerland, although if you plan to spend a lot of money in one store you might ask for a discount (except in department stores and supermarkets). Value added tax (VAT) is always included and there are no hidden extras: the advertised price is the price you pay. Swiss shopkeepers are usually scrupulously honest and most shops exchange goods or give refunds without question. The Swiss customer is usually very critical and he demands top quality, durability, after sales service and value for money – all features of most Swiss products. Although prices may be higher than in many other countries, goods may be of superior quality and therefore comparisons aren't always valid. Most Swiss shops accept euros and may also accept other major foreign currencies.

Cartels are common and aren't illegal unless shown to be harmful (a new law designed to prevent the harmful economic and social effects of cartels came into force in 1996). Consequently, the prices of some goods and services can be up to 50 per cent higher than in most EU countries. This makes shopping in Switzerland's neighbouring countries rewarding. Sales and prices of most goods in Switzerland are strictly regulated and prices for branded goods are fixed to protect small shop owners. Stores can, however, sell branded goods under their own name at lower prices or sell goods at reduced prices during official sales, e.g. in January and July. Many Swiss prefer to shop in their local village or town and happily pay higher prices in return for the convenience of shopping locally. There are large indoor shopping centres in all areas, where you can do all your shopping under one roof and cities and most large towns usually have a traffic free shopping street or town centre. Many Swiss manufacturers provide factory shops where you may shop at generous discounts, although hours are usually restricted and some shops are only open one day a week or month.

Most shops hold sales (*Sonderverkauf/Ausverkauf, soldes*) in January and July, when goods are available at bargain prices. If you intend to have a shopping spree, it's definitely worth waiting for the sales. Around Christmas time, storage areas are provided in many towns, where shoppers may leave their purchases free of charge (while they buy more). Some major cities, e.g. Zurich, produce monthly shopping guides. Finally, don't panic if you're pounced on by an army of shop assistants – it's just the natives way of being friendly. If you don't want their help, tell them that you're just looking and hopefully they will go away.

For those who aren't used to buying articles with metric measures and continental sizes, a list of comparative weights and measures are included in

Appendix D. American Women's Clubs (see **Appendix A**) and other women's clubs are an excellent source of shopping information, particularly for those hard to find imported foods.

SHOPPING HOURS

Shopping hours in Switzerland are usually from around 8 or 9am to 6.30 or 6.45pm Tuesdays to Fridays and from 8am to between 4 and 6pm on Saturdays. On Mondays most shops open from between 1 and 2pm until around 6.30 or 6.45pm, although some are closed all day. Many towns have late night shopping until 8 or 9pm on Wednesday, Thursday or Friday (in Zurich shops can now stay open until 8pm from Monday to Friday); larger shopping centres also have extended shopping hours. In smaller towns, all shops and businesses close for lunch, e.g. from noon until 2pm. Local shops, for example those located in villages, close for a half or full day a week and may close earlier on a Saturday, e.g. 2pm. It's customary for certain businesses to be closed on the same day, for example most hairdressers (*Coiffeur*) are closed on Mondays and pharmacies (*Apotheke, pharmacie*) on Thursdays. Shops generally close at 4 or 5pm the day before a public holiday, even if it's a late shopping day.

All shops are closed on Sundays except bakeries, some of which open from around 10am to noon. However, a recent law allows stores to open on six Sundays or official holidays a year (stores are often open on a few Sundays before Christmas). Geneva and Zurich airports have shopping centres open from 8am to 8pm every day and some motorway (*Autobahn, autoroute*) shopping centres are open every day of the year, with the possible exception of Christmas day. In major cities there are vending machines in most main railway stations (*Hauptbahnhof, gare centrale*) containing essential foods and you can usually find shops in the vicinity (around 100 metres) that are also open longer than normal (e.g. 7am to 10pm), including Sundays and public holidays. Grocery stores near border crossings are usually open on Sundays and shops in many holiday resorts (including special tourist areas of some major cities) are open on Sundays and public holidays throughout the season. At Christmas time, many major stores hold shopping evenings exclusively for the disabled.

SHOPPING CENTRES & MARKETS

There are many large modern indoor shopping centres (*Einkaufszentrum, centre commercial*) in Switzerland. These often contain over 100 shops including supermarkets, department stores, furniture stores, restaurants, banks and a post office, plus many of the small specialist shops you'd expect to find in a small town. The main attractions, in addition to the wide choice of shops, are protection from inclement weather and free parking, meaning you can simply wheel your purchases to your car (parking is expensive and difficult in most city and town centres, particularly on Saturdays). Most banks are open on Saturdays in shopping centres. Shopping centre stores periodically issue books of discount coupons (*Einkaufsbon/Bezugsschein, bon d'achat*) to attract customers.

Most towns have markets on various days of the week, with Wednesdays and Saturdays the most popular. These vary from fruit and vegetable markets to flea/curiosity (second-hand goods) markets. In major cities there are markets on most days of the week. Food markets usually open around 6am and may close as early as 11am, while curiosity markets often operate from 10am to 4pm or even until 9pm in summer. Check with local tourist and information offices.

SUPERMARKETS

Many foreign foods can be found in local supermarkets (*Supermarkt, supermarché*) if you look hard enough, but don't overlook the many delicious local foods on offer. One of the advantages of living in central Europe is being able to sample the bewildering choice of continental food and beverages on offer. Don't despair if you cannot find your favourite food as there are many other delicacies available. The German, French and Italian-speaking parts of Switzerland all offer excellent regional and ethnic specialities. Most department stores sell imported foods, particularly Globus, Jelmoli and Manor (see **Department & Chain Stores** below) and all major towns have a variety of delicatessens and imported food shops. A number of companies that import American and British foods also advertise in the English-language press in Switzerland (e.g. Taste of America – ▢ www.tasteof america.ch).

Among the best value-for-money supermarkets are Coop, Denner Discount (particularly for wine, beer, cigarettes and perfumes), EPA (Unip), Jumbo, Migros, Pick Pay, Uniprix and Waro, all of which have branches throughout Switzerland. Prices in village shops are generally higher than in supermarkets, although many villages have a reasonably priced Volg store. Migros, one of the largest companies in Switzerland, has the lowest prices. It also has the most outlets and accounts for some 15 per cent of food and non-food (cleaning products, toiletries, fashion, etc.) sales. The Coop has around 20 per cent of the food market and Denner some 3 per cent. Migros **doesn't** sell spirits, wine or tobacco and sells mostly own-brand goods (although more branded goods are appearing). Migros and the Coop operate mobile shops in some areas (ask your neighbours or at your local branch).

Most supermarkets provide only small plastic carrier bags, and charge from SFr. 0.20 to 0.40 for larger, more sturdy bags. This may be irritating, but is intended to decrease waste pollution and is to be applauded. Copy the Swiss and take a bag with you when shopping. Some supermarkets provide free boxes. Supermarket trolleys require a deposit of SFr. 1 or 2, which ensures that most customers return them to a collection point rather than abandoning them in the car park (or taking them home). Many items such as tea and coffee contain stamps on their labels, which can be collected and exchanged for books, pictures and games (etc.) when you've collected 'a few million'. Stamp catalogues can be obtained from manufacturers (addresses are printed on labels).

Migros offers regular customers a client reward scheme where you receive a client card (called a 'cumulus card') and earn one point for each franc spent. Every three months you receive a booklet with special discount offers and vouchers worth SFr. 0.01 per point collected, so effectively you receive 1 per cent discount on your purchases. Coop has a similar scheme called 'Supercard' where you can collect points and benefit from discounts on specific articles.

Most supermarkets have a coffee bean grinding machine for their customers' use. If you live in a farming community, you can buy unpasteurised milk from your local dairy by the bucket full (you supply the container). It's cheaper than buying milk by the carton from a supermarket, but it should be boiled before use. Many farms sell potatoes and other vegetables in bulk, and allow you to pick your own fruit during the harvest season.

Supermarkets sell beer, soft drinks and mineral water by the crate, where you pay a deposit on the crate and bottles, which are usually returnable. Many people also have drinks delivered to their homes, rather than struggle home with heavy crates from the supermarket. Ask your neighbours about deliveries.

See also **Shopping Abroad** on page 362 and **Home Shopping** on page 361.

DEPARTMENT & CHAIN STORES

Switzerland has many excellent department (*Warenhaus, grand magasin*) and chain stores. One of the most famous and exclusive Swiss department stores is Globus, part of a group which includes ABM (Au Bon Marché), Herren Globus (menswear), Interio (home furnishings and furniture) and Office World – all of which are now owned by Migros. Manor and Jelmoli (including Innovation and Grand Passage) are department store chains with outlets in most Swiss cities and large towns. Manor is noted for their own-label, high quality, value-for-money clothes. Other department stores include the Loeb (Berne), EPA, Unip and Bon Genie. The Coop and Migros also have large DIY/Shopping centres.

Jumbo, a do-it-yourself (DIY) and hardware store chain, also merits a special mention. Besides selling hardware and household goods, Jumbo also stock motoring accessories, bicycles and skis at competitive prices (plus food in some stores). Obi, is another DIY and hardware store chain that offers a large selection of hardware and is often used by professionals. One of the largest discount houses for TV, video, hi-fi, photographic, computer and household goods is Eschenmoser. They publish a comprehensive catalogue and have sales in January and July at their stores in Basle, Berne and Zurich. Media Markt is a good source for inexpensive CDs and electronic equipment, while Inter Discount operate a large chain of stores selling hi-fi, video, photographic, radio, computer and other electronic equipment at competitive prices. Shop around for electronic and computer equipment, as prices for similar items can vary considerably; don't forget to compare the guarantee period, which can vary from six months to two years.

Many department stores (e.g. Globus, Jelmoli, Loeb and Manor) provide account cards, some of which double as credit cards where the account balance can be repaid over a period. Card holders may take advantage of special offers and discounts. Some account cards can be used in other franchised stores and businesses, e.g. Globus and the Jelmoli J-Card. Some stores won't give a foreigner an account card until he has a C permit. Department stores and many smaller shops provide a free gift wrapping service, particularly at Christmas time, and will deliver goods locally or send them by post (both within Switzerland and world-wide). Some stores have a 'Mister Minit' department, where on-the-spot shoe repairs, key cutting and engraving is done.

Migros deserve a special mention for the high quality and range of its products (mostly own brand) and services, plus a reputation for limiting price increases. Migros stores come in three sizes, denoted by the number of Ms displayed outside:

M	Food store only;
MM	Food and household goods, sometimes a restaurant;
MMM	Complete department store selling food, household goods, furniture, clothes, hi-fi, electrical goods; sports equipment and often has a restaurant.

Migros (plus some other stores) provide discounts on all purchases on the opening day of a new branch and on special anniversaries, plus many special offers. They also operate do-it-yourself stores, a travel agency, book and record stores (Ex Libris), petrol stations and banking services (M-Bank, now with ATMs in its supermarkets called M-Bancolinos) services (among other things). Migros doesn't accept credit cards apart from its own M-card (Migros bank), the EC-Direct (debit) card, and the Postcard. The same applies to a lesser extent the Coop (🖥 www.coop.ch), which operates a bank, electronics stores (Radio TV Steiner, Inter Discount) and other ventures.

NEWSPAPERS, MAGAZINES & BOOKS

You may not have been much of a newspaper (*Zeitung, journal*), magazine (*Magazin/Zeitschrift, revue/périodique*) or book (*Buch, livre*) reader at home, but not being able to obtain your favourite English-language reading can be an unexpected deprivation abroad. However, newsagents in Switzerland probably stock the widest selection of foreign newspapers in the world, although British and American newspapers and magazines are expensive. If you enjoy reading, it's advisable to stock up on magazines before your arrival and during holidays abroad. Take out subscriptions to your favourite magazines as, assuming you can find them, they will be much more expensive in Switzerland.

English and other European newspapers are sold at kiosks in most large towns. English daily newspapers are usually on sale at most railway stations the day after publication and at main railway stations and international airports on the day of publication. If you're hooked on English Sunday newspapers, they're

Beyond Chocolate

understanding Swiss culture

by Margaret Oertig-Davidson

Go beyond Swiss chocolate, beyond the initial fun and adventure of a new country and a new career to immerse yourself in the cultural attitudes of Switzerland's fascinating, multifaceted society.

These insights are based on extensive interviews with Swiss and international people who know well the ups and downs of life in Switzerland. These observations enable newcomers to better understand the perspectives of their Swiss neighbours, friends and international business colleagues.

Discover the different attitudes and potential misunderstandings about friendship, neighbourliness, being professional, giving and getting compliments and criticism, parenting, schooling, being polite, entertaining, negotiating, decision making, business etiquette, team work, leadership, making plans, and much much more.

English edition: ISBN 3-905252-06-6, German edition ISBN 3-905252-10-4, illustrated softcover editions, each CHF 38.00, Euro 26.00. See the introduction, excerpts, table of contents and reviews on **www.bergli.ch.**

Bergli Books, Rümelinsplatz 19, CH-4001 Basel.
Tel. +41 61 373 27 77, Fax +41 61 373 27 78, e-mail: info@bergli.ch

available at many main railway stations and airports from around 11am on Sundays. To save a wasted journey, telephone first, as they sometimes don't arrive – if they aren't at your local railway station, they're usually also unavailable at airports. **Note, however, that they're expensive.**

Major foreign European newspapers are available on the day of issue in Basle, Geneva and Zurich and perhaps a day later in other cities. Some English-language daily newspapers are widely available on the day of publication including *USA Today, International Herald Tribune* (printed in Zurich), *Wall Street Journal Europe* and the *European Financial Times* (printed in Frankfurt). Many English and foreign newspapers produce weekly editions including the British *International Express, Guardian Weekly,* and *Weekly Telegraph.* Many foreign newspapers can be purchased on subscription at a large saving over kiosk prices. When sent airmail from within Europe, e.g. from the UK, they usually arrive a few days after publication. English-language monthly magazines published in Switzerland include *Swiss News,* and *GT Magazine.* The *Swiss Review of World Affairs,* published by the *Neue Zürcher Zeitung,* has been replaced by an English-language interactive news section on their website (⌨ www.nzz.ch).

There are no national newspapers in Switzerland, but a wide variety of regional newspapers (over 200) and some 2,000 magazines plus professional and specialist journals. Most cantons have an official daily or weekly newspaper or booklet containing a wealth of local information. It includes announcements of

job vacancies, local and official events, meetings, church services, plus advertisements for houses and apartments (for rent and sale), small ads., restaurants and entertainment. You will get a number of free local newspapers delivered to your home.

There are many excellent English-language bookshops in Switzerland (such as those advertising in this book) including all the major cities, although the selection may be a bit limited when compared with a major bookshop in the UK or the US. However, most will order any English-language book in print at no extra cost. A small selection of English-language paperbacks is also usually available in Swiss bookshops and at news kiosks. You can also buy books via the Internet (e.g. 💻 www.amazon.co.uk).

FURNITURE

Furniture (*Möbel*, *meubles*) in Switzerland is generally quite expensive compared with many other European countries. There is, however, a huge choice and the quality is invariably good. Exclusive modern and traditional furniture is available everywhere, although not everyone can afford the exclusive prices. If you want reasonably priced, good quality, modern furniture, you need look no farther than Ikea, a Swedish company manufacturing furniture for home assembly (which helps keep down prices). Ikea has stores at Aubonne (west of Lausanne), Spreitenbach (southwest of Zurich), Lyssach (between Berne and Zurich), Dietlikon (east of Zurich), Centro Lugano-Sud (Grancia, Lugano) and Basle/Pratteln. An annual catalogue is delivered to local homes and is also available from stores.

Another excellent furniture and home furnishings chain is Interio, now part of the Migros group. Like Ikea they offer good quality modern furniture for home assembly (as well as pre-assembled furniture) at reasonable prices from their stores in Basle/Pratteln, Geneva/Vernier, Lausanne/Morges, Lucerne/Emmenbrücke, St. Gallen/Abtwil, Zurich/Dübendorf and Zurich/Spreitenbach, plus numerous other 'Wohngaleries' and 'Wohnboutiques' selling household accessories. Migros and Manor sell reasonably priced, good quality furniture. Migros are particularly good value, especially for quality leather suites. One of the largest furniture store chains in Switzerland is Möbel Pfister, which has its flagship store in Suhr (Aargau) in northern Switzerland and branches throughout the country. They offer a huge choice with a wide quality and price range. If you need carpets at reasonable prices, Möbel Pfister sell large-sized remnants (*Restposten*, *surplus*) at bargain prices – typically 50 per cent reduction. Most carpet shops and department stores also offer their remnants for sale cheaply.

A rare exception to fixed prices in Switzerland is when you're buying a large quantity of furniture. Don't be reticent about asking for a reduction as many stores will give you a 10 to 20 per cent discount. Considerable savings can also be made on furniture when shopping abroad (see page 362).

HOUSEHOLD GOODS

Large appliances such as cookers and refrigerators are usually provided in rented accommodation, although not always in French-speaking areas. Dishwashers (mechanical type, not the wife/husband) are sometimes installed and private washing machines are rare. **When looking for kitchen units or appliances such as a refrigerator, washing machine or dishwasher, note that the standard Swiss unit width isn't the same as in other countries.** The standard width of kitchen appliances in Switzerland is 5cm less than across the rest of Europe (to reduce foreign competition) and consequently domestic prices for dishwashers, washing machines and dryers are much higher than the European average. If you can tailor your kitchen to accommodate foreign appliances, you will save a lot of money by buying them abroad. However, check the latest Swiss safety regulations before shipping these items to Switzerland or buying them abroad, as they may need expensive modifications.

If you already own small household appliances, it's worthwhile bringing them to Switzerland as usually all that's required is a change of plug (but check first). If you're coming from a country with a 110/115V electricity supply, e.g. the US, then you will need a lot of expensive transformers (see page 103). Don't bring a TV to Switzerland without checking its compatibility first, as TVs from the UK, France and the US won't work (see page 138). Smaller appliances such as vacuum cleaners, grills, toasters and electric irons aren't expensive in Switzerland and are of excellent quality.

If you need kitchen measuring equipment and cannot cope with decimal measures, you will need to bring your own measuring scales, jugs, cups and thermometers. Foreign pillow sizes, e.g. British and American, aren't the same as in Switzerland and the Swiss use duvets and not blankets to keep warm in winter (besides central heating).

LAUNDRY & DRY CLEANING

All towns and shopping centres have dry cleaners (*Chemische Reinigung, nettoyage à sec*), most of which do minor clothes repairs, invisible mending, alterations and dyeing. **Note that express cleaning may mean a few days rather than hours, even at a dry cleaners where cleaning is done on the premises.** You usually pay in advance and it's quite expensive (better to buy washable clothes), particularly for leather and suede. Cleaning by the kilogramme with no pressing is possible in some places and much cheaper.

If you live near the French border it might be worthwhile to take your clothes to a French dry cleaner. Not only can they do the job much quicker (usually 24 hours) but they also charge considerably less.

There are self-service launderettes (*Wäscherei, blanchisserie*) in major towns and cities, but they're expensive at around SFr. 10 to wash and dry a 5kg load. They are, however, rare in smaller towns, as (communal) washing machines are provided in most rented accommodation (the Swiss don't usually wash their dirty linen in public).

SECOND-HAND BARGAINS

There isn't a very active second-hand (*gebraucht, occasion*) market in Switzerland (only foreigners buy used goods) except in antiques, motor cars, gold and gem stones, and asking prices are generally higher than in other countries. There is, however, a local second-hand furniture and junk store (*Brockenhaus, broccante*) in most towns, and many also have a Salvation Army (*Heilsarmee, armée du salut*) shop. These usually have restricted opening hours. You can find second-hand stores and flea markets on the Internet (🖵 www.fundgrube.ch). There are special weekly newspapers in some areas devoted to bargain hunters, for example *Fundgrueb* and *Inseraten Markt* in German-speaking areas, and *Aux Trouvailles* in French-speaking areas. Advertising is usually free, as advertisements are financed by newspaper sales, although you must buy a copy to insert an advertisement.

The classified advertisements in local newspapers and adverts on shopping centre, supermarket and company bulletin boards, may also prove fruitful. Many expatriate clubs (see **Appendix A**) and large companies publish monthly magazines or newsletters containing small ads., where everything from furniture to household apparatus and cars are advertised for sale. Sales are held in many towns and villages, e.g. for children's clothes and toys, usually in autumn and spring.

HOME SHOPPING

Home shopping isn't as common in Switzerland as it is in many other countries, although you will receive some unsolicited mail-order catalogues with your junk post. A few large chain stores also publish mail-order catalogues, for example Ackermann and Jelmoli. Beware of some mail-order companies (e.g. selling records and books) who offer attractive gifts to members as an inducement to recruit new members. Prices are often high, particularly when compared with the special offers available in many shops, and it's costly to resign your membership – whether you've received any benefits or not. **Make sure you know what you're signing.**

Many major stores abroad publish catalogues and will send goods anywhere in the world, for example Fortnum & Masons, Habitat and Harrods in the UK. Many provide account facilities or payment can be made by international credit cards. Although many foreign mail-order companies won't send goods abroad, there's nothing to stop you obtaining catalogues from friends or relatives and ordering through them. Buying goods mail-order from the US can result in a 25 to 50 per cent saving, even after paying postage and VAT. Most mail-order companies also have websites where you can order catalogues and goods.

Internet

Shopping via the Internet has taken off in a big way in recent years and is now the fastest-growing form of retailing. Many Swiss companies offer Internet shopping, but the real benefit comes when shopping abroad, when savings can be made on a wide range of products (you can buy virtually anything via the Internet). However, when comparing prices take into account shipping costs, insurance, duty and VAT. Nowadays, shopping on the Internet is usually very secure and even safer than shopping by phone or mail-order (in many cases the trader never even sees your credit card details). To find companies or products via the Internet, simply do a search using a search engine such as Google (🖳 www.google.com) or for Swiss websites 🖳 www.search.ch.

Online grocery shopping is provided by Migros (🖳 www.migros-shop.ch), Coop (🖳 www.coop.ch) and Le Shop (🖳 www.leshop.ch), probably the best Internet grocery shopping site, offering everything from fresh produce to alcohol, including imported products from around the world. They offer a monthly billing service, next day delivery via the post, and a flat SFr. 12 delivery fee anywhere in Switzerland. Other good Swiss Internet sites include www.directmedia.ch, which sell CDs, movies and videogames online, and www.dvdworld.com, where you can rent a selection of DVDs for less than a video store post-free – and you can keep them for a whole week!

If you purchase a small item by post from outside Switzerland, you may have to pay VAT (*MWSt*, *TVA*) of 7.6 per cent on delivery or at the post office on collection. Goods sent from EU countries (usually above a minimum value) should be free of local value added tax (see **Shopping Abroad** below). Gift parcels from abroad that don't exceed SFr. 100 in value are exempt from VAT, but must be clearly marked in customs declarations.

When you purchase a large item abroad and have it shipped to Switzerland by air freight, you should have it sent to your nearest airport. The receiving freight company will notify you when it has arrived. You must provide them with details of the contents and cost (an invoice copy) so that they can clear the goods through customs. They will deliver the goods to you with the bill for VAT and freight, payable on the spot, unless you make alternative arrangements.

The cost of air freight within Europe or even from North America is usually reasonable, however, the delivery and handling charges from a Swiss airport to your home can be as high as the air freight costs to Switzerland! If possible, it's a lot cheaper to collect goods yourself after they've been cleared through customs. **Ensure that goods sent by air freight are fully insured.** It's sometimes better to have goods sent by post (excluding local taxes), rather than importing them personally, when it's often a long and difficult process to obtain a refund.

SHOPPING ABROAD

Shopping abroad makes a pleasant change from all those boring Swiss shops full of diamond necklaces, gold watches and *haute couture* fashions. It can also save you a lot of money and makes a pleasant day out for the family. Don't forget your passports or identity cards, car papers, dog's vaccination papers and euros. Most shops in border towns gladly accept Swiss francs, but usually give a lower exchange rate than a bank.

Many foreigners and Swiss, particularly those living in border areas (e.g. Basle, Geneva and Lugano), take advantage of the generally lower prices outside Switzerland and do their weekly shopping abroad (the Swiss spend around SFr. 2 billion a year shopping abroad). Almost half the residents of Geneva (one-third of whom are foreigners) regularly do the bulk of their shopping in France and overall around 15 per cent of Swiss residents regularly shop abroad. Germany, France and Italy all have a lower cost of living than Switzerland (although salaries are also much lower). A combination of lower prices, a favourable exchange rate and low Swiss VAT, mean that savings of a third or more can be made on many items. Many foodstuffs (and wine) are up to 50 per cent cheaper in France, Germany and Italy (overall savings are around 30 per cent). This means that if you spend SFr. 200 a week on groceries and alcohol in Switzerland, you can save up to SFr. 3,000 or more a year!

Prices in Germany are lower for most goods and you will often save around 25 to 30 per cent after paying Swiss VAT and receiving the German VAT refund. The best buys in Germany include electrical, electronic and photographic equipment; household appliances; optical goods and services; furniture; sporting goods; car parts, servicing and accessories; alcohol; and meat products. Buying a car abroad, e.g. in Germany or Italy, can also yield large savings. **Note that in all countries except Germany there are minimum purchase levels, below which you're unable to reclaim local VAT.**

Shops in Germany normally close at 2pm on Saturdays, except for the first Saturday of the month when they're open until 5pm (plus the four Saturdays before Christmas). On weekdays, shopping hours are much the same as in Switzerland, except for Wednesday, when shops usually close at 1pm. In many German towns bordering Switzerland, most shops are open until 4pm on Saturdays especially to cater for the influx of shoppers from Switzerland. **Prices may be slightly higher in border towns than in larger inland German cities.**

Of course, not everything is cheaper abroad and it's often wise to compare prices and quality before buying. Bear in mind that if you buy goods that are faulty or need repair, you may have to return them to the place of purchase, which could be a hassle with customs paperwork. When buying goods outside Switzerland on which you intend to reclaim the foreign VAT, the procedure is as follows:

1. Obtain a receipt for your purchase and inform the shop assistant that you'd like a form to reclaim the tax. The shop will complete the tax reclaim form (*Ausfuhrschein/Zollschein, fiche d'exportation/feuille d'exportation*) and enter the tax rate and total amount to be refunded. Write your name and your Swiss address on the form. If you wish to claim your tax refund by post, check that the vendor will reimburse the tax by post.

2. Have the form stamped by the local customs border official in the country of purchase before entering Switzerland. The local customs official might want proof that you don't live in the country, e.g. a Swiss residence permit. **If you're flying back to Switzerland with your purchases, e.g. from the UK, you may need to carry them as hand baggage in order to have your tax reclaim form stamped.**

3. At the Swiss customs post, present your receipt to the official and tell him what you've purchased. He'll determine the import duty and Swiss VAT to be paid, if any. Swiss customs officials sometimes query your country of residence, so make sure you have your Swiss residence permit handy.

4. To reclaim your VAT, return the form in person to the vendor or send it by post (keep a copy of the receipt and tax form). This must usually be done within a limited period, e.g. six months for goods purchased in Germany.

   Some shops in border areas will deliver goods to your home in Switzerland within a certain radius, in which case you won't pay local VAT but may be charged for delivery. For expensive purchases, a shop may send someone to accompany you to the border and return your local tax on the spot, on receipt of the stamped tax reclaim form.

DUTY-FREE ALLOWANCES

The Swiss customs regulations allow duty-free purchases up to SFr. 300 with the following restrictions (amounts per person and per day):

- 1 l/kg of butter and cream;
- 5 l/kg of milk, cheese, yoghurt and other dairy products;
- 2.5 kg of eggs;
- 20 kgs of any vegetable or fruit;
- 2.5kg of potatoes (including crisps!);
- 20kg of flour or flour-based products (bread, cakes etc);
- 3.5kg of meat and meat products. This may include a maximum of 500g of fresh or frozen meat (oxen, sheep, lamb, horses, goats, kids and pigs).

People over 17 years can also import the following:

- 2 litres of wine or champagne under 15° proof **and** 1 litre of alcohol over 15° proof (if you import more than one litre, duty on the excess amount is likely to equal or exceed its cost);
- 200 cigarettes **or** 50 cigars **or** 250g of pipe tobacco (doubled for visitors domiciled outside Europe).

There are regulations prohibiting the importation of meats from certain countries and occasional restrictions on the import of some meats due to an outbreak of swine fever or foot and mouth disease. If in doubt, check with the Federal Veterinary Office, Schwarzenburgstr. 161, CH-3003 Berne (☎ 031 323 85 24, ✉ beratung@bvet. admin.ch). On no account may you exceed the limit on meat imports.

General Information

- The total value of duty-free goods permitted is SFr. 300. At the Swiss border you must declare what you've purchased and, if asked, produce receipts to verify the place of origin and the price paid. When you exceed the permitted tax-free limit, you're liable to pay VAT of 7.6 per cent on **ALL** your purchases, including the duty-free allowance.

- Customs duty on goods imported above the duty-free allowance is calculated by weight, depending on the category of goods. This is payable in addition to the 7.6 per cent VAT.

- Duty-free goods and petrol can also be purchased in the town of Samnaun (Graubünden). La Cure, a village on the Swiss-French border in the Jura hills above Nyon, also harbours a duty-free 'shop' (*Bar de la Dôle*).

- Never attempt to import illegal goods. Don't agree to bring a parcel into Switzerland or to deliver a parcel in another country, without knowing exactly what it contains. A popular trick is to ask someone to post a parcel in Switzerland (usually to a *poste restante* address) or to leave a parcel at a railway station or restaurant. **THE PARCEL USUALLY CONTAINS ILLEGAL DRUGS!**

Swiss customs officials are usually reasonable and flexible and unless you're a big-time smuggler, will treat you fairly. See general **Customs** notes on page 76.

Leaflets in English can be downloaded from the website of the Federal Customs Office (🖳 http://www.customs.admin.ch/e/private/rv/reisen_einkaufen.php).

EMERGENCY RATIONS

All residents of Switzerland are requested to keep an emergency food supply (*Notvorrat, provisions de secours*) in their nuclear shelter. The food supply includes 1 to 2kg per person of sugar, rice or pasta, oil or fat, protein rich food, carbohydrate rich food and food of your choice (if the bombs don't get you the food will!). To this must be added drinks (two litres a day), fuel, cleaning materials, assorted extras such as, medicines, rubbish sacks, spirit stove (for cooking), methylated spirits and iron tablets. Don't forget essentials such as baby food, nappies (diapers), diabetic treatments, drugs and vitamin tablets. Washing powder is also one of the essential requirements, although most shelters have no running water and no toilet facilities. You should take a radio (although reception may be impossible). Most Swiss also keep a good supply of wine in their shelters.

The necessary foods are listed in a pamphlet available from your community or from the Bundesamt für wirtschaftliche Landesversorgung, Belpstr. 53, CH-3003 Berne (☎ 031 322 21 11). Foods can be stored only for a limited period and must be replaced periodically (see pamphlet).

RECEIPTS

When shopping in Switzerland, always insist on a receipt (*Quittung/Kasse–bon*, *quittance*) and retain it until you've left the store or have reached home. This isn't just in case you need to return or exchange goods, which may be impossible without the receipt, but also to verify that you've paid if an automatic alarm sounds as you're leaving the shop or any other questions arise. When you buy a large object which cannot be wrapped, a sticker should be attached as visible evidence of purchase, in addition to your receipt. In supermarkets, the cashier usually sticks your receipt to goods with sticky tape.

It's advisable to keep receipts and records of all major purchases made while resident in Switzerland, particularly if your stay is only for a limited period. This may save you both time and money when you finally leave Switzerland and are required to declare your belongings in your new country of residence.

CONSUMER ASSOCIATIONS

The independent Swiss Consumer Association provides free product information and legal advice, and publishes books and monthly or bimonthly magazines in local languages, available on subscription and from news kiosks. The association has three main offices, serving the main language regions of Switzerland, plus local advisers in many areas.

* **French** – Fédération Romande des Consommateurs, rue de Genève 7, Case postale 2820, CH-1003 Lausanne (☎ 021 312 80 06 or ☎ 0900 57 51 05 for advice and information, SFr. 2.13 per minute).
* **German** – Stiftung für Konsumentenschutz, (☎ 0900 900 440, SFr. 2.10 per minute, 💻 www.konsumentenschutz.ch).
* **Italian** – L'Associazone Consumatrici della Svizzera Italiana, Via Lambertenghi 4, CH-6900 Lugano (☎ 091 922 97 55, 💻 www.acsi.ch).

Another publication worthy of special mention is *Ktip*, a German-language consumer magazine which has rapidly established itself as the best-selling subscription publication in Switzerland. It costs around SFr. 28 a year or SFr. 51 for two years (20 issues) from K-Tip, Wolfbachstr. 15, Postfach 431, CH-8032 Zurich (☎ 01 266 17 17, 💻 www.k-tip.ch).

18.

ODDS & ENDS

This chapter contains miscellaneous information. Most of the topics covered are of general interest to anyone living and working in Switzerland, although not all subjects are of vital importance. However, buried among the trivia are some fascinating snippets of information.

ALARMS

There are various alarms for the Swiss population in times of peace (*Alarmierung der Bevölkerung in Friedenszeiten, alarme de la population en temps de paix*), with which all residents of Switzerland should be familiar. Alarms are occasionally tested, when announcements are made in advance in the communities concerned. The following information is provided at the back of Swiss telephone directories, where it's listed in French, German and Italian. Some communities and cantons may have additional alarm signals.

General Alarm

The general alarm (*allgemeiner Alarm, alarme général*) is a continuous oscillating high frequency tone for one minute. Information is broadcast on radio DRS (frequency 103) and local radio in the Swiss national and other languages, including English. Instructions will be given by the authorities on what action to take. Inform your neighbours (or ask them what's going on).

Radioactivity Alarm

The radioactivity alarm (*Strahlenalarm, alarme radioactivité*) is an interrupted oscillating high frequency tone for two minutes. Signifies **IMMEDIATE DANGER**. Close all doors and windows and seek shelter **IMMEDIATELY** in the nearest nuclear shelter. Take emergency rations (see page 365) with you if they aren't already stored in your shelter, plus a transistor radio and listen for further instructions (if you can hear anything in your bunker).

Water Alarm

The water alarm (*Wasseralarm, alarme eau*) is an interrupted low frequency tone for six minutes. Warning of a danger of floods in the local area. Listen to local radio and TV for information. If you're in the danger area, evacuate **IMMEDIATELY** and seek out high ground. There may also be local regulations concerning water alarms.

All Clear

The all clear (*ende der gefahr, fin du danger*) is announced via radio, TV and loudspeaker vehicles.

The famous Swiss underground shelter plays an important role in Switzerland's civil defence plans and all new houses built in Switzerland must have one. The Swiss take all this 'bunker business' extremely seriously. No doubt they have a master plan to arise from their bolt-holes after the radiation has dispersed and conquer what's left of the world? (They cannot bear the thought of leaving all those lovely Swiss francs behind.)

BUSINESS HOURS

The usual business hours (*Geschäftsstunden, heures de bureau*) for offices (not shops or factories) vary, but are generally from 8 to noon and 1.30 or 2pm to 5 or 6pm, Mondays to Fridays. Many close for lunch, which may extend from 11.30 or noon to 2pm, and most businesses are closed on Saturdays. Switchboards may be unmanned (unwomanned?) at lunch time, during which telephones may be unanswered or be connected to an answering machine. Government offices are usually open from around 8 to 11.45am and from 2 to 4pm.

CHILDREN

There are various laws in Switzerland governing the behaviour of children in public places. Children under 16 years old, which is the legal age of sexual consent in Switzerland, aren't permitted in public places after 10pm. unless accompanied by an adult. Those under 16 aren't allowed in bars, night clubs or casinos. Switzerland is generally a very safe place for children, although they should be informed of the danger of 'talking to strangers'.

CITIZENSHIP

A child born to a foreigner in Switzerland has the right of Swiss citizenship (*Schweizer Nationalität/Schweizer Staatsbürger, nationalité suisse/citoyen suisse*) only when his parents are married and one is a Swiss citizen. From 1992, the foreign wife of a Swiss citizen has no longer been automatically entitled to Swiss citizenship. To qualify for Swiss citizenship, a foreigner married to a Swiss citizen must have been married three years and have been living in Switzerland for five years. A foreigner who isn't married to a Swiss citizen must be a resident of Switzerland for 12 years, including three of the last five years, in order to qualify for Swiss citizenship. The number of years spent in Switzerland between the ages of 10 to 20 count double.

Following an application to become a Swiss citizen, an 18-month investigation is carried out to determine whether you're suitable. If you survive the inquisition you must then pass a general knowledge quiz on Switzerland – failure to answer correctly means no lovely red Swiss passport (as a consolation, a tasty chocolate Swiss passport is available from sweet shops). Foreigners who take Swiss citizenship no longer automatically lose the nationality of their country of origin, as dual nationality is now accepted (at least by the Swiss).

In 1994, the Swiss voted against easing the naturalisation process for young second generation foreigners who have spent all or most of their lives in Switzerland.

CLIMATE

It's almost impossible to give a general description of the Swiss climate, as it varies considerably from region to region (like the Swiss people themselves). Probably no country in Europe has such diverse weather conditions in such a small area. The Alps, extending from east to west, form a major weather division between the north and south of Switzerland, and separate weather forecasts are usually given for each area. The climate north of the Alps is continental with hot summers and cold winters, although prolonged periods when the temperature is below freezing are rare during daytime (unless you live on top of a mountain). At high altitudes, it's frequently warm during the day at any time of the year, although cold at night, even in summer. In winter it usually snows everywhere at some time (even in the lowlands), but it generally thaws by spring, except above 2,000 metres. Many areas often experience heavy fog and mist, particularly in autumn, caused by temperature inversions. In winter, storms are apt to cause avalanches, mudslides, rockfalls and floods in some areas.

In Ticino, south of the Alps, a mild Mediterranean climate prevails and even in winter it's significantly warmer here than elsewhere in Switzerland. Spring and autumn are usually mild and fine in most areas, although it can be dull and wet in some regions. Spring in Ticino is particularly warm and pleasant. Generally Switzerland has more rainfall than most other regions of Europe (although Valais is particularly dry) and the country is noted for its low humidity and lack of wind. Most areas suffer occasionally from the *foehn*, a warm oppressive south wind often blamed for headaches, fatigue, vertigo, bad tempers and other minor irritating complaints. You can even buy a gadget to ease its unpleasant effects. High ozone levels caused by summer smog are becoming more common and creating health hazards in some areas.

The daily weather forecast in winter includes the snow limit (*Schneegrenze, limite d'enneigement*), which is the lowest level (in metres) where snow will fall and where freezing point will occur (*Nullgradgrenze, limite du degré zéro*). Generally Swiss weather forecasts are surprisingly accurate. Average afternoon temperatures in Centigrade and Fahrenheit (in brackets) are:

Location	Spring	Summer	Autumn	Winter
Geneva	14 (58)	25 (77)	14 (58)	4 (40)
Lugano	17 (63)	28 (83)	17 (63)	6 (43)
Zurich	12 (53)	22 (71)	11 (52)	0 (32)

The Swiss weather forecast is available by telephone in the local language (162), via the Swiss television teletext service and in all daily newspapers. The daily pollen count (*Pollenbericht, pollen bulletin*) is reported from March to July on the Swiss television teletext service and in daily newspapers. Daily weather reports for around 25 Swiss resorts are displayed at major railway stations. The weather in major European cities is also given on Swiss television teletext. Avalanche bulletins are given on telephone service number 187.

CRIME

Compared with other western countries, Switzerland has a low crime rate, although in common with other countries there has been a sharp increase in the last decade, particularly crimes against property (much of which is due to refugees and other migrants). However, despite the fact that the number of murders has doubled since the 1960s (to a grand total of around 18 a year in 2001), violent crime remains relatively rare. Negligence is the cause of many thefts, with mopeds and bicycles being the main target (over 100,000 are stolen each year!). The Swiss are too trusting for their own good and often leave doors, windows and even safes open for their friendly neighbourhood thief (if you're a crook, you shouldn't be reading this).

Switzerland has a growing drug problem and the open drug scene in some cities (e.g. Zurich) is conspicuous in a country where cleanliness and order abound. Most of the recent increase in crime and violence (and burglaries) is associated with drug dealers (many of whom are foreigners) and addicts. Zurich and other Swiss cities have been losing the drug war for many years. Many observers put the blame on Switzerland's tolerant attitude towards drug addicts, which some claim acerbates the problem and serves to attract foreign addicts. The use of hard drugs is one of the few problems that Switzerland has on the same scale as other European countries. Over 40 per cent of crimes in Switzerland are committed by foreigners and Swiss prisons contain a high proportion of foreigners, although 25 per cent are non-residents who come to Switzerland simply to commit crimes. Prison overcrowding is widespread and a growing problem.

Like most countries, Switzerland has professional thieves who do a good business breaking into private houses and apartments. Don't leave cash, cheques, credit cards, passports, jewellery and other valuables lying around or even hidden in your home (the crooks know **all** the hiding places). Good door locks will help but won't keep the professionals out (they will drill them out). It's better to keep your valuables in a safety deposit box (costing from SFr. 50 to 100 a year) and ensure you have adequate house contents insurance (see page 270). Most apartment blocks in Switzerland are fitted with a security system, allowing residents to speak to callers before giving them access to the building. In addition, most apartment entrance doors have a spy-hole, so that occupants can check a visitor's identity before opening the door.

There are pickpockets in major cities and tourist centres, so don't walk around with your wallet or purse on display and never keep your wallet in your back trouser pocket. Some theft insurance doesn't cover pickpocket thefts, only robbery with violence (so tell your insurance company that you were robbed at gun point!). Mugging and crimes of violence are fortunately still rare in Switzerland and you can safely walk almost anywhere, day or night (most Swiss think a mugger is someone who makes large cups). Remember to lock your car and put any valuables in the boot or out of sight, particularly when parking overnight in a public place, and look after your expensive skis and other belongings in ski resorts.

The Swiss compensate for the lack of serious crime by making many trivial offences unlawful, such as hanging bedding from your windows at the wrong time or washing your car on a Sunday. All fines (sometimes referred to as administrative measures – the Swiss have many euphemisms for unpleasant things like taxes and fines) over SFr. 50 are entered in a canton register. Single fines over SFr. 200 are entered in a central criminal register (*Strafregister, casier judiciaire*) and too many entries in the **BIG BLACK BOOK** may prejudice your residence permit. If you're fined for an offence, you may have the option of doing community service at weekends, rather than pay a fine.

What you may be unaware of as a foreigner (and hopefully will remain so) is the infamous Swiss imprisonment on remand (*Untersuchungshaft, prévention*), whereby anyone can be imprisoned on suspicion of committing a crime and kept there for months without charge or trial. (I hope this doesn't apply to foreigners who advertise this stain on Switzerland's civil rights' record!) Despite the exemplary behaviour of the Swiss and most foreign residents in Switzerland, it was discovered in 1990 that the federal police had compiled over 900,000 secret files on its Swiss and foreign residents, who were apparently perceived as a threat to national security (Swiss xenophobia knows no bounds).

ECONOMY & TRADE

Despite its limited size and severe shortage of raw materials, Switzerland is one of the most productive, competitive and prosperous countries in the world. Swiss products are renowned for their quality, reliability and after sales service, and a strong emphasis is given to the refinement and finishing of products, and high quality specialisation. Switzerland's success is due to a combination of technical know-how; enterprising spirit; hard work (particularly by the foreign labour force); virtually no strikes; high investment in plant and equipment; and an overriding pro-business mentality. Like Japan, it's largely dependent on imports, particularly raw materials, semi-finished and finished products, energy sources and food. The majority of Swiss companies are leaders in their fields.

Switzerland's most important industry is precision mechanical and electrical engineering, which produces highly specialised equipment and tools (comprising some 45 per cent of total exports), particularly machine tools, and textile and printing machinery. This is closely followed by the chemical and pharmaceutical industries, tourism, the textile and clothing industries, and watch making. The Swiss food industry is also prosperous and Swiss chocolate (much of which is now manufactured abroad – is it still Swiss?) and cheese, among other foods, are exported all over the world. (Nestlé is the largest food company in the world.) Despite the fact that only a quarter of Switzerland's surface area is productive, Swiss farmers produce around 70 per cent of the country's food.

It's the service sector, however, which contributes most towards balancing the budget, in particular the major Swiss banks and insurance companies. The tourist industry is also important and is one of the country's largest employers, providing work directly or indirectly for some 300,000 people (8 per cent of the workforce). Tourism is Switzerland's third-largest export source (after the machine and chemical industries) with foreign tourists spending around SFr. 12 billion in 2002 (some 4 per cent of GDP). The Swiss workforce consists of some four million people or around 55 per cent of the population (55 per cent men and 45 per cent women), some 25 per cent of whom are foreigners. Around 62.8 per cent are employed in the services sector; 23.7 per cent in industry, trades and construction; and 13.5 per cent in agriculture and forestry.

Switzerland's rejection of the EEA (and hence the European Union) could prove an obstacle to future growth and prosperity in the long term, as few western countries are so dependent on the outside world for their economic survival. It cannot afford any kind of isolation, either with regard to energy or raw materials, or in relation to capital and labour markets. For this reason, Switzerland's foreign exchange system has always been based on a free market, opposition to all forms of protectionism, and a policy of low customs duties with almost no restrictions on imports.

Agricultural products are virtually the only exception. Most food imports are subject to high duties in order to protect the livelihood of Swiss farmers and ensure sufficient food production in times of need (due to their high production costs, Swiss farmers cannot compete with imports). Swiss farmers receive almost 80 per cent of their income from federal subsidies (the highest level in the world), which the government wants to cut by up to 30 per cent. Despite the duties on imported food, Switzerland imports more agricultural products per capita than any other European country. Other important benefits of the Swiss farming policy are safeguarding the traditional Swiss way of life, particularly in mountainous regions, and the protection of the environment. Agriculture is also considered a vital prerequisite for the tourist industry. Nevertheless, every resident of Switzerland pays over SFr. 1,000 a year to subsidise Swiss farmers.

The Swiss economy remains strong and competitive, despite the strength of the Swiss franc (which has wiped millions of francs off the profits of Switzerland's multinationals in the last decade), high labour costs and ever increasing competition. However, Swiss companies are feeling the pinch and are increasingly being forced to move production and other facilities abroad, reduce prices and shave their profit margins. The Swiss are constantly striving to improve their products to meet world demand and are quick to incorporate the most advanced technical innovations (who but a Swiss would invent a prayer mat for Muslims with a built-in compass, calibrated to point towards Mecca from anywhere in the world!).

Switzerland spends more per capita on research and development than any other country, is second only to the US in the number of computers per head, and is sixth in the world in the value of advanced technology exports. It's significant that (per capita) the Swiss have produced more Nobel prize winners (around 25) and registered more patents than any other country. A 'Made in Switzerland' label remains a significant attraction to many buyers, who gladly pay a premium for Swiss quality and durability. However, ominous signs for the future of Swiss industry include the sharp drop in foreign investment and the increasing number of Swiss companies transferring investment and manufacturing abroad. In recent years, Swiss companies have redoubled their efforts to build ties with companies located within the European Union.

GEOGRAPHY

Switzerland is situated in the central Alpine region of Europe and has borders with five countries: Italy (734km/456mi) to the south, Austria (164km/102mi) and the Principality of Liechtenstein (41km/25mi) to the east, Germany (334km/207mi) to the north and France (573km/356mi) to the west. Due to its 'isolationist' policies, Switzerland has been described as the only island in the world surrounded entirely by land! It's a small country; the maximum distance from east to west is just 348km/216mi and from north to south only 220km/137mi. The total area is 41,290km^2 (around 15,940mi^2). The Alps, mainly in the central part of the country, reach altitudes of more than 4,000m (13,123ft). Geographically Switzerland can be divided into three main regions:

- The alpine massif, which includes the whole of southern Switzerland, covering some 60 per cent of the country and containing around 20 per cent of the population. Approximately one-fifth of the total alpine range lies within Switzerland.

- The central plateau (Mittelland) north of the alpine massif consists of some 30 per cent of the land area and is home to around two-thirds of the population.

- The Jura mountains in the northwest make up the remaining 10 per cent of Switzerland, with some 15 per cent of the population.

The highest point in Switzerland is the Dufour Peak of the Monte Rosa (4,634m/15,203ft) and the lowest Lake Maggiore (195m/639ft above sea level). The Swiss Alps contain the crossroads formed by the St. Gotthard, Grimsel, Furka and Oberalp passes and are the source of both the Rhine and Rhône rivers. Due to its central position, Switzerland has long been an important link in communications and transport between northern and southern Europe, a fact that has been decisive in determining the course of Swiss history.

GOVERNMENT

Switzerland is the most politically stable country in the world. The Swiss constitution (reviewed and updated in 2001) provides both the confederation and cantons with the system of a democratic republic, in the form of either direct or representative democracy. Switzerland's foreign policy is neutral. A number of important recent referendums (e.g. EEA membership and Swiss UN troops, both of which were rejected) have shown only too clearly that the Swiss government is increasingly out of step (at least in terms of foreign policy) with its people. However, Switzerland's foreign policy isn't entirely isolationist and in 1992 it became a member of the IMF and the World Bank (it's also a member of the Council of Europe, GATT and the OECD). In 2002, the Swiss voted to become a member of the United Nations.

In Switzerland, power is 'devolved' **upwards** from some 3,000 communities (*Gemeinde, commune*), each of which has a local council or municipal authority. A Swiss citizen is first and foremost a citizen of the community (written in his passport) where he was born, which remains ultimately responsible for his welfare throughout his life. In a community, the executive is the administrative council headed by the mayor, with legislative matters being handled by the municipal council. The community levies local taxes and has self-rule in all matters that aren't the responsibility of either the federal government or the canton. These include the administration of public property such as forests; water, gas and electricity supply; bridges, roads and administrative buildings; schools (primary education); and the civil defence, fire, health and local police departments. Several communities make up a borough or county (*Bezirk, district*).

Next in line are the 26 cantons (*Kanton/Stande, canton*), six of which rank as half-cantons (half a canton is better than none). Each canton has its own written constitution and is in effect a sovereign state subject to federal law. The canton government consists of an executive state council of five to nine members (each head of a department) and a legislative grand council of varying size, depending on the canton. Each canton is responsible for its own civil service; citizenship; church matters; education; finances and income tax; fire service; labour department; land usage; law and order; libraries; public health; public transport; roads; stock exchange supervision; and water and electricity supply.

The federal government is directly responsible for the armed forces; civil, criminal and industrial law; currency; customs and federal taxes; fishing, forestry and hunting; foreign policy; hydroelectric power; monetary controls; pensions; post and communications services; and railways. Legislative power is exercised by the federal assembly (*Bundesversammlung, Assemblée Fédérale*), consisting of two chambers of equal status:

- **The Council of States** (*Ständerat, Conseil des Etats*) comprises 46 representatives of the cantons. The 20 'full' cantons have two representatives each and the six half-cantons one each.

- **The National Council** (*Nationalrat, Conseil National*), is elected for a four-year term and consists of 200 direct representatives of the people. The number of members allocated to each canton depends on their size and population. This results in five cantons with one member only and therefore no proportional representation.

Both chambers hold four regular sessions a year, each of three weeks duration, and bills must be debated and passed by both chambers. Members of both chambers aren't professional politicians and hold other jobs, although most are self-employed or high-ranking corporate executives with the time and money to be part-time politicians. Politicians are paid around SFr. 70,000 a year and a proposal has been put forward to double their salary, meaning fewer members would need to follow other careers. As you'd expect in Switzerland, few federal politicians are women (possibly because they've had the right to vote only since 1971), although this is changing. The men of half canton Appenzell Innerrhoden steadfastly refused to give women the right to vote in community and canton elections until being overruled by the federal government in 1990.

The federal assembly elects the seven federal councillors (comprising the federal executive), who serve for four years and head the departments of foreign affairs; the interior; justice and police; defence and sport; finance; economics and environment, transport and energy (including communications). Re-election of federal councillors is permitted. Each year the assembly elects one of the councillors as president of the confederation (who remains anonymous to everyone but his/her spouse). The highest judicial authority is the Federal Supreme Court, which sits in Lausanne and consists of 30 members elected by the federal assembly.

The Swiss system of democracy, although not perfect, is among the best. Almost everyone is represented through proportional representation, with the notable exception of the 1.4 million foreigners who comprise around 20 per cent of the population. Local communities and cantons have real powers that cannot be usurped or vetoed by the federal government and all important decisions must be decided by the people through referendums (see page 384). The system functions well because politicians of all parties work together for the greater benefit of the majority, rather than indulging in petty squabbling and party politics. However, Swiss politics are also terminally boring, although the EEA/EU issue has injected a modicum of interest and the Swiss are beginning to debate issues with some passion. You can find out more about Swiss politics on the Internet (💻 www.socio.ch/poli/).

LEGAL ADVICE

Many towns and all major cities offer free or inexpensive legal advice for foreigners in English and other languages. Advice encompasses both criminal and civil law, e.g. the interpretation of house rental or purchase contracts. Ask your community or local information office for the address of your nearest legal office (*Notariat*). The Information Centre for Women (INFRA) is a nation-wide organisation run by women for women. It provides women with information and help on almost any subject, including contraception, births, divorce and employment. INFRA usually has English-speaking assistants and if necessary will provide the names of specialists and groups who can provide further help. With regard to divorce, Swiss private international law applies only when either spouse is a Swiss citizen or has been residing in Switzerland for more than two years.

If you have reason to complain about faulty goods or bad services and your initial attempts at redress fall on deaf ears, try writing a letter in English to the manager or managing director. This often has surprisingly positive results (see also **Consumer Associations** on page 366). Even when dealing with government bureaucrats or officials, you can be successful if you protest loudly and long enough. The Swiss usually submit meekly to all rules and regulations, and therefore bureaucrats are often dumbfounded when faced with an assertive foreigner. Legal advice and services may be provided by your embassy or consulate in Switzerland, including, for example, an official witness of signatures (Commissioner for Oaths).

MILITARY SERVICE

If you work in Switzerland, you may notice that your Swiss male colleagues have a habit of disappearing for a few weeks every few years. They aren't entitled to more holidays than foreigners, but are simply doing their military service (*Militärdienst, service militaire*). Switzerland has a 'citizen' army of part-time soldiers and can muster up to 220,000 men at arms in 48 hours to defend the homeland (only brigade commanders and above and instructors are full-time professionals, a total of around 3,000). However, don't be concerned as foreign residents aren't liable for military service. If you become a Swiss citizen, military service will depend on your age and whether you've already served in a foreign army (if you have, you won't be trusted and will be exempt). You will probably be unaware of it as a foreigner, but success and promotion in the army often opens the door to position and power in Swiss industry, government and finance. The Swiss army was cut by around a third in the last few years, from 600,000 to 400,000 and then again to 220,000.

All Swiss males must serve at least 260 days from the age of 20, when they undergo a basic 21-week training course, after which they become 'active' troops. Most ranks (soldiers and non-commissioned officers) must complete a number (around six) of 19-days-refresher courses, usually every year, and after this stay in the 'reserve' until age 30 when military service ends (the exception being senior officers, who serve until they're 50). Senior NCOs and officers undergo additional periods of training. The total length of military training is around one year and includes annual target practice when not on active duty.

Military service isn't compulsory for women, although they can volunteer to serve in the women's military service.

To speed up mobilisation in the event of a war, Swiss soldiers keep their uniforms, gas masks, arms and ammunition at home – a sure-fire recipe for civil war in less disciplined countries. An unusual feature of the Swiss armed forces is that in peace time they have no general, one being appointed only in the event of a threat of war. Anyone who's unfit for military service must serve in the auxiliary services, e.g. the civil defence or ambulance service. In 1991, Switzerland finally recognised the status of conscientious objector, prior to which anyone who refused to serve in the army was imprisoned. An alternative civil service (390 days) has now been established for those who object to military service on religious or moral grounds. Swiss citizens living abroad aren't liable for military service, but are required to pay a military exemption tax (*Militärpflichtersatz, taxe d'exemption du service militaire*) of a percentage of their salary, even if they never intend to return to Switzerland. The tax also applies to anyone excused service on medical, moral or religious grounds. Swiss employers usually pay employees their full salary while on military service, except in extreme circumstances when they're unable to do so.

Although the majority of Swiss proclaim that they loathe military service, whenever the question of abolishing conscription or the army is raised in a referendum, they vote to retain it. However, in 1989, 35.6 per cent voted to abolish the army, which shocked the complacent military and political establishment to the core, although in a second referendum in December 2001, only 23.2 per cent voted to abolish the army. However, fears in military circles that a future referendum could prove terminal have led to a reduction in the length of military service and the number of personnel. In 1994, the Swiss voted against allowing their troops to volunteer for UN peacekeeping missions. The army has been reformed twice over the last ten years, with one of the goals being the reduction of costs. Switzerland's defence budget for 2003 was SFr. 4.6 billion (around 1.6 per cent of its GDP) – a lot of money for a country without an enemy in the world and which hasn't fought a foreign campaign since 1515! There are, however, plans to slash the military budget in the coming years by reducing manpower, putting equipment and vehicles into storage, and closing camps.

PETS

If you intend to bring a pet (*Haustier, animal domestique*) with you to Switzerland, check the latest regulations in advance. Make sure that you have the correct papers, not only for Switzerland but for all countries which you must pass through to reach Switzerland. If you need to return prematurely, even after a few hours or days, to a country with strict quarantine regulations, your pet will be put into quarantine. On 28th March 2000, the UK introduced a pilot 'Pet Travel Scheme (PETS)' which replaced quarantine for qualifying cats and dogs. Under the scheme, pets must be micro-chipped (they have a microchip inserted in their neck), vaccinated against rabies, undergo a blood test and be issued with a 'health certificate' ('passport'). **Note that the PETS certificate isn't issued until six months *after* the above have been carried out!** Pets must also be checked for ticks and tapeworm 24 to 48 hours before embarkation on a plane or ship.

There's generally no quarantine period for animals in Switzerland. For entry into Switzerland, all dogs and cats over five months old must have an international health certificate stating that they've been vaccinated against rabies (*Tollwut, rage*). You must have an official letter stating that your pet was in good health before the vaccination, which must have been given at least 30 days and not more than one year before entering the country. Certificates are accepted in English, French, German and Italian. Dogs and cats under five months of age may be imported from many countries (Europe excluding Turkey, Australia, New Zealand and the US) without a vaccination, but require a veterinary attestation of their age and good health. Dogs and cats from countries which don't require rabies vaccinations (Australia and New Zealand) can be imported without a vaccination certificate. People who are resident in Switzerland aren't allowed to import dogs whose ears or tails have been cut, although those coming to live in Switzerland can import such dogs when they enter the country.

In Switzerland, dogs must have a rabies vaccination every two years from the age of six months. A vaccination for distemper (*Staupe, morve/maladie carré*) is recommended every two years, but isn't mandatory. If you plan to take your dog abroad, it must have had its rabies vaccination at least six weeks before travelling. Cats aren't required to have regular rabies vaccinations, although if you let your cat roam free outside your home it's advisable to have it vaccinated annually. Areas usually become active rabies areas in three to four-year cycles. If your area is active, there are strict rules for pet owners, for example dogs must be kept on a lead. Don't let your children play with wild or strange animals, or approach a pet or wild animal that's acting strangely, as it could have rabies. Report the incident to the police as soon as possible. If your child is bitten by an animal that could have rabies, he'll require a series of anti-rabies injections. The authorities set anti-rabies vaccine in bait (chicken heads) for foxes twice annually; don't touch them or let your dog get at them.

A dog needs a licence when it's six months old, available from your local community office on production of its international health certificate. In some cantons owners may require private liability insurance (see page 271) before a dog licence is issued. A card is issued by the insurance company, which must be produced when applying for a licence. When you obtain your dog licence, you're given a small aluminium tag inscribed with the year, licence number and canton. It must be attached to your dog's collar and be worn at all times in public places. If a dog is found without a licence tag, it will usually be taken to a refuge. They will try to find the owner or someone to take care of it, otherwise it may be put down. Licences must be renewed annually by 31st May, when an announcement is made in local newspapers by your community. They cost between SFr. 60 and 150 a year depending on your community. If you have two or more dogs, the cost of licences can be astronomical in some areas. Owners of unlicensed dogs are fined. If you move home within Switzerland, you must re-register your dog in your new community.

If you plan to leave your pet at a kennel or cattery (*Tierheim, refuge pour animaux*), book well in advance, particularly for school holiday periods. Dogs left at kennels must be inoculated against kennel cough (*Zwingerhusten, toux cannine*). All vaccinations must be registered with your veterinary surgeon (*Tierarzt, vétérinaire*) and listed on your pet's international health certificate. Dogs must be kept on a lead (*an der Leine, (tenir) en laisse*) in all public places. There are special areas and parks where dogs are allowed to roam free. Owners of dogs that foul public footpaths may be fined, so take a shovel and plastic bag with you when walking your dog (no joke!). Plastic bags and containers are provided in some towns and some also provide special toilet areas. Brackets or hooks are provided outside many shops and shopping centres, where you can secure your dog while shopping. Dogs require half-price tickets on public transport and are allowed into most restaurants.

Birds (except canaries) need a special import license, obtainable from the Bundesamt für Veterinärwesen, and are be put into quarantine until it's established that there's no danger of parrot fever (psittacosis). Rabbits also need special permission and must undergo a quarantine period of around 15 days. Guinea-pigs, golden hamsters, rats, mice, aquarium fish and canaries may be imported without a health certificate. An import licence and a veterinary examination is required for some domestic animals, e.g. horses. Dangerous animals, for example poisonous snakes, man-eating tigers, teddy-bears, etc., require a special import licence. Note also the following:

- Some apartments have regulations forbidding the keeping of dogs, cats and/or other animals.

- Most major cities and towns have veterinary hospitals (*Tierspital, hôpital pour animaux*) and a veterinary surgeon is on 24-hour call for emergencies. Ask the telephone operator (111) for the number.

- A brochure regarding the keeping of dogs is published by some cantons.

- In some cantons you need special permission to be allowed to have a dog of a potentially dangerous breed (e.g. Bullterrier, American Staffordshire Terrier, Pitbull Terrier, Staffordshire Bullterrier, Rottweiler, Dobermann, Dogo Argentino, Filo Brasileiro and crosses of these breeds).

- The death of a dog or horse should be reported to your community and your vet. Your community or vet will arrange to collect and cremate the body of your pet for a small charge, as you aren't permitted to bury a dead pet in Switzerland. You can also have a pet cremated privately and keep the ashes.

- If you take your dog to some countries, e.g. Italy, it must wear a muzzle.

- If you want to take your pets from Switzerland to a country without rabies, e.g. Australia, Ireland, New Zealand or the UK, it may need to go into quarantine for a period. **Check in advance with the authorities of the country concerned.**

- Rats and mice aren't allowed into Switzerland and officially don't exist (except as pets). If you happen to catch or kill a rat or mouse that has eluded the border patrols, your community may pay you a reward (e.g. SFr. 1).

For the latest regulations regarding the importation or keeping of pets in Switzerland contact the Federal Veterinary Office (*Bundesamt für Vetrinärwesen, Office Vétérinaire Fédéral*), Schwarzenburgerstr. 161, CH-3097 Berne (☎ 031 323 85 24, 🖳 www.bvet.admin.ch).

POLICE

Switzerland has no uniformed federal police force (*Polizei, police*), as law and order is the responsibility of the cantons and police uniforms vary from canton to canton. Besides canton police, Switzerland also has city and town police, and a non-uniformed federal police force. All police are armed, efficient and courteous, particularly when giving you a speeding ticket. However, all isn't sweetness and light. In recent years, Amnesty International has accused the Swiss police of 'unjustifiable and liberal use of violence', particularly against foreigners and Swiss citizens of non-European descent. Law enforcement is generally strict, particularly for any number of trivial offences. There are a significant number of foreigners living and working illegally in Switzerland, and you can be stopped by special plain clothes police and asked for your passport or identity card at any time, particularly if you drive a car with foreign registration plates.

You will rarely be able to find a policeman on the streets in towns or cities unless he is directing traffic (another indication of the low crime rate) and if you need one you will usually need to phone or visit the local police station. The large number of foreigners in Switzerland take their cue from the Swiss and are generally law-abiding – which is just as well, as their meal-ticket (residence permit) can easily be cancelled.

POPULATION

The estimated population of Switzerland in 2002 was 7,320,900 including 1,486,000 (20.3 per cent) foreigners, living in an area of 41,290km² (some 15,950mi²). The population density of 176 inhabitants per km² is one of the highest in the western world. When the uninhabited areas are excluded, the average population density rises to around 250 people per km². This figure reaches 400 inhabitants per km² in the central plateau, which incorporates the main centres of population. In 2002, the canton of Basle (city) had 5,045 inhabitants per km², Geneva 1,405 and Zurich 711. The city of Geneva has over 11,000 inhabitants per km², making it one of the most densely populated cities in the western world.

Over 50 per cent of the Swiss population live in urban areas, although less than 25 per cent live in cities with 30,000 inhabitants or more. The largest Swiss cities (2001) are Zurich (population 340,900), Basle (164,900), Geneva (176,000), Berne (122,500) and Lausanne (115,600). In sharp contrast to the cities, the population density is only 26 inhabitants per km² in canton Graubunden and 53 in canton Valais. Geneva has the highest proportion of foreign residents at around 38 per cent.

REFERENDUMS

Direct democracy, as practised in Switzerland, results in numerous national referendums, meaning that the people have a direct say in all important (and many insignificant) decisions. Referendums are also held at the canton level, although their use varies from canton to canton. The voting age is 18 for federal elections and variable for canton elections. The following types of national referendums are held in Switzerland:

- **Obligatory Referendum** – A change or addition to the constitution proposed by the federal government.

- **Optional Referendum** – A change in the law demanded by a minimum of 50,000 voters nation-wide or by eight cantons.

- **Popular Initiative** – A new article or change in the constitution registered by a petition signed by 100,000 voters.

A change in the legislation requires a majority vote by the electorate, while a change in the constitution must be approved by a majority of the votes cast by the people **and** a majority of the Council of States (canton representatives). The decision of the voters is final at all levels (communal, canton and federal), although providing the requirements are met, an issue can be put before the voters repeatedly, perhaps couched in different terms. Many people believe that Switzerland has too many referendums and that it's too easy to call one. Voting isn't compulsory and the turnout is often low, e.g. between 30 and 50 per cent, unless a particularly important or controversial issue is at stake (political apathy is rife in Switzerland). Of the 70 per cent of the population eligible to vote, only some 40 per cent actually vote (around 30 per cent of the population). Votes are usually decided by something over half of the votes cast, i.e. 15 per cent of the population or 25 per cent of eligible voters.

A foreigner will usually be unaware that a referendum is taking place, unless the issue is of national interest and widely publicised. Recent referendums have involved joining the UN, abolishing the army and limiting the foreign population, all of which are unique, these questions having been put to the people of no other country. Foreigners hardly ever have voting rights in Switzerland, irrespective of how long they've been residents (particularly when the Swiss are voting on whether to throw them out!). In some cities (e.g. Zurich), foreigners have even had the effrontery to petition for voting rights at the community level (they've so far been unsuccessful). It took Swiss women some 700 years to secure the vote, so foreigners can look forward to success sometime around the year 2700.

RELIGION

Approximately 41.8 per cent of the Swiss population are Roman Catholics, some 33 per cent Protestants, 7 per cent other religions (e.g. old Catholic, Jewish, Islamic and Hindu) and 7 per cent have no religion. Besides local Protestant and Catholic church services conducted in local languages, there are English churches and English-language services in all major cities, e.g. Catholic, Anglican, Church of England and International Protestant. There are also bible study groups in many areas and Jewish, Islamic, Greek Orthodox and other religious centres in the major cities. In major cities, services are often held in languages other than the local Swiss language. In addition to the established mainstream religions, Switzerland is also home to some 600 religious movements, cults and pseudo-religious organisations.

The curriculum of Swiss state schools includes compulsory religious education, which may be segregated by denomination when the class entails more than simple bible study. Parents can, however, request that their children are excused from religious education classes. Although the Swiss constitution includes freedom of conscience and belief, certain radical sects are banned. Contact your community, tourist, or information office for information regarding local places of worship and service times.

SMOKING

Smoking isn't permitted in cinemas, theatres, on most public transport, in many public buildings (e.g. post offices), or in doctor's and dentist's waiting rooms. However, it's permitted in restaurants in Switzerland, but it's compulsory for them to have a non-smoking section, although some don't or the non-smoking section is poorly separated from smokers. Smoking on local trains is limited to smoking compartments (*Raucher, fumeur*), where the seats in older trains are usually upholstered in red (for danger?), while compartments with green seats are reserved for non-smokers (*Nichtraucher, non fumeur*). Despite the fact that many Swiss are extremely anti-smoking and health conscious, Switzerland ranks around third-highest (per head of population) in the world smoking league.

SOCIAL CUSTOMS

All countries have their own particular social customs and Switzerland is no exception. As a foreigner you will probably be excused if you accidentally insult your host, but you may not be invited again. The following are a few Swiss social customs:

- When introduced to someone, use the formal form of address (*Sie, vous*). Don't use the familiar form (*du, tu*) or call someone by their Christian name until invited to do so. Generally the older or more important person, e.g. your boss, will invite the other person to use the familiar form of address and first names (usually after around 50 years' acquaintance in Switzerland).

- After you've been introduced to a Swiss, address him or her as Mrs. (*Frau, Madame*) or Mr. (*Herr, Monsieur*) followed by his or her family name and shake hands **without** gloves (unless it's 20° below freezing). When saying goodbye, it's a formal custom to shake hands again.

- It's customary to say good day on entering a small shop and goodbye on leaving. Even the checkout cashier in a supermarket will often (usually apathetically) do this.

- If you're invited to dinner, take along a small present of flowers, a plant or chocolates. If you take flowers, there must be an odd number and you should unwrap them before presenting them to your hostess. Flowers can be tricky, as to some people, carnations mean bad luck, chrysanthemums are for cemeteries and roses signify love. Maybe you should stick to plastic, silk or dried flowers – or perhaps a nice bunch of weeds.

- Don't arrive late for an invitation and don't overstay your welcome (your Swiss host will probably fall asleep around 9pm or earlier, which is your cue to leave).

- The Swiss say good appetite (*en Guete, bon appétit*) before starting a meal. If you're offered a glass of wine, wait until your host has made a toast (*Prost/zum Wohl, santé*) before taking a drink. If you aren't offered a (another) drink, it's time to go home.

- It's customary to telephone in advance before dropping in on a Swiss family, unless they're relatives or close friends. Privacy is respected in Switzerland.

- Always introduce yourself before asking to speak to someone on the telephone and don't telephone at meal times (whenever they are?) or after 9pm.

- If you're planning a party, it's polite to notify your neighbours (so they don't call the police **too** early).

- If you do a Swiss a favour, he'll usually feel obliged to repay you with a gift. The habit of doing favours for nothing is generally un-Swiss and a Swiss may expect you to reciprocate if he does you a favour.

- Although the Swiss are usually formal in their relationships, their dress habits, even in the office, are often extremely casual. There are generally no office dress rules and many employees wear jeans or shorts (in summer) with sandals or clogs. You aren't usually expected to dress up for dinner.

TIME DIFFERENCE

Like most of the continent of Europe, Switzerland is on Central European Time (CET), which is Greenwich Mean Time (GMT) plus one hour. The Swiss change to summer time in spring (usually the end of March) when they put their clocks forward one hour; in autumn (usually the last weekend in October) clocks are put back one hour for winter time (spring forward, fall back). Time changes are announced in local newspapers and on radio and TV. The international time difference in winter between Switzerland and some major cities is shown below:

SWITZERLAND	LONDON	JO'BURG	SYDNEY	AUCKLAND	NEW YORK
1200	1100	1300	2200	2400	0600

The time can be obtained by calling the 'speaking clock' on ☎ 161 or via teletext.

TIPPING

In Swiss hotels and restaurants, a service charge of 15 per cent is included in all bills and tipping (*Trinkgeld*, *pourboire*) has officially been abolished. In most major cities and towns, including Basle, Berne, Geneva and Zurich, a 15 per cent service charge is included in taxi hire costs. A service charge is always included in the price of hairdressing. No tipping is generally the rule, although there are a few exceptions, notably railway and hotel porters, wash and cloakroom attendants, and garage petrol pump attendants, e.g. when they clean your windscreen or check your oil. People do, of course, reward good service and if you intend to become a regular customer it often pays to sweeten the staff. Large tips are, however, considered ostentatious and in bad taste.

TOILETS

Last, but not least, when you need to go to the little girls' or boys' room, you will find Switzerland has the cleanest and most modern public toilets in the world. Some even have revolving, self-disinfecting seats, automatic bidets, automatic soap dispensers, taps and hand dryers, and even on occasion **fresh real cotton towels** (free of charge). Public toilets are found everywhere and are generally free, although those located at some railway stations and motorway stops may cost SFr. 0.20 or 0.50. Toilet humour is frowned upon , so don't write on the walls!

19.

THE SWISS

Who are the Swiss? What are they like? Let us take a candid and totally prejudiced look at the Swiss people, tongue firmly in cheek, and hope they forgive my flippancy or that they don't read this bit (which is why it's hidden away at the back of the book).

The typical Swiss is scrupulously honest, narrow-minded, industrious, pessimistic, boring, hygienic, taciturn, healthy, insular, tidy, frugal, sober, selfish, spotless, educated, insecure, introverted, hard working, perfect, religious, rigid, arrogant, affluent, conservative, isolated, private, strait-laced, neutral, authoritarian, formal, responsible, self-critical, unfriendly, stoical, materialistic, impatient, ambitious, intolerant, unromantic, reliable, conscientious, obstinate, efficient, square, enterprising, humourless, unloved (too rich), obedient, liberal, thrifty, stolid, orderly, staid, placid, insensitive, patriotic, xenophobic, courteous, meticulous, inventive, prejudiced, conventional, intelligent, virtuous, smug, loyal, punctual, egotistical, serious, bourgeois, cautious, dependable, polite, reserved or shy, law-abiding and a good skier.

You may have noticed that the above list contains 'a few' contradictions, which is hardly surprising as there's no such thing as a typical Swiss. Apart from the many differences in character between the French, German, Italian and Romansch-speakers of Switzerland, the population encompasses a potpourri of foreigners from all corners of the globe. Inevitably when you're certain you have the Swiss neatly labelled and pigeonholed, along comes yet another friendly, humorous and fun-loving Swiss who ruins all your preconceptions. Nevertheless I refuse to allow a few misfits to spoil my argument . . .

With 'all' the above characteristics, it will come as no surprise to discover that the Swiss aren't always the best companions with whom to share a deserted island. On the other hand, the characteristics that often make the Swiss so solemn and serious are the foundation of Switzerland's political and financial stability. A revolution or two might make life more exciting, but would do little for the economy or the strength of the Swiss franc. However, there are a few contradictions to the virtuous Swiss image, for example they're often reluctant to admit they're wrong about anything (their way of admitting a mistake is to say that **you** weren't wrong). They rarely compliment anyone on anything, but are generally quick to complain, particularly about trivia.

The Swiss are rather uncommunicative and tend to meet everything foreign with reserve, the general consequence of which is an innate distrust of foreigners (unless you're a tourist). It's difficult to become close friends with the Swiss (even for other Swiss). They rarely start a conversation with strangers, not just with foreigners but even with other Swiss. In fact the Swiss have taken the art of non-conversation to new heights. Rumour has it that the French and Italian-speaking Swiss are more open, less stressed and more friendly than their German-speaking countrymen. Most foreigners, however, notice little difference. In fact, social contact of any kind between the Swiss and many foreigners is rare, and the vast majority of foreigners in Switzerland count few Swiss among their close friends. This is particularly true in cantons such as Geneva, where a third of the population are foreigners, another third Swiss from other parts of Switzerland and only a third are born locally. Surprisingly, some foreigners **actually marry Swiss citizens**, although they usually meet abroad.

The Swiss love their guest worker (*Gastarbeiter, traivailleur étranger*) as only those who **know** they're superior can (we all need someone to look down upon). It's so convenient to have someone to blame for your troubles (and to do all the dirty manual jobs), whether it's unemployment, crime, pollution, housing shortages or social problems – the guest worker makes a useful scapegoat. Even Swiss with foreign names find themselves the victims of xenophobia. (Foreigners in Switzerland will be pleased to hear that the Swiss government is concerned about their nationals living in other European countries becoming second-class citizens after their rejection of membership of the EEA.)

You may be unaware that you have Swiss neighbours, except when they complain. They won't welcome you when you move into a new house or apartment and if you can speak the local language, it's up to you to invite them round for coffee and introduce yourself. Don't expect your neighbours to drop round for a cup of sugar; the Swiss are much too reserved to do such a thing and anyway, they never run out of anything. Only close friends or relatives call on each other without making appointments. In business the Swiss are even more formal. After many years, colleagues may still address each other as Herr Zürcher or Madame Guisan, using the formal *Sie* or *vous* form of address. Young Swiss are, however, less formal than their parents. The Swiss aren't so strict with foreigners and if you speak to them in English, you may find yourself on first name terms after a relatively short period. You can get away with a lot by being an eccentric foreigner (at least I hope so), as we're all a little strange to the Swiss.

To many foreigners, the Swiss don't appear to be the merriest of people. This is often difficult to understand considering the beautiful country they inhabit and the high standard of living and quality of life they enjoy. Switzerland has been unkindly referred to by some foreigners as a robotic paradise (or 'land of the living dead'), where many people lack spontaneity and soul, are devoid of a sense of fun and zest for life, and are afraid to open their hearts for fear of looking foolish. This may in part be due to the fact that only some 15 per cent of Swiss consume alcohol daily – it's enough to make anyone dull!

There's no truth in the rumour that laughter is forbidden (*Lachen ist Verboten, défense de rire*) although you may sometimes wonder if there's a tax on humour. The Swiss don't even laugh when you tell them they have no sense of humour! It may come as a big surprise that the Swiss have their **very own** book of jokes in English called, *Tell me a Swiss Joke* – **and** the pages aren't blank. Of course all the jokes could be borrowed (joke!)? Maybe their lack of humour is all the fault of a local wind called the *Foehn*, which gives people headaches and makes them grumpy. Of course not all Swiss lack a sense of humour, although the minority that appreciate a joke are usually foreigners masquerading as Swiss (or Swiss who have worked abroad). Life is taken seriously in Switzerland and if the foreigners followed their example, perhaps they too would be rich. Many Swiss, particularly among the ultra-conservative German-speakers, believe it's sinful to be lazy, to retire early or to enjoy yourself.

The Swiss are **very, very** careful with their money. There's over SFr. 2,500 billion deposited in Swiss banks (although not all Swiss owned) and the Swiss are second only to the Japanese in savings per capita. Maybe they've worked out a way of taking it with them or have installed Bancomats in heaven (all Swiss go to heaven). Alternatively, Hoffman La Roche may have discovered the secret of eternal life. It's no coincidence that the Swiss are pioneers in cellular therapy, rejuvenation and revitalisation. Their meanness is the one characteristic that they deny most vehemently, but then nobody likes to be thought of as a penny-pincher. Be wary if a Swiss invites you to dinner as he may split the bill with you (or leave you to pick up the tab). To be fair (who's trying to be fair!), although the Swiss don't believe in wasting money, it's rumoured that they're gracious and generous hosts in their own homes – if only you could get an invitation.

The Swiss don't approve of flaunting their wealth or their poverty, which officially doesn't exist. Incredibly, some 600,000 inhabitants of Switzerland are considered to live below the official poverty level (probably all foreigners), although most of Switzerland's 'poor' would be considered wealthy in many third world countries. The little old man sitting next to you on the tram could easily be one of the 100,000 or so millionaires in Switzerland. 'If you've got it, flaunt it' isn't the Swiss way of doing things. In fact, modesty is taken to extremes; for example if a Swiss tells you he is a fair skier, it usually means he is not quite as good as the world cup stars.

The Swiss are very law-abiding (except with speed limits). Any Swiss loitering in town at 3am is more likely to be waiting for the green light to cross the road than preparing to rob a bank. In fact anyone out at 3am is probably a foreigner preparing to rob a bank, as all Swiss will have been in bed since early evening. The Swiss slavishly follow all rules and regulations and delight in pointing out your transgressions: they're world leaders in robotics – there are over five million in Switzerland (Ouch!). In Switzerland, rules (however trivial) certainly **aren't** made to be broken, and if you use the IN door to EXIT, or park an inch or two over the authorised parking line, it will be quickly brought to your attention by an upstanding Swiss citizen. Solzhenitsyn left Switzerland, where he arrived after deportation from Russia, complaining that Swiss bureaucracy was worse than Russia's (even the usually placid Swiss were taken aback by this pronouncement). In Switzerland, everything that isn't illegal is forbidden; everything else is compulsory. Switzerland is often described as a benevolent police state and heaven help anyone who steps out of line.

The Swiss like everything to be spotless and are obsessed with cleanliness (it being next to godliness). They employ an army of guest workers to clean up after them and not only vacuum clean their tunnels and footpaths, but scour the streets **between** villages. Swiss streets are so clean you could eat off them and are cleaner than the average kitchen hand in some countries. Swiss banks (colloquially known as laundromats) even wash dirty foreign money so their citizens won't become contaminated.

Switzerland isn't exactly a land of milk and honey for the dedicated career woman, who's considered something of an eccentric. Most Swiss men think that a women's place is in the home, particularly the kitchen (not the bedroom judging by the low birth-rate). What they think of women politicians is unprintable! They don't think much of politics and politicians in general – but then who does? Swiss women didn't obtain the right to vote until 1971 and Swiss marriage laws, which were heavily biased in the husband's favour, were finally revised in January 1988 (after 81 years) to give a wife equal rights with her husband. Swiss women are among the least emancipated in Western Europe and the majority appear to like it that way. The Swiss are slow to make changes, both individually and as a nation. However, they're usually quick to embrace new technology, particularly when it will make them rich(er).

The Swiss have enjoyed the good life for so long that they've forgotten what it's like in the real world. However, Switzerland's seemingly permanent prosperity and stability was threatened in the early 1990s by the recession, which shook the Swiss to the core. Among the biggest concerns facing the Swiss are unemployment; drug addiction; asylum seekers and refugees; the environment; provision for the elderly (pensions); relations with the EU; inflation; crime; housing; and taxation (not necessarily in that order). Many Swiss are fearful of what the future may hold. The only certain thing is that (like everyone else) they must adapt to the challenges of the new millennium and can no longer afford to live in cloud cuckoo (clock) land.

Despite their idiosyncrasies, most foreigners could learn a lot from the Swiss, who excel in many things. They're excellent skiers, the world's best hoteliers and have the best public transport services in the world. They're also the world's most prolific flag flyers and best *hornussen* players. In business they're among the world's best bankers and insurance salesmen, and are renowned for the quality of their products, from precision machinery and watches to cheese and chocolate. Switzerland is the most ordered and stable (financially and politically) country in the world. If we turned the operation of the world economy over to the Swiss the rest of us could relax and organise the parties.

The Swiss political system is a (boring) model of democracy, where co-operation and compromise are preferred to obstruction and obstinacy (members of the Swiss Radical Party are actually liberals). Swiss politicians even ask the opinion of the Swiss people when important issues are at stake. It hardly seems credible, but the Swiss could give politicians a **good** name – not only can you believe them most of the time, even government statistics are usually accurate. Finally, despite the famous words of a former British Chancellor of the Exchequer, most inhabitants of Zurich are of average height and bear little resemblance to gnomes. They do, however, have lots of treasure.

The Swiss are a nation of diverse peoples who don't always see eye to eye, although generally Switzerland is a prime example of unity in diversity. However, nothing is guaranteed to bring the Swiss closer together than **being made fun of by a bloody foreigner!** (Pssst! Don't **Tell** the Swiss, but **William** their national hero, didn't exist.)

20.

MOVING HOUSE OR LEAVING SWITZERLAND

When moving house or leaving Switzerland, there are numerous things to be considered and a 'million' people to be informed. The checklists contained in this chapter are intended to make the task easier and may even help prevent an ulcer or nervous breakdown – provided of course you don't leave everything to the last minute.

MOVING HOUSE WITHIN SWITZERLAND

When moving house **within** Switzerland the items mentioned below should be considered:

- You must usually give your landlord at least three months notice before vacating rented accommodation (refer to your contract). If you don't give your landlord sufficient notice or aren't resigning on one of the approved moving dates, you will need to find someone to take over your apartment (see page 101). **Your resignation letter must be sent by registered post to reach your landlord by the last day of the month at the latest.** This will also apply if you have a separate contract for a garage or other rented property, e.g. a holiday home, in Switzerland. Arrange a date with your landlord for the handover.
- Inform the following:
  - Your employer.
  - Your present community eight days before moving house and your new community within eight days of taking up residence (see **Resident's Control** on page 78).
  - Your electricity, gas, telephone and water companies.
  - Your insurance companies (for example health, car, house contents and private liability); banks, post office, stockbroker and other financial institutions; credit card and hire purchase (credit) companies; lawyer; accountant; and local businesses where you have accounts.
  - Your family doctor, dentist and other health practitioners. Health records should be transferred to your new doctor and dentist, if applicable.
  - Your family's schools. If applicable, arrange for schooling in your new community. Try to give a term's notice and obtain a copy of any relevant school reports or records from your children's current schools.
  - All regular correspondents, subscriptions, social and sports clubs, professional and trade journals, and friends and relatives. Give or send them your new address and telephone number. Free address cards are available from post offices. Arrange to have your post redirected by the post office (see **Change of Address** on page 119).

- If you have a Swiss driving licence or a Swiss registered car, inform your canton's motor registration office within 14 days of moving. If you're moving to a new canton, you will receive a refund of your road tax from your previous canton. You're required to re-register your car in a new canton within 14 days and to return your old registration plates to your former canton's motor registration office.

- Your local consulate or embassy if you're registered with them (see page 81).

● Return any library books or anything borrowed.

● If moving cantons, arrange to settle your income tax liability in your present canton (see page 292).

● Re-register your dog in your new community (see page 380).

● Arrange shipping for your furniture and belongings (or transport, if you're doing your own move).

● Arrange for a cleaning company and/or decorating company for your apartment, if necessary (see page 101).

● If applicable, ensure the return of your deposit from your landlord.

● Cancel the milk and newspapers.

● Ask yourself (again): 'Is it really worth all this trouble?'.

LEAVING SWITZERLAND

Before leaving Switzerland for an indefinite period, the following items should be considered **in addition** to those listed above.

● Give notice to your employer, if applicable.

● Check that your own and your family's passports are valid.

● Check whether there are any special entry requirements for your country of destination by contacting the local embassy or consulate in Switzerland, e.g. visas, permits or inoculations. An exit permit or visa isn't required to leave Switzerland.

● You may qualify for a rebate on your income tax and federal old age and survivors insurance (see page 259). Your employer and community will assist you with these. Tax rebates are normally paid automatically.

● Your private company pension contributions will be repaid in full (see page 261). Before your pension fund will repay your funds, you must provide a statement from your community office stating that you've de-registered and are leaving Switzerland.

- Arrange to sell anything you aren't taking with you (e.g. house, car and furniture) and to ship your belongings. Find out the exact procedure for shipping your belongings to your country of destination (see page 98). Check with the local embassy or consulate of the country to which you're moving. Special forms may need to be completed before arrival. If you've been living in Switzerland for less than a year, you're required to re-export all imported personal effects, including furniture and vehicles (if you sell them, you should pay duty).

- If you have a Swiss registered car that you intend to take with you, you can retain your Swiss registration plates for up to one year until your Swiss insurance expires. When you re-register your car abroad, your Swiss registration plates must be returned to your former canton's motor registration office or can be destroyed, in which case you must provide **official** proof. If you don't return them, the Swiss authorities won't be pleased – and have long memories.

- Pets may require special inoculations or may need to be placed in quarantine for a period (see page 380).

- Contact Swisscom well in advance to recover your telephone deposit, if applicable (see **Moving or Leaving Switzerland** on page 133).

- Arrange health, travel and other insurance (see **Chapter 13**).

- Depending on your destination, you may wish to arrange health and dental check-ups before leaving Switzerland. Obtain a copy of your health and dental records and a statement from your health insurance company stating your present level of cover.

- Terminate any Swiss loan, lease or hire purchase (credit) contracts and pay all outstanding bills (allow plenty of time, as most Swiss companies are slow to respond).

- Check whether you're entitled to a rebate on your road tax, car and other insurance. Obtain a letter from your Swiss motor insurance company stating your no-claims bonus.

- Sell or let your house, apartment or other property.

- Check whether you need an international driving licence or a translation of your Swiss or foreign driving licence for your country of destination (see page 210).

- Give friends and business associates in Switzerland an address and telephone number where you can be contacted.

- If you will be travelling or living abroad for an extended period, you may wish to give someone 'powers of attorney' over your financial affairs in Switzerland so that they can act on your behalf in your absence. This can be for a fixed period or open-ended and can be limited to a specific purpose only. **You should, however, take legal advice before doing this.**

● Buy a copy of *Living and Working in ********* before leaving Switzerland. If we haven't published it yet, drop us a line and we'll get started on it right away!

Gute Reise/Bon Voyage!

APPENDICES

APPENDIX A: USEFUL ADDRESSES

Embassies & Consulates

Embassies are located in the capital Berne, consulates and missions in Geneva and Zurich (plus a few other towns). Embassies and consulates are listed in telephone directories under *Konsulate/consulat* or *ambassade*. A selection of embassies is listed below.

Berne

Albania, Pourtalèsstrasse 65, CH-3074 Muri b. Bern (☎ 031 952 60 10).

Algeria, Willadingweg 74, CH-3006 Berne (☎ 031 352 69 61).

Argentina, Jungfraustr. 1, CH-3005 Berne (☎ 031 356 43 49).

Austria, Kirchenfeldstr. 77-79, CH-3006 Berne (☎ 031 356 52 52).

Belarus, Quartierweg 6, CH-3074 Muri b. Berne (☎ 031 952 76 16).

Belgium, Jubiläumsstr. 41, CH-3005 Berne (☎ 031 350 01 50).

Bosnia-Herzegovinia, Jungfraustr. 1, CH-3005 Berne (☎ 031 351 10 77).

Brazil, Monbijoustr. 68, CH-3023 Berne (☎ 031 371 85 15).

Bulgaria, Bernastr. 2, CH-3005 Berne (☎ 031 351 14 55).

Cameroon, Brunnadernrain 29, CH-3006 Berne (☎ 031 352 47 37).

Canada, Kirchenfeldstr. 88, CH-3005 Berne (☎ 031 352 63 81).

Chile, Eigerpl. 5, CH-3007 Berne (☎ 031 371 07 45).

China, Kalcheggweg 10, CH-3006 Berne (☎ 031 352 73 33).

Colombia, Dufourstr. 47, CH-3005 Berne (☎ 031 351 54 34).

Costa Rica, Schwarztorstr.11, 3007 Berne (☎ 031 372 78 87).

Croatia, Thunstrasse 45, CH-3005 Berne (☎ 031 352 02 75).

Cuba, Gesellschaftstr. 8, CH-3012 Berne (☎ 031 302 21 11).

Czech Republic, Muristr. 53, CH-3006 Berne (☎ 031 352 36 45).

Denmark, Thunstr. 95, CH-3016 Berne (☎ 031 352 50 11).

Ecuador, Ensingerstr. 48, CH-3016 Berne (☎ 031 351 17 55).

Egypt, Elfenauweg 61, CH-3006 Berne (☎ 031 352 80 12).

Finland, Weltpoststr. 4, CH-3015 Berne (☎ 031 351 30 31).

France, Schosshaldenstr. 46, CH-3032 Berne (☎ 031 359 21 11).

Germany, Willadingweg 83, CH-3006 Berne (☎ 031 359 41 11).

Ghana, Belpstr. 11, CH-3001 Berne (☎ 031 381 78 52).

Grèce, Jungfraustrasse 3, CH-3006 Berne 6 (☎ 031 352 16 37).

Hungary, Muristr. 31, CH-3006 Berne (☎ 031 352 85 72).

India, Kirchenfeldstr. 28, CH-3005 Berne (☎ 031 351 11 10).

Indonesia, Elfenauweg 51, CH-3006 Berne (☎ 031 352 09 83).

Iran, Thunstr. 68, CH-3006 Berne (☎ 031 351 08 01).

Ireland, Kirchenfeldstr. 68, CH-3005 Berne (☎ 031 352 14 42).

Israel, Alpenstr. 32, CH-3006 Berne (☎ 031 356 35 00).

Italy, Elfenstr. 14, CH-3006 Berne (☎ 031 352 41 51).

Ivory Coast, Thormannstr. 51, CH-3006 Berne (☎ 031 351 10 51).

Japan, Engestr. 43, CH-3026 Berne (☎ 031 302 08 11).

Jordan, Belpstr. 11, CH-3001 Berne (☎ 031 381 41 46).

Kazakhstan, Alleeweg 15, CH-3006 Berne (☎ 031 351 79 69).

North Korea, Pourtalèsstr. 43, CH-3074 Muri b. Berne (☎ 031 951 66 21).

Portugal, Weltpoststr. 20, CH-3015 Berne (☎ 031 352 83 29).

South Korea, Kalcheggweg 38, CH-3015 Berne (☎ 031 351 10 81).

Lebanon, Thunstr. 10, CH-3074 Muri b. Berne (☎ 031 950 65 65).

Libya, Tavelweg 2, CH-3006 Berne (☎ 031 351 30 76).

Liechtenstein, Willadingweg 65, CH-3016 Berne (☎ 031 357 64 11).

Luxembourg, Kramgasse 45, CH-3008 Berne (☎ 031 311 47 32).

Macedonia, Kirchenfeldstr. 30, CH-3005 Berne (☎ 031 352 00 02).

Madagascar, Egelbergstrasse 9, CH-3006 Berne (☎ 031 368 18 63).

Mexico, Bernastr. 57, CH-3005 Berne (☎ 031 357 47 47).

Monaco, Hallwylstr. 34, CH-3006 Berne (☎ 031 351 18 75).

Morocco, Helvetiastr. 42, CH-3005 Berne (☎ 031 351 03 62).

Netherlands, Kollerweg 11, CH-3011 Berne (☎ 031 352 70 63).

Nigeria, Zieglerstr. 45, CH-3014 Berne (☎ 031 382 07 26).

Norway, Bubenbergplatz 10, CH-3011 Berne (☎ 031 310 55 55).

Pakistan, Bernastr. 47, CH-3005 Berne (☎ 031 352 29 92).

Paraguay, Kramgasse 58, CH-3008 Berne (☎ 031 312 32 22).

Peru, Thunstr. 36, CH-3005 Berne (☎ 031 351 85 55).

Philippines, Kirchenfeldstrasse 73, CH-3005 Berne (☎ 031 350 17 17).

Poland, Elfenstr. 20a, CH-3016 Berne (☎ 031 352 04 52).

Portugal, Weltpoststr. 20, CH-3015 Berne (☎ 031 351 17 73).

Romania, Kirchenfeldstr. 78, CH-3005 Berne (☎ 031 352 35 22).

Russia, Brunnadernrain 37, CH-3006 Berne (☎ 031 352 05 66).

Saudi Arabia, Kramburgstr. 12, CH-3006 Berne (☎ 031 352 15 55).

Slovakia, Thunstr. 99, CH-3006 Berne (☎ 031 352 36 46).

Slovenia, Schwanengasse 9, CH-3011 Berne (☎ 031 312 90 09).

South Africa, Alpenstr. 29, CH-3006 Berne (☎ 031 350 13 13).

Spain, Kalcheggweg 24, CH-3006 Berne (☎ 031 352 04 12).

Sweden, Bundesgasse 26, CH-3011 Berne (☎ 031 328 70 00).

Thailand, Kirchstr. 56, CH-3097 Liebefeld (☎ 031 970 30 30).

Trinidad & Tobago, Elfenauweg 24, CH-3006 Berne (☎ 031 352 19 35).

Tunisia, Kirchenfeldstr. 63, CH-3005 Berne (☎ 031 352 82 26).

Turkey, Lombachweg 33, CH-3015 Berne (☎ 031 351 16 91).

Ukraine, Feldeggweg 5, CH-3005 Berne (☎ 031 352 23 16).

United Kingdom, Thunstr. 50, CH-3015 Berne (☎ 031 359 77 00).

Uruguay, Kramgasse 63, CH-3011 Berne (☎ 031 311 27 92).

USA, Jubiläumsstr. 93, CH-3001 Berne (☎ 031 351 70 11).

Venezuela, Morillonstrasse 9, CH-3023 Berne 23 (☎ 031 371 32 82).

Yugoslavia, Seminarstr. 5, CH-3006 Berne (☎ 031 352 63 53).

Zaire, Sulgenheimweg 21, CH-3001 Berne (☎ 031 371 35 38).

Geneva

Afghanistan, rue de Lausanne 63, CH-1202 Geneva (☎ 022 731 14 49).

Algeria, rte de Lausanne 308, CH-1293 Bellevue (☎ 022 774 19 19).

Angola, rte de Pré-Bois 29, CH-1215 Geneva 15 (☎ 022 788 51 74).

Australia, Rue de Moillebeau 56-58, CH-1211 Geneva 19 (☎ 022 918 29 00).

Austria, rue Jean-Sénebier 20, CH-1205 Geneva (☎ 022 312 06 00).

Bahrain, ch. William-Barbey 51, CH-1292 Chambésy (☎ 022 758 21 02).

Bangladesh, rue de Lausanne 65, CH-1202 Geneva (☎ 022 732 59 40).

Belgium, rue de Moillebeau 58, CH-1209 Geneva (☎ 022 730 40 00).

Belize, rue Pedro-Meylan 1, CH-1208 Geneva (☎ 022 786 38 83).

Brazil, place Cornavin 12, CH-1201 Geneva (☎ 022 732 09 30).

Burkina Faso, av. Eugène-Pittard 16, CH-1206 Geneva (☎ 022 704 18 18).

Cameroon, rue de Nant 6, CH-1207 Geneva (☎ 022 736 20 22).

Cap Verde Republic, av. Blanc 47, CH-1202 Geneva (☎ 022 731 33 36).

China, Chemin de Surville 11, CH-1213 Petit-Lancy (☎ 022 792 25 37).

Congo, rue Michel-Servet 12, CH-1206 Geneva (☎ 022 702 90 90).

Cyprus, Rue Pedro-Meylan 1, CH-1208 Geneva (☎ 022 736 34 16).

Czech Republic, ch. de la Gabiule 110, CH-1245 Collonge-Bellerive (☎ 022 855 95 70).

Denmark, rue de la Gabelle 9, CH-1227 Carouge (☎ 022 827 05 00).

Dominican Republic, rue Grenus 16, CH-1201 Geneva (☎ 022 738 00 18).

Egypt, rte de Florissant 47 ter, CH-1206 Geneva (☎ 022 347 63 79).

El Salvador, rue de Lausanne 65, CH-1202 Geneva (☎ 022 732 70 36).

Ethiopia, rue de Moillebeau 56, CH-1209 Geneva (☎ 022 733 07 59).

Finland, Grand-Rue 25, CH-1211 Geneva (☎ 022 311 83 75).

France, rue J.-Imbert-Galloix 11, CH-1205 Geneva (☎ 022 319 00 00).

Georgia, rue Richard-Wagner 1, CH-1202 Geneva (☎ 022 919 10 10).

Germany, ch. du Petit-Saconnex 28C, CH-1209 Geneva (☎ 022 730 11 11).

Ghana, rue de Moillebeau 56, CH-1209 Geneva (☎ 022 919 04 50).

Greece, rue Pedro-Meylan 1, CH-1208 Geneva (☎ 022 735 37 47).

Grenadines, av. de Frontenex 8, CH-1207 Geneva (☎ 022 707 63 00).

Guatemala, rue de Vieux-Collège 10, CH-1211 Geneva 3 (☎ 022 311 40 22).

Honduras, ch. Taverney 13, CH-1218 Le Grand-Saconnex (☎ 022.710 07 60).

Iceland, rue du Mont-de-Sion 8, CH-1206 Geneva (☎ 022 347 16 52).

India, rue du Valais 9-11, CH-1202 Geneva (☎ 022 731 51 29).

Iran, ch. du Petit-Saconnex 28a, CH-1209 Geneva (☎ 022 919 05 20).

Iraq, ch. du Petit-Saconnex 28a, CH-1209 Geneva (☎ 022 918 09 80).

Italy, rue Charles-Galland 14, CH-1206 Geneva (☎ 022 346 47 44).

Ivory Coast, av. Cardinal-Mermillod 6, CH-1227 Carouge GE (☎ 022 343 90 09).

Jamaica, rue de Lausanne 36, CH-1201 Geneva (☎ 022 731 57 80).

Japan, ch. des Fins 3, CH-1218 Le Grand-Saconnex (☎ 022 717 31 11).

Kuwait, av. de Ariana 2, CH-1202 Geneva (☎ 022 918 01 30).

Lithuania, av. du Bouchet 18, CH-1209 Geneva (☎ 022 734 51 01).

Luxembourg, ch. de la Rochette 13, CH-1202 Geneva (☎ 022 919 19 29).

Malaysia, rte de Prés-Bois 20, CH-1215 Geneva 15 (☎ 022 710 75 00).

Malta, Parc Château-Banquet 26, CH-1202 Geneva (☎ 022 901 05 80).

Mauritania, rue des Eaux-Vives 94, CH-1207 Geneva 24 (☎ 022 736 42 00).

Mexico, rue de Candolle 16, CH-1205 Geneva (☎ 022 328 39 20).

Monaco, rue de Candolle 8, CH-1205 Geneva (☎ 022 708 01 01).

Myanmar Union, av. Blanc 47, CH-1202 Geneva (☎ 022 731 75 40).

Netherlands, Rue Ferdinand-Hodler 23, 1211 Geneva 3 (☎ 022 787 57 30).

New Zealand, ch. des Fins 2, CH-1211 Geneva (☎ 022 929 03 50).

Nigeria, Rue Richard-Wagner 1, CH-1202 Geneva (☎ 022 730 14 14)

Norway, rue de Jargonnant 2, CH-1211 Geneva 6 (☎ 022 736 16 12).

Oman, Chemin de Roilbot 3A, CH-1292 Chambésy (☎ 022 758 96 60).

Panama, rue de Lausanne 72, CH-1202 Geneva (☎ 022 715 04 50).

Peru, rue des Pierres du Niton 17, CH-1207 Geneva (☎ 022 707 49 17).

Philippines, av. Blanc 47, CH-1202 Geneva (☎ 022 731 83 20).

Portugal, rte de Ferney 220, CH-1218 Grand-Saconnex (☎ 022 791 05 11).

Qatar, rte de Ferney 149B, CH-1218 Le Garand-Saconnex (☎ 022 798 82 56).

Republic of Rwanda, rue de la Servette 93, CH-1202 Geneva (☎ 022 919 10 00).

Romania, Chemin de la Perrière 6, CH-1223 Cologny (☎ 022 752 10 90).

Russia, rue Schaub 24, CH-1202 Geneva (☎ 022 734 79 55).

Saudi Arabia, rue de Lausanne 263, CH-1292 Chambésy (☎ 022 758 22 74).

Senegal, Route de Berne 25, CH-1010 Lausanne (☎ 021 652 18 42).

Sierra Leone, quai Gustave-Ador 62, CH-1207 Geneva (☎ 022 735 85 78).

South Africa, rue du Rhône 65, CH-1204 Geneva (☎ 022 849 54 54).

Spain, rue Pestalozzi 7, CH-1211 Geneva 16 (☎ 022 734 46 06).

Sri Lanka, rue de Moillebeau 56, CH-1209 Geneva (☎ 022 919 12 51).

Sudan, av. Blanc 47, CH-1211 Geneva 19 (☎ 022 731 26 63).

Sweden, Rue Rodolphe-Toepffer 8, CH-1207 Geneva (☎ 022 700 47 00).

Syria, rue de Lausanne 72, CH-1202 Geneva (☎ 022 732 56 58).

Taiwan, rue de Moillebeau 56, CH-1209 Geneva (☎ 022 919 70 70).

Thailand, rue de l'Athénée 6, CH-1205 Geneva (☎ 022 319 87 00).

Togo, rue Rudolphe-Toepffer 11 Bis, CH-1206 Geneva (☎ 022 346 52 60).

Turkey, rte de Pré-Bois 20, CH-1215 Geneva 15 (☎ 022 798 12 32).

United Arab Emirates, rue Moillebeau 58, CH-1209 Geneva (☎ 022 918 00 00).

United Kingdom, rue de Vermont 37-39, CH-1202 Geneva (☎ 022 918 24 00).

USA, Rue Versonnex 7,CH-1207 Geneva (☎ 022 840 51 60).

Vietnam, ch. Taverney 13, CH-1218 Le Grand-Saconnex (☎ 022 798 98 66).

Yemen, ch. de Jonc 19, CH-1218 Le Grand-Saconnex (☎ 022 799 05 10).

Zurich

Austria, Seestr. 161, CH-8002 Zurich (☎ 01 283 27 00).

Bahamas, Bahnhofplatz 9, CH-8023 Zurich (☎ 01 226 40 42).

Belgium, Basteiplatz 5, CH-8022 Zurich (☎ 01 212 11 55).

Brazil, Bürglistr. 6, CH-8002 Zurich (☎ 01 206 90 20).

Burkina Faso, Weinbergstrasse 29, CH-8006 Zurich (☎ 01 261 06 25).

Croatia, Bellerivestr. 5, CH-8008 Zurich (☎ 01 422 83 18).

China, Bellariastr. 20, CH-8002 Zurich (☎ 01 201 10 05).

Costa Rica, Stockerstr, 10, CH-8002 Zurich (☎ 01 201 13 52).

Cyprus, Talstr. 83, CH-8001 Zurich (☎ 01 211 30 23).

Czech Republic, Dufourstr. 22, CH-8008 Zurich (☎ 01 262 15 81).

Denmark, Bürglistr. 8, CH-8002 Zurich (☎ 01 289 30 60).

Djibouti, Othmarstr. 8, CH-8008 Zurich (☎ 043 268 09 18).

Estonia, Bergstr. 52, CH-8712 Stäfa (☎ 01 926 88 37).

Finland, Kronenstr. 42, CH-8006 Zurich (☎ 01 350 25 66).

France, Mühlebachstr. 7, CH-8032 Zurich (☎ 01 268 85 85).

Gambia, Rütistr. 13, CH-8952 Schlieren (☎ 01 731 10 10).

Germany, Freigutstrasse 15, CH-8002 Zurich (☎ 0 201 72 22).

Greece, Bellerivestrasse 67, CH-8034 Zurich (☎ 01 388 55 77).

Grenada, Claridenstrasse 20, CH-8002 Zurich (☎ 01 206 29 34).

Guatemala, Tödistr. 17, CH-8002 Zurich (☎ 01 202 58 15).

Haiti, Forchstr. 182, CH-8032 Zurich (☎ 01 381 69 89).

Hungary, Voltastr. 65, CH-8044 Zurich (☎ 01 262 39 32).

Iceland, Bahnhofstr. 44, CH-8001 Zurich (☎ 01 215 12 60).

India, Mühlestrasse 41, CH-8803 Rüschlikon (☎ 01 772 81 51).

Ireland, Claridenstr. 25, CH-8002 Zurich (☎ 01 289 25 15).

Italy, Tödistr. 67, CH-8002 Zurich (☎ 01 286 61 11).

Ivory Coast, Löwenstr. 17, CH-8001 Zurich (☎ 01 211 88 44).

Japan, Utoquai 55,CH-8008 Zurich (☎ 01 991 62 18)

Latvia, Gessnerallee 36, CH-8001 Zurich (☎ 01 211 79 75).

Lesotho, Bleicherweg 45, CH-8002 Zurich (☎ 01 201 44 45).

Luxembourg, Seegartenstr. 2, CH-8000 Zurich (☎ 01 383 63 55).

Madagascar, Kappelergasse 14, CH-8001 Zurich (☎ 01 212 85 66).

Malaysia, Fraumünsterstr. 29, CH-8001 Zurich (☎ 01 210 06 66).

Malta, Limmatquai 3, CH-8001 Zurich (☎ 01 252 70 50).

Marshall Islands, Limmatquai 1, CH-8001 Zurich (☎ 01 261 16 20).

Mauritania, Bahnhofstr. 52, CH-8001 Zurich (☎ 01 214 62 92).

Mexico, Tödistr. 17, CH-8002 Zurich (☎ 01 209 70 10).

Monaco, Chapfstrasse 48, CH-8126 Zumikon (☎ 01 919 04 16).

Morocco, Bahnhofstr. 73, CH-8001 Zurich (☎ 01 211 74 32).

Nepal, Bleicherweg 33, CH-8002 Zurich (☎ 01 201 45 15).

Netherlands, Allmendstrasse 140,CH-8027 Zurich (☎ 01 488 28 88).

Norway, Utoquai 37, CH-8008 Zurich (☎ 01 251 69 39).

Panama, Löwenstr. 40, CH-8001 Zurich (☎ 01 225 14 88).

Peru, Löwenstr. 69, CH-8001 Zurich (☎ 01 211 82 11).

Portugal, Zeltweg 13, CH-8032 Zurich (☎ 01 261 33 66).

Rwanda, Zürichstr. 31, CH-8700 Küsnacht (☎ 01 914 14 91).

Senegal, Schifflände 22, CH-8001 Zurich (☎ 01 251 19 45).

Seychelles, General Guisan-Quai 22, CH-8002 Zurich (☎ 01 285 79 29).

South Africa, Wiesenstr. 7, CH-8008 Zurich (☎ 043 488 60 01).

Spain, Hotzestrasse 23, CH-8042 Zurich (☎ 01 368 61 00).

Swaziland, Lintheschergasse 17, CH-8001 Zurich (☎ 01 211 52 03).

Sweden, Gotthardstrasse 21, CH-8022 Zurich (☎ 01 252 38 30).

Thailand, Talacker 50, CH-8001 Zurich (☎ 01 211 70 60).

Turkey, Markusstrasse 10, CH-8006 Zurich (☎ 01 363 87 55).

United Kingdom, Hegibachstrasse 47, CH-8032 Zurich (☎ 01 383 65 60).

USA, Zurich America Center, Dufourstr. 101, CH-8008 Zurich (☎ 01 422 25 66).

Vanuatu, Basteipl. 5, CH-8001 Zurich (☎ 01 212 70 73).

Yugoslavia, Alfred Escher-Str. 4, CH-8002 Zurich (☎ 01 202 02 73).

Basle

Austria, Lange Gasse 37, CH-4052 Basle (☎ 061 271 35 35).

Belgium, Gerbergasse 1, CH-4001 Basle (☎ 061 261 69 22).

Bolivia, Sevogelplatz 2, CH-4052 Basle (☎ 061 312 44 45).

Brazil, Freie Str. 1, CH-4001 Basle (☎ 061 261 76 61) .

Cap Verde Republic, Rümelinspl. 14, CH-4001 Basle (☎ 061 269 80 95).

Czech Republic, Unterwartweg 15, CH-4132 Muttenz (☎ 061 462 00 01).

Ecaudor, Wallstrasse 8, CH-4002 Basle (☎ 061 272 03 03).

Finland, Lichtstr. 35, CH-4056 Basle (☎ 061 696 48 14) .

France, Aeschengraben 26, CH-4051 Basle (☎ 061 276 56 77).

Germany, Schwarzwaldallee 200, CH-4058 Basle (☎ 061 693 33 03).

Hungary, Hirzbodenweg 103, CH-4052 Basle (☎ 061 319 51 48).

Italy, Schaffhauserheinweg 5, CH-4058 Basle (☎ 061 689 96 26).

Jamaica, Güterstr. 141, CH-4153 Reinach BL (☎ 061 711 80 40).

Luxembourg, Steinengraben 28, CH-4051 Basle (☎ 061 206 91 01).

Malaysia, Centralbahnstr. 17, CH-4051 Basle (☎ 061 271 27 12).

Mali, Spalenberg 25, CH-4051 Basle (☎ 061 261 13 73).

Monaco, Wartenbergstr. 40, CH-4052 Basle (☎ 061 319 51 19).

Netherlands, Aeschengraben 9, CH-4002 Basle (☎ 061 206 31 00).

Norway, Peter Merian-Str. 45, CH-4052 Basle (☎ 061 205 33 33).

Philippines, Innere Margarethenstr. 2 , CH-4051 Basle (☎ 061 278 99 88).

San Marino, Sternengasse 18, CH-4002 Basle (☎ 061 331 82 97).

Sweden, Neubadstr. 7, CH-4015 Basle (☎ 061 281 00 42).

Thailand, Aeschenvorstadt 71, CH-4051 Basle (☎ 061 206 45 65).

Togo, Unterer Heuberg 19, CH-4051 Basle (☎ 061 261 10 45).

Tuvalu, Elisabethenstr. 42, CH-4010 Basle (☎ 061 273 49 20).

Uruguay, Lange Gasse 15, CH-4052 Basle (☎ 061 277 52 42).

Government

Central Compensation Office (OASI/DI), av. Edmond-Vaucher 18, CH-1211 Geneva 28 (☎ 022 795 91 11☐ www.ahv.ch).

Federal Aliens Office, Quellenweg 9/15, CH-3003 Bern-Wabern (☎ 031 325 95 11, ☐ www.imes.admin.ch).

Federal Office for Social Insurance, Effingerstr. 33, CH-3003 Berne (☎ 031 322 90 11, ☐ www.bsv.admin.ch).

Federal Veterinarians Office, Schwarzenburgerstr. 161, CH-3097 Liebefeld-Berne (☎ 031 323 85 09, ☐ www.bvet.admin.ch).

Head Customs Office, Monbijoustr. 40, CH-3003 Berne (☎ 031 322 65 11 ☐ www.zoll.admin.ch).

Swiss Broadcasting Corporation (SBC), Postfach, CH-3000 Berne 15 (☎ 031 350 91 11, ✉ info@srgssrideesuisse.ch ☐ www.srg.ch).

Swiss Bureau for the Prevention of Accidents, Laupenstr. 11, CH-3008 Berne (☎ 031 390 22 22, ☐ www.bfu.ch).

Switzerland Tourism, PO Box 695, CH-8027 Zurich (☎ 0800 100 20 30, ☐ www.myswitzerland.com).

Swiss Radio International, Giacomettistr. 1, CH-3000 Berne 15 (☎ 031 350 92 22, ☐ www.swissinfo.org).

Miscellaneous

Association of Swiss Private Clinics, Moosstr. 2, CH-3073 Gümligen-Berne (☎ 031 952 61 33 ☐ www.privatkliniken.ch).

The Automobile Club of Switzerland (ACS), Wasserwerkgasse 39, Postfach, CH-3000 Berne 13 (☎ 031 328 31 11 ☐ www.acs.ch).

British Swiss Chamber of Commerce, Freiestr. 155, CH-8032 Zurich (☎ 01 422 31 31☐ www.bscc.ch).

English Teachers Association of Switzerland, ETAS Administration, rue de l'Hôpital 32, CH-1400 Yverdon (☎ 024 420 32 54, ☐ www.e-tas.ch).

Mobility Carsharing Schweiz, Gütschstrasse 2, CH-6000 Lucerne 7 (☎ 041 248 22 22, ⌨ www.mobility.ch).

Pro Infirmis, Feldeggstr. 71, Postfach 1332, CH-8032 Zurich (☎ 01 388 26 26, ⌨ www.proinfirmis.ch).

Pro Senectute Schweiz, Lavaterstr. 60, CH-8027 Zurich (☎ 01 283 89 89, ⌨ www.pro-senectute.ch).

REGA Administration und Secretariat, Rega Center, Postfach 1414, CH-8058 Zurich-Flughafen (☎ 01 654 33 11 or 1414 in an emergency, ⌨ www.rega.ch).

Swiss Accidents and Insurance (SUVA), Fluhmattstr. 1, CH-6002 Lucerne (☎ 0848 83 08 30, ⌨ www.suva.ch).

Swiss-American Chamber of Commerce, Talacker 41, CH-8001 Zurich (☎ 01 211 24 54, ⌨ www.amcham.ch).

Swiss Camping Association, Bahnhofstr.2, CH-3322 Schönbühl (☎ 031 852 06 26, ⌨www.swisscamps.ch).

Swiss Hotel Association (SHV), Monbijoustr. 130, CH-3001 Berne (☎ 031 370 41 11, ⌨ www.swisshotels.ch).

Swiss Red Cross, Rainmattstr. 10, Postfach 8263, CH-3001 Berne (☎ 031 387 71 11, ⌨ www.redcross.ch).

Swiss Spas, Avenue des Bains 22, CH-1400 Yverdon-les-Bains (☎ 024 420 15 21, ⌨ www.heilbad.org).

STA Travel, Ankerstr. 112, Postfach, CH-8026 Zurich (☎ 01 297 11 11, ⌨ www.statravel.ch).

Swiss Travel Savings Fund, Neuengasse 15, CH-3001 Berne (☎ 031 329 66 33⌨ www.reka.ch).

Swiss Youth Hostels, Schaffhauserstr. 14, CH-8042 Zurich (☎ 01 360 14 14, ⌨ www.youthhostel.ch).

Touring Club of Switzerland (TCS), ch. de Blandonnet 4,Case postale 820, CH-1214 Vernier (☎ 022 417 27 27, ⌨ www.tcs.ch).

Transport Club of Switzerland (VCS), Lagerstr. 18, CH-3360 Herzogenbuchsee (☎ 062 956 56 56, ⌨ www.verkehrsclub.ch).

Clubs & Organisations

There are many clubs and organisations in Switzerland for foreigners, a selection of which is listed below. Your embassy or consulate in Switzerland may be able to provide you with a list of clubs and organisations. Information about expatriate clubs is also available from Anglo-Phone on ☎ 157 5014.

Allgemeine Lesegesellschaft, Mrs. Ruth Marzo, Münsterplatz 8, CH-4001 Basle (☎ 061 261 43 49, ✉ lesegesellschaft@balcab.ch).

American Citizens Abroad (ACA), Mr Karl Jauch, 5 rue Liotard, CH-1202 Geneva (☎ 022 340 02 33, 🖳 www.aca.ch).

American Club of Ticino, c/o CA Rezzonico, Via Torricelli 30, CH-6900 Lugano.

American Club of Zurich, Ms Susan Suter, Hinteracherweg 7, CH-8303 Bassersdorf (☎ 043 266 08 60, 🖳 www.acz.ch, ✉acz info@freesurf.ch).

American International Club of Geneva, Mr Pierre Imfeld, Hotel Intercontinental, Case postale 371, ch. Petit-Saconnex 7-9, CH-1211 Geneva 19 (☎ 022 910 25 80, 🖳 www.amclub.ch).

American Women of Ticino, c/o Jonsi Andrews, Casa Mimosa, CH-6914 Carona (☎ 091 649 66 13, ✉ jonsi@bluewin.ch).

American Women's Club of Basle, Postfach 2161, CH-4002 Basle (☎ 061 272 33 46, 🖳 www.esccb.orp/americanwomensclub/home.html).

American Women's Club of Lausanne, 6, av. Eglantine, CH-1006 Lausanne (☎ 021 320 2688, ✉ awc-lausanne@span.ch).

American Women's Club of Zurich, Mrs. Sue Rickenbacher, Schöntalstr. 8, CH-8004 Zurich (☎ 01 240 44 55, 🖳 www.awc zurich.org).

Anglo-Swiss Circle, St. Gallen, John Waygood, Quellenstr. 17, CH-9016 St. Gallen (☎ 071 288 31 81, 🖳 www.angloswiss-sg.ch).

Anglo-Swiss Club Basle, Anitra & Howard Green, Kornackerweg 16, CH-4132 Muttenz (☎ 061 461 45 36, 🖳 www.fasc.ch).

Anglo-Swiss Club Fribourg, Rose-Marie Coombs, La Bataille, CH-1566 St. Aubin (☎ 026 677 25 67, ✉ coombs@netplus.ch).

Anglo-Swiss Club Geneva, Mrs. Rosemarie Schaer, rue de Contamines 11, CH-1206 Geneva (☎ 022 346 65 53).

Anglo-Swiss Club Lausanne, Mr. David Willingham, route de Taillepied 112, CH-1095 Lutry (☎ 021 791 11 24, 🖳 www.anglo swissclubs.ch, ✉david.willingham@tetralaval.com).

Anglo-Swiss Club Locarno, Mr. Claudio Roncoroni, via ai Saleggi, CH-6600 Locarno (☎ 091 751 44 39).

Anglo-Swiss Club Lucerne, Mr. John Askins, Altegghalde 1, CH-6045 Meggen (☎ 041 377 34 12, ⊠ jaskins@centralnet.ch).

Anglo-Swiss Club Solothurn, Mr.Rinaldo Wolf, P.O.Box 120, CH-4501 Solothurn (☎ 032 622 20 71, ⊠ wolfies@bluewin.ch).

Association for International Development, c/o Mr. C. Ritchie, P.O. Box 120, CH-1218 Grand Saconnex.

Basel Expats, Mr Nigel MacGeorge, Thannerstrasse 34, 4054 Basle (☎ 061 206 88 08, 💻 www.baselexpats.com).

Basle Mingles Social Club (💻 http://groups.yahoo.com/group/baselmingles).

Bharatiya Association Berne, Mr. Indre Jain, Postfach 71, CH-3000 Berne 15 (☎ 031 385 64 09, 💻 www.geocities.com/soho/gallery/3893).

Big Ben Club, Mrs. Natalie Torriani, Via Massagno 24, CH-6900 Lugano (☎ 091 921 44 30, ⊠ nlbelet@yahoo.com).

The Book Nook, c/o Leslie Guggiari, Ticino (☎ 091 605 39 28).

British-American Club, av. Avant-Poste 4, CH-1005 Lausanne (☎ 061 311 4204).

British Circle, Mrs. Janet Keene, Ringmauergasse 5, CH-4310 Rheinfelden (☎ 061 831 49 59, ⊠ janetkeene@compuserve.com).

British Residents' Association Basel, Mrs. Angela Meier-Jones, Brunnrainstrasse 10, CH-4132 Muttenz (☎ 061 461 73 62, ⊠ angie meir@gmx.ch).

British Residents' Association Berne, Mrs. Judy Chisholm, Hildanusstrasse 14,CH-3013 Berne (☎ 031 951 93 00, ⊠ judy chisholm@bluemail.ch).

British Residents' Association Geneva, Mr. Michael Rogers, chemin des Gonthiers 7, CH-1295 Mies (☎ 022 755 57 33, ⊠ mrogers@ wwfint.org).

British Residents' Association Neuchâtel, Mrs.Anne Droz, Avenue du Mail 34, 2000 Neuchâtel (☎ 032 724 03 42).

British Residents' Association Tessin, Mr. John Peters, case postale 251, 6906 Lugano (☎ 091 971 63 89, ⊠ leshiboux@bluemail.ch).

British Residents' Association Zurich, Mrs.Joanna Koch, A.Landstrasse 89, CH-8802 Kilchberg (☎ 01 715 41 46, ⊠ joanna koch@gmx.net).

British Residents' Association of Switzerland, Mrs. Robin Walker, Chemin des Roches 9, CH-1009 Pully (☎ 021 728 62 55).

British Swiss Chamber of Commerce, Freiestr. 155, CH-8032 Zurich (☎ 01 422 31 31).

Canadian Club of Basle, Mrs. Mary Müller-Vance, Therwilerstr. 97, CH-4153 Reinach (☎ 061 711 0048).

Catholic Women's Club, Mrs. Julie Schütz, rue Grand-Pré 40, CH-1202 Geneva.

Centrepoint, Im Lohnhof 8, CH-4051 Basle (☎ 061 261 20 02, 🖳 www.centrepoint.ch).

Club International Montreux, Case postale 228, CH-1820 Montreux.

Commonwealth Association of Geneva, Mr. Derrick Deane, Case postale 69, CH-1211 Geneva 20 (☎ 022 791 35 03, ✉ deaned@who.ch).

Cornell Club of Switzerland, Dr. Jürg Hari, Kirchacherstrasse 32, CH-8606 Bubikon(☎ 055 243 14 73, 🖳 www.cornellclub.ch, ✉ juerg.hari@swissonline.ch).

Dänischer Verein CUK, Mr. Flemming Vilhelmsen, Ueberlandstr. 341, CH-8051 Zurich (☎ 01 321 2823).

Danish Club Basle, Mrs. Agnethe Christensen, Tiefenmattstrasse 12, 4434, Hölstein (☎ 061 951 29 19, ✉ agnethe.christensen@bluewin.ch).

Die Dänische Kolonie in der Schweiz, Mr. Lennart Bisgaard, Feldheimstrasse 43 CH-6260 Reiden/LU.

English Club of Berne, Laupenstrasse 17, CH-3008 Berne (☎ 031 381 63 34).

English Club Biel/Bienne, Postfach 3462, CH-2500 Biel/Bienne 3 (🖳 www.englishclubbienne.ch).

English Club Zofingen/Langenthal, Mrs. Doris Pavel, Hausmattweg 25, CH-4802 Stengelbach.

English Club Toggenburg,Doris Züger, Grubenstrasse 46, CH-9500 Wil (☎ 071 911 97 86, ✉ mail@ectw.org).

English-Speaking Club, Mr. Horst Schiel, Meilistr. 18, CH-8400 Winterthur (🖳 www.fasc.ch).

English-Speaking Club, Mr & Mrs A. & D. Feltoe, Postfach 418, 5004 Aarau (☎ 062 824 26 86, 🖳 www.fasc.ch).

English-Speaking Club, Mr. Otto Goebel, Nordstrasse 3, CH-7000 Chur (☎ 081 284 75 88).

English-Speaking Club, Mr. K.A. Prevost, Beckenburgstr. 10, CH-8212 Neuhausen.

English-Speaking Club Baden/Brugg, Mrs. Fiona Hadfield-Hart, Boldistrasse 19, CH-5415 Nussbaumen b.Baden (☎ 056 282 08 14, 💻 www.brugg-online.ch, ✉ fhadfield_hart@yahoo.com.)

English-Speaking Club of Zurich, Mr. Jürg Meier, P.O. Box 7321, CH-8023 Zurich (☎ 01 860 95 24, 💻 www.escz.ch, ✉ esczinfo@freesurf.ch).

English Theatre Group of Zug, Mrs. Fiona Schaller, P. O. Box 2110, CH-6302 Zug (☎ 041 741 28 86).

European Women's Management Development, Mrs. Susanne Köchli, IBM Consulting Group, Bändliweg 21, Postfach, CH-8010 Zurich.

Familienzentrum Robinson, Mrs. Susi Ebner, Dorf 30, CH-8704 Herrliberg (☎ 01 991 63 10, 💻 www.zsz.ch/vereine/fa_club_herrliberg).

Federation of Anglo-Swiss Clubs, Mr. Laurent Belet, via Massagno 24, CH-6900 Lugano (☎ 091 921 44 31, 💻 www.angloswissclubs.ch).

Friends of Ireland, Bern, Mrs. Paddy Quinche, Tägetlistr. 8, CH-3072 Ostermundigen (☎ 031 931 29 78).

Geneva English-Speaking Club, Mr. Victor Wolff, Rue du Vélodrome 3, CH-1205 Geneva (☎ 022 781 49 41).

Geneva Irish Assoc., Mr. John Donnelly, Cité Universitaire, av. de Miremont 46, CH-1206 Geneva.

Harvard Club of Switzerland, c/o Bellevue Holding AG, Seestrasse 16, CH-8700 Küsnacht (☎ 01 267 67 77, ✉ cps@bellevue.ch).

Indian Association, Venkatraman Narasimhan, av. Adrien-Jeandin 12, CH-1226 Thônex.

International Club of Basle, Mr. George Imanidis, Postfach 650, 4001 Basle (💻 www.centrepoint.ch/icb).

International Club of Berne, Mrs. Maren Kuster, Postfach 242, CH-3065 Bolligen(☎ 031 922 02 62, ✉ mark.us@freesurf.ch).

International Club of Lausanne, Gabi Cruise, Promenade de l'Europe, CH-1203 Geneva 5 (☎ 022 345 67 16, ✉ icl@urbanet.ch).

International English-Speaking Club La Chaux-de-Fonds, Mrs. Sannemarie, Oldenziel, Les Allées 19, CH-2300 La Chaux-de-Fonds (☎ 032 9133861, ✉ sannemarie@hynatec.com).

International Men's Club of Zug, Mr. Joop Hubbeling, Flachsacher 18, CH-6330 Cham (☎ 041 780 75 50, ✉ jhubbeling@bluewin.ch, 🖳 www.imcz.com).

International Men's Club of Zurich (IMC), Mr. Josef Brogle, c/o ARKU, Zeltweg 81, CH-8032 Zurich (☎ 01 261 02 19, 🖳 www.zimc.ch).

International Women's Group of Lugano, c/o Mrs. Nathalie Belet, Via Massagno 24, CH-6900 Lugano (☎ 091 923 21 10, ✉ nlbelet@ yahoo.com).

International Women's Club of Lucerne, Mrs. Björg Jakob, Stegenhalde 30, CH-6048 Horw (☎ 041 340 10 56, 🖳 www.swiss cities.com/iwel).

Irish Swiss Association, Zurich, Mrs. Anne Heatly, Lüssiweg 18, CH-6300 Zug.

Library in English, 3, rue de Monthoux, CH-1201 Geneva (☎ 022 732 80 97).

Neuchâtel English Speaking Ladies Group, Mrs. Carole Clark, Avenue de la Gare 6, Neuchâtel (☎ 032 725 46 62, ✉ carole. clark@freesurf.ch).

Nordisk Club Schweiz, Mr. Sven-Erik Gunnervall, St.Gallerstrasse 41 A, CH-9034 Eggersriet (☎ 071 877 36 84, ✉ sgnorden@bluewin.ch).

Odd Fellows Haus, Grosspeterstrasse 5, CH-4052 Basle.

Pirate Ship Productions, Mrs. Bev Meyer, Etzelstrasse 17, CH-8800 Thalwil (☎ 01 721 04 64, ✉ zemo@access.ch).

Professional Women's Group Basle, c/o Centrepoint, Im Lohnhof 8, CH-4051, Basle (🖳 www.centrepoint.ch/pwg).).

Rhine Valley Irish Club, Mr. William Foley, Akazienweg 17, 4147 Aesch (✉ foley@datacomm.ch).

Saleem Ismail, Assoc. Friends of India, Mettliweg 2, CH-4148 Pfeffingen.

Semi-Circle Theatre Group Basle, Ms. Chris Comerci, Bahnhofstr. 27, CH-4104 Oberwil (☎ 061 401 07 68).

Six to Eight, Mrs. Leona Foldi, ch. des Crêts-de-Champel 11, CH-1206 Geneva (☎ 022 346 74 87, ✉ lfoidi@informaniak.ch).

Skandinavisk Club Zurich, Mrs. Annemarie Bratt, Postfach 4436, CH-8022 Zurich.

Society for International Development, Mr. Cyril Ritchie, ch. Rojoux 15, CH-1231 Conches.

Stanford Club of Switzerland, Mr. Manuel Ebner, Eschenweg 9, CH-8704 Herrliberg (✉ manuel.ebner@ebnerfamily.com).

Swedish Women's Educational Assoc., Ms Eva Ebbeson, Horbenstr. 3, CH-8356 Ettenhausen TG.

Swedish Women's Educational Assoc., Mrs. Britt Leopold, rue de la Servette 59, CH-1202 Geneva (☎ 022 740 45 66).

Swiss American Society of Berne, Mr. Fred Moser, P.O. Box 5, CH-3000 Berne 26 (☎ 031 301 55 45).

Swiss American Society of Lucerne, Richard Bosshardt, Schwanenplatz 7, CH-6004 Lucerne (☎ 041 410 10 64, ✉ rmboss@everyware.com).

Swiss American Society of Sankt Gallen, c/o Jack Bates, Ruppen, CH-9450 Altstätten.

Swiss British Society, c/o Englisches Seminar der Universität, Nadelberg 6, CH-4051 Basle (☎ 061 267 27 90).

Swiss Friends of the USA, c/o Dr. Alfred Reber, Postfach, CH-8034 Zurich.

Swiss-USA Association, Case postale 2184, CH-1211 Geneva 2.

Toastmasters International Club Berne, Mr. Graham Tritt, Schaufelacker 11, CH-3033 Wohlen (☎ 031 325 98 36, 🖥 www.community.ch).

Toastmasters International Club Zug, Mr. Marc Ebnöthes, P.O. Box 1010, CH-6301 Zug (☎ 01 761 12 03, 🖥 www.swisscities.com/toast/zug).

Toastmasters International Club Zurich, Jane Bircher, Mühlebrückestr. 20, CH-8400 Winterthur (☎ 052 233 37 46).

United Nations Women's Guild, Villa Les Feuillantines, 13, av. De la Paix, CH-1211 Geneva 10 (☎ 022 917 33 86, ✉ cfnu.unwg@bluemail.ch).

Wednesday Club, Mr. Herbert Maassen, rue Poterie 8, CH-1202 Geneva. (✉ wdcge@greenmail.ch).

The Women's Activity Club, The learning tree cooperative school, Winterthurerstrasse 18, CH-8610 Uster (☎ 043 305 92 50).

Zug International Women's Club (ZIWC), Mrs Lesley Nussbaumer, Dachlissen, CH-8932 Mettmenstetten (☎ 01 776 89 36, 🖥 www.ziwc.ch, ✉ info@ziwc.ch).

Zurich Comedy Club, Mrs Irene Münger, Grenzsteig 13, 8802 Kilchberg (☎ 01 715 27 04, 💻 www.zcc.ch).

Zurich Young People's Theatre (ZYPT), Mrs. Beverly Meyer Zemo, Etzelstrasse 17, CH-8800 Thalwil (☎ 01 721 04 64, ✉ zemo@access.ch).

Appendix B: FURTHER READING

One of the most useful Swiss publications for anyone seeking information about anything in Switzerland is *Publicus*, the *Swiss Year Book of Public Life* (*Schweizer Jahrbuch des Öffentlichen Lebens, Annuaire Suisse da la vie publique*), also available on CD-ROM. It contains the addresses and telephone numbers of federal and canton government departments, charitable organisations, embassies and much more, and is available from Schwabe & Co. AG, Farnsburgerstr. 8, Postfach, CH-4132 Muttenz 1 (☎ 061 461 27 61).

In the lists on the following pages, the publication title is followed by the author's name and the publisher's name (in brackets). Note that some titles may be out of print, although you may still be able to find a copy in a bookshop or library. Books prefixed with an asterisk (*) are recommended by the author.

Travel & Tourism

All About Geneva, Scott Charles

*Baedekers AA Switzerland (Baedeker) AA

*Berlitz Discover Switzerland (Berlitz)

Blue Guide Switzerland, Ian Robertson (A & C Black)

*Camping in Switzerland (Swiss Camping Association)

Essential Switzerland, Gerry Cranshaw (Automobile Association)

*Fodor's Switzerland, E. Fodor (Hodder & Stoughton)

Frommer's Switzerland & Liechtenstein (Macmillan Publishing)

Guide Gastronomique Schweiz/Passeport Bleu Suisse

*Insight Guides Switzerland (APA Insight Guides)

Karen Brown's Switzerland: Charming Inns & Itineries, Clare & Karen Brown (Karen Brown's Guides)

*Let's Go Austria & Switzerland (Macmillan)

*Michelin Green Guide to Switzerland (Michelin)

*Michelin Red Guide Switzerland (Michelin)

Off The Beaten Track: Switzerland (Moorland Publishing)

*Swiss Hotel Guide (Swiss Hotels Association)

The Swiss Travel Trade Directory (Urs Meierhofer Publications)

Switzerland, A Phaidon Cultural Guide (Phaidon)

*Switzerland: A Travel Survival Kit, Mark Honan (Lonely Planet)

Switzerland at its Best, Robert S. Kane (Passport Books)

Travel Bugs: Switzerland (Sun Tree)

Economy & Government

An Outline History of Switzerland, Dieter Fehrni (Pro Helvetia)

George Mikes Introduces Switzerland (Andre Deutsch)

How Switzerland is Governed, Prof. Hans Huber

Modern Switzerland, Prof. J. Murray Luck (Sposs Inc.)

The Referendum - Direct Democracy in Switzerland, Kris W. Kobach (Dartmouth)

*The Social Structure of Switzerland, René Levy (Pro Helvetia)

The Swiss Army (La Place de la Concorde Suisse), John Mcphee (Faber & Faber)

The Swiss Constitution, Nicholas Gillet (YES Publications)

Swiss Foreign Policy, Daniel Frei (Pro Helvetia)

*Switzerland (Auge International)

*Switzerland Inside Out, Lydia Lehmann (Bergli Books)

*Switzerland Land, People, Economy, Aubrey Diem (Media International)

Switzerland's Political Institutions, Oswald Sigg (Pro Helvetia)

*Switzerland: People, State, Economy, Culture (Kümmerly + Frey)

*Why Switzerland?, Jonathan Steinberg (Cambridge University Press)

Hiking & Climbing

Adventuring in the Alps, W. E. & M. Reifsnyder (Sierra Club)

The Alpine Pass Route, Jonathan Hurdle

Footloose in the Swiss Alps, William Reifsnyder (Sierra Club)

*Grosse Freizeit und Ferienbuch (Kümmerly + Frey)

*Grosser Wander-Atlas der Schweiz (Kümmerly + Frey)

*Walking in Switzerland, Brian Spencer (Moorland Publishing)

*Walking Switzerland - The Swiss Way, Lieberman (Cordee)

100 Hikes in the Alps, Harvey Edwards (The Mountaineers Seattle)

Miscellaneous

*Berne, Peter Studer, Walter Däpp, Bernhard Giger & Peter Krebs (Bergli Books)

*Christmas in Switzerland (Bergli Books)

Cooking in Switzerland, Mariane Kaltenbach (Wolfgang Hölker)

Culture Shock Switzerland, Shirley Eu-Wong (Kuperard)

Cupid's Wild Arrows, Dianne Dicks (Bergli Books)

Dance and Ballet in Switzerland, Jean-Pierre Pastori (Pro Helvetia)

*Handbook of Swiss Traffic Regulations (Federal Department of Justice and Police)

*Inside Outlandish, Susan Tuttle (Bergli Books)

*Laughing Along with the Swiss, Paul Bilton (Bergli Books)

Malice in Wonderland, Eugine V. Epstein (Benteli)

A Pain in the Alps, Eugine V. Epstein (Benteli)

*The Perpetual Tourist, Paul N Bilton (Bergli Books)

Southwards to Geneva, Mavis Coulson (Alan Sutton Publishing)

*The Surprising Wines of Switzerland, John C. Sloan (Bergli Books)

The Swiss and the British, John Wraight (Michael Russel)

Swiss Cooking, Anne Mason (Andre Deutsch)

The Swiss Financial Year Book (Elvetica Edizioni SA)

Swiss Meals on Wheels, Diana Nial (Littlestone)

Swiss Theatre Scene, Roland Maurer (Pro Helvetia)

*Switzerland by Rail, Anthony Lambert (Bradt Publications)

*Switzerland for Beginners, George Mikes (Andre Deutsch)

Switzerland: An Inside View (Scalo Publishers)

Switzerland: Through the Eyes of Others (Scalo Publishers)

Take Me to Your Chalet, Eugine V. Epstein (Benteli)

*A Taste of Switzerland, Sue Style (Bergli Books)

Tell Me a Swiss Joke, René Hildbrand (Benteli Publishers Bernee)

*Ticking Along With The Swiss, Dianne Dicks (Bergli Books)
*Ticking Along Too, Dianne Dicks (Bergli Books)
Who Put the WIT in SWITzerland, Eugine V. Epstein (Benteli)
Xenophobe's Guide to the Swiss, Paul Bilton (Ravette)

Appendix C: Useful Websites

Swiss Websites

Basler Zeitung (🖳 www.baz.ch): The online version of Basler Zeitung, covering mainly the northwest of Switzerland. Many articles are translated into English.

Bluewin Route Planner (🖳 www2.bluewin.ch/routenplaner): Find your destination on online maps of all towns and villages in Switzerland, with route planner.

Comparis (🖳 www.comparis.ch): Provides interactive comparisons of insurance premiums, telephone charges and bank charges in Switzerland.

Educa (🖳 www.educa.ch): Covers all levels of the Swiss education system.

Federal Office Of Immigration (🖳 www.auslaender.ch): Provides information on work and residence permits.

Feiertagskalender (🖳 www.feiertagskalender): Lists all Public Holidays for eacb canton of Switzerland

Inforoute (🖳 www.inforoute.ch): Actual traffic information on Swiss motorways, alpine passes and tunnels.

Immopool (🖳 www.immopool.ch): Comprehensive database of apartments and houses for rent or sale.

Matterhorn (🖳 www.matterhorn.ch): Search engine for holiday homes all over Switzerland. With online booking system.

Meteo Schweiz (🖳 www.meteoschweiz.ch): Actual and historic weather and climate information on Switzerland.

Museumspass (🖳 www.museumspass.ch): A portal which provides access to information on museums in Switzerland.

My Switzerland (🖳 www.myswitzerland.ch): Website of the Swiss tourist office. Comprehensive information and links to accommodation, transport, sports facilities, events etc.

NZZ (🖳 www.nzz.ch): Biggest national newspaper in Switzerland, mainly Zurich focused.

SBB (🖳 www.sbb.ch): The website of the Swiss Railway company. With train schedules and personalized timetables.

Search (🖳 www.search.ch): Search engine for Swiss websites. Also shows actual sports news.

SSR Travel (🖳 www.ssr.ch): Finds the cheapest flight from Switzerland to any destination of your choice. Also provides last minute travel and hotel bookings.

Swiss Banking (🖳 www.swissbanking.ch): Website of the Swiss Bankers' association. Explains the Swiss banking system.

Swissconnex (🖳 www.swissconnex.ch): A portal that links to many sites covering health, tourism, sports and business.

Swiss Government (🖳 www.admin.ch): The website of the Swiss government with links to all state departments.

Swiss Helpdesk (🖳 www.swisshelpdesk.org): Provides written answers to your own specific questions about Switzerland.

Swissinfo (🖳 www.swissinfo.org): National and international news provided by Swiss Radio International.

Switzerland Insight (🖳 www.switzerland-in-sight.ch): Provides information on Switzerland's history, the political system, the culture and society – and on the history of chocolate production in Switzerland.

Telsearch (🖳 www.telsearch.ch): Swiss online telephone book.

The English Show (🖳 www.theenglishshow.ch): Magazine style local radio show broadcast in English.

Youth Hostels (🖳 www.youthhostel.ch): List all youth hostels in Switzerland, with online reservation system.

General Websites

Au Pair Forum (🖳 www.aupair-forum.com): Experiences of au pairs and tips for those thinking of becoming one.

Australia Shop (🖳 www.australia.shop.com): Expatriate shopping for homesick Australians.

British Expatriates (🖳 www.britishexpat.com and www.ukworld wide. com): Two sites designed to keep British expatriates in touch with events in and information about the UK.

Direct Moving (🖳 www.directmoving.com): General expatriate information, tips and advice, and numerous links.

Escape Artist (🖳 www.escapeartist.com): One of the most comprehensive expatriate sites, including resources, links and directories covering most expatriate destinations. You can also subscribe to the free monthly online expatriate magazine, Escape from America.

ExpatAccess (💻 www.expataccess.com): Aimed at those planning to move abroad, with free moving guides.

ExpatBoards (💻 www.expatboards.com): A comprehensive site for expatriates, with popular discussion boards and special areas for Britons and Americans.

Expat Exchange (💻 www.expatexchange.com): Reportedly the largest online 'community' for English-speaking expatriates, including articles on relocation and a question and answer facility.

Expat Forum (💻 www.expatforum.com): Provides cost of living comparisons as well as over 20 country-specific forums.

Expat Mums (💻 www.expat-moms.com): Information for expatriate mothers.

Expat Network (💻 www.expatnetwork.com): The UK's leading expatriate website, which is essentially an employment network for expatriates, although it also includes numerous support services and a monthly online magazine, Nexus.

Expat Shopping (💻 www.expatshopping.com): Order your favourite foods from home.

Expat World (💻 www.expatworld.net): Information for American and British expatriates, including a subscription newsletter.

Expatriate Experts (💻 www.expatexpert.com): Run by expatriate expert Robin Pascoe, providing advice and support.

Global People (💻 www.peoplegoingglobal.com): Includes country-specific information with an emphasis on social and political issues.

Living Abroad (💻 www.livingabroad.com): Includes an extensive list of country profiles, which are available only on payment.

Outpost Information Centre (💻 www.outpostexpat.nl): Contains extensive country-specific information and links operated by the Shell Petroleum Company for its expatriate workers, but available to everyone.

Real Post Reports (💻 www.realpostreports.com): Includes relocation services, recommended reading lists and 'real-life' stories written by expatriates in cities throughout the world.

Save Wealth Travel (💻 www.savewealth.com/travel/warnings): Travel information and warnings.

Trade Partners (💻 www.tradepartners.gov.uk): A UK government-sponsored site providing trade and investment (and general) information about most countries, including the USA.

The Travel Doctor (⌨ www.tmvc.com.au/info10.html): Includes a country by country vaccination guide.

Travelfinder (⌨ www.travelfinder.com/twarn/travel_warnings.html): Travel information with warnings about danger areas.

World Health Organization (⌨ www.who.int): Health information.

The World Press (⌨ www.theworldpress.com): Links to media sites in practically every country in the world's media.

World Travel Guide (⌨ www.wtgonline.com): A general website for world travellers and expatriates.

Yankee Doodle (⌨ www.yankeedoodleiow.com): Import American products.

Websites for British Expatriates

British Expatriates (⌨ www.britishexpat.com and www.ukworld wide. com): These websites keep British expatriates in touch with events and information in the United Kingdom.

Trade Partners (⌨ www.tradepartners.gov.uk): A government-sponsored website whose main aim is to provide trade and investment information for most countries. Even if you aren't intending to do business, the information is comprehensive and up to date.

Websites for Women

Career Women (⌨ www.womenconnect.com): Contains career opportunities for women abroad plus a wealth of other useful information.

Expatriate Mothers (⌨ http://expatmoms.tripod.com): Help and advice on how to survive as a mother on relocation.

Spouse Abroad (⌨ www.expatspouse.com): Information about careers and working abroad. You need to register and subscribe.

Third Culture Kids (⌨ www.tckworld.com): For expatriate children.

Women Abroad (⌨ www.womanabroad.com): Advice on careers, expatriate skills and the family abroad. Opportunity to subscribe to a monthly magazine of the same name.

Worldwise Directory (⌨ www.suzylamplugh.org/worldwise): Run by the Suzy Lamplugh charity for personal safety, the site provides practical information about a number of countries with special emphasis on safety, particularly for women.

APPENDIX D: WEIGHTS & MEASURES

Switzerland uses the metric system of measurement. Those who are more familiar with the imperial system of measurement will find the tables on the following pages useful. Some comparisons shown are only approximate, but are close enough for most everyday uses. In addition to the variety of measurement systems used, clothes sizes often vary considerably with the manufacturer (as we all know only too well). Try all clothes on before buying and don't be afraid to return something if, when you try it on at home, you decide it doesn't fit (most shops will exchange goods or give a refund).

Women's Clothes

Continental	34	36	38	40	42	44	46	48	50	52
UK	8	10	12	14	16	18	20	22	24	26
USA	6	8	10	12	14	16	18	20	22	24

Pullovers

	Women's						Men's					
Continental	40	42	44	46	48	50	44	46	48	50	52	54
UK	34	36	38	40	42	44	34	36	38	40	42	44
USA	34	36	38	40	42	44	sm	med	lar	xl		

Men's Shirts

Continental	36	37	38	39	40	41	42	43	44	46
UK/USA	14	14	15	15	16	16	17	17	18	-

Men's Underwear

Continental	5	6	7	8	9	10
UK	34	36	38	40	42	44
USA	sm	med		lar	xl	

Note: sm = small, med = medium, lar = large, xl = extra large

Children's Clothes

Continental	92	104	116	128	140	152
UK	16/18	20/22	24/26	28/30	32/34	36/38
USA	2	4	6	8	10	12

Children's Shoes

Continental	18 19 20 21 22 23 24 25 26 27 28 29 30 31 32
UK/USA	2 3 4 4 5 6 7 7 8 9 10 11 11 12 13
Continental	33 34 35 36 37 38
UK/USA	1 2 2 3 4 5

Shoes (Women's and Men's)

Continental	35 36 37 37 38 39 40 41 42 42 43 44
UK	2 3 3 4 4 5 6 7 7 8 9 9
USA	4 5 5 6 6 7 8 9 9 10 10 11

Weight

Avoirdupois	Metric	Metric	Avoirdupois
1oz	28.35g	1g	0.035oz
1lb*	454g	100g	3.5oz
1cwt	50.8kg	250g	9oz
1 ton	1,016kg	500g	18oz
2,205lb	1 tonne	1kg	2.2lb

Length

British/US	Metric	Metric	British/US
1in	2.54cm	1cm	0.39in
1ft	30.48cm	1m	3ft 3.25in
1yd	91.44cm	1km	0.62mi
1mi	1.6km	8km	5mi

Capacity

Imperial	Metric	Metric	Imperial
1 UK pint	0.57 litre	1 litre	1.75 UK pints
1 US pint	0.47 litre	1 litre	2.13 US pints
1 UK gallon	4.54 litres	1 litre	0.22 UK gallon
1 US gallon	3.78 litres	1 litre	0.26 US gallon

Note: An American 'cup' = around 250ml or 0.25 litre.

Area

British/US	Metric	Metric	British/US
1 sq. in	0.45 sq. cm	1 sq. cm	0.15 sq. in
1 sq. ft	0.09 sq. m	1 sq. m	10.76 sq. ft
1 sq. yd	0.84 sq. m	1 sq. m	1.2 sq. yds
1 acre	0.4 hectares	1 hectare	2.47 acres
1 sq. mile	2.56 sq. km	1 sq. km	0.39 sq. mile

Temperature

°Celsius	°Fahrenheit	
0	32	(freezing point of water)
5	41	
10	50	
15	59	
20	68	
25	77	
30	86	
35	95	
40	104	
50	122	

Notes: The boiling point of water is 100°C / 212°F.

Normal body temperature (if you're alive and well) is 37°C / 98.4°F.

Temperature Conversion

Celsius to Fahrenheit: multiply by 9, divide by 5 and add 32. (For a quick and approximate conversion, double the Celsius temperature and add 30.)

Fahrenheit to Celsius: subtract 32, multiply by 5 and divide by 9. (For a quick and approximate conversion, subtract 30 from the Fahrenheit temperature and divide by 2.)

Oven Temperatures

Gas	Electric	
	°F	°C
-	225–250	110–120
1	275	140
2	300	150
3	325	160
4	350	180
5	375	190
6	400	200
7	425	220
8	450	230
9	475	240

Air Pressure

PSI	Bar
10	0.5
20	1.4
30	2
40	2.8

Power

Kilowatts	Horsepower	Horsepower	Kilowatts
1	1.34	1	0.75

Appendix E: Map Of Switzerland

The map opposite shows the 26 Swiss cantons (listed in alphabetical order below). Cantons Appenzell Inner-Rhodes and Appenzell Outer-Rhodes; Basle-Town and Basle-Country; and Nidwalden and Obwalden, rank as half-cantons, and have only one seat in the Council of States (all other cantons have two seats). The letters in brackets are the official canton abbreviations, as shown on vehicle license plates.

Aargau/Aargovia (AG)

Appenzell Inner-Rhodes (AI)

Appenzell Outer-Rhodes (AR)

Berne (BE)

Basle-Town (BL)

Basle-Country (BS)

Fribourg (FR)

Geneva (GE)

Glarus (GL)

Grisons/Graubunden (GR)

Jura (JU)

Lucerne (LU)

Nidwalden (NW)

Obwalden (OW)

Neuchâtel (NE)

St. Gallen (SG)

Schaffhausen (SH)

Solothurn (SO)

Schwyz (SZ)

Ticino (TI)

Thurgovia (TG)

Uri (UR)

Valais (VS)

Vaud (VD)

Zug (ZG)

Zurich (ZH)

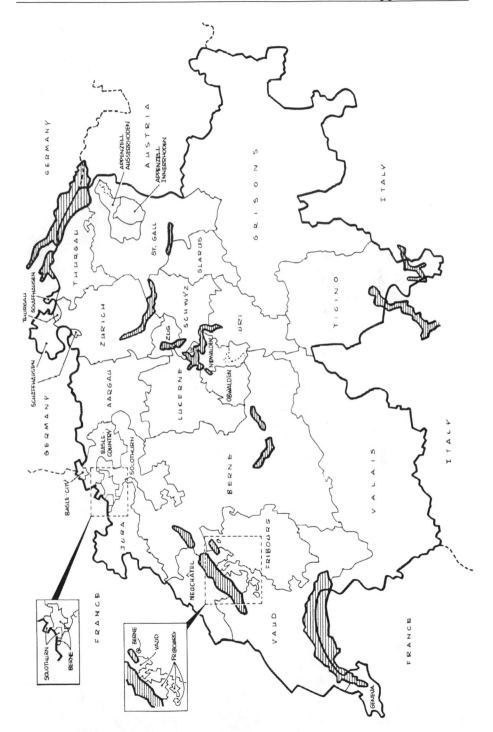

INDEX

F

G

H

T

Tax

LIVING AND WORKING SERIES

Living and Working books are essential reading for anyone planning to spend time abroad, including holiday-home owners, retirees, visitors, business people, migrants, students and even extra-terrestrials! They're packed with important and useful information designed to help you **avoid costly mistakes and save both time and money.** Topics covered include how to:

- Find a job with a good salary & conditions
- Obtain a residence permit
- Avoid and overcome problems
- Find your dream home
- Get the best education for your family
- Make the best use of public transport
- Endure local motoring habits
- Obtain the best health treatment
- Stretch your money further
- Make the most of your leisure time
- Enjoy the local sporting life
- Find the best shopping bargains
- Insure yourself against most eventualities
- Use post office and telephone services
- Do numerous other things not listed above

Living and Working books are the most comprehensive and up-to-date source of practical information available about everyday life abroad. They aren't, however, boring text books, but interesting and entertaining guides written in a highly readable style.

Discover what it's really like to live and work abroad!

Order your copies today by phone, fax, mail or e-mail from: Survival Books, PO Box 146, Wetherby, West Yorks. LS23 6XZ, United Kingdom (☎/▤ +44 (0)1937-843523, ✉ orders@ survivalbooks.net, 💻 www.survivalbooks.net).

BUYING A HOME SERIES

Buying a Home books are essential reading for anyone planning to purchase property abroad and are designed to guide you through the jungle and make it a pleasant and enjoyable experience. Most importantly, they're packed with vital information to help you **avoid the sort of disasters that can turn your dream home into a nightmare!** Topics covered include:

- Avoiding problems
- Choosing the region
- Finding the right home and location
- Estate agents
- Finance, mortgages and taxes
- Home security
- Utilities, heating and air-conditioning
- Moving house and settling in
- Renting and letting
- Permits and visas
- Travelling and communications
- Health and insurance
- Renting a car and driving
- Retirement and starting a business
- And much, much more!

Buying a Home books are the most comprehensive and up-to-date source of information available about buying property abroad. Whether you want a detached house, townhouse or apartment, a holiday or a permanent home, these books will help make your dreams come true.

Save yourself time, trouble and money!

Order your copies today by phone, fax, mail or e-mail from: Survival Books, PO Box 146, Wetherby, West Yorks. LS23 6XZ, United Kingdom (☎/▤ +44 (0)1937-843523, ✉ orders@ survivalbooks.net, ▯ www.survivalbooks.net).

ORDER FORM

ALIEN'S GUIDES / BEST PLACES / BUYING A HOME / DISASTERS / WINES

Qty.	Title	Price (incl. p&p)*			Total
		UK	Europe	World	
	The Alien's Guide to Britain	£5.95	£6.95	£8.45	
	The Alien's Guide to France	£5.95	£6.95	£8.45	
	The Best Places to Buy a Home in France	£13.95	£15.95	£19.45	
	The Best Places to Buy a Home in Spain	£13.45	£14.95	£16.95	
	Buying a Home Abroad	£13.45	£14.95	£16.95	
	Buying a Home in Britain	£11.45	£12.95	£14.95	
	Buying a Home in Florida	£13.45	£14.95	£16.95	
	Buying a Home in France	£13.45	£14.95	£16.95	
	Buying a Home in Greece & Cyprus	£13.45	£14.95	£16.95	
	Buying a Home in Ireland	£11.45	£12.95	£14.95	
	Buying a Home in Italy	£13.45	£14.95	£16.95	
	Buying a Home in Portugal	£13.45	£14.95	£16.95	
	Buying a Home in Spain	£13.45	£14.95	£16.95	
	How to Avoid Holiday & Travel Disasters	£13.45	£14.95	£16.95	
	Renovating & Maintaining Your French Home	Autumn 2003			
	Rioja and its Wines	£11.45	£12.95	£14.95	
	The Wines of Spain	£15.95	£18.45	£21.95	
				Total	

Order your copies today by phone, fax, mail or e-mail from: Survival Books, PO Box 146, Wetherby, West Yorks. LS23 6XZ, UK (☎/▤ +44 (0)1937-843523, ⊠ orders@survivalbooks.net, ▣ www.survivalbooks.net). If you aren't entirely satisfied, simply return them to us within 14 days for a full and unconditional refund.

Cheque enclosed/please charge my Amex/Delta/MasterCard/Switch/Visa* card

Card No. _ _ _ _   _ _ _ _   _ _ _ _   _ _ _ _

Expiry date _____   Issue number (Switch only) _____

Signature _____   Tel. No. _____

NAME _____

ADDRESS _____

_____

* Delete as applicable (price includes postage – airmail for Europe/world).

Swiss customers can order from Bergli Books, 4001 Basel (☎ +41 (0)61 373 2777, ▤ +41 (0)61 373 3778, ⊠ info@bergli.ch, ▣ www.bergli.ch).

ORDER FORM

LIVING & WORKING SERIES / RETIRING ABROAD

Qty.	Title	Price (incl. p&p)*			Total
		UK	Europe	World	
	Living & Working Abroad	£16.95	£18.95	£22.45	
	Living & Working in America	£14.95	£16.95	£20.45	
	Living & Working in Australia	£14.95	£16.95	£20.45	
	Living & Working in Britain	£14.95	£16.95	£20.45	
	Living & Working in Canada	£16.95	£18.95	£22.45	
	Living & Working in the Far East	Winter 2003			
	Living & Working in France	£14.95	£16.95	£20.45	
	Living & Working in Germany	£16.95	£18.95	£22.45	
	Living & Working in the Gulf States & Saudi Arabia	£16.95	£18.95	£22.45	
	Living & Working in Holland, Belgium & Luxembourg	£14.95	£16.95	£20.45	
	Living & Working in Ireland	£14.95	£16.95	£20.45	
	Living & Working in Italy	£16.95	£18.95	£22.45	
	Living & Working in London	£11.45	£12.95	£14.95	
	Living & Working in New Zealand	£14.95	£16.95	£20.45	
	Living & Working in Spain	£14.95	£16.95	£20.45	
	Living & Working in Switzerland	£16.95	£18.95	£22.45	
	Retiring Abroad	£14.95	£16.95	£20.45	
				Total	

Order your copies today by phone, fax, mail or e-mail from: Survival Books, PO Box 146, Wetherby, West Yorks. LS23 6XZ, UK (☎/▤ +44 (0)1937-843523, ✉ orders@ survivalbooks.net, 💻 www.survivalbooks.net). If you aren't entirely satisfied, simply return them to us within 14 days for a full and unconditional refund.

Cheque enclosed/please charge my Amex/Delta/MasterCard/Switch/Visa* card

Card No. _ _ _ _   _ _ _ _   _ _ _ _   _ _ _ _

Expiry date _____   Issue number (Switch only) _____

Signature _____   Tel. No. _____

NAME _____

ADDRESS _____

_____

* Delete as applicable (price includes postage – airmail for Europe/world).

Swiss customers can order from Bergli Books, 4001 Basel (☎ +41 (0)61 373 2777, ▤ +41 (0)61 373 3778, ✉ info@bergli.ch, 💻 www.bergli.ch).

OTHER SURVIVAL BOOKS

Survival Books publishes a variety of books in addition to the *Living and Working* and *Buying a Home* series (see previous pages). These include:

The Alien's Guides: *The Alien's Guides to Britain* and *France* provide an 'alternative' look at life in these popular countries and will help you to avoid the most serious gaffes and to appreciate more fully the peculiarities (in both senses) of the British and French.

The Best Places to Buy a Home: *The Best Places to Buy a Home in France* and *Spain* are the most comprehensive and up-to-date sources of information available for anyone wanting to research the property market in France and Spain and will save you endless hours choosing the best place for your home.

How to Avoid Holiday and Travel Disasters: This book is essential reading for anyone planning a trip abroad and will help you to make the right decisions regarding every aspect of your travel arrangements and to avoid costly mistakes and the sort of disasters that can turn a trip into a nightmare.

Renovating & Maintaining Your French Home: New for 2003 is the ultimate guide to renovating and maintaining your dream home in France, including essential information, contacts and vocabulary and time and cost-saving tips.

Retiring Abroad: This is the most comprehensive and up-to-date source of practical information available about retiring to a foreign country and will help to smooth your path to successful retirement abroad and save you time, trouble and money.

Wine Guides: *Rioja and its Wines* and *The Wines of Spain* are required reading for lovers of fine wines and are the most comprehensive and up-to-date sources of information available on the wines of Spain and of its most famous wine-producing region.

Broaden your horizons with Survival Books!

Order your copies today by phone, fax, mail or e-mail from: Survival Books, PO Box 146, Wetherby, West Yorks. LS23 6XZ, United Kingdom (☎/🖨 +44 (0)1937-843523, ✉ orders@ survivalbooks.net, 🖳 www.survivalbooks.net).